W9-CDU-375

GHOSTS OF THE ORPHANAGE

GHOSTS
OF THE
ORPHANAGE

A Story of Mysterious Deaths,
a Conspiracy of Silence, and
a Search for Justice

CHRISTINE
KENNEALLY

PUBLICAFFAIRS

New York

Copyright © 2023 by Christine Kenneally

Cover design by Pete Garceau
Cover photograph copyright © Ian MacLellan
Cover copyright © 2023 by Hachette Book Group, Inc.

Hachette Book Group supports the right to free expression and the value of copyright. The purpose of copyright is to encourage writers and artists to produce the creative works that enrich our culture.

The scanning, uploading, and distribution of this book without permission is a theft of the author's intellectual property. If you would like permission to use material from the book (other than for review purposes), please contact permissions@hbgusa.com. Thank you for your support of the author's rights.

PublicAffairs
Hachette Book Group
1290 Avenue of the Americas, New York, NY 10104
www.publicaffairsbooks.com
@Public_Affairs

Printed in the United States of America

First Edition: March 2023

Published by PublicAffairs, an imprint of Perseus Books, LLC, a subsidiary of Hachette Book Group, Inc. The PublicAffairs name and logo is a trademark of the Hachette Book Group.

The Hachette Speakers Bureau provides a wide range of authors for speaking events. To find out more, go to www.hachettespeakersbureau.com or email HachetteSpeakers @hbgusa.com.

PublicAffairs books may be purchased in bulk for business, educational, or promotional use. For information, please contact your local bookseller or Hachette Book Group Special Markets Department at special.markets@hbgusa.com.

The publisher is not responsible for websites (or their content) that are not owned by the publisher.

Print book interior design by Amy Quinn.

Library of Congress Cataloging-in-Publication Data
Names: Kenneally, Christine, author.
Title: Ghosts of the orphanage : a story of mysterious deaths, a conspiracy of silence, and a search for justice / Christine Kenneally.
Description: First edition. | New York : PublicAffairs, 2023. | Includes bibliographical references and index.
Identifiers: LCCN 2022026574 | ISBN 9781541758513 (hardcover) | ISBN 9781541758506 (ebook)
Subjects: LCSH: Orphanages—United States—History. | Catholic Church—United States—History. | Child abuse—United States—History.
Classification: LCC HV978 .K46 2023 | DDC 362.73/2—dc23/eng/20221011
LC record available at https://lccn.loc.gov/2022026574

ISBNs: 9781541758513 (hardcover), 9781541758506 (ebook)

LSC-C

Printing 1, 2023

To the truth tellers

CONTENTS

ACT I

Chapter 1	3
Chapter 2	19
Chapter 3	37
Chapter 4	51

ACT II

Chapter 5	73
Chapter 6	93
Chapter 7	115
Chapter 8	129
Chapter 9	139
Chapter 10	149
Chapter 11	159
Chapter 12	179
Chapter 13	195
Chapter 14	205
Chapter 15	223
Chapter 16	239
Chapter 17	249
Chapter 18	257

ACT III

Chapter 19	271
Chapter 20	281
Chapter 21	295
Chapter 22	307
Author's Note	*321*
Acknowledgments	*325*
Notes	*329*
Index	*351*

ACT I

The virtue of discretion is one of the most necessary virtues in religious life. A discreet Sister is a pillar in a house. One who lacks discretion can do considerable harm.

—*Reports of Provincial Superior of Official Visits to St. Joseph's Orphanage, April 16, 1947*

CHAPTER 1

IT WAS A FREEZING DAY IN JANUARY 2016 WHEN I PASSED THROUGH A long-locked door and first set foot into what had once been St. Joseph's Orphanage. The beautiful, spooky old hulk of a building was dark and frigid, and as I walked through the hallways, the sound of my feet against the worn wood floors was amplified in the long corridors.

In the cold winter light, the basement dining room, once an optimistic yellow, had an uneasy green tinge. Here and there the paint blistered. I tried to picture all the children sitting here at their little tables, eating their food and keeping their heads down, dreading the consequences if they got sick.

I walked up the stairs, above the lattice-panel doorway that led to the confessional, past the polished wood posts, past exposed brick and moldering mortar. A dark corridor ran the length of the building, as it did on each of the three other floors. Polished by generations of children, the floor still reflected a dull gleam. To one side opened a room of cupboards, their wooden shelves blanched with dust, the children's numbers still clearly marked: 53, 19, 34 . . .

After years of talking to former residents and reading their words, I felt like I already knew every nook and corner. Here in the confessional, on one side of the wooden grill, a young boy told a priest that another priest had touched him. The priest's reaction to this story was angry and dismissive.

Now, I knew, he was also an accused abuser. Here at this bench in a side room, children were pulled in from the corridor and deputized as godparents in quick baptismal ceremonies conducted over abandoned newborns. Here on this floor, a young girl had been forced to troop up and down the hallway, staggering with exhaustion in the middle of the night. Here was the freezing bathroom where a nun swung a girl by her back brace until she bounced off the walls. Here at the elevator door, a girl had clutched each side of the doorway in a mad panic as two nuns behind her tugged her into the small space.

Here, finally, on the top floor, was a pinched, steep staircase caked in dust, and at the top of it, the attic. Every inch of the building below had been assigned a clear purpose. But the vast, eerie attic, with its immense crisscrossing beams and dark rafters, felt almost like a forest, a wild place.

It occurred to me as I stepped nervously across the loft that the Sisters of Providence had probably been frightened of the attic, too. Even when they punished children there, they often went up in pairs. Except maybe for Sister James Mary, who had seemed so energized by rage and hatred and control. Here among the statues and old chests, she had strapped an unhappy teenage girl named Sally Dale into a chair and told her that the chair was electric and would fry her. I stood on the loft and looked around. I tried to conjure up Sally, to see her in the chair. I wanted to tell her that I knew what happened to her. She had not been forgotten. Her words had lived on. But all that was left were echoes and dust.

In the fall of 1994, Sally Dale of Middletown, Connecticut, received an invitation in the mail. A two-day reunion would be held at the Hampton Inn in Colchester, Vermont, for "survivors" of St. Joseph's Orphanage, which struck Sally as an odd word to use. She hadn't been in touch with anyone from the orphanage for a long time. She thought about the place as little as possible. But she was curious to see some of the old faces and find out who was still around.

Her husband Bob would drive. Bob had looked after Sally since they married and treated her son and daughter from her first marriage as if they were his own. Now that the children were grown, she didn't have to worry about leaving them as she always had when they were young. She and Bob lived on the ground floor of a triplex, with her son, Rob, and his wife in an apartment above them. When Rob returned late from night shift at the prison, Sally always waited up. She left the front door open a crack and the light turned on. Only when she heard Rob call out, "Good night, Ma!" did she go to bed.

On Saturday, September 18, the first day of the reunion, Sally was only a few steps inside the hotel conference room when a man exclaimed, "You little devil!"

It was Roger Barber, who had been a boy at St. Joseph's with his two sisters. *Little devil*, that's what they used to call her. She hadn't thought of it in so long.

"Sal, you look good for everything you went through," one of Barber's sisters said.

"You were our Shirley Temple of the orphanage!" said the other. She reminisced about the way Sally used to sing "God Bless America" and "On the Good Ship Lollipop" when she was little.

Sally remembered some of those things. She sometimes remembered bad things, too, such as times when the nuns hit her. But it was long ago. She recognized few of the fifty or sixty people in attendance. Debbie Hazen was there, and so was Katelin Hoffman, along with Coralyn Guidry and Sally Miller, but many of those women had lived at St. Joseph's after Sally left. Some of the women recognized each other not by name but by the numbers that nuns used to identify them: *Thirty-two! Fourteen!*

The first day's events began with Philip White, a tall, friendly looking man who explained that he was a lawyer. He introduced Joseph Barquin, who was a resident of the orphanage in the early 1950s, and some other people who were there to help. One man spoke about the Bible and turning to God in times like these, and two therapists said they were available for anyone who wanted to talk. Local journalists were on hand, too.

Sally still remembered some of the little boys she had cared for in the orphanage nursery at that time, but if she had looked after Barquin, she didn't recall. He stood up and told everyone about a nun taking him into a closet and doing terrible things to him. He still had scars. Roger Barber spoke next. He said that a nun told a group of older boys to rape him. As the morning went on, more of the former residents told their stories, and more of them became increasingly upset. Some began to melt down in the meeting room and the hotel's hallways. One lanky, weathered man stood up and addressed another man before the whole crowd. He said he had come that day because back in the orphanage he bullied the man. He felt bad about it his whole life and wanted to say he was sorry. Then one woman spoke about how nuns wiped her face in her own vomit, and Sally started to remember that the same thing had happened to her. She could hear the voice of one sister telling her after she threw up her food, *You will not be this stubborn! You will sit and you will eat it.*

One woman said she'd watched a nun hold a baby by its ankles and swing its head against a table until it stopped crying. As Sally listened to the awful stories, something ruptured inside her. She shook her head and began to say, "No, no, no, no, no, it's not true." But it was too late. The spell was broken. Her memories of St. Joseph's were already flooding back.

Though the reunion would go for two days, Sally could barely stay for one. She left that first afternoon with a crushing headache. Bob drove her home, and the next morning she had diarrhea and was unable to speak without heaving. She had spent that night sitting bolt upright, remembering things she hadn't thought about for decades, saying, "No, no, no, no, no." When Bob asked her why she was saying no, she just replied, "No."

MORE THAN TWENTY YEARS LATER, I MET SALLY'S SON, ROB DALE, IN another state, in a tavern at the busy intersection of two highways. The place was loud and a little louche. Rob slid into the large booth of paneled dark wood, placing an old, battered briefcase beside him.

Relief was my dominant emotion. It had taken two years to find Rob. He had worked as a correctional officer for twenty years, specializing in organized crime and intelligence. Now, he kept the details of his life out of the public domain. One of the first things he said to me was that he'd called a lawyer we both knew before he agreed to meet. He wanted to make sure I could be trusted. For all that, he had a lighthearted presence and an open, cheery face.

Rob had been worried that I would take his mother's stories and write about her as if she were crazy. There had been times, he told me, when she told him things that made him think, *That's not sane.* In the early 1990s, he started to think she might be going mad. She told him stories from her days at St. Joseph's Orphanage, and he'd say, "Mom, that doesn't sound right." But Sally was adamant. "Bobby, that really happened," she said. "I'm telling you the truth. This is what happened."

Rob didn't exactly disbelieve Sally, but he didn't want to believe her stories either. He loved his mother and told me how strong she was. She barely reacted if she had a broken bone. It was a kind of strength, to be sure, but also the result of specific training.

"My mother wanted a family so badly," Rob said. She was loving and always kind to children, welcoming neighborhood kids and baking them cookies. Sally had been odd about food herself. She was particular about her house, too. It was full of happy knickknacks, like small china animals, but everything was always exactly where it was supposed to be. When Rob used to tease her by taking one little item and putting it in another room, she'd notice within seconds of entering. There were other signs that Rob recognized only later. Every summer, Sally took him to a local pond and taught him how to swim. She told him that as a child she'd been thrown into Lake Champlain and told to swim or drown. He was so young himself when she told him that, he said, the extreme nature of the story didn't register.

I told Rob that when she was very little, Sally was famous in her world for her singing voice. He laughed at the idea. "My mother loved Shirley Temple. She loved her to death! Oh my goodness." Sally knew all the tunes from all the movies, Rob said. But she'd only hum them. She never sang.

After a few hours, Rob took the briefcase and put it on the table. Sally had given it to him before she died. It contained documents from her fight for justice and letters she had written in the 1990s about everything she saw at the orphanage. It included stories about children that Sally said had died or were even killed at the orphanage. My call had prompted Rob to read Sally's letters for the first time. He found them painful and intensely moving.

I spent a long time looking for traces of Sally's life and proof of the stories she told. In the previous few years, I walked through the cemetery she used to hide in. There at that spot, on that gray stone embedded in the soft green grass, that was where she sat. I crossed the black track where the old railway line used to be and wound my way down a steep slope to the shore of Lake

Champlain. That was how she made her way to the water to swim. I tracked people all over the country who once knew her or were known by her, or who had once lived the kind of life she had lived. I hunted dates and times and events, and much more elusive, ways to test the veracity of the stories Sally told. Was this extraordinary story, this staggering claim, this insane assertion—was this kind of thing even possible? Did it happen? Could it ever have happened?

I found my way to Sally because for the previous five years I had been talking to people like her. They were mysterious, private, intense voyagers from another realm. Before that point in my life, I'd lived and traveled in different countries. I had a doctorate. I was a mother. I had worked for years as a journalist and thought of myself as a relatively worldly adult. I also believed that the world was a singular, knowable, real place.

NOW I KNOW THAT SOME PEOPLE HAVE ALWAYS MOVED FREELY BETWEEN the reality that is plain to see and its hinterlands: the institutions, the orphanages, the places where things happen behind closed doors and stay hidden.

It may come as no surprise that priests belong to this privileged caste of travelers to unseen worlds. They have themselves made such claims for thousands of years. Their promise has always been to lead us over a starry bridge that only they can see. But in fact, many have slipped unseen between the known world and unknown places, like orphanages, where they used their immense power to bend and twist and shape the reality of the children who lived there. If you grew up Catholic, you have almost certainly met a man who had such power.

I came across such a man when I was fourteen years old, though I didn't know it until much later. My best friend, who I will call Lisa, asked if I wanted to go with her to a theater camp run by a priest, a close friend of Lisa's family. The prospect was more exciting than I could express. Lisa and I attended a girls-only Catholic school run by nuns, and here was the promise of a whole weekend with a bunch of teenagers, actual boys, and initiation into the world of acting. I was afraid to admit that I wanted to learn how to act. It seemed to me that you had to think pretty highly of yourself to say something like that out loud. Nevertheless, I asked my parents if I could go, and fortune smiled upon me.

The camp was held at a rural property near Lancefield, Victoria, in Australia. It was owned by Father Glennon, a priest in his forties. *Call me Michael!* he said. He had thick blond hair, a gaunt face, and a constant patter. He picked me and Lisa up in his van, and her parents came out front to wave us goodbye. Lisa sat beside him in the favored front seat all the way to Lancefield. The property, Glennon explained, was for spiritual retreats. A house, which was more of a large hall, sat on a huge tract of bushland. It was a lonely, cold place not far from where scientists had discovered an ancient bed of giant bones in the 1970s. Titanic marsupials had lumbered through the landscape tens of thousands of years before. Were they still alive, they would have recognized the ancient, spooky gum trees around us. Inside the big hall was a huge room with a fireplace where the kids threw down their sleeping bags and talked into the small hours.

I don't recall what time it was when Lisa and I, plus a cute boy with dark hair, found ourselves sitting with Michael Glennon in front of the fire. Glennon was delivering a friendly sermon, some kind of spiritual monologue that I normally would have paid obedient attention to, but I was distracted by the cute boy who was looking at me. Then Glennon said to all three of us that it was very beautiful when people loved each other, and that love was very special. He added something about trust and the free expression of love, and how it was a nice idea for the four of us to go into the next room, his bedroom, the only room there with a door that closed, and take off all our clothes. Being naked in front of each other, he said, was a good way to show that we trusted each other.

My presence at the theater camp that weekend had been pretty touch-and-go to begin with. My parents were not thrilled by the idea. I grew up in a Catholic suburb, went to Catholic school, and received the Holy Spirit via communion wafer every Sunday, and my parents had always been the most religious adults I knew. On one rare occasion when the local priest visited our home, I believe that even he had been taken aback by their reverence.

Much of this came from my father. He was raised by his grandparents, literally born in the middle of the nineteenth century, and his way of seeing the world had always leaned toward theirs. He was staunchly conservative, obedient unto the one true God, and often authoritarian with his children. He and my mother, as it turned out, had heard some odd things about Father Glennon and initially balked at the idea of letting me go. Eventually, in the face of my dramatic insistence, and the fact that Glennon was, after all, a priest, they allowed it.

There's a cruel irony for parents who believe there is a kingdom of heaven and want to guarantee their child's place in it, because there is great pressure to control what is ultimately out of their hands. It was a duty my father took seriously even though, inevitably, he would have to let go one day. But how could he know if this was the day?

There are no good answers for parents, but as it turned out, my father had prepared me for such a day. Life with Dad, as difficult as it sometimes was, had equipped me with tools that I didn't know I had. I can't explain this even now because I believe in a scientifically verifiable universe, but at that moment in front of the fire, when the priest asked me and my fourteen-year-old friend, the daughter of his close friends, to take off our clothes and prove we knew what trust was, my father—at that moment an hour away and fast asleep—took over my body. At least, that's what it felt like. I heard him thunder the word *No* out of my mouth. And that was it.

Glennon looked shocked, and then he grew cold. The conversation took on a sour note. Shortly after that, his rap about the meaning of love and trust ended. I grabbed my sleeping bag and lay down by myself on one of the couches in the room full of buzzing, happy kids. The next morning, one of the cool, older girls mocked me because I had apparently crawled right inside my bag, pulled it up over my head and not moved for the next eight hours.

Glennon did not glance in my direction for the rest of the weekend. I tried once the following morning to get his attention, but he pointedly did not hear me. I could feel the kids around us cringing at my low status. Before acting camp ended, Glennon held a mass, and as his eyes swept over the crowd of admiring kids, they always bounced away from where I was. Looking back, I wonder at the effort of it. For him to so successfully not look at me, he must have been aware of where I was every second. At the time, though, I mostly felt confused and hurt. There was no mention of acting the whole weekend.

I learned later that Glennon had already been convicted for assaulting a ten-year-old girl before my time at the camp. Did Lisa's parents know this? Had they not believed it? Did they suggest that Lisa take a friend with her? Was I their hedge, just in case?

In the three years after my visit to Lancefield, Glennon was charged with raping seven boys and one girl between the ages of twelve and sixteen, all of whom visited the camp in the years before I did. He went to jail, and yet more than ten years later after his release, he was brought up on twenty-four more counts, including the rape of a child under ten years old. He told at least one boy, after raping him, that if the boy told his parents what Glennon had done, Glennon would kill his parents and take custody of the boy. Another victim testified that Glennon said he had lost track of how many people he had raped.

Glennon was the subject of at least five trials and pleaded not guilty in all but one. He was convicted many times over. By his final conviction in 2003, now in his sixties, his hair still thick but his gaunt face turned spectral, he was sentenced for what would be the rest of his natural life. A reporter at that trial noted that when the guilty verdict was read out, Glennon shook his head in disbelief.

It was also reported after the legal proceedings that Glennon had regularly visited a boys' orphanage called St. Augustine's on the outskirts of a neighboring city. An immense building, half college, half chateau, it was run by the Christian Brothers and set on 620 acres of farmland that had been given to the religious order by the government. Glennon, it was said, provided counsel to the young residents.

When this was first reported, few would have understood what it likely meant, even in context of the grotesque details of Glennon's trial. For much of the twentieth century, St. Augustine's had been a satellite unto itself. Most of the thousands of boys who disappeared from rural hamlets and larger cities across the state had probably never heard of the place before they woke up one day inside it. Once inside, the boys may as well have been on the moon. Each morning they lined up to receive a dot of toothpaste on their toothbrushes. If they lost their toothbrush, they had to use their finger. When the bells rang, they lined up for their food, and to go to church, and to learn. On Saturdays, when they assembled to watch a film, the boys who were deemed undeserving were lined up in the same room but made to stand with their backs to the show.

The brothers who lived at St. Augustine's, who allowed the child rapist Michael Glennon to come and go, wore tunics equipped with a special pouch that housed a strap, three strips of leather sewn together, eleven inches long and half an inch thick. One brother used to leap into the air, both feet off the ground, before he brought the strap back down onto the hand of a child. Another named his own strap "the red terror." Each night the brothers prowled the halls, and boys rocked themselves from side to side to put themselves to sleep.

At different times over the decades, a canny, desperate, outraged child would escape from St. Augustine's to tell people in the world outside what was happening to him. Survivors from the home have reported that dozens and dozens tried. But even if they managed to break free from this horrifying and altogether separate reality, they never got far. The runaway was always caught, and the police or his relatives or his local priest returned him. Then his head was shaved, and he was really punished.

If one of those boys had told Sally Dale of St. Joseph's in Vermont, more than ten thousand miles away, what he had experienced, she would have been surprised to learn that the boy existed at all, but she would not have blinked at his story. The Australian children of St. Augustine's in the antipodes had more in common with Sally and her fellow orphans in the far American north than any other child who lived free in their own neighborhoods or states, or even their country. Those boys and Sally were citizens of the same realm.

Ultimately, though, the boys never knew of Sally's existence, nor she of theirs. But we can now say that they each understood something secret and profound about the difference between the world that most of us think we live in and the other worlds that only some people know.

FOR MOST OF THE TWENTIETH CENTURY, AN INVISIBLE ARCHIPELAGO stretched across the Western world. On each island in the chain stood a large, dark manor, some of red brick, some of stone. Most stood two to four stories tall, and all were utilitarian, though often graced by the statue of a saint or an architectural note, a pretty gable here, a cupola there. The hulking great buildings sat on the edge of their towns, high on a hill, by the river on the outskirts, or in the fields where few lived. They loomed large and solitary, and if the people in the nearby town thought of them at all, they thought of them as one-off institutions. Few understood that they belonged to an enormous, silent network. In fact, between St. Augustine's in Victoria, Australia, and St. Joseph's in Vermont, United States, existed thousands of other institutions like them: Smyllum Park orphanage in Lanarkshire, Scotland; the Bon Secours Mother and Baby Home in Tuam, Ireland; the Mount Providence Orphanage in Montreal, Canada.

Most institutions were religious, but many were not. All told, they composed the twentieth-century orphanage system, through which millions of children passed and from which relatively few records remain.

There are many reasons why the orphanage system, which was once so enormous, is now so obscure. All those reasons, diverse as they are, are strung between two poles: the active concealment of crime on one end and the impact of tremendous trauma on the other. The truth—a truth I struggled to accept for years—is that the cover-up of crimes was profuse, intentional, and effective. The destruction of evidence, the hiding of records, and the obscuring of facts and systems and prior warnings were all carried out by people who committed criminal acts or by their colleagues, who sought to protect them or the reputation of their church. The impact of the malefactors' work is evident today and remains formidable.

The trauma inflicted by the orphanages is unique and particular, and not yet fully understood by modern psychology or psychiatry. Certainly, everywhere the islands of the orphanage archipelago existed, shattered travelers now live. These people were once marooned, but found a way home. Yet even as they escaped, a spell was cast upon them. Most of the survivors could not talk about what happened to them in that other place, or if they did talk about it, like the mythical seer Cassandra, no one believed them.

The orphanages left marks on the bodies of former residents, on their lifelong choices, on the way they raised their children, and on the geography of their adult lives. Some moved as far away as they could as soon as they could. Others stayed in the same town, but if you took a map and ran a pencil over their daily movements, you'd see that there was a particular street or a neighborhood that was never marked. If the town were, say, Burlington,

Vermont, you'd find lines through the center of town, around the university campus, along the interstate, and down to the lakeshore, but stark against the messy scribble, you'd also see a clean wide space, and at the center of that space, you'd see a big building on a bluff overlooking the lake: St. Joseph's Orphanage.

IN THE 1990S, THE SILENCE OF SURVIVORS BEGAN TO BREAK EVERYWHERE. Former residents reached out to one another, or to lawyers, or to law enforcement. They created activist groups and support groups. They began to write letters and lobby representatives and call on the media. An awakening dawned in many communities where orphanages had once stood. Shortly afterward, however, the history of American orphanages split from the history of orphanages in other countries.

It took me a long time as a journalist to understand what happened in the United States. I took my first steps into the orphanage archipelago from outside the country, in places that primarily engaged in the experience of the former residents of orphanages with government inquiries and journalism.

I entered that world because of the determined work of others, usually former residents of orphanages. When I first fumbled my way into this new territory, some of my friends had a vague sense of those places. When I mentioned it, they might get a dreamy look and say, *Yeah, there was a place like that near where I grew up, I once asked my mother about it*, or *I wondered about that place! I remember driving by and seeing children in the yard there.* Still, I found it hard to see the larger story beyond the gripping tale of the one person I was talking to or the terrible and specific history of the single institution I was reporting on.

I understood intellectually that there had, in fact, been many institutions. By 2010, a considerable number of newspaper reports had documented abuse stories from orphanages all over the world. In Australia, a radical group of archivists launched a historic website that aimed to identify all the orphanages in the country. But few people comprehended the enormity of it. The vast whole eluded the basic tools of journalism not to mention the reach of the law, traditional ideas about justice, and the limits of basic, human psychology. In every sense, it was too big.

As the years went by, my lens widened, and I became increasingly disturbed by what I saw. Looking back from the 2010s, I finally began to see not just one or two or ten of these places, but an entire fantastic world, a massive network, thousands of institutions, millions of children connected to one another if not by an explicit system of transport or communication, then by the overwhelming sameness of their experiences: the same schedules, the same cruelty, the same crimes committed in the same fashion, then covered up by the same organizations. In many cases, the sameness had roots in a shared history and culture, including systems of operation, abstract notions of personal responsibility and obedience, and attitudes toward children, and women, and sex. Irish and French Catholicism, for example, had sent many people across the world to become avatars of their religion in a new place. Sometimes, though, the institutions were uncannily alike simply because inside such strange places, with little transparency to the outside world, there are only so many grooves along which human pathology and human tragedy run.

I began to focus on the Catholic orphanage system, partly because I was raised Catholic and partly because the Catholic Church is remarkable—ironically—for its record-keeping as well as its criminality. It still took years to glimpse the full outline of that dark underworld.

Over time, I became overwhelmed by the sense that those of us lucky enough not to know it were in a fraught position. We had unwittingly been party to a great mystery, a huge heist, a secret murder, many murders probably. I lost count of the stories I heard—too many to fully grasp. Some I could document, some I couldn't. But each was uniquely harrowing. The more that happened, the more I was struck by the immensity of the underworld and the monster that stood astride it.

What does this widespread, hidden trauma cost us? What does society pay by letting it continue to loom over a large group of people, and at best, registering only some of its impact? An extraordinary number of children experienced profound trauma in twentieth-century institutional childcare in the United States, Canada, Australia, the United Kingdom, Ireland, and other countries. A significant number are still alive today, and for many, it affects everything about their lives. But they are not the only victims.

Many survivors had children who also had children, and the shadow of institutionalized abuse and exploitation looms over them, too, even those who never knew that their parents or grandparents once lived in an orphanage. The cost of not acknowledging what happened, let alone attempting a true reckoning, is immense in any terms you choose: economic, social, or legal.

The Adverse Childhood Experiences (ACE) study launched in 1995 and is still renowned for its rigorous attempt to construct a scientific understanding of the long-term, widespread impact of childhood adversity. Its findings subvert some of our most basic ideas about abuse: the notion that it happens in "distinct categories," for example, and that one form is inherently worse than another. In fact, it's not possible to determine which type of abuse causes more harm when there is more than one type of abuse. It appears that most harm is caused by a number of compounded adverse childhood experiences. The great challenge posed by the ACE study is what to do now about social systems that are built on the old ideas, like our contemporary system of childcare, and when that goes wrong, our system of justice.

The ACE study tells us what orphanage survivors could have told us long ago if we had only listened. The true history of orphanages provides one of the darkest and most complete natural experiments on the nature and consequences of abuse, and on the behavior of abusers. Take a group of people at their most vulnerable, make them subject to an organization with almost zero transparency to the outside world, build weak to nonexistent systems of oversight, and give the organization social status or exemption from taxes—then what does the abuse look like? It is profuse, complicated, and category-busting. It is the act, and it is the denial of the act. It causes emotional, physical, social, and economic harm and increased risk across the span of lifetimes and down generations.

The true history of America's orphanages—and many others across the world—teaches us about the cost of letting abuse occur. It also teaches us about abusers and criminality, and where unlimited corruption of institutional power leads. These lessons are not just historical, they pertain to acts that are happening right now. The organizations that ran orphanages still deny the full reality of what happened inside them, still refuse to take true responsibility for the consequences, and still sit on the records. They will rewrite history, if they are allowed to. They will rewrite reality, too.

In 2019, after many of the events of this book had occurred, and many Americans had been reminded, if not educated, about the impact of life in a twentieth-century orphanage, and St. Joseph's Orphanage in Vermont in particular, the current bishop of the Diocese of Burlington, Christopher Coyne, did a curious thing.

In response to a formal investigation and renewed activism, Coyne publicly and individually in private addressed survivors of the extreme events that occurred at St. Joseph's and the cover-up that followed. As leader of the diocese, he made a number of reparative acts. Then in April 2019, once much of the initial hubbub and press attention died down, a spokesman for the Diocese of Burlington announced that Coyne planned to recommend a man for canonization. The man had been born in France in 1816. He had become a priest and voyaged to America in 1853, ultimately taking up residence in Burlington, Vermont.

Canonization is a long and complicated process, but if successful, the subject is declared a saint. Miracles are attributed to them; they are beatified, elevated above all others, seen as beyond reproach. In a hundred years, or maybe just a decade, good Catholics around the world would pray to them for their own miraculous intercession for help and healing. The man that Coyne nominated for sainthood? Louis deGoesbriand, the first bishop of Burlington. Among his many acts as bishop, in 1854, he founded St. Joseph's Orphanage.

How do you investigate a cold case that has been actively concealed by the oldest institution in the world? How do you investigate ten thousand cold cases? It was overwhelming, but I took a grim comfort in the refusal of some survivors to be defeated, no matter what they had been through.

Sally Dale refused defeat—though I don't know if it ever consciously occurred to her that way. The boys of St. Augustine's who later testified about what happened to them refused, too. So did a girl from St. Catherine's, who grew up to start a revolution. So did a haunted boy I spoke to in jail. So did hundreds of brilliant children from orphanages all over the world. They had survived events that most people would tremble to contemplate, and if I learned anything from all of them and their experiences over decades and continents, it was this: if you want to take on a two-thousand-year-old monster, you're going to have to play a long game.

CHAPTER 2

T HE TWO-STORY MANOR SITS NORTHEAST OF THE HILL CREST, WHERE IT
begins to wind down to the bay. When you stand across the road to survey the grand Victorian whole, you can't see the nearby water, but you can tell
it's there from the lightness of the air. There are two reasons for this. Rozelle
Bay, glinting in Sydney's perfect summer light, lies at the bottom of the hill
to the right. A few blocks beyond the house, Jubilee Park stretches down to
the water on the other side. It's not all grand houses on this street but there
are plenty here, with their pretty balconies, plastered arches, and yellow sand-
stone. Miniature box hedges mark parking spaces on the road. They probably weren't here sixty years ago, but the money that paid for them has clearly
flowed through this street, one way or another, since the house was built.

Even if you didn't know the history of this place and the wealthy solicitor
who first lived there in the late nineteenth century, you can tell it was one of
the first, one of the most admired.

Go in.

The iron palisade gate swings open without a sound. A tessellated tiled
path takes you to the front door, where a frangipani tree throws gentle
shade. Here on the porch must be where the little ones were lined up. Chins
high, eyes down, ready for inspection.

Enter.

The hallway that runs from the entrance has two enormous rooms to each side, and a decorated arch halfway along. The staircase rises on the left. If you stand next to it, you can glimpse part of the atrium at the back of the house. Light fills the space. Next to you, on the side of the staircase, there is a paneled door.

The house is quiet, you are alone. Open it.

The cupboard under the stairs is smaller than you think it will be. The dark wood columns and lustrous balustrade of the staircase are lovely, like everything else here. But the cupboard is more afterthought. There are shelves and a jumble of brushes, dust pan, and other cleaning tools inside. A small amount of light marks the vent at the bottom of the outside wall; it sits where the earth comes up against the brickwork.

Shut the door of the cupboard under the stairs. Open it again.

Now there is a small boy sitting in the dusty space. He is pale and dirty, and his face is a mess. He has sandy hair and he has soiled himself. He's not alone. There are two other boys, one on either side of him. They all hold hands tightly. The boy stares at you. He has been crying but now he is too scared to talk. The cupboard smells of fear.

WHEN GEOFF MEYER LIVED AT ROYLESTON, HE WAS NEVER THERE FOR long, maybe a few months at a time, sometimes a few days. Nevertheless, the big house was the grim station to which he was always returned. Every time he came back, he cringed at the iron gate, which squealed loudly when he passed through. As he walked from the gate to the front door, where the matron stood waiting, waves of dread swamped him. Officially, Royleston was known as a Home for Wayward and Abandoned Boys, but Meyer knew it as the Boys' Depot, a place for the storage of spare children.

Regularly, Meyer lined up with the other boys on the front porch in order of height. Strangers arrived and walked up and down the line, eventually choosing one of them. It was always women who came to choose, and when one of them fixed on Meyer, he left with her.

The idea was that Meyer would become part of the woman's family, at least for a while. Thus he would go to live in a new suburb or on a farm, where he milked cows or fed chickens or cleaned from morning to night.

Most of the time, Meyer noticed, he was fostered out to a family with a child the same size as he was. He always left Royleston with two suitcases of new clothes paid for him by the government, but after the first day, Meyer never saw those clothes again.

When the season was done or the need was met, Meyer was returned to Royleston, where the food was rotten and the punishment was rich. If Meyer threw up after eating weevil-ridden porridge, he was forced to eat his own vomit. For other infractions, he was flogged or made to scrub the veranda tiles with a toothbrush. Sometimes the matron took him into the attic and did strange, painful things to his private parts.

When one of his fellow residents wet the bed, the matron draped the boy's wet sheets over his head and made him walk around the dormitory. As the sad little wet ghost wandered about, the other boys stood there, watching and laughing, trying to trip him up. Meyer noticed that a boy would participate in this laughter until he himself wet the bed. Meyer never laughed. He was too small, and he was afraid of what would happen to him if he did. He had his uses, though. He was fast as well as little, so he usually found himself acting as a lookout for bigger boys.

No one called Meyer by name at the Depot. He answered to "Hey you," but mostly the matron and the other adults called him terrible words. Sometimes the other boys called him *threepence* because he was so small. He didn't mind that one so much. At Royleston, none of the boys knew each other's names. They weren't even really allowed to talk to each other.

As bright and sunny as the big house was, the boys of Royleston existed in a strange gray state of unknowing. They knew very little about each other and almost as little about themselves. Who were their parents? They didn't know. Did they have brothers or sisters? Usually, they didn't know. What had they, the wayward boys, done, to end up in this place of punishment? They didn't know. They were given to understand that they were at Royleston because they were bad, but really they had no idea why.

Sometimes the boys at Royleston played cricket with the Catholic lads from nearby Westmead. The Catholic boys told Meyer about the "fathers" from their school. These men weren't like normal fathers, Meyer learned, but were grown men without wives or families who looked after the boys. The fathers were touching them, the boys told Meyer.

At the time Meyer didn't understand that the Catholic boys were telling him and the other boys from Royleston what was happening to them so they would report to someone in authority and get help. Meyer had no one to tell. Even the idea of telling made no sense to him.

ONE DAY THE MATRON MADE MEYER GET INSIDE THE CUPBOARD UNDER the stairs. It was the place he hated most at Royleston. It didn't take much to be put there. Minor infractions, acts of rebellion, unsanctioned expression. If Meyer didn't smile when he was lined up on the veranda for inspection, he was put under the stairs.

This time he and two other boys hunched together in the small, musty space. They held hands as feet thumped up and down the stairs above them. Meyer didn't know how long he would be in there. More than once he had sat under the stairs for three days. There was no food or water there. There was no toilet. Meyer had to do it in his pants.

This time, the hours passed, and the house gradually became quiet. When it was completely dark and still and there was hardly any noise, the door to the cupboard opened. This was strange. Before, Meyer was always released into the blinding light of the day. In fact, it was so dark under the stairs, that when Meyer eventually emerged, dirty and blinking, the light hurt his eyes as much as if someone was standing there and pressing on them. It felt like torture.

But the person who opened the door now wasn't there for Meyer. Instead, he took one of Meyer's nameless companions and then shut the cupboard door. Meyer never saw that boy again.

Twice more this happened. Meyer was banished to the cupboard with other boys. One of them was taken into the darkness outside the cupboard and, each time, that was the last time Meyer saw that boy. He never understood why. No one fostered boys in the middle of the night.

I MET MEYER IN 2012. EARLIER THAT YEAR I HAD LEARNED ABOUT A GROUP of people known as care leavers, or more casually, "homies," who grew up in orphanages between the 1930s and 1980s. They were having a hard time getting their personal information from the government.

They weren't after tax returns or historic deeds or birth certificates to validate genealogies they already knew. They simply wanted basic facts that had been withheld from them at an early age—the kind of information that most of us cannot imagine not knowing—like their real names, or when their birthdays were, or if they had siblings.

I first learned that the orphanages existed from a group of archivists who were gathered at a conference in Brisbane, Australia. The archivists were often on the other end of requests for help from former orphanage residents, and had come to feel that the former residents' plight was a human rights issue. I struggled to imagine what it was like not to know these things about oneself. The rest of us live our lives firmly embedded in a web of information. We know where we were born. We know whether our parents liked each other. We know what it is like to be a child and see an adult brush their teeth. As adults, we belong to interconnected groups like a family, neighborhood, or religious community, and we have experiences that constantly reinforce what we know. Together, the bits and threads that bind us add up to a complex, unquantifiable body of information, providing not only a medical and personal history but a sense of self. Yet for the children sent to live in these twentieth-century homes, that information was systematically and utterly erased so that, for a very long time, they didn't know it should have been there in the first place.

When I looked for more information, all the archivists I asked directed me to Leonie Sheedy. Once a resident of St. Catherine's Orphanage in Geelong, sister home to St. Augustine's, Sheedy was a small, dynamic woman who was equal parts funny, frank, and angry. I met her in Sydney in an aging but well-kept white brick house set on a busy road in Bankstown. It was the office of an organization that Sheedy cofounded, the Care Leavers Australasia Network, or CLAN.

Sheedy appeared to know nearly everyone who had passed through the orphanage system in Australia, and as far as I could tell, she had pursued with an inexhaustible drive every public figure or politician who might have had the smallest bit of influence on their plight.

Sheedy told me that in the early 1990s, her cofounder Joanna Penglase, then a doctoral student as well as a survivor of the twentieth-century child welfare system, wrote to more than 150 newspapers in her state, asking that survivors get in touch. Slowly, one by one, they reached out. Sheedy and Penglase then established CLAN. In the years that followed, many more of Australia's ex-orphans found their way to the organization. Most were so ashamed of the fact that they had grown up in an institution, Sheedy told me, that she was the first person they'd told.

SHEEDY CAME TO KNOW THOUSANDS OF HOMIES' STORIES AND CONNECTED dozens of them with each other—kids who'd grown up side by side in the same place and then left, never to see each other again. Her newsletter classifieds read like ads for former selves: "Michael would like to get in touch with anyone that remembers him in Renwick in the 1950s"; "If anyone can remember my nickname Debbie Wobble Head from the Ballarat Children's Home, it would be nice to have some contact."

The orphanage residents told Sheedy they had been placed in a home because calamity had befallen their family. They had lost their father to war or their mother to illness. They had been given up by their parents because they were poor or disabled, or their parents were divorced or had never been married. Some parents believed they were ensuring a better life for their kids by placing them in an orphanage or a small, privately run home. Some children were surrendered by parents who didn't want them, or they were taken from parents who had committed crimes, struggled with addiction, or abused them. Only rarely was it the case that both parents had died. They told Sheedy they had been taken by strangers in the middle of the night or had fled out the back door when strange men arrived and began to grab their siblings.

The stories they told Sheedy about life in an orphanage were chillingly similar, even as each also had its own painful details. There had been few celebrations in the institutions and little news of the outside world. Some children attended the local school but wore special clothes that made it clear where they were from. Some were schooled inside the institution and never left the grounds. Many were not taught to read or write or do basic math. They were blamed if they became ill, and if it wasn't completely debilitating, their illness was often ignored. They told vividly similar stories about floggings, punches to the face, forced labor, sexual assault, and emotional torment. They were forced to hit each other and put into solitary confinement for days at a time. In some homes, they were not allowed to look one another in the eye. Their names were arbitrarily changed.

Up until the 1970s, children in some homes were subject to medical experimentation, some with substances that had failed safety tests in animals, and some that caused fever and vomiting in infant subjects in the study. At the St. Joseph's Broadmeadows home in Melbourne, run by the Catholic Sisters of St. Joseph, babies in the 1940s were injected with a trial herpes simplex vaccine, which failed to provide any protection against infection. Another group in the same home was later injected with a trial influenza vaccine. In another home in Melbourne, a trial whooping cough vaccine was given to children.

Home staff were expert at placing children in no-win situations and then punishing them as if they had control over the outcome. At the Ballarat Orphanage in Victoria, boys lined up to have their shoes inspected. If a boy's heels were worn away, he was smacked. In homes all over the country, night after night, children who wet the bed were sent to bed the following night with no protective garments or access to a toilet. At one Catholic orphanage, a girl let her younger sister jump into bed with her so that when the little girl peed, only the older sister would be punished.

The former residents told Sheedy that while some carers had been kind, they usually didn't last in the job. As awful as the abuse was, it was the absence of affection that was most devastating. When children entered institutions, they were taken from a place where they were at least claimed and, in many cases, loved by adults. One man said that children showed each other pictures of their mothers, which in reality were photos cut from magazines.

In many homes, staff controlled every connection a child had with the outside world. When children were moved to another institution, as they often were, no one explained why. One girl entered a Sydney home with her three-year-old brother and woke one morning to find he was gone. No one told her where. Staff confiscated letters, and children were falsely told their parents were dead or never wanted to see them again.

At St. Catherine's, where Sheedy had grown up, one girl didn't know she had any family until the day she and a younger girl were called into the head nun's office and introduced to a man and a woman. "This is your new mum

and dad," she was told. The nun told her that the visitors had adopted both
her and her sister, indicating the small girl. "My sister?" she said.

THE DAY THAT SHEEDY INTRODUCED ME TO GEOFF MEYER, HE OPENED THE
front gate for me, lifting it carefully so it wouldn't squeak. He was seventy-
six years old, on the short side, and wore a Fair Isle jumper and slicked-down
hair. He was courtly and jokey, and called me "mate." He looked like everyone's granddad. Meyer's wife died three years before, but he stayed active
on the CLAN committee and mowed the lawn to help out. Since he left
Royleston more than half a century before, he hadn't eaten any vegetables
except spinach, which had not been served there. He told me that he often watched people on the streets, wondering how many of them were once
wards.

Meyer told me that he had been fostered out eight times, and each time
he returned, the sound of the squealing front gate "frightened the living Jesus out of me because I knew what I was in for."

On his final foster placement at age nine, Meyer was sent to an older
woman in an outer suburb of Sydney. When she enrolled him at the local
school, he learned the date of his birthday for the first time. Everyone at the
school knew Meyer was a ward because the assistant principal made him and
another boy stand up as he said to the class, "They are under child welfare
because their mothers never loved them." During arithmetic one day, Meyer
told me the man "lost the plot completely." He said, "Geoff Meyer, stand up.
I want you to sing a song. I want you to sing 'I'll Take You Home Again,
Kathleen.'" But Meyer rebelled—"I said, 'No!'"—so the teacher slammed
Meyer's head into the wall. For years, Meyer had migraines and his head
twitched uncontrollably. When it jerked hard toward his shoulder, the other
students laughed at him.

Most of Meyer's foster mothers beat him. The last one whipped him with
horse reins, but when he showed the welts to government inspectors, they
told him he was a liar. After school, he trained as a motor mechanic, then
took off for the city, taking the clothes he was wearing, a tennis racquet, a
cricket bat, and 24 pounds and 18 shillings. He had no friends, acquaintances, or family that he knew of. He had no idea how to find a job or a

place to stay, but thanks to the woman who had placed him in school, he had learned when he was born and had never forgotten it, so he timed his escape exactly. He ran away on May 10, 1954, his eighteenth birthday.

Meyer said that, not long after he ran away, "I started to get it into my brain to find out if I had any family." He guessed that the best place to look was the Department of Child Welfare. "I'm a state ward," he told a young man at the local office. "I'm looking to see if I've got a mother and father." The young man went into another room and returned after five minutes, and said, "I think you might have a sister." He disappeared again. An older man came out and said, "I think you had better leave." Meyer thought he had misunderstood. "I think you had better leave," the man repeated. Meyer refused, and they argued back and forth, the man dismissing Meyer with no explanation and Meyer refusing to budge. Then the man said, "Get out or I'll call the fucking police." Meyer left, asking himself why he was always in trouble.

He found work. One day on the train where young women cadged cigarettes off the working lads, he met a girl named Marion and gave her his whole pack. They were married and had four children and, as the years passed, eleven grandchildren. Meyer never told any of them that he had been a state ward. When his children asked him about his childhood, he changed the subject. But when he retired, he started to go to the state records offices to see what he could find. Even then, he didn't tell his wife. "It felt very, very private," he said. He found his birth certificate and discovered that his mother was Maisie Aileen Meyer and his father was Leo Joseph Meyer, an American sailor. There was no information about why he was made a state ward and no record of contact from his parents after it happened.

As he looked for records about his life and family, Meyer was told different things by different departments. Some officials were good to him. Others clearly didn't care. One said his information had been lost in a flood. Another said it was a fire. He looked at files in the records offices but had to insist that he was legally entitled to a copy. When he received copies, they took months to get to him and were missing papers from the sets he had seen at the records office. The files also included information that he was not supposed to see, like the names and addresses of all his foster parents.

When Meyer's wife was at work one day, he tracked down one of his foster mothers from 1941 to 1943, a Mrs. Little of Bexley. "She was the only one who ever showed me love," he said. "Not a hug or anything like that, but she never hit me." She told Meyer that the only reason she gave him back was because she was summoned to make submarine nets for the war effort. "She gave me a picture, God bless her," Meyer said. "It was me with her son—the only photo I ever had of me as a child."

When he was sixty-eight, Meyer saw a newspaper notice seeking state wards. The ad asked: "Did you grow up in a children's home?"

Meyer still hadn't told his wife about his time at Royleston or what happened to him, but he said to her that day, "I think I'm going to ring this number up. It may just lead me somewhere."

Shortly thereafter, Meyer ended up at the Bankstown office with Leonie Sheedy. "She started talking to me, and I talked, and then the more I talked the more she was getting out of me, and I had never talked like this before."

When Meyer left Sheedy that day, he felt extraordinary. "I felt like Superman walking in the air," he told me. "I felt like Jesus Christ walking on the water." Meyer's conversation with Sheedy reframed his entire life. "I thought I was the reason all that stuff happened," he told me. "All that time, I thought it was only happening to me, but it was happening all over the place." When he got home that day, he told his wife about his experience at CLAN. She asked him, "What really went on in your life?" So he began to tell her, too.

By the time I visited the Royleston Depot in 2012 on a hot summer day, it had been sold a few times over and was by then a privately owned bed and breakfast. I booked a room for the night. When I first arrived, I stood across the road on the warm concrete. For a long time I just looked. It was so hard to resolve the lovely architecture before me with the mad, terrifying world that Meyer had described.

I walked down the narrow street beside the old Depot. Four ghost gum trees towered over the back fence and behind them was a small parking lot and a building. Earlier, Meyer had told me that both had been built since he lived there.

Meyer had returned to Royleston only once as an adult. He had gone back with his granddaughter, who by then knew, like the rest of Meyer's family, that he had lived there once as a ward of the state. They pretended to be interested in booking a room. The proprietor let them in, and they looked around. It was the back that most interested Meyer.

Meyer believed that the boys whose hand he had held but whose names he had not known, the three boys who one by one had been taken from the cupboard beneath the stairs under the cover of darkness, were still there at the back of the Depot, pressed beneath the earth and now held down by the asphalt and cars. He believed the boys had been killed, and though it seemed that hardly anyone but him knew they had once existed, he believed that beneath this pretty, gentrified, wealthy world, not far from the roots of the ghost gum trees, the lost boys lay.

Meyer understood there was little he could do with his idea. He had spent most of his life not being believed about any of the details of the strange world he had come from. He was disappointed to find that the place had changed so much, and to see that there was asphalt and concrete between him and what might have remained of those boys. The asphalt may as well have been a plate of steel. No one was going to hear his story and have either the authority or the will to breach the ground cover and look.

The day I visited the Royleston bed and breakfast, I was the only person there apart from the woman who ran the place. I looked inside the cupboard under the stairs. It was so small, so ordinary. Nothing remained of its former role as cramped jail cell for terrified children. I retreated upstairs to the large room I had booked. There was no trace of the former occupants there either. I lay on top of the bed covers and thought about Meyer and the thousands of children who had passed through this place. It was hard to process—all that brazen abuse behind firmly locked doors, creeping adults in dark dormitories, and the whole network that Sheedy told me about, of which this large, beautiful house was one node.

When Meyer and I first spoke, he showed me the files he had painstakingly gathered about his life, a reasonably thick wedge of papers that included his intermediate school certificate. He had to pay to get a copy, but he was proud that he now had something to show his grandchildren. There was a state inspector's report from when he was ten years old, a year after he was assaulted by his teacher. It described him as an overanxious worrier. There was only one record from before that time, with nothing about the assault or the ensuing years of medical treatment. For Meyer, the missing files would be proof of an otherwise invisible life, a deeply important symbol. But he also wanted them so he could sue the state government for compensation.

Meyer was likeable and modest; he didn't look like he had once lived in hell, making his stories all the more surreal. They seemed to belong less to another time than another universe, one designed by Hans Christian Andersen, where children scrubbed vast expanses of floor with toothbrushes and adult women did inexplicably awful things to frightened little boys.

I didn't doubt that the Royleston matron had taken Meyer into the attic and molested him, or that his foster mothers used him as cheap labor, or that the local Catholic boys whispered to him about creepy fathers who touched their private parts. But it was different when Meyer spoke about murdered children. Looking back, I suspect that my attention was drawn to what felt tractable, what seemed extraordinary but plausible. It was not my intention to treat the stories about missing boys differently from the other stories Meyer told me. But I did. How else, I have asked myself since, could I even begin to process the rest of the fantasia that Meyer described?

IN THE EARLY 2000S, THE RELENTLESS ACTIVISM OF LEONIE SHEEDY AND Joanna Penglase led to an Australian Senate inquiry. For the first time, a national government in the orphanage archipelago attempted to reckon with how many children it had placed in homes and what had happened to them since they left.

The inquiry estimated that at least 500,000 children from Australia's relatively small twentieth-century population had been placed in hundreds of different institutions. Even now, most people whose lives have been untouched by institutional care imagine that orphanages were full of children who had lost both parents. The popular idea of orphans and orphanages has been shaped by Shirley Temple films, Babar books, and an endless line of *Little Orphan Annie* productions. Fictional orphans are plucky, resourceful, and resilient, and despite experiencing great tragedy, they are winsome enough to attract adults who want to adopt them and create a new family. Orphanages in the popular imagination may be stern, even cold places. The children in them are generally thought to be firmly locked behind the high walls of the institution until they are lucky enough to be adopted. If a villain walks the hallways, they are usually more mean-spirited than predatorial.

In reality, the residents of orphanages were overwhelmingly not orphans. Usually one or both parents were still alive. In many cases a parent, usually the mother, voluntarily placed their child in care because they were unable to care for them. The child may have been born out of wedlock and the father did not want to be involved, or he was sick, in jail, at war, or dead. In her book, *Orphans of the Living*, CLAN cofounder Joanna Penglase wrote that it's hard to know now how or why a parent chose a particular institution for their child. In many cases, it would have been a referral from the parish priest or pastor. One woman chose a large institution because she thought there would be regular welfare checks on the children. She was wrong, Penglase observed. Penglase's own mother chose a small home-based situation for her because she'd heard about it by chance.

If not given up voluntarily, children were taken by the state—often the police—who deemed them to be in danger in the family home. Many children only spent one or two years at an orphanage and were taken out again once their single parent had remarried and was able to bring them home. In some cases, a member of their extended family was able to look after them. For some children, the walls of an orphanage were somewhat porous, as a parent or a grandparent visited every weekend.

The inquiry's 2004 report found that many former residents had died, often from drug- and alcohol-related causes, but those who remained were a significant, living demographic. Most were between sixty-five and ninety years old, and many had built careers in institutions like the navy, nursing, or the religious orders that ran their homes. Some were visibly successful, like former senator Andrew Murray, who had been a British child migrant sent to Zimbabwe (and later immigrated to Australia). Many were not. The last three people to be executed in Australia before capital punishment was outlawed had spent time in orphanages.

Using testimony from more than six hundred former residents and care leaver experts, the inquiry reported that an "abnormally large percentage" of care leavers had attempted suicide, and many had experienced homelessness. There was a well-worn path from children's homes to prison. One survey found that 65 percent of one state's female prison population were care leavers. Former residents had a high incidence of mental illness. They suffered ailments like arthritis and ligament damage from hours on their knees scrubbing floors. Many had dental issues because their teeth had not been looked after, and hearing loss from being boxed on the ears. Some women still cleaned their houses obsessively. Most were noticeably short, which was usually attributed to malnutrition. They lived in terror of homes for the elderly, yet a number of them ended up placing their own children in care. One man traced five generations of wards in his family, beginning in 1865 with a young male ancestor who spent time in a former naval battleship turned floating reformatory.

The former residents of urban and suburban orphanages were mostly poor white children. Sometimes they included Indigenous children who had been taken from their families as part of a separate assimilationist policy. Many Indigenous children were also taken from their families and sent to live with white families or in mission boarding schools. The practices in such schools included devastating individualized abuse and acts of systemic cultural genocide, such as punishing children for speaking in their native tongue. Those children came to be known as Australia's "stolen generation." Other orphanages, many on the Australian west coast, housed local children with children from the United Kingdom who had been spirited away from their families and sent to the other side of the globe. They were officially designated "child migrants," although most of them had no idea why they had been institutionalized, let alone moved to Australia.

I wrote about the void of personal information and the way it haunted orphaned children their whole lives. Many of their records had been destroyed, and there was little clarity about what had been lost and what was not kept in the first place. While it was intimidating for a former orphanage resident to enter a neutral institution like a public records office to search for personal documentation, many had to return to the place where they had been abused and ask nicely for help.

"People get rotten drunk in order to read their files," Sheedy told me. In the Senate inquiry, one woman described opening her files at home alone and being committed to a psychiatric ward a week later. Sheedy herself had been hungry for knowledge. She was eight and a half months pregnant when she got her file. Like the records of many others, it bore witness to the disdain with which institutionalized children were treated, describing her as "mentally slow." It was too much. "I fell in a heap," she told me. "Luckily my husband picked me up. Lots of people don't have a supportive person."

The overzealous application of privacy laws meant that many people received files with their missing siblings' names redacted, even though it was the government who made the sibling disappear in the first place. One man received a rare photo of a children's party with all the little faces at the table whited out, except for his own.

EVENTUALLY THE GOVERNMENTS OF CANADA, ENGLAND, SCOTLAND, IRE-land, Austria, New Zealand, and other countries held inquiries, too. All documented a comprehensive, entrenched culture of cruel practices across hundreds and hundreds of institutions. Together, the thousands of individual stories they told make up a vast and terrible mesh of corroboration.

In orphanages all over the world, children who wet the bed were paraded with wet bedclothes and sheets, while non-bedwetters were encouraged to laugh at them. Children in orphanages everywhere stood for hours holding their boots or some other item with their arms straight out. If they dropped them, they were beaten. They stood facing a wall in the middle of the night, and if they slumped forward and touched the wall, they were beaten. They walked up and down the hallways, back and forth for hours at night, and if they didn't stay awake, they were beaten.

No part of a child's body in any orphanage in any country was off-limits. Hair, heads, ears (they "spin it as hard as they can . . . you can kind of hear it cracking"), legs, spines, genitals, skin, the soles of feet. Children were held under cold showers and had their heads submerged in baths. They were shoved upstairs and pushed, kicked, dragged, and thrown downstairs. Hands and bodies were hit with straps, metal scissors, wooden crucifixes, rulers with a metal strip, and two-by-fours.

Emotional abuse was endemic. *You are society's garbage* was a constant refrain. Everywhere, children were shamed if they fell ill. They were made to eat their own vomit. Letters into and out of orphanages were censored and destroyed, and as if the dehumanization could not be greater, it was also common in religious and nonreligious institutions to address children by number, not name. This practice has also been documented in cults and with political prisoners and hostages to, in the words of psychiatrist and trauma specialist Judith Herman, "signify the total obliteration of [someone's] previous identity and [their] submission to the new order."

Yet all the government inquiries, despite their enormous reach, did little to account for the death stories. Australia's Senate inquiry did not formally pursue the question, though it dutifully recorded a number of accounts. One man, who described being told as a child that his brother had died of asthma, said that he had previously been told that the warden of the home regularly took his brother's inhaler away to torment him. Another saw a Christian Brother punch a boy and then throw him down the stairs. He learned a short time later that the boy had died. One woman reported that sometimes the police came to her orphanage when one of the girls had died, as if it were a regular occurrence. Once a baby died there, she said, and the nuns told her what to say to the police, "which meant lying."

The more I learned, the more Meyer's memory of the missing boys nagged at me. He was the first person I met who had looked me in the eye and told me about his life, seamlessly including the likely murder of children among all the other pedestrian details about cigarettes, clothing, and public transport. I had been so moved by Meyer's determination and his inexplicable sweetness that I had begun to look for more people like him. It was a while, though, before I noticed that I had put his story of the missing boys aside. It had not been a conscious choice, but it was a consequential act. It bothered me that I had done something so potentially meaningful without realizing it.

When I considered Meyer's story of the missing boys, I worried about possible motivations for claiming that children died or disappeared. To be sure, what the former residents of orphanages had been through was impossibly awful. It had happened when they were young, without support and even without the language to process and understand and explain to others. Maybe talking about death, claiming that there had been deaths, was the only way to really communicate how bad it had been?

But why did I suppose that death was a metaphor, and that someone needed an additional reason to invoke it? When I was told stories of abuse, including acts of cruelty far beyond my experience of the world, I believed they were likely literally true. But the death stories automatically existed in a wholly different category for me. I know I am not unusual in this regard. Death is frightening and final. Once it occurs, there's usually no going back. We all instinctively feel this way. It is reflected in all cultures.

The law reflects it, too. Murder is one of the few crimes in most jurisdictions for which there is no statute of limitations. If you kill someone and run, the law is unforgiving. If you help a killer to run, the law will not forget.

While death rightly exists in its own psychological and legal category, the causes of death may be more mundane and don't necessarily get the same special treatment—a beating that went too far, a shove down the stairs, the withholding of medical care. Death reliably occurs without controversy or clarion call when the body is treated in these ways. The mind may struggle to parse it, but the body is still subject to cause and effect.

When I first spoke to Meyer, it didn't occur to me that the red line had really been crossed at Royleston. It was such a serious charge, I thought—without thinking—that a mountain of direct evidence would be required to even contemplate it. If it had been crossed, I assumed, there would have been an investigation. The killers would have been caught. By now we would all know about it. But there had been no such investigation. So there must have been no murder.

Slowly, it dawned: If I believed what the former residents of orphanages were saying, if I believed even half of their stories about what had happened to them and what they had seen, the sheer numbers of children who were whipped, slapped, cut, hit, thrown, crushed, and launched into thin air, then it made no sense to assume that children were not killed. It was illogical.

Of course, you needed more than logic to prove such a crime. But I could no longer dismiss it as a whisper.

I circled back to Leonie Sheedy. Had she heard other stories like Meyer's? Were children killed at orphanages? If they had been killed, how was it possible that we didn't already know about it? I don't recall if it was Sheedy's tone of voice on the phone or her expression as she looked at me in response to the question. All I remember was the spirit of her reply: *Are you kidding me?*

CHAPTER 3

I N Adelaide, South Australia, in a small, slightly disorganized house in Northfield, Therese Williams led me through a small, dark anteroom to sit in the kitchen. Williams warmed up some bread and left the oven on to keep the room warm. She was over seventy years old and had spent years in an orphanage on the west coast of Australia, around the same time that Sally Dale grew up at St. Joseph's in Vermont. As we settled in, she handed me a few sheets of paper on which she had written the story of her life. She offered to read it out loud. She was anxious to give me as much detail and to be as accurate as she could.

"I was taken to Nazareth House in Geraldton, Western Australia, on the thirty-first of January 1948, being at the age of six years and seven months," she read. "The person who referred me was Monseigneur Irwin, parish priest of Northampton, Western Australia. The reason given was illness of Mother."

Overseeing Nazareth House was a Mother Frances, Williams said. "Sister John Fisher was in charge of the elderly women. Sister Kieran was the junior primary teacher, Sister Veronica was the other primary teacher, and Sister John Boscoe and Sister Albina were in charge of the children after school hours."

The names were burned into Williams's memory. She recited a long list of orphan girls as well. But the one she wanted to talk about most was Eileen Sinnott, who had been, "short, beautiful, placid, very well-mannered, very kind."

Williams had a slight build. She was earnest and a little self-conscious, but occasionally her voice rose and became so intense that all the shadows in the room suddenly seemed to deepen. She read, "The incident causing the injury and subsequent death of Eileen Sinnott took place shortly before my seventh birthday, which is on the twenty-seventh of June. Eileen and I were close friends, and Eileen always protected me from bullying by all the girls and tried to shield me from the violence often inflicted on us by Sister Albina. It seems to me that Sister Albina targeted certain individuals depending on their appearance or their place of origin."

When Leonie Sheedy first phoned Therese Williams, she checked more than once to confirm that my visit would be welcome, and that Williams didn't feel pressured or obligated. But Williams was determined to tell her story. By the time I met her, I had learned that in the pantheon of orphanage employees, a few were known to be unusually kind or gentle. Invariably they did not last long. Then there was a sizable group in the middle who, as they performed their day-to-day duties, may have committed some terrible life-shaping acts, sometimes intentional, sometimes not. There was also a handful of epic figures whose sadism was legendary and whispered about for generations. Sister Albina was one of those.

She grabbed girls by the hair and slammed their heads repeatedly into a wall. She sneered and bristled and blasted the girls with contempt, calling them "Northampton dogs" or "Belfast rats." She thrashed the five-year-olds who woke up with wet sheets. When Williams and the other girls went swimming, she got the older girls to hold Williams's head underwater. Eileen Sinnott would yell, "Leave her alone!" But it did no good. When Williams came up spluttering and gasping, Sister Albina smiled.

Who was this woman? Where did she come from? Did she have siblings? Did she read? Was she lonely? Williams knew nothing about her or about the other nuns at Nazareth House. They were actors on a stage, like costumed, one-dimensional, pantomime villains.

Nazareth House itself was host to a constant parade of horrors that would seem almost farcical had they not been true. The girls labored in the laundry, doing work the nuns took in and were paid for, and it was said that one of the younger girls lost her arm in the mangle machine. Because the orphanage sat right near the coast, the girls ate local crayfish that they were told to put live into a pot of boiling water. One of the girls later described the whistling sound of air escaping the cooking crayfish, which sounded to her young ears like screaming. A priest who occasionally came to Nazareth House to shoot pigeons one day, for no apparent reason, started shooting seagulls instead. He shot so many that dead seagulls were splayed and splattered across the grounds. He told the girls to pick them up. Eventually a nun asked him to leave. The girls helped the nuns look after older people in the home. One later said that when she tried to feed an old man who seemed to be refusing to eat, the nun she was with said, "You stupid girl. He's dead."

Williams told me that every day the girls walked two by two in line to chapel for rosary at five o'clock in the afternoon. One day, as she walked hand in hand with Eileen Sinnott, Sister Albina rushed toward them. For no reason that Williams could understand, the nun, who wore thick boots, kicked Sinnott in the belly with such force that the girl flew from Williams's grasp. Sinnott landed with a scream and curled into a ball, clutching her stomach as blood began to spurt from her mouth. Williams looked at me as she explained, "It was all over, and the gravel was red, and we were just staring at her, like that, just staring at her."

The next thing Williams remembered, it was evening, and she was waiting in a room. She said she "went blank" in the intervening hours and didn't know what happened. Later, all the girls were called together into the refectory where a red-eyed Mother Superior was saying to the senior girls that she was very sorry. Then another nun made the girls stand on the stairs while she delivered a lecture about what had happened to Sinnott.

Sinnott, like most of the girls at Nazareth House, was English. She was part of the child migrant program that took children from England and sent them to Australian institutions. Many children were taken from their families with all ties severed and no knowledge about how to find them again. They were promised "oranges and sunshine," but they understood little of what was going on. Some of them left England thinking they were going on a day trip. Sinnott, along with a group of girls and Sister Albina herself, had sailed on the SS *Asturias* at the end of 1947 from Southampton, England, to the west Australian coast. Williams was unusual at the time for being one of the Australian-born children at Nazareth House.

On the stairs that night, the nun told Williams and the other girls that Sinnott had actually fallen while on the boat to Australia and hurt herself then. She also said that Sinnott had undergone an appendectomy on the ship. Most importantly, Williams said, "We were not to speak to anyone outside Nazareth House about anything that happened there."

Williams never saw Sinnott or Sister Albina again. Sinnott had been taken to the hospital, and another girl told Williams that Sister Albina was seen getting into a taxi with two suitcases shortly afterward. Neither returned to Nazareth House. Weeks later, on Williams's birthday, one of her friends at Nazareth House told her that Sinnott had died.

WILLIAMS LEFT NAZARETH HOUSE THE YEAR AFTER SINNOTT'S DEATH. She never understood why she was sent there in the first place, nor did she understand why she was sent home. But nothing about her life was the same. Before she'd gone to the orphanage, she and her sisters had run freely in the bush. Her family had originally come from Ireland, and she and her parents lived in a tent until her parents built a house from clay and stones gathered in a local creek bed. Williams tried to teach baby cockatoos how to speak. Her brother used to light beehives on fire, then she and her sisters would grab the honeycomb and run for their lives.

The day Williams's mother drove her home from Nazareth House, she vomited for the entire journey. Once there, she spoke with a British accent, and only in a whisper, and her family couldn't understand a word she said. She had somehow become unrecognizable, even to her own mother, who was now angry at her most of the time.

Not long after, Williams was sent to work for her board at a convent run by the Presentation Sisters. When she turned sixteen, Williams decided to become a Presentation nun herself, not knowing what else she could do. The sisters educated her and trained her as a teacher, and she stayed with them for fifteen years. Eventually she left the order and continued to work as a teacher in the Catholic school system.

For most of her adult life, Williams didn't know there was anything wrong with her. Making a lopsided face, she said she didn't realize that people might have found her strange. She only understood looking back that she had, in fact, been angry *all* the time. Years later, a priest friend gave her some books on personal development. "You know, healing the past, that kind of thing." Williams came to see that she was full of bitterness.

Before I met with Williams, I studied the testimony of other former residents of Nazareth House. The day I visited, I read a brief story out loud, in which a former resident described being made to strip naked before being publicly strapped. "See! It happened," said Williams. She had seen such things herself and never forgotten them, yet despite everything she had just told me, her tone was still one of wonder. With tears in her eyes, she put her hands against her mouth and shook her head. "Even when you say these things, they are hard to believe."

When she was forty-seven, Williams had a dream that had once haunted her as a child. She was climbing a mountain but could never reach the top. This time, forty years after Eileen Sinnott died, Williams climbed her dream mountain again. She finally she put her foot on the summit, which then broke away from the mountain. Williams had never cried in her adult life, but the morning after her dream she woke up weeping. She didn't stop for weeks.

Williams never forgot Sinnott, though she rarely spoke of her. She told me she had attended a mass in the 1960s where the priest gave a sermon about a young girl who had been at Nazareth House in the same period that Williams was there. The girl had had a ruptured spleen and she was in terrible agony before she died, the priest said. He attached some moral to the story, Williams told me, laughing mirthlessly. She couldn't remember what it was. "Something about forgiveness?"

In 2002, Williams entered Towards Healing, a program offered by the church for former residents like her. She told the nun who ran the program about Sinnott. The nun later sent her a few things: a photo of Sinnott's gravestone and a small sheet of paper that said Sinnott had died of liver cancer.

In 2003, Williams finally told a friend about Sinnott for the first time, another Presentation nun she'd known from her time in the order. The friend's immediate response was not, "Surely it didn't happen." Instead, Williams said, "She believed me! She didn't think I was lying."

But the friend still cautioned her. "Don't tell anybody else because it will damage the church."

I DID WHAT I COULD TO VERIFY WILLIAMS'S TALE. SINNOTT HAD INDEED existed, I found, and she had died as a child. According to her funeral notice in the *Geraldton Guardian*, she was buried on June 26, 1948, the day before Williams's birthday. I tracked down women who had been at Nazareth House at the same time—Williams remembered all their names correctly—but of the few I found, none wanted to talk. I even found a reference to Sinnott's death in a book that had been published in 1998. Other women whom Williams hadn't spoken to since the 1940s had also been telling people about Sinnott, but their versions differed. A number claimed she was killed at the hands of a nun. One said she was thrown down the back stairs by a nun before chapel. Another said that the girls were told Sinnott died of cancer that had come on suddenly. One said Sinnott wasn't pushed but fell. In a different account, another woman said the girls had been told to say Sinnott had very bad asthma. One woman said it all began when Sinnott was "just laughing and joking with her little mate."

I had begun the search wondering how time and trauma and memory would get in the way of recalling what really happened. Before I met with Williams, Leonie Sheedy told me that I would meet a woman who would tell me about a child who died. By that point, I had enough of a sense of Sheedy to believe that if she said something was there, it would be there. But how much, I wondered, could this woman really tell me? What was it even like to go through something like that as a young child? Would she remember exactly what happened? Would it be more impressionistic? Did she even know the name of the child she said had died?

I was amazed to see that Williams, in fact, had a memory like a steel trap. Had she written down all the names and whispered them to herself every night since, she would not have had better recall. Did her training as a teacher help her recall? Had her anger kept the story alive? Williams *was* a very special person. When she was small, alone, and in danger, Eileen

Sinnott had looked after her. Then Sinnott's life had been taken, so Williams had carried Sinnott with her all this time.

Williams was not unique. Her sincerity and lucidity, the sure-footed way she went through the events of her story, the texture of the whole. These were qualities I encountered again and again in my reporting. Leonie Sheedy, it turned out, knew a lot of people like Williams.

MONTHS LATER, I FLEW TO THE OTHER SIDE OF THE CONTINENT TO MEET with a man named Gordon Lyle Hill, who went by Peter Hill but was known to everyone as Hilly. He grew up in an orphanage in rural Victoria in Australia's southeast. We met in a city that was about as far away from his old orphanage that Hilly could get and still be on the same continent.

We sat in the corner of a cafe with our backs against a wall. Hilly, a tanned, wiry man with long white hair who had worked outdoors most of his life, plunked down an old briefcase when he came in. He illustrated his story with the treasures inside: his birth certificate, a small award for volunteer labor, his parents' marriage certificate, a 1950s photograph of young boys, and a small set of coins (two shillings and a ha'penny) that the nuns gave him when he left the orphanage at age seventeen, before Australia's currency went metric. The coins had been handed to Hilly in an envelope with scribble marks on it, which he couldn't understand at the time because he'd never been taught how to read.

Hilly was raised in an institution run by the Poor Sisters of Nazareth near Ballarat, Victoria. There, he was known as number twenty-nine. "I didn't even know I had a name until I was about eleven," he told me.

Hilly spent most of his young life believing that he was alone in the world. It was only when he was about to get married that he had an inkling that he must have some brothers and sisters. Eventually, he found that he had at least nine siblings, some of whom had been at the orphanage with him, though he had no idea at the time who they were to him. It wasn't until 2012 that he learned how old he was. "It was only through my brother and a couple of other people that I could get records because I had no education," he said.

At the orphanage, Hilly had worked in the gardens and cleaned the building, and the only time he spent in a classroom was "to bloody well clean the blackboards on the wall and pick up the papers." The children who learned how to read and write were the ones who were visited by a parent, uncle, or brother once a month. They weren't supposed to talk to Hilly or any of the children like him. "We used to call ourselves 'the drones,'" Hilly said. He knew what a drone was from watching the orphanage beehives. "A drone is the one that goes out and works."

Hilly walked me through a history of the scars all over his body, like the puncture mark in the soft part of his hand, where a nun had plunged a knife, and the cigarette burns from the "bloody priests." He explained why he had no bottom teeth (a nun knocked them out when he was nine), and he grabbed my hand and pressed it against an odd patch of skin on the back of his head. That's where the nuns used to apply two big pads, and with other pads on his arms and legs, gave him electric shock treatment. Hilly described the machine that had been connected to the pads, with its wind-up dynamo. According to Hilly, it was a "mind bending type of thing" that they used "if you rebelled or anything." It happened to Hilly four different times, and where the pads had been applied, Hilly lost his hair and it never grew back. That's why he wore it long, to cover the scars.

Hilly told me about a night when he was eight years old, sometime around 1952. He knew it was the early 1950s because a babies' wing was being built at the time. He was in bed in a locked-up dormitory with about thirty-five other boys. Some of the older boys were in charge. It was about nine o'clock on a very cold night, and the boy in the bed next to Hilly started to have a coughing fit. The older boys yelled at the coughing boy. They told him to "shut up" or else there would be trouble. If the older boys didn't yell at the younger boy, Hilly explained, then the nun, who slept in a small room off the side of the dormitory, would open a glass partition and start yelling at them.

But the boy kept coughing. "It sounded like he had a very, very bad cold," Hilly said. One of the older boys said, "Shut up or I'm going to get up there and bloody knock your head off." It didn't work; the boy kept coughing.

After that, Hilly surmised, the older boy must have got out of his bed and taken one of the iron casters that were placed under the legs of the beds to protect the wooden floor. "This thing came flying over and hit this kid," Hilly said. "All I heard was a clunk and he stopped coughing. He didn't cough no more."

Hilly told me that when the nun came through the next morning, all the boys were supposed to be kneeling beside their bed to pray, but she said to the older boy, "You've still got a kid in bed." Someone whipped back the younger boy's bedding, said Hilly, and the nun grabbed the younger boy by the arm and the leg, and she pulled him.

"She thought he would stand up when she let go but he just went clunk on the wooden floor," said Hilly. "He must have been dead for a while because he was stiff as a board."

Hilly saw a lump on the boy's temple and a caster beside his bed. Later the nuns told the other children that the boy died of pneumonia. Hilly still dreams about it. "At night when I have nightmares, I have something flying through the air," Hilly said. He wakes up ducking.

THERESE WILLIAMS AND PETER HILL COULD NOT HAVE BEEN MORE COMpelling or clear. But I couldn't pin their stories down to confirm them. Documents were hard to obtain unless the church had been forced by law to surrender them, or I could find the right archival entry. People who were present when a death occurred had scattered far and wide. Many were uncontactable, uninterested, or dead. Everywhere but inside the mind of the traumatized prime witness, time had rolled on. Evidence had been destroyed, either with malice aforethought or for no other reason than that someone cleaned up.

Most of the orphanage death stories were six or seven decades old, which put them at the outer limit of investigation, not just for journalists, but for legal authorities. As with any cold case, the more time between a crime and its investigation, the more time perpetrators have had to destroy evidence and get their story straight. Like all investigators, cold case investigators look for facts and motives, but they must search for them beneath a thousand instances of action and intent that have since accrued like sedimentary layers.

I spoke to another man, Rod Braybon, who spent seven years at a Salvation Army home called Bayswater in Melbourne, Australia, in the 1950s. When he was sixteen years old, Braybon moved almost seamlessly from the children's home to Pentridge, a notorious maximum-security prison, after being convicted of robbery. His path was not unique. In fact, so direct was the bridge from places like Bayswater to the prison system, Braybon said, that when he walked into Pentridge, it was like walking back into the children's home. There were at least thirty men there he knew from the old days. Compared to the children's home, he said, prison was "a piece of cake."

A book about Braybon's life, *Salvation*, described his experience of the disappearance of a number of boys, in two cases after an out-of-control beating that ended with a lot of blood. Braybon reported the missing boys to the police in 2009, telling them about one in particular, Ray Dewar, a little boy with red hair who was assaulted by a caretaker with a big piece of wood. Braybon saw Dewar beaten to the ground, heard him screaming for it to stop, watched him trying to protect himself, and then saw Dewar silenced by a final blow to the head. Dazed and bleeding, Dewar was then helped away by another caretaker. Braybon never saw him again.

The police told Braybon that they had inquired about Dewar and learned that he had, in fact, been returned to his parents. "That's a little bit awkward," Braybon observed. He explained to the police that the reason the boy was in the home in the first place was because both of his parents had been killed in a car accident. Braybon told me that the police checked again, and they conceded that Braybon was right. The boys' parents were deceased. "Well, where is he now?" Braybon wanted to know. The police replied that they did not know.

Braybon had the impression that even though the police were responding to his claims, they didn't really believe that what he was saying had happened, or that it was even possible. Their basic position was that it simply *wouldn't* have happened. In fact, the police had taken the claims of Braybon and others seriously enough to conduct a forensic investigation at the home, but the search was limited to only part of the huge area of the home. Perhaps unsurprisingly, they found nothing. The further the inquiry went, the more Braybon had the sense that the investigators really didn't want to find anything.

If Braybon's impressions were correct, it would have been entirely consistent with the way orphanages had always been treated. To imagine that even *one* death took place in the way that Braybon described would require people to step fully into the eerie otherworld that few people in the twenty-first century know about. Even when they were functioning and ubiquitous, orphanages were opaque to the rest of society. State interference was, for most of the institutions' existence, minimal.

But the invisibility of the world of orphans, and the reluctance of the state to see them at all, let alone with any kind of clarity, was only part of the problem. The stories that emerged from them belonged to a unique set of human experiences that were so universally shunned and shut down that modern mental health is only beginning to understand them. Like victims of incarceration and torture in a gulag or death camp, or like victims of childhood sexual abuse in other contexts, orphans could take years, often decades, to report what happened to them.

The nature of this lag in reporting was not well understood when stories began to emerge in the 1990s. There was enormous anxiety about the memory of victims and the reliability of stories from the distant past, especially stories from childhood. The question of how people cope with disturbing memories through repression was vexing, especially given that the mechanisms of repression were not themselves fully understood.

If these problems were not complex enough, power dynamics also played a role. At the heart of all the orphanage cases, the balance of power between the two parties could not have been more off. The accused were some of the most venerated people in society. The victims were traditionally some of the most powerless. When children from an orphanage died, their names and any record of their existence often became undiscoverable, if not entirely lost. Yet the ghosts of their tormenters, long dead, still wandered freely, hounding everyone else who remained.

GEORGE—NOT HIS REAL NAME—AND I MET ON AN INTENSELY BRIGHT DAY in a big pub in the outer suburbs of Melbourne. George's daughter drove him and stayed for a while, chatting nervously and checking me out, until he told her to go. George had brought a bag full of books, papers, and photographs, including a photo of when he arrived in Australia (the photographer said he'd give him and his friends sixpence if they smiled). We spread out on a big table in the dark, air-conditioned room, and he told me that he was known as a fountain of knowledge. He was eighty-one and the very soul of joviality.

In the 1940s, George had been sent from England to Bindoon in Western Australia, about fifty miles out of Perth, the state capital. It was a region of dramatic escarpments and ridges, red and yellow soil, and relentless heat. Today the area teems with opencut mines of bauxite, sand, and iron ore.

The buildings of Bindoon were built by immigrant workers and the young boys who lived there. Children as young as ten spent long days using picks and shovels to clear the ground, mixing lime, laying cement, even working a quarry, using dynamite to blast rocks—all in heat of one hundred degrees or more.

The boys' labors were directed by Brother Keaney, an Irish immigrant who had been a policeman before he joined the Christian Brothers. He was known in Perth as "the orphans' friend," and also as "Keaney the builder"—a name he had given himself.

According to George, a more accurate moniker might have been "Keaney the sadist." The priest flogged naked boys in public, and in private, addressed them as Colleen, Betty Anne, or Bridgette. On Sundays, he took tea on the veranda with his good friend, the local commissioner of police, and together the men watched the boys work.

For decades, Bindoon was Keaney's own child-slave kingdom. Outside the orphanage, he was hailed as a savior. Inside, he was so hated that there were, according to local legend, at least two attempts to kill him. Once, George told me, someone tried to blow Keaney up with dynamite. Another time, the immigrant workers at the quarry put arsenic in his tea. Keaney consumed enough of the poison that his hair turned white, so the story went, but not enough to die.

Bindoon was one of four homes for boys—including Castledare, Clontarf, and Tardun—run by the Christian Brothers in Western Australia. At different times, Keaney ruled over two of them. While the policeman-turned-seminarian was the best-known brother, he was only one of the monsters in charge.

A 1998 government report on the Christian Brothers homes gives the strong impression that few boys left them without having been raped. The term "sexual abuse," the report noted, was too weak to describe the "exceptional depravity" of the homes run by the brothers. One boy at Tardun was the object of a competition between the brothers to see who could rape him one hundred times. The report said the boy tried to beat his own eyes in response. It is hard to know what this actually meant. Did he punch himself in the eyes? His hope, apparently, was that he could make them less blue because the brothers liked blue eyes.

George left Bindoon and returned twenty-six years later to the nearest city to find it full of homeless men. They were all ex–child migrants from the orphanages, he said. For all of them, even after they were finally free of the brothers and the nuns, life was haunted and hard.

By the time I met George, I had already heard a handful of stories about deaths at Bindoon and the other Christian Brothers homes. There was even a report from 1940 that mentioned a large number of sprained and broken limbs sustained by the boys at one of the homes, and the death of a twelve-year-old boy who died from tetanus. George knew many of the same stories and others that he had only heard a few years before.

GEORGE TOLD ME THAT ONE NIGHT IN 1949, A BOY NAMED SIMON DARNELL lay in his dorm at Tardun, situated in a small town in remote Western Australia. Darnell lay next to an Irish boy named Kevin Glasheen. A brother at the home, a notorious molester, prowled the dorms of Tardun at nine o'clock every night. That night, he began to harass the Irish boy. Darnell heard the boy say, "Oh no, not you again, Brother. God help me."

Somehow the Irish boy ended up on the balcony next to the dorm. The next morning, he was found dead, his body below the balustrade. An official report from the time noted that a boy named Kevin Glasheen died from a broken skull when he accidentally fell over a balcony.

Simon Darnell, the terrified boy in the next bed, told George the story many years later. George told me that he thought the boy ran out and threw himself off the balcony to get away from the brother. But no one, except presumably the brother, saw it happen. He could have pushed the boy over the edge. No one would have known.

When George repeated the words of the young Irish boy to me—"Oh no, not you again, Brother. God help me"—he said them with an Irish accent. For one disorienting second, it was like hearing a recording of the last minutes in the life of a child murdered in 1949. Kevin Glasheen uttered those words. Simon Darnell heard them. Decades later, Darnell repeated them for George as he had heard them. Now, in another city and another time, George replayed them for me. It chilled me. I felt sick thinking about it.

WHEN GEORGE AND I SAID GOODBYE AT THE PUB, HE'D PRESSED ONE OF HIS books on me. He wanted me to read it and get back to him. In the meantime, I found a record that stated four boys at the Christian Brothers homes, including Kevin Glasheen, died from a broken skull. The deaths had been recorded at the time they occurred, but no coroner's inquest or police inquiry was conducted into any of them.

A few days later, George phoned back. He sounded so upset that at first I couldn't understand what he was saying. George said he didn't want to be a part of the story anymore. His daughter didn't want him stirring stuff up. I was bewildered by the reversal. He didn't want to talk about what had changed. He sounded enraged and demanded that I send his book back straight away. It was as if I had taken it from him. Sure, I said, I would send the book back. George wanted me to agree to not pursue the story, not just his version, but the whole thing. I would not agree. Then he told me his son was a police officer in the very state where he had been incarcerated as a child. He said I would have to deal with his son if I didn't drop it. I told him I wasn't going to drop it. We went around and around. In the end he hung up.

Although we would later reconnect and discuss some of the facts of the story again, the call stunned me at the time. I turned it over and over, trying to make sense of it. I had a nagging sense that there was something in it that I'd heard before. Then it came to me: the moment when George had reproduced the voice of the young Irish boy about to die in that remote place of terror.

This felt like the same thing. Again, it was as if a hole had been ripped in time, and someone was phoning me direct from Bindoon in the 1940s. Maybe the voice I heard on the phone was a voice that George had himself heard a lot. It was saying, *How dare you? Do not question this. Let it go. You'll be sorry.*

I had met a lot of people who were witnesses of the orphanage world. I had met others who were gatekeepers. George appeared to be both. He also seemed to be terrified.

CHAPTER 4

THERE WERE YET MORE STORIES, MORE STATES, MORE HOMES, DIFFER-
ent media. Sheedy passed me a cassette tape that contained a detailed
description, with names, about a death in a place called St. John's, run by
the Sisters of Mercy in Goulburn, New South Wales. The tape had been
recorded by a man who had quietly told his story by himself in his living
room, and then put the tape away. His wife found it in a drawer only after
he died. The man described scrubbing the marble steps of the home he had
lived in, pilfering toast from the priest's supper plate, and seeing a child stab
another to death, an incident that was then covered up by the nuns. He
named the young murderer and I looked for him. But by the time I tracked
him down, he, too, had died.

Another man who, like Rod Braybon, spent years at a Salvation Army
home, shook with such intensity as he told me about a beating he had witnessed that he believed had resulted in a death, it left me feeling like I had
witnessed the violence. He was willing to talk more, but when his attention
was diverted, his wife begged me not to ask him any more questions. When
he became overwhelmed by the worst memories, she said, it made her life so
much harder.

Others told me stories about a child who suddenly wasn't there one morning, or a boy who was badly beaten and then disappeared, or a patch of yard

where the children never stepped. I read news articles from Ireland, Scotland, and Canada about people who grew up in orphanages and told similar tales, a rumor about a disappearance here, someone's secondhand story about an eyewitness to murder there. I spoke to an Irish man who grew up at a Christian Brothers school in Artane, near Dublin, Ireland. He told me that he saw a boy fall through a stairwell from the fourth floor. He recalled looking up to see one of the brothers looking down over the railing. The official line was that the boy had been playing and fell. Other children said that the boy was running from the brother, who regularly abused him. "The whole thing didn't make sense," he said. The boy died.

It was impossible to hold the whole idea in my head. I got in the habit of creating lists and then unaccountably losing them. Regularly, I would sit down and start again, listing details from these and other cases: Therese Williams, the falling boy, Pentridge, the drowned boy, Gilbert, Peter Hill, the frozen boy.

Except for Sheedy and her organization, almost everyone else's reaction to the death stories was bewilderment, at least at the beginning. Even the people who were well acquainted with the violations and violence of orphanages and the Catholic Church became hazy or skeptical when the subject turned to death, negligent homicide, or murder.

When I asked him about the deaths, an Irish academic who was familiar with the world of violence and abuse in Christian Brothers homes in Ireland said, "It's hard to know." He'd heard stories, he said, but most were from very early in the twentieth century, and he was reluctant to give them much credence. "There was a requirement by the state if there was a death in the school to have an inquiry," he said. "And by and large they did. Certainly, in some of the schools there was a high enough death rate, but it was mainly through diseases and mostly pre-independence." Why was he confident that where disease was claimed, the cause of death had in fact been disease? Was it reasonable to trust an institution that lied and lied again about the rape of children to be scrupulous in their infirmary note-keeping?

CANADA, I LEARNED, WAS THE ONLY COUNTRY TO HAVE CREATED A SPECIAL Missing Children Project to investigate the stories of dead or missing children in residential schools. It was started by the Assembly of First Nations and became part of the Truth and Reconciliation Commission, whose final report was published in 2015. It began with the fact that thousands of Indigenous Canadian children who had been forced to go to residential schools simply never returned home. Like Australia's Indigenous children in mission schools, the Canadian children who eventually did return from residential schools reported extreme abuse and targeted punitive treatment designed to destroy their connection with their ancestry and their culture.

The Missing Children Project took testimony from witnesses and reached out to the public, asking people to be in contact if they knew of a child who had disappeared or died in a residential school, or if they knew of sites where residential schools may have buried children. They identified the documentation for more than six hundred deaths that had occurred since the 1940s and thousands more preceding that time.

Many children who died were not named by the schools, nor was their date of death noted, and for almost half of the children, the cause of death was not recorded. Where an explanation for death was given, some children were said to have run away and then frozen to death. Many died of tuberculosis or in other epidemics, which were not uncommon. There were drownings, accidents, fires in residential buildings, and suicides. Other children died and disappeared in more mysterious circumstances. Often their parents had no idea what happened to them.

Kimberly Murray, Ontario's first assistant deputy attorney general for Indigenous Justice, and Mohawk of Kanesatake, led the project. In 2018 she told me about former residents who recalled witnessing other children beaten to death in front of them. The residents didn't know the name of the child who died but they never forgot what they saw. For a number of these cases, Murray's team found a record from the school that noted the death of a child at the same time, but which did not include a cause of death. They found records about a child falling to his death from a window. There were survivor stories from all over the country about dead babies being placed in incinerators.

Murray asked me if I'd heard about the story of an electric chair in St. Anne's School in Northern Ontario. Former residents of the school, run by the Grey Nuns and the French-speaking priests of the Oblates of Mary

Immaculate, had told Murray about a homemade electric chair that was used on the children up to the early 1960s. Earlier, the former residents had reported the use of the electric chair and other abuse to the government, but they were told they were making it up. It was simply too outlandish. Later, Murray's team found a letter in French in the church's own records from the time that mentioned the chair and proved its existence.

The Missing Children Project was unique in the world for taking the death stories seriously when it did. In other government inquiries, the investigative body restricted its focus to sexual abuse, and the death stories out of orphanages and other residential institutions seemed more like one-off hallucinations or misinterpretations rather than patterned and predictable events, as the stories of sexual abuse were. It was understood that sexual and physical violence were inevitable outcomes in a world of grotesque negligence and dehumanizing brutality. Yet for many, the deaths still had a powerful aura of unreality.

IN 2002, THE *BOSTON GLOBE* BLEW OPEN THE STORY OF SEXUAL ABUSE BY Catholic priests in the United States with its Spotlight investigation of the Archdiocese of Boston and its cover-up of longtime sexual abuse of children by many of its priests. The series released a flood of similar claims all over the country, and then all over the world. In its wake, one diocese after another was exposed for the same crimes, endemic sexual attacks on children, and subsequent cover-ups. The effect was revolutionary. One famous victim's attorney told me that before the Spotlight investigation, the assumption made by judges, juries, and the public was that it was impossible for a priest to molest a child. After the exposé, he said, that reversed completely. Most people assumed that any allegations against priests were probably true.

If anyone knew about orphanages, and the abuse and likely murder that occurred in them, I figured it would surely be the Americans who had been at the forefront of the revolution for so long. I pitched the story to *BuzzFeed News*, who threw their support behind the investigation. I began to report the story in the United States.

For a long time, I kept hitting walls. No one seemed to know what I was talking about. It was extraordinary to me how many people who were deeply immersed in the world of sexual abuse investigation and litigation against the church didn't know much about the orphanages. Some told me that such places had never existed in the United States. Many assumed that America's orphanages and childcare institutions had shut down in the nineteenth century, ending in 1870 instead of 1970. I spoke to so many people— seasoned, grizzled experts—who I thought would know but did not, that even I started to wonder if, in fact, the orphanages had all closed over a hundred years ago.

Documentation was scarce. Unlike other countries, the United States had no large-scale government inquiries into institutionalized sex abuse, let alone the other depravities of orphanage life. The White House hosted a conference in 1909 on the Care of Dependent Children and concluded that institutional care was not preferred, and that there was much about it to be criticized. Where possible, foster care and other kinds of family settings were recommended for children in need. Despite this seemingly contemporary approach, the number of orphanages only increased in the next few decades. Isolated reports and white papers followed over the years. The message in most was that institutions were not good for children and were quite likely bad. But they had little impact.

In the early 1990s, some limited scholarship about orphanages was produced. But with only a small number of books published on the subject, America's historians largely ignored it. Some orphanage stories had been investigated by law enforcement, but the endeavor was usually weak or hamstrung. Certainly, across the world, accounts of cooperation between police, public officials, and institutional staff to cover up past crimes were legion.

In the small number of cases where American courts had been asked to judge the orphanage system and its consequences, they had ultimately, with a few exceptions, remained indifferent. If an institution settled privately with a victim, it was typically for only a few thousand dollars. Most rare were the cases where government bodies pursued institutions and held them legally responsible for many of the children.

Really, it was no surprise then that the stories of American orphans were rarely told and barely heard, let alone recognized in any formal way by the government, the public, or the law. The orphanages of the twentieth century and their many thousands of residents had slipped so quickly into the

American subconscious that most people, not just those who worked in related worlds, assumed that orphanages belonged to a bygone era. But that was not the case.

I spoke to Terry McKiernan, the founder and president of Bishop Accountability.org, Inc., an organization with the quietly revolutionary mission of collecting every priest file, legal report, church document, newspaper article, and magazine piece on priest sex abuse, and creating a database of offenders and the credibly accused in the United States and other countries. Even McKiernan with his ten-thousand-foot view of the world of Catholic abuse hadn't come across much about the orphanages. He sent me some depositions from an orphanage litigation in Vermont in the 1990s. He had tracked them down after reading a series of articles in the *Burlington Free Press* by a journalist named Sam Hemingway. The case sounded bizarre.

On December 3, 1997, in the office of a law firm in Burlington, a lawyer named Robert Widman had questioned a woman who had once lived in a local orphanage:

"When you were in the classroom, was there ever any effort to make the children make animal noises?" asked Widman.

"Yes, there was," she said.

"Can you describe that for us, please?"

"I was made to bark like a dog for one of the . . . for the nuns," she replied. "One of the nuns that was in the classroom. It seemed like to be for her to, to have fun with, you know, to intimidate you or at her pleasure."

"How many times did this occur?"

"It occurred every single day, and every single, every morning, every afternoon."

. . .

"What kinds of sounds did the other children, were the other children required to make?"

"Oh, there was birds, there was horses, there, you know . . . roosters."

ACTUALLY, MOST AMERICAN STATES WERE HOME TO ORPHANAGES. EVEN midsized cities, like Burlington, Vermont, and Albany, New York, had more than one. Before the orphanage era, the same children would have had to fend for themselves. If they were lucky, relatives could take care of them, though many lived on the streets. But from the 1850s, a silent network of buildings, often purpose-built, spread across the nation and absorbed hundreds of thousands of its children. At their peak in the 1930s, there were as many as 1,600 orphanages in the United States, some of which housed more than 1,500 children at a time. Their numbers steadily declined from that point on, but in the 1950s, it's likely there were still many hundreds of them. The institutions were often religious. Hundreds were run by the Catholic Church, but not all were Catholic. There were Protestant and Jewish orphanages, and some, like Mooseheart in Illinois, were founded by fraternal orders like the Loyal Order of Moose. Typically, the institutions, no matter their denomination, had a relationship with the state, which in some cases paid them a fee for each child. It is likely that more than five million Americans passed through these institutions in the twentieth century.

As they were elsewhere in the world, American orphanages were designed to care for children in cases of ordinary and exceptional tragedy. They had lost their fathers in the Civil War, the Great Depression, World War I, or World War II, and their mothers simply could not care for them. Most were not orphans at all. In some states the children were Indigenous or the children of settlers and the devastated tribes of America, whose parents were deemed somehow incompetent. Some had alcoholic fathers or mothers, who had themselves ended up in mental health institutions. In the 1950s, many "orphans" were the children of two otherwise robust parents whose main transgression was that they had divorced or that one was Catholic and one was not. Children were taken—voluntarily or involuntarily—from their single working mothers or widowed parents. One institution was called a

"Half-Orphan Asylum." Children stayed at an orphanage anywhere from a few weeks to years, until someone was able to come for them, or they were old enough to walk out themselves, or less commonly, they were adopted. Around the middle of the century, many of the institutions changed their names. St. Joseph's Orphan Asylum became St Joseph's Child Care Center, but in significant ways, they stayed the same.

By the 1960s and 1970s orphanages were shutting down in response to financial struggles and, in some cases, increasing criticism from a professionalized welfare community. With the advent of the contraceptive pill, legalized abortion, more state support for families in need, and changing ideas about family size, there was also a smaller population of children in need. In the case of Catholic orphanages, the number of nuns, the poorly paid carers who did most of the work in the institution, was decreasing. It is likely that the trend to deinstitutionalization, which began in 1955 and saw thousands of people with mental health issues and developmental disorders released from institutions into the community, also influenced the waning support for orphanages in professional and broader communities, but there is not much scholarship on this topic.

The orphanages were replaced primarily by the foster care system and, in some cases, by small group homes, an attempt to create a kinder, more family-like situation. By the 1990s, many destitute or disadvantaged American children who might have otherwise lived in an orphanage were likely in foster care. The orphanages had always placed some children in local families, often to work on farms or help with babies, and in the 1970s foster care became the sole mission of some as they transformed into placement agencies.

During the orphanage era, institutions were usually controlled from the top down. In Catholic institutions, a resident priest probably lived in the building, with an order of nuns to do all the childcare, and local townsfolk to staff the kitchens and maintain the grounds. Not much remains of communication between the orphanages, but it is clear that at least some of them were in touch, sometimes sending children from one place to the other through an unseen network.

Given modern efforts to acknowledge injustices in American history, it is extraordinary that the orphanage system has remained invisible. We know a great deal about the long-lasting legacy of many catastrophic practices from the nineteenth and twentieth centuries and before. Yet we know next to nothing about the millions of lives affected by this perverse system of warehousing children—and worse.

It's not just orphans who have kept silent. State governments and religious organizations have been so keen to forget what happened that, even though substantial money passed through orphanages, it's hard to find definitive numbers to describe the system. More than a decade into the twenty-first century, orphanages remained a significant but almost wholly missing part of American history.

BECAUSE ORPHANAGES SHAPED THE LIVES AND FAMILIES OF MANY ADULTS who are still alive today, in small pockets of the country, stories from the inside lived on—in the archives of local newspapers and in self-published memoirs, on tribal reservations where people talk about intergenerational pain and intimately understand its impact, and in the remnants of court cases buried deep in state and federal archives. In 2014, as I began to ask about orphanages in the United States, the evidence was rapidly disappearing.

Slowly, I found people who had spent time in an orphanage or a mission school. They told me hair-raising stories about little girls who were peeling potatoes one night and then never seen again, about the sounds of babies crying in places where they shouldn't have been. It was hard to find pieces of the larger context for the stories to fit into.

I met Ken Bear Chief, a man who had for years been on his own journey to expose the abuse and deaths of children in the Catholic-run mission and boarding schools of the American West. We traveled together for some days visiting the sites of stories and rumors he had heard. We spoke to members of the Blackfeet Nation about the accidental 2007 discovery of the skeletal remains of more than two dozen children at the site of the Willow Creek boarding school, northwest of Browning, Montana, which closed in 1909. There were so many stories.

Ken Bear Chief introduced me to a woman who spent time at St. Mary's Mission, in Omak, Washington, on the Colville Reservation. She and I stood together in the church at St. Mary's Mission and gazed at a spot on the wooden floor where, she told me, years before she had watched a priest and some nuns put something beneath the floorboards. As they did it, she heard a baby cry. She believed the clergy buried a child there. Years later she reported the incident to the FBI. The agent told her that he couldn't believe it had happened. He said she must have imagined it. Later, Bear Chief wrote to the FBI to follow up. The story should be investigated, he said. They never responded.

It was a long time before I came across a significant body of records that had been left by a group of survivors. The actions of survivors in Burlington, Vermont, and elsewhere in the 1990s had generated so much material, they preserved large pieces of a long-gone institution. It was like finding the archaeological ruins of a medieval fortress. The overall shape and many smaller details were still apparent.

The little girl who had barked like a dog had lived at St. Joseph's in Burlington, Vermont, and the more I read of her story and the other stories McKiernan had sent, the more determined I became to learn more. Eventually, I had thousands of pages of litigation from numerous sources that took many months to plough through.

St. Joseph's was a house of horrors, though not in the usual sense. That is not to say that children didn't literally fly down stairs, sent airborne by rage-filled women; that they weren't whipped, hung out windows, or humiliated; and that there weren't any number of stories that either began or ended with a pool of blood. Rather, it was the usual implication of the phrase—that a house of horrors is unique—that was not right. To be sure, St. Joseph's was its own epic tragedy, but it was also part of a vast network of similar islands that connected poor Geoff Meyer at Royleston, the boys of St. Augustine's, Therese Williams at Nazareth House, and more people from more institutions in more countries.

St. Joseph's became a kind of ground zero for the world's orphanage story because what remained was, in a sense, the most complete archaeological site I had come across. This was because in the 1990s, decades after the orphanage had closed, many of its former inhabitants had found the strength to come forward and describe what they had been through—and to speak out on behalf of the fellow orphans who had not survived. In response, the church pursued an aggressive legal strategy to divide and conquer, to deny them the strength and credibility that their numbers should have brought.

Although much evidence of abuse at St. Joseph's had been definitively smashed and scattered in the 1990s, pieces remained. The challenge in the mid 2010s was to work out where to find them and fit them back together.

Early on, I came across the testimony of Sally Dale, who said she had witnessed at least two deaths, events that she thought may have been murder. I also learned about Robert Widman, the lawyer who took on the oldest institution in the world before the Spotlight investigation changed everything.

I found Widman alive and well in Florida. He told me that for a few years after the release of the film *Spotlight*, which told the story of the historic investigation by the *Boston Globe*, he could not watch it. When he eventually did, he cried throughout. *Oh my God, I knew all these people*, he thought. As he listened to the actor playing Richard Sipe in the film—the Benedictine monk-turned-psychotherapist who had been a frequent expert witness in sex abuse cases against the church—Widman remembered talking to Sipe in the 1990s for his own case. At the time that Widman watched the film, he hadn't thought about the St. Joseph's case in years. Yet for at least a decade before the *Globe's* investigation, at a time when entirely medieval ideas of subservience were practiced unchallenged in modern America, Widman had been one of a small group of lawyers and journalists across the country who had risked their jobs, reputations, family life, and mental health to stand up to the church Goliath and defend the victims of its priests and nuns. They had all failed.

I DID NOT FULLY UNDERSTAND THE STORY OF ST. JOSEPH'S IN BURLINGTON the first time Widman and I met. I had begun to read witness accounts, but it was frustratingly hard to sync the stories together—how many deaths were claimed, who saw them, and when in the forty-odd years covered by the litigation they had occurred. Some people had changed their names more than once in that time. Transcripts of witness depositions are usually very long documents, but when courts file them, they typically retain only the pages that mention the key stories or facts that were deemed relevant to the final ruling. Already I had come across horrifying tales about a boy who drowned and a child who froze, and I had turned the page . . . only to find that the next page was missing. I frantically tried to cross-reference the story in other depositions and track down the witness. Sometimes I found more. Often I found only a whisper of the original story.

When I first asked Widman about the death stories at St. Joseph's, our conversation didn't go anywhere. It took time to work out where he stood on the matter and how to make sense of it in my own mind. The larger picture was a puzzle. On the one hand, it would be hard to overstate the irrational courage and extreme zeal of the attorneys, journalists, and whistleblowers, like Widman, who took on the church before the Spotlight investigation. Those people had grappled with ideas that most found unthinkable, and they backed victims who no one else believed. With little support from anyone, they went into battle against a two-thousand-year-old entity that had crushed uncountable foes. Their role in the history of American justice was not heralded at the time, but it was, and will always be, enormously important. And yet, huge questions remained unanswered.

I spoke to Richard Sipe, who had been so instrumental in the *Boston Globe* Spotlight investigation, and who was still out there working as an expert witness in cases against the church. Sipe had counseled many Catholic priests and ex-priests, and more than anyone in the world, he spoke from a place of expertise and integrity about the ways a large percentage of Catholic clergy were not celibate and were often abusive.

Sipe told me about the Catholic Church's institutionalized sadism, its glorification of suffering, and how commonplace abuse was in its institutions. But it was his stories about a fundamental quality of arrogance in the church that made me believe the worst was possible. When I told him about the murder stories I had heard, and the ways I had tried and failed to verify them, Sipe said, "You have a wonderful, wonderful tiger by the tail here," and he began to talk about the accuracy of official documents.

The cause of death on the death certificate for a priest who died of an AIDS-related illness in Sipe's monastery was recorded as starvation, he told me. A bishop who died in similar circumstances was described as a salesman on his death certificate, Sipe said. At a hospital where Sipe had worked long ago, some of the junior nurses, who were also novices, needed study credits in order to be fully licensed. The head of the hospital, who was both a nun and head of the order to which the novices belonged, simply took the novices' files and gave them the credits they needed. Just like that. "This is the important thing," Sipe said. "The sense of power, and the sense of necessity, and the justification."

SALLY DALE'S DEATH STORIES, FOR ME, CAME TO REPRESENT THEM ALL. THEY were cold cases, twice over. They had gone unreported and uninvestigated for more than half a lifetime. Then the courts of Vermont chewed them over and set them aside in the 1990s, and they had receded once more from view. Since then, a critical change had occurred: the hidden history of orphanages had been revealed over much of the world, if not in America. Each of Sally's stories, and every other death story, represented a terrible criminal act, or at least the possibility of one. But they were also part of something that was much larger and more systematic, as was clear from the many similarities among stories from around the globe.

St. Joseph's was its own house of horrors *and* it was an outpost in a grim and complex netherworld. It became clear that where evidence had gone missing or a witness had died or documents had been destroyed in one place, orphans from elsewhere could at least illuminate what might have happened. Occasionally they might point to where evidence could be found.

They could speak to the whole experience, too, not merely the assaults and sexual abuse, but the life. Together, the orphans of St. Joseph's, Nazareth House, and Bindoon, and the children of the Sisters of Providence, St. John of God, and all the others could speak with an authority that no one else had.

I talked to as many survivors from St. Joseph's as I could find, tracking down every death story as far as I could go. Throughout, I was haunted by the idea that the child abuse sex scandal that had cost so many millions of dollars and left such a foul stain might not be the worst thing that had happened in the Catholic Church. It might only be the tip of the iceberg.

IN OCTOBER 2019, I DROVE TO THE SOUTHERN STATE CORRECTIONAL FAcility in Springfield, Vermont. The facility was a gray brutalist fortress on a rocky hill above the Black River. Tunnels of barbed wire sat on top of an enormous fence next to the main building. As I walked through the large parking lot to the visitor's door, I saw men moving in a distant yard, wearing jumpsuits in different shades of orange.

A young caseworker escorted me to the interview room, a small internal space with a green linoleum floor, brick walls painted all one color, and a tiny table next to a glass window that looked onto a corridor. On the other side of the corridor the window of a control room with a bank of monitors showed staff walking in and out. If I felt unsafe, the caseworker told me, I could wave at someone in the control room. I was there to talk to Anthony Giallella, who was serving an eleven-year sentence for the sexual abuse of a minor. Giallella shuffled in through a different door. I wasn't allowed to take in a recorder, a computer, or any kind of device.

One year earlier, *BuzzFeed News* had published my orphanage investigation. It told the story of St. Joseph's of Burlington, Vermont, and the missing history of America's orphanages. It was based on hundreds of interviews and documents totaling tens of thousands of pages, including police records, government files, depositions, handwritten diaries, and letters. It identified multiple stories of torture and suspicious death at American orphanages, including six at St. Joseph's alone.

The article was viewed by six million people. Many wrote to say that it had validated something about the country's history, or their own, that they had known deep down, if not consciously. The state's attorney general launched a criminal investigation and a restorative justice process, in which the survivors joined forces once again to revisit the terrible past and to make new meaning from it. Together they changed US history.

Yet painful mysteries remained. Someone I spoke to mentioned Giallella. It was said that he had reported an entirely different death story at the orphanage that I had, by that point, spent years investigating. He wasn't the only person who came forward to tell a tale I'd never heard before, or to provide the missing piece of a puzzle—published or unpublished—that I had wrestled with. Yet there was something about Giallella's story that stood out. It seemed not just believable, but tractable. That was how I ended up sitting there on the day before Halloween, across from the man. He was in his eighties, hunched, and unwell. He wore dark glasses and spoke from a place of strange, unfocused intensity.

Giallella's father had dropped him at the orphanage with his two brothers and sister sometime around 1940. He and his brother Bob had been a handful, he said, as if that explained it. He was not even two years old.

He remembered being driven to the orphanage by his father and seeing the great building looming and a crowd of boys playing outside in the yard. He remembered becoming an altar boy and serving mass sometimes two or three times a day. He remembered the windows from the nuns' rooms that looked directly into the dorms. He didn't draw the comparison, but he described a setup much like the one we sat in that day.

Giallella remembered sitting in front of a girl named Marie St. Pierre in the orphanage classroom. She used to tell him about a man who brought candy and ice cream to the orphanage, and who had sex with lots of the girls there. He spoke about Sister Pauline, who would hit the boys upside the head with a rolled newspaper. He described how awful it was to have soap forced into his mouth and his head held underwater in a sink, until another boy taught him to hold his breath and cover his ears—he leaned forward and mimed having his head held down with his hands firmly clasped over his ears, mouth tight shut. If he didn't get too many demerits during the week, he got to watch a movie on the weekend with the other children, like an Abbott and Costello film, or *Bambi*.

At night, Giallella and his mates used to crawl down the long dormitory hallway and sneak downstairs to the kitchen. He stole a whole loaf of bread, he told me, and quietly returned to share it with his friends. One night, Giallella snuck into the kitchen and struck gold. There were ice creams in the pantry. He gorged what he could and took two extra to hide under his pillow until morning. When he woke the ice cream had melted everywhere, and he was caught.

Giallella described scenes of lurid sexual abuse that he had personally experienced at the orphanage—he held his hands up above his head, wrists crossed over. It was so sadistic I would not have believed him, except that by that point I'd read the testimony of half a dozen men who had been assaulted by the same person that Giallella named, an unconstrained serial sadist of epic dysfunction.

When he was in his mid-teens, Giallella's mother, who he hadn't seen since he was one year old, came to take him out of the orphanage. He shrugged at me, still confused as to why she had come. He felt kind of lonely at first, he said, and wanted to go back to St. Joseph's.

WHEN HE WAS ABOUT TEN YEARS OLD, GIALLELLA WAS CALLED INTO A BIG room. At times, he thought it may have been the girls' dormitory. Other times he said it was the attic. Sister Jane of the Rosary stood there with two men Giallella had never seen before. On the floor lay a girl wrapped in plastic. She was wrapped up "real good," he said. Blond hair peeked out the top of the wrapping. She was dead. Sister Jane looked at Giallella, "You did this," she said.

The nun made Giallella help the men carry the body of the girl out of the back of the orphanage. They headed toward the baseball field and turned right at the tallest tree. There, Giallella and the adults squeezed through the hole in the wooden fence between the orphanage and the cemetery next door. They walked in a fairly straight line across the cemetery toward what Giallella called, "a little house."

Once they got there, Sister Jane unlocked the door and the men entered. When they reappeared, they no longer had the body of the girl with them. Sister Jane shut the door.

Giallella moved back and forth between describing the events of that day and the haunting he had suffered since. He told the story of the girl with the same concreteness that he spoke about stealing food from the pantry. But then he would get vague and confused.

The blond girl. I could have dreamed it, he said. *Kids disappeared. I dreamed about her. She was floating in the air. She had this glowing beautiful face. She was like an angel. I think of it. Was it real? I started having dreams that I did it. I still see her. That blond hair.*

After I spoke to Giallella, I drove back to Burlington and wandered up and down the fence of Lakeview Cemetery, where it abutted the old St. Joseph's Orphanage property. What Giallella described must have occurred almost seventy years before. He said I would find the hole in the fence if I found the tallest tree. But if there had been an enormous tree on the orphanage side of the fence, it was gone now. I peered through the fence at the back of the orphanage. There were no traces of a baseball field either. I could not see any holes or traces of old holes mended, and the fence, which seemed old, was made of iron. It was a long shot, obviously.

Then again, cemeteries are quiet places. Time moves more slowly inside their boundaries than in the towns around them. Later, I showed satellite photos to other men who had been boys at the orphanage around the same time that Giallella was there. They pointed out exactly where the baseball field had once been and where the tall tree was—the tree that a boy had once unforgettably sent a baseball soaring over—and they told me that if you walked from that spot to the side fence, which had once been wooden, there was a hole that everyone knew about, through which the children sometimes escaped.

I went back to the cemetery and worked out where the tree had been. I realized that if you walked in a relatively straight line from the hole in the fence toward the middle of the cemetery, you ended up at a mausoleum that looked a lot like a little house.

For a while I worried that Giallella's story had been influenced in some way by the *BuzzFeed News* article. But then I spoke to two other people who had also heard it. Giallella had told them, too, about the dead girl that he helped place in the little house. Like me, they had initially balked. It was too awful. It couldn't be real. If it had happened, we would have known about it by now.

But as they came to know Giallella and understood more of what he'd been through, they found the story of the girl compelling. Both came to believe that Giallella was telling the truth. One of them even tried to get help, to get someone to investigate, but nothing was done. All of that happened more than fifteen years before I wrote about St. Joseph's Orphanage.

"I hope it's a dream," Giallella had said when we first spoke. Later on the phone, he told me: "I wish you could find the body. It's a dice game until you find the body."

He told me again about nuns sleeping with the boys. He laughed and mentioned that he'd once tried to burn the place down. He wasn't without empathy. "You take care of thirty or forty kids? You go out of your mind, I guess." We went through the story of the dead girl once more, punctuated irregularly by his disbelieving laugh, "She told me I did it!" As we neared the end, his voice shook. "I told you, ma'am, you've got to find a body!"

I returned again to the mausoleum that lay at the end of the invisible path that started at the orphanage's tall tree. It stood about eight feet tall and maybe a bit over six feet across. It was constructed from enormous blocks of bluestone.

At the front, two large, rusted doors bulged slightly outward, but they had been secured by two thick planks of wood. Above the doors, three layers of bluestone simulated a roof. In the center of the bottom layer, the word *Lewis* had been carved.

The Lakeview records listed fourteen mausoleums at the cemetery, most of which had been opened since the 1950s. If there had been an extra body in one of them, I presumed, it would have already been found. Some had glass in their doors or filigree metal, making it possible to see inside. There was only one that had not been opened—as far as anyone knew—since the 1920s: the Lewis Mausoleum.

I set about trying to find the owner of the mausoleum, but in 2020, the global COVID pandemic shut everything down. I live in Melbourne, the city of the world's longest lockdown, which made it harder. In the end it took me two years to find the family, the last remaining of the Lewis kin. They gave me permission to look inside the mausoleum, but I did not find the body. Giallella's girl was not there. Yet I didn't find closure either.

I still think about her and Giallella. I recall how it felt when he spoke about her, plastic-wrapped, floating. It was like she was there in the tiny brick room with us, aloft, watching. The experience had verged on the extremely claustrophobic. The girl had never left him, though she was hardly Giallella's only ghost.

Once, he told me, when he had grown big enough that he was no longer willing to simply take the physical abuse of the nuns, Sister Pauline hit him with her rolled up newspaper one final time. In response, he said, "I decked her." Probably as terrified by what he had done as the nun must have been, and big or not, Giallella was promptly dragged into the orphanage attic and tied with his arms behind him to a thick wooden beam. One of the nuns then stood in front of him.

In the orphanage archipelago, it was normal for kids like Giallella to be faced with unhinged grown-ups, ranging from the bitterly authoritarian or sexually abusive to the ones who allowed themselves to lose all adult control only on special occasions. This day, however, was different. There was something about the nun standing in front of Giallella that was so outside normal, even orphanage-normal, that it was hard for the young boy to process. He almost fainted from fear, he told me, but because he was tied standing up, he couldn't. There was nothing he could do, nowhere else to go, when the nun before him leaned in, bit him hard on the shoulder, and then growled, *I am the Devil.*

ACT II

Règlement de visite à l'Orphelinat St. Joseph, Burlington, Vermont
29 nov 1939

In closing the visit of St. Joseph's Orphanage, Burlington, Vermont, I the undersigned Provincial Superior of the Institute of the Daughters of Charity, Servants of the Poor, attest and prescribe that which follows:

1. The prescriptions of the Questionnary of the Sacred Congregation are followed
2. The Rule is well observed
3. The spirited exercises are made regularly
4. There is a family spirit among the Sisters
5. The books are kept neatly and well
6. Order and neatness reign everywhere and the offices are well kept and well provided for
7. The children look happy and are well cared for

. . .

May our Celestial Mother Mary watch over every soul that will ever find shelter under this dear roof

Made and passed at St. Joseph's Orphanage, Burlington, Vt, this twenty nine day of November nineteen hundred and thirty nine

Sr Margaret of Scotland, Prov Sup
Reports of Provincial Superior of Official Visits
to St. Joseph's Orphanage, November 29, 1939

CHAPTER 5

You have priests in the house, who you meet occasionally. Be respect-
ful and discreet with them, they will appreciate you more. Between
us do not speak of priests unless necessary.

—Reports of Provincial Superior of Official Visits
to St. Joseph's Orphanage, December 6, 1945

I<small>T IS</small> 1948. S<small>OUTH OF</small> L<small>ONE</small> R<small>OCK</small> P<small>OINT, THE EASTERN SHORE OF</small> L<small>AKE</small> Champlain rises in a series of terraces and slopes up to a plateau along which North Avenue runs. The avenue undulates gently, and as it heads away from town, it crosses an invisible line between the New North End and the Old North End.

Two lines of tall elms run along the avenue, separating a cluster of modest houses on one side and a series of monuments on the other: the gothic chapel of the Lakeview Cemetery; the Lakeview Sanitarium, a retreat for those with "select cases of mild derangement" and "nervous troubles"; and between the two, the old Providence Orphan Asylum, later called St. Joseph's Orphanage.

Both the cemetery and the sanitarium feature winding paths, landscaped lawns, and pretty groves. The orphanage is a massive redbrick block. In the back, a large annex projects out toward the lake, and in the front, more than fifty windows face North Avenue, not counting those in the eaves or the cupola. Narrow white columns mark the grand front door, which opens onto a foyer for visitors, and a visiting parlor on the right. The parlor regulations are mounted on the wall: *1. Visiting hours are the second and fourth Sundays of each month, from one to three-thirty; 2. Visits should not last longer than a half hour without special permission; 3. The children are not allowed to eat in the parlor; and 4. Relatives and friends desiring to see the children must come to the parlor. It is strictly forbidden to go to playgrounds in search of them.* A gothic script in the glass above the foyer entrance proclaims, *God Will Provide.*

Inside the grand building lives one chaplain, twenty-nine Sisters of Providence, mostly French-speaking women from the mother house in Montreal, Canada, and more than 150 children. Occasionally a silent line of boys or girls marches by the front door on their way to a classroom or the basement dining room. On most days, they inhabit the yard outside or the floors above, each defined by an immensely long hallway that looks longer still in the deep shine of the wooden floor. Today is different. Most of the children are going about their normal routines, but one girl is separate, waiting. Her bright red hair is set in wavy curls framing a round face. She is nine years old, and her name is Sally. Once she had sung like an angel, but nowadays she has a reputation for being stubborn. Today, though, in a promising moment of early spring warmth, none of that matters because the most incredible thing is about to happen.

Earlier, Sally had been sent to the office of Vermont Catholic Charities, situated in the little stone house next to the orphanage, to talk to Harriet Parker, a Catholic social worker. Parker has known Sally since she was two years old, and they have never gotten along. A few years before, Sally told Parker that when she was down at the lake, Brother Foster and another brother played what they called "tea party" with the girls in the water. They moved the girls' bathing suits and touched them on "that bad place." But, Parker said, Sally had an imagination. The nuns told her so. Sally also told Parker that another priest had lifted up her skirt, but Parker just laughed.

According to Parker, the nuns said Sally was a rebellious devil child. Even Sally could not deny that she often caused trouble. When all the girls kneeled to pray in the hallway, Sally often laughed, and if an older girl in charge slapped her, Sally would slap her right back. She refused to eat her own vomit, and when it came to chores, sometimes she was a real slowpoke on purpose.

But in the most recent meeting Sally had with Parker, a miracle occurred. A woman Sally had never seen before sat in the room with a girl. Parker introduced them as Mrs. Pelkey and her daughter, Nancy, who was seven years old. She asked Sally if she would like to go home with the Pelkeys. If they liked her, Sally might become Nancy's big sister. Would Sally like that? Sally liked it very much. Parker told her she'd have to be a good girl and not be so defiant or stubborn. Sally readily agreed.

So now here she is, waiting to leave the orphanage. Sally knows, because she has been told, that she is the devil's own child, and that she will pay for the sins of her parents. All the bad things that have happened to her—and that will continue to happen to her—are of course her own fault. That's what the nuns told her, anyway. Yet somehow, despite all that, Sally is about to get the only thing she has ever wanted. She is going to live with a real mother and a father and another little girl. Sally is going to be part of a family.

Watchfulness is serious duty for all the Sisters who have to deal with children either at work, in school, or elsewhere. It must be done nobly and openly, as a mother cares for a child she loves. The children's souls are pure and innocent, but the devil is wicked and he is always alert to entrap them. His one hope is to spoil a child's soul, knowing of old, that if he can soil a youthful soul, he will make a bad man. Let us not allow him to harm our dear children.

*—Reports of Provincial Superior of Official Visits
to St. Joseph's Orphanage, November 29, 1939*

EIGHT YEARS EARLIER, AT MIDSUMMER IN THE MIDDLE OF WORLD WAR II, Sally arrived at St. Joseph's with three other siblings. She was two years old and covered in bruises, surrendered by her mother, who had been chased down by a local probation officer. For a while, she lived across the road in a house with Mrs. McGrath under the supervision of the Mother Superior. Sally's older sister, Sherry, had been absorbed into the big orphanage building with the nuns. Her brother, Ronald, disappeared around the same time, though how much time he spent at the orphanage and how much he was off somewhere else in the world, Sally never really knew. Joanna, the baby, was taken by a local family.

As Sally adjusted to regular mealtimes and the enormous dog at Mrs. McGrath's house, the orphanage priest, a social worker, the attorney general, and a probation officer engaged in a flurry of letters and reports about her young parents, Henry and Ramona Fredette, both already well known to the state and the local Red Cross, and neither of whom had made a great impression on anyone.

The ferociously quarrelling couple had separated. Henry had been court ordered to pay ten dollars from his weekly salary of nineteen dollars and eighty cents from Foley's Laundry to his estranged wife for the maintenance of their children. Now that the three older children had been taken from their mother and placed at the orphanage, most of that money was to be redirected.

Accordingly, much of the correspondence circled around money. Permission to get the children baptized was also a concern. Henry and Ramona had planned to baptize their children but instead had heated and irresolvable fights about who would fill the role of godparent, ensuring the children's belief in God the Father, Almighty Creator of heaven and earth, and renouncing Satan and all his works and empty promises.

Henry visited his children at St. Joseph's once. He felt so awful afterward that he decided it was easier for all of them if he didn't go again. He was praised, though, for his regular payments and willingness to send Ronald to the nuns, though the boy had begged to be left with his grandparents. Ramona, known for hitching rides into town by a nearly impassable road from her parents' farm near Clarendon Gorge and hanging out on the streets with her sister, was judged less kindly. First married to Henry and a mother of four by twenty-one, Ramona married again and was expecting another child a few years after Sally was left with the nuns.

Ramona visited St. Joseph's a few times, but then she, too, stopped. When a social worker asked her why, Ramona complained that she never heard from her children. When she sent gifts or clothes for them in care of the sisters, the children never wrote back to thank her. When she visited the orphanage, the children didn't wear the clothes she had sent. When she gave Ronny money to buy toothpaste because his teeth were so dirty, nothing seemed to happen. It was so upsetting to her, she explained, that she decided not to visit.

Ramona was open to the idea of taking her children back, she said. But she felt the children's father should take some responsibility. She could probably take two of them, she told the social worker, Ronny and Joanna, or perhaps Ronny and Sherry. But she did not like Sally. She never had. The girl was too like her father. Even when she was born, the doctor who delivered her had exclaimed, "Jesus Christ! Fredette all over!" Sally was "bold and greedy and forward," Ramona said, and she wet the bed. If Ramona took her daughter back and Sally wet the bed again, spoiling the bed and making the house smell, Ramona declared, "I would kill her."

By letting your pupils know your grievances against their parents, by blaming them, by ridiculing them, by making remarks, in class, on their behavior, on the notes that they write to you, etc. . . . If you want your students to obey you, respect their parents.

—*Teaching Advice, Daughters of Charity,*
Servants of the Poor, Second Edition,
Providence Mother House, Montreal, 1936

LIFE AT THE ORPHANAGE OFFERED SALLY AN EXPERIENCE OF CONNECTION that life with Ramona had not. Mrs. McGrath loved Sally and found her to be an entirely normal, lively child. Sister Jane of the Rosary became her orphanage mother when Sally was sent to live with other children in the orphanage nursery. Sally missed Mrs. McGrath but became attached to Sister Jane, who called her "sweetheart."

Like all the sisters, Sister Jane dressed in black with a long veil and a white band across her face. She wore a gold ring, a cross around her neck, and a big set of wooden beads that hung off her waist and clacked when she moved. She was known to all the girls for her constant companion: a thick razor strap that the girls called "the green pill," bitter medicine for any child who came near it. She was also known for her sore feet, often sitting at the end of the hallway and complaining, "Oy, oy, my bunion." Then Sally or one of the other girls untied her shoes because Sister Jane couldn't reach them.

It took Sally a long time to understand that a human woman with a recognizable human body lived beneath Sister Jane's robes. She would have had a hard time explaining what, exactly, she thought was under there. It was just that the nuns were different. Discovering that a nun had hair, for example, just like the girls, had come as a disorienting shock.

Sister Jane spoke differently, too. Only a few of Sally's young companions knew about different languages that had names like *French* and *English*. For the rest, the nuns' incomprehensible utterances were simply part of their alien being. In later years, some of the older girls learned a few common phrases: *Maudit Crisse! Qu'est-ce que c'est ça?* (*Curse Christ! What is this?*) or *Fermez la bouche!* (*Shut your mouth!*)

Sister Jane discovered that Sally could sing, and bold little Sally Fredette soon became St. Joseph's authentic Shirley Temple. When a visitor came to the orphanage, even late in the evening after Sally had fallen fast asleep, she was trotted out to delight and impress. Her hair was curled, she learned how to tap dance, and she sang "Stars and Stripes Forever" or "God Bless America." Left to her own devices, Sally preferred "On the Good Ship Lollipop," which she sang to herself over and over. If the girls behaved during the week, their reward was to watch a Shirley Temple film. Sally adored the pint-sized cutie-pie, who often played the role of a little orphan girl who finally finds a family to love.

Once, Sister Jane told Sally, she had taken her to the parlor and introduced her to a woman she described as her mother. As a matter of fact, Sister Jane said, Sally's mother had been coming to the orphanage every Sunday but asked to see only Sherry, not Ronald or Sally. The implication was that Ramona hadn't asked to see Sally this time either, but that Sister Jane had taken matters into her own hands. Sally had no memory of the day. Sister

Jane said that she wasn't sure if Sally had understood that the woman was her mother. She must have recognized something about her though. Sally, who was still very little, grabbed her brother's hand and told the woman, "I hate you."

My dear sisters let us be on guard against making remarks about others, officers or meddling in any way. I have grace of state but for the task assigned me, hence why venture where grace cannot follow me? Doing so is both harmful to others, and very harmful to the one who speaks.

—Reports of Provincial Superior of Official Visits to St. Joseph's Orphanage, November 29, 1939

WHEN SALLY WAS AROUND FOUR YEARS OLD, A GREAT BURST OF ACTIVITY drew in every single person at the orphanage. All the children were taught songs and given lines to recite, and then were assembled in the gym. As they got ready, an excited nun came to the door and said, "He is here, he is here!"

The man who entered the gym had a big hat on his head and a cross around his neck and wore what looked to Sally like a long purple dress. He was seated in a special chair, and the nuns flocked and flapped about him, bending to kiss his ring. Some of the children thought that maybe Jesus had come to visit, but the man turned out to be Bishop Brady of the Diocese of Burlington.

That day, the girls with pretty hair and the boys in little sailor outfits or blazers and bow ties held new toys and sat for photos with the nuns and strange men in black dresses. When it was her turn to look at the camera, Sally, who had been seated in pride of place in the front row in a shiny dress and dark stockings, placed a tiny hand on each of her knees, leaned forward, and gave the camera a frank but inscrutable look.

Later she was taken back to the nursery, where tensions were running high. To be sure, the atmosphere in the nursery was always taut, and it seemed to Sally that she was always being punished for something. It was impossible for her and her fellow orphans to comprehend how much the bishop meant to the women of the order, how radiant and glorious his presence, how godlike the man. Sally's brand of boldness, so valuable when there were other visitors to impress, was not appreciated. She played up, and Sister Mary Vianney, the nun in charge, became enraged. She grabbed Sally by the arm and hurled her into one of the nursery walls, throwing her with such force that Sally's head left a dent in the plaster.

Sally never forgot the moment, in part because her head left a hole in the wall. It was also because just as she hit the wall and fell to the floor, Bishop Brady, who was touring the building, came into the room.

Sr. Mary Vianney, defensive, told the bishop that Sally was a *very bad and evil child*.

But the bishop was unexpectedly unmoved by the nun's condemnation. He patted Sally on the head and said that he didn't believe it.

He told the nun, "This child is very honest. If she is going to do something wrong, she will always do it right in front of all of you."

Then he gestured at another little girl: "Do you know what she's thinking or what she's doing?"

Sally was just mischievous, said the bishop.

"Wouldn't you rather have one like her rather than one over there sitting in the corner and not know what she's doing or thinking?"

Bishop Brady told the nun that he never wanted to see anything like that happen again.

It was extraordinary. The bishop, who was so important and who had never met Sally before, had been able to tell at a glance that she didn't mean harm, that all she wanted was to be herself.

After Bishop Brady left, Sister Mary Vianney locked Sally in the nursery closet for a long time. There she sat, afraid, in pain, and oblivious to the nursery nun's deep humiliation. She didn't spare a thought for the other girl, either—the quiet, well-behaved one who, according to a prince of the church, might be harboring evil thoughts. The feeling of the great man petting her head, though, the reassurance, the validation, stayed with her for a very long time.

Sisters ours is a beautiful field, all ready to seed in the Master's blessed service. Those dear young souls are like soft wax, on which our example takes print. They will forget every other lesson but they will never forget what they saw us do.

—Reports of Provincial Superior of Official Visits to St. Joseph's Orphanage, November 29, 1939

IN THE BIG GIRLS' DORM, SISTER JANE BURST IN EVERY MORNING AT FIVE-thirty, shaking her wooden clappers, two bits of hinged wood that in other circumstances might have made music. She clap-clapped and hollered, *Let us bless the Lord! Let us bless the Lord!*

Sally obediently scrambled out of bed with the other girls and knelt on the floor, responding, *Let us bless His holy name.*

Life in the first and second nursery had been highly regimented, but here, with the big girls, each day was, even more so, exactly like every other.

After prayers, Sally folded her pajamas under her pillow, tucked her sheets as tight as possible, and arranged her gray blanket and white bedspread in perfect symmetry. In this dormitory the girls' beds were fanned out in a crescent shape. Next to each was a small bureau with a single drawer, in which nothing was kept. At the foot of the bed, a chair held Sally's neatly folded clothes from the night before. She got clean socks and underpants from her box in the hall closet. Each of the fifty hall boxes was marked by the girls' numbers, which the nuns often used instead of their names. They called Sally *la rouge*, though, for her flaming red hair and freckles. Sometimes the other girls called her *Sal*.

The girls who had wet their beds had their sheets draped around them, although sometimes one of the nuns pushed the bedwetter's face into the cold patch first. Sometimes the bedwetters' sheets were hung out the window so that everyone knew what they had done. Sally and the other girls sang funny songs about the bedwetters, and pointed at them and laughed. Sally didn't like to do this but was worried about what would happen to her if she didn't.

Two by two, from youngest to oldest, Sally and the girls then walked silently to mass, a long and solemn affair. After mass they filed into the basement dining room. Sally stood by her chair until the dining room nun clapped her clappers and led the grace. Then she lined up for oatmeal, coffee, and milk. At the table she stood in silence until the nun shook her clappers once more, and she and all the other girls sat and ate and talked. Next came morning chores, and then school in the classrooms on the first floor of the orphanage.

By now Sally's career as the real-life Shirley Temple of St. Joseph's Orphanage—and Sister Jane's pet—was long over. Overnight, her voice, which had been so powerful, became strained and cracked so that she could hardly talk, let alone sing. Where she had once been outgoing, she became needy and shy. Though Sally had been toilet-trained in the nursery, she had gone through a period when she wet her pants during the day. Sometimes she soiled herself.

All this had occurred, the orphanage social worker noted, when Sally was transferred from the care of Sister Jane to that of Sister Paul, who did not especially like Sally or find her at all charming. When Sally was returned to Sister Jane's care, she stopped wetting herself, but didn't sing again.

Chronique
De
l'Orphelinat Saint Joseph
Burlington, Vermont
Du 1es juillet 1944—1 es juillet 1945

Baptême de l'enfants
1er octobre—L'eau baptismale coule sur le font de six enfants de la nursery—No 2, nommement: Michael, Anthony et Robert Giallella âgés respectivement de 8, 6 et 4 ans; Dora, Philippe et Nancy Perrier, âgés de 5, 2 et 2 ans

AROUND THE TIME THAT SALLY LOST HER VOICE, OTHER THINGS HAPPENED at the orphanage for which there were no formal reports. One quiet night when everyone was supposed to be asleep, Sally watched events unfold in the big girls' dorm that she knew should not have happened. Normally, the bedtime routine was as regimented as the morning routine. After folding clothes and washing up, Sally said her prayers. She thanked God for all the good people in the world. Without them she would not have had a roof over her head, the nuns said, or food in her stomach. Then she got into bed, where she was supposed to stay for the night, not getting up again, not even to go to the toilet.

Sally positioned herself in the bed in the way that the nuns had taught her: lie on one side, put her hands together in prayer, place her head upon her hands on the pillow, and face the same direction as everyone else. Even after she had fallen asleep, she was supposed to stay in control of her body. If her hands slipped under the covers, the nighttime nun woke her with a flicked finger to the head or a solid whack. Or she pulled Sally off the bed and made her kneel for a few hours, or whipped her before sending her back to bed, hands in prayer resting on the pillow under her face.

The routine only changed in exceptional circumstances, such as when a terrific thunderstorm erupted one night, and the nuns rushed in and hurried the children out of bed and onto their knees to pray as the cataclysm raged about the building. God was angry, Sister Jane told Sally, because the girls had been bad.

One night Sally saw the nuns deviate from these strict rules. A girl was quietly taken out of her bed and led into one of the nun's bedrooms. It happened the next night with another girl, and then again. Sally noticed that sometimes when the girls came back from the nun's bedroom they were crying, but sometimes they had a lollipop.

After many nights of silent watching, it was suddenly Sally's turn. The nun appeared beside Sally, took her from her bed, and brought her into the nun's own bedroom. Then the nun took off her white bonnet and long white nightgown. She did things to Sally with her hands. She made Sally do things to her. Sally hated it. She told her no.

The nighttime nun took Sally into her bedroom a couple of times. Then another nun did the same thing. Sally stopped sleeping. She forced herself to stay awake because she was afraid the nun would return and take her again.

It happened to Sally five times, until one night a storm erupted inside her. She vomited all over the nun and her bed. The nun was furious. She beat Sally black and blue, and in the morning she pointed to Sally in front of all the other girls and told them what a foolish child she was for falling out of bed in the middle of the night.

Since this house is a home for orphans exclusively, let us do all in our power to make life happy and cheerful for them, while giving them a training that will fit them to face the world and its dangers. Treat them with dignity and courtesy always. You must correct them, but by reasoning with them, never any punishments based on ridicule. Ridicule leaves a wound in a child's memory that time cannot heal.

—Reports of Provincial Superior of Official Visits to St. Joseph's Orphanage, October 20, 1941

THE OTHER THING THAT HAPPENED AROUND THE TIME SALLY LOST HER voice occurred in broad daylight as a nun walked Sally through the yard to show her the difference between the boys' and the girls' sides of the orphanage. It was a late summer afternoon and no one else was around. Sally and the nun had just emerged from the back of the building, and the nun was pointing out where the kitchen and the boiler room were, when a boy was thrown through a window high above them.

The first thing Sally heard was the smashing glass. Then she looked up to see a boy where he should not have been, up high in the air. He fell and hit the ground, rising again briefly into the air before hitting the ground once more. Then he stopped moving. Sally looked up and saw a window on the fourth floor, out of which the boy had come. A nun stood there with her hands pushed out.

Baffled, Sally said to the woman next to her, "Sister?"

The nun took hold of Sally's ear, turned her around, and walked her back to the other side of the yard. She told Sally that she had a vivid imagination. "We are going to have to do something about you, child."

Charity in words is God's holy law. The most influential member of a community is the one who is master of her tongue because she prevails by her silence, and her conduct inspires confidence. Let us beware about remarks about priests, about those in authority, about our sisters, about the children and their families. No inquisitive questions about those who come and go. Easy to give a blow to a reputation, but very hard to repair that blow, yet Heaven will only be opened to us when all is repaired. Let us ponder on those truths.

—Reports of Provincial Superior of Official Visits to St. Joseph's Orphanage, October 20, 1941

THE INCIDENT OF THE BOY WHO WAS THROWN THROUGH THE WINDOW stayed with Sally. She didn't know what to do with it or how to think about it. She was just really worried about the boy. It took her two days to find a way to talk about him. She went back to the sister who was with her in the yard that day and asked if the boy was okay.

"Don't, Sally!" The nun replied. "Don't start with your imagination again."

Sally stopped thinking about the boy that day. She had other things to worry about.

Silence is the seal of all religious houses; without it, no religious spirit can be attained.

—Reports of Provincial Superior of Official Visits to St. Joseph's Orphanage, October 20, 1941

SALLY DRESSED IN HER SUNDAY BEST AND MADE SURE SHE SMILED WHEN visitors arrived. She knew that if she didn't, the strap or banishment to the attic awaited. The attic at St. Joseph's was a huge, spooky space that ran for almost two hundred feet from one end of the orphanage to the other. It contained chests with parasols and funny old dresses with bustles. A half-wall with cupboards and hooks—numbers beside them—cut across the middle, and along its entire length, large timber struts supported the planks of a loft.

When Sally was little, the nuns shut her in the "dark menagerie," the closet next to the nursery. The closet had a light with a dangling cord, but the nuns twisted the bulb so that no matter how many times Sally tried to turn it on, it never worked. When Sally was too big for that, they sent her to cry by herself in the attic. It was terrifying. Mice lived up there. Pigeons and bats flew through the rafters. Old statues draped in sheets were stored in the loft. When the wind blew, the sheets rustled, and the statues appeared to move.

When the nuns were really angry, they took Sally to the pad box at one end of the vast attic, where the rubber sheets for children who wet the bed were stored. The nuns walked Sally over, made her get inside the pad box, and then locked her in.

When Sally was in the box, the nuns told her not to cry or do anything. Indeed, it was impossible to do anything. Sally couldn't sit up straight or lie down in the box, so she scrunched herself up. It was painfully uncomfortable. Left by herself, she had no idea how much time was passing, but it felt like hours.

She wasn't the only child who received such treatment. She often heard other children crying or screaming from the attic, "Let me out! Let me out!"

It is painful to remark that some sisters do not follow the Rule for their "borders." Some wear them too high and too wide which is due to the way they are ironed. Sisters let us always be faithful to the Rule #413 of Customary which says "the bandeaux will be 6 1/2 inches wide including the hems, and extend forward of the camail not more than 2 inches." Let us faithfully follow this Rule and it will shield us from very unflattering remarks.

—Reports of Provincial Superior of Official Visits
to St. Joseph's Orphanage, November 4, 1942

SALLY'S MOST URGENT DAILY PROBLEM, OR AT LEAST THE ONE THAT BEGAN every day, was the milk. When she drank her daily glass, her stomach cramped, and she threw up. It felt terrible, and the nuns got so angry with her. They said it was her stubbornness. But Sally couldn't help it.

Every morning, she avoided the milk as long as she could. She ate her cereal but didn't drink her milk. She talked to the other girls. She stared at the milk. Finally, she did what she had to. Sally drank the milk.

Straight away her stomach clenched and jumped, and a short time later she turned to the side and threw up on the floor. The nun in charge made Sally get down on the floor and scrape up her vomit and put it back in her bowl. Then she made her eat it.

It happened all the time. Sally drank her milk, threw up, and scraped it up. Then the nuns made her eat it again. It tasted disgusting.

Sally did not understand why she vomited all the time or why she had to eat her vomit, and one day the unfairness of it all overwhelmed her. She scraped her vomit into her bowl but refused to eat it. The nun in charge insisted, but Sally did not budge.

The nun did not let it go. She kept telling Sally to eat what was in her bowl, but Sally refused, so the nun hauled her out of the dining room and up the staircase to the Mother Superior. The dining room nun explained that Sally was a stubborn, evil child because she wouldn't eat what was in her bowl.

Mother Superior simply responded that the nun should leave Sally and the bowl with her. Sally would not leave the room until she had cleaned it.

Sally sat in Mother Superior's office for ages. Once the flush of outrage had worn off, it quickly got boring. Still, she refused to give in. The hours ticked by, but Sally did not empty her bowl.

Mother Superior walked in and out of the room, and each time she asked:

"You're going to eat it, Sally?"

"No, I'm not," Sally replied.

"Yes, you are," Mother Superior said.

Finally, Mother Superior came over and asked Sally when she was going to clean her bowl. Sally couldn't believe it!

Would the Mother Superior eat her own vomit? Sally asked.

The older woman paused at this. For the first time that day, she came over and looked in Sally's bowl. After that, she beat a quick retreat.

Sally had no idea what happened, only that soon after she was able to leave Mother Superior's room, and she didn't have to clean her bowl anymore.

Eventually Sally had worked out how to not show everyone what she was thinking all the time. She began to sneak her glass of milk over to another girl, who happily drank it and then slid the glass back to her. After that, Sally almost never threw up. Sometimes, when she was actually ill, she vomited even if she didn't have any milk. When that happened, Sister Jane of the Rosary rubbed Sally's face in it instead.

Chronicles
Of
St. Joseph's Orphanage
Burlington, Vermont
July 1st 1947 to July 1st 1948

Birthday
February 19—The birthday of our Mother Foundress was marked by a catastrophe for our senior boys. The Gamelin Hobby Shop caught fire during the noon hour while the boys were working in the building. The fire started by the chimney, but was soon controlled by the City Fire Department. There was very little loss, however the boys felt very sad, because they are sure to miss the pleasant hours spent in the shop.

THE MORE SALLY GOT INTO TROUBLE, THE MORE HER RELATIONSHIP WITH Sister Jane deteriorated. The nun was old and tired. Sally was no longer so cute. Without Eva and Irene, the only women at the orphanage who were not nuns and who regularly worked with the children, Sally may not have survived. She knew they really loved her.

Eva DuPaul, the seamstress, had been at St. Joseph's since 1910, when she was only five years old herself. Small and meek, she was a true creature of the nuns and the institution. Sometimes when girls were banished to the attic, Eva would keep them company. When she was middle-aged, she tried to teach herself how to ride a bicycle, and in the vast attic space, she cycled around and around one of the banished girls, wobbling but happy, as the girl clapped and cheered her on. Irene McGowan, a housekeeper, had family in the area, but she too entered St. Joseph's Orphanage as a resident in 1906 when she was two years old. Even though she didn't have the authority of a nun, she had a certain power because the nuns depended upon her. Eva and Irene seemed to regard Sally as one of them.

The day that Sister Jane had caught Sally running and giggling among the beds, she took her to the little bedroom off the sewing room and made her lie facedown, dress yanked up, panties pulled down. Then she sent in Eva to whip her.

When Eva came into the little room, she looked at Sally and stood frozen for a few long moments. The strap lay beside her on the bed. Then she left.

Irene came in next. She had her own special name for Sally—"Fryface." She was not gentle like Eva. She never hesitated to order Sally around and punish her when needed. She even spoke sharply to the nuns. But this time, she just looked at Sally and didn't do anything either.

Even Sister Jane, usually so quick to punish, came in but did nothing except say that Sally was "a little puppy with brown eyes."

At last Sally heard Sister James Mary arrive and announce that she had no problem performing the task. The nun was one of the few Vermont natives in the order, though her family were French-Canadian. She taught English classes at the local school, worked as a companion in the big girls' dorm, and organized the girls choir at the orphanage. Entering the room, she brought the strap down hard on Sally, from the back of her neck all the way down to her ankles. Once, twice. Ten times. Too many times to count.

Sally recoiled with each downstroke but tried her best to hold back the tears. The silence only enraged Sister James Mary, who kept hitting her. On and on, the blows kept coming. The nun had a shrill, screaming voice. "You will cry!" she insisted.

Eventually Sally did. She began to weep.

Sally couldn't twist around far enough to see the damage that Sister James Mary had done. But when Irene looked, she gasped.

"How many times do we have to tell you?" Sister Jane of the Rosary demanded from above. "If you cry, you cry alone. If you smile the whole world smiles with you."

Irene brought Sally across the long hallway, and down the marble stairs, past the foyer and into the office of Mother Superior herself. She showed Mother Superior Sally's wounds. "It wasn't right to do that to a little girl."

Mother Superior replied that Sally was going to end up in reform school anyway.

The next time Sally was sent to Irene and Eva for a beating, Irene said she would deal with the child herself.

Irene hit her, but only on her bottom. Sally was so overwhelmed with gratitude that the next day, she told Irene that she loved her.

Chronique

De

l'Orphelinat Saint Joseph
Burlington, Vermont
Du 1es juillet 1948 au 1 es juillet, 1949

Seminaristes
July 1—Two seminarians from St Johns Seminary, Brighton, Mass, domiciled in Rutland, VT, return this summer to supervise the boys during the months of July and August. They are Rev Brothers Jos Pray and Edward Foster both admirable for piety; dedication and kindness.

THE MOMENTOUS DRIVE TO WEBSTERVILLE, WHERE THE PELKEYS LIVE, doesn't take too long. They wind east and through stark, still, wintry forest until they arrive at the tiny town next door to Graniteville, renowned across the world for an enormously deep hole and the granite mined from it, the source of virtually all of America's tombstones.

By now Sally has been whipped black and blue countless times. She has been locked in a variety of tiny spaces, left for days, threatened with death, and witness to as much horror and injury as some of her country's soldiers. She has been tortured with the same dark creativity used to torment political prisoners in authoritarian regimes. She has watched adult women, empowered by adult men, all of them empowered by the ancient Catholic magisterium, lie, torment, abuse, and lie again.

The falling boy was the first dead child that Sally believes she has seen, but he was not the last. She has seen other little ones disappear and fears there will be more to come. There will eventually be a group of children whose absence she will never be able to explain. But Sally doesn't know this yet. The Pelkeys know none of it either. They would hardly believe it if someone sat them down and laid it out point by point.

The Pelkeys believe that Sally is a sweet and lively little girl, a potential big sister, a fun friend. Sally doesn't disabuse them. It's impossible to know what Sally believes, if she thinks that's who she really is. It's probably fair to imagine that it's who Sally believes she can be.

CHAPTER 6

Everything Sally knows about how orphans should behave in a real family she learned from Harriet Parker, the St. Joseph's social worker, and from Shirley Temple films. These were the lessons from Harriet Parker: *Don't be so defiant. Don't be so stubborn. Don't be the way you are at the orphanage.*

The lessons from Shirley Temple are different. One: orphans who are exquisitely winsome and resolutely and adorably confident, even when people are cruel to them, get adopted. Two: grown men, sometimes whole groups of them, stare at teeny-tiny orphan girls in baby minidresses with dumbstruck, mesmerized longing. Three: even when an orphan is so cute she can barely articulate a word without her lips forming into a precious pout, she can still move through people's lives like a moral beacon, an avenging angel, a baby-voiced avatar of justice.

It's hard to apply all of these lessons in Sally's new world. Yet somehow life as a real girl in a real family starts out pretty fun. The Pelkey house is on the main street of Websterville, a small village a few miles from Barre. It has three bedrooms and two living rooms. Sally and Nancy sleep in bunk beds, Nancy on bottom, Sally on top. Nancy has two brothers, but Sally is there to be her companion. The girls play outside behind the apple trees, they ride their bikes, they play with dolls. They even start to dress alike. They play hide-and-seek, though Sally will never hide in the closet like Nancy does. They walk to and from the Upper Websterville Elementary School together and attend the same third grade class. Sally is a little outspoken, which sometimes makes the teacher holler, but she does fine with her schoolwork. Sally and Nancy play happily together, and if anybody threatens Nancy, Sally is her avenging angel. She defends her new little sister, even to the point of a fistfight with Linda, the town bully (no blood is drawn, but both girls walk away with solid facial bruising).

Mr. Pelkey, who works at the nearby granite quarry, never raises a hand. Mrs. Pelkey is often very affectionate. Sally wants Mrs. and Mr. Pelkey to become her mother and father, so she tries as hard as she can to be a good girl. She wants to help around the house, but Mrs. Pelkey doesn't need her to wax the floors or scour the kitchen. The family encourages her to play and even to get dirty, which is confusing. Living in an actual house is so different for Sally. There are no enormous pots in the kitchen, in which a child can sometimes fit. There is no cavernous attic or electric chair. When there is a storm, no one tells Sally it is her fault.

The Pelkeys ask Sally about her life at the orphanage. Occasionally she tells them she did a lot of work there. But she doesn't tell them anything else, not about Sister Jane or the nighttime nuns. She doesn't talk about the falling boy. She is pretty sure that if she does, the Pelkeys will think she is a liar. She doesn't even think about any of it. Of course, none of it goes away, not the beatings, the creepy secrets, or the children who disappeared. They're all still there inside her, quiet, waiting, trying to be good.

THE SECOND TIME A BOY AT ST JOSEPH'S DISAPPEARED RIGHT BEFORE SALly's eyes, it happened at Lake Champlain, which had always been Sally's favorite place. The lake wasn't far from the orphanage, but it was another world. In the summer Sally and the other girls walked out the back of the building and down the huge green hill through fields of scattered wildflowers, edged by dark pink sumac. At the bottom they arrived at the edge of a thick line of oak, black locust, cottonwood, and pitch pine, then they plunged down a steep, winding path, crossed over a railway track, and continued down through the trees. The small wood stopped so abruptly that when they came out the other side, it was like they had walked through a solid green wall.

On the other side of the wall was North Beach, where the water was clear and lovely and tiny fish darted. When the girls chased each other through it, they looked as if they were running on its surface.

Wading in the shallows one day, Sally watched two nuns and a boy in a rowboat head out from the shore and go as far as the breakers, a pile of rocks that jutted out from the jetty, where the water was deep. The screaming boy sat in the front of the boat. Sally watched the nuns row out, stop the boat, and throw the boy in the water. Then she watched them row back.

The same thing had happened to Sally a few years before. She had been taken out into the deep water and tipped into it. The nuns said they were teaching the children to swim, but it was not clear how this would help the children learn. Many came out of the water screaming or in a state of silent terror. But Sally was fine. The day she was thrown in, she discovered that she was, in fact, a strong swimmer. She made her way back to the beach on her own with some pride. Maybe the boy would be fine, just like she had been?

After the nuns threw the boy in, Sally stood and watched, waiting and wondering what happened to him. She watched until the whistle blew, but she did not see the boy swim back. She waited and she waited, but she did not see him come up again.

When the children trudged back up the hill, Sally asked a nun if the boy had drowned.

"Oh, don't worry," the nun said. "He's gone home for good."

Mrs. Pelkey gives Sally different colored underwear, green, blue, and pink, each with lace. Sally wants to be a good girl but cannot let this fantastic opportunity go by. Each day at school, she picks up her skirt and shows the boys the new color. She prefers to play with the boys, though she is told she isn't supposed to. She likes their hard games and their attention. Sometimes she plays down behind the barn with the rowdiest boy in the neighborhood. She is in a lot of trouble when they are found.

At school Sally loves coloring, for which she always gets high marks, though she is finding the other subjects increasingly difficult. She thinks she is too dumb to do any of the other work well. Sometimes she cheats.

Since Sally arrived in Websterville, Mrs. Pelkey has been trying to help her. She encourages her to play, although nothing in the world can induce Sally to hide in the closet. She lets Sally know she doesn't have to be such a good girl. But she also teaches her not to be so forward with strangers. She tries to get Sally to have better table manners, too. Sally still wants to be good but finds it hard to take the lessons on. She doesn't really like to brush her hair or clean herself, and she's hard on her clothing. Sometimes she walks in her sleep.

After Sally has been with the Pelkeys for many months, Mrs. Pelkey falls ill. Sally doesn't know what's going on, but she can tell bad things are coming. At least when Mrs. Pelkey has to go to the hospital, Sally knows what to do. She washes and waxes the bathroom like it's never been cleaned before. But there are strange rumblings. More and more, Sally can feel all the ways she doesn't fit and isn't normal. She isn't interested in going to church and stops going to confession. She is not alone in this. Nancy doesn't really go either, and Mrs. Pelkey doesn't seem to care. Sometimes Sally goes outside and refuses to come back into the house.

The more she likes the Pelkeys and the more comfortable she feels in their home, the more afraid she is that she will lose them. It's hard to stay still with all those feelings, and Sally can see herself withdrawing. Now, when Mr. and Mrs. Pelkey tell her what she needs to do, she starts arguing with them and refuses to behave. When Nancy is annoying, Sally says mean things to her. She even hits her once. For a bit of fun, she throws a bunch of stones at the neighbors' garage.

WHEN SALLY IS TEN YEARS OLD, WHEN SHE HAS BEEN WITH THE PELKEYS for one and a half years and hardly ever thinks about the orphanage anymore, she and Nancy come home from school to find Mrs. Pelkey crying. Mr. Pelkey is nowhere to be seen. Sally's suitcase is sitting on the floor, packed. Nancy stands by, dumbfounded. Mrs. Pelkey gives Sally a beautiful, expensive doll with rosebud lips and shiny hair.

They get in the car and drive away, and at some point, out of the clear blue sky, suddenly Harriet Parker, the social worker, is there. Parker grabs Sally by the arm and says, "You're coming with me now." Mrs. Pelkey doesn't say anything. She just keeps crying. Parker tells Sally she is coming back to St. Joseph's. No one will explain why.

Sally is utterly confused. She hasn't done anything; it makes no sense. She loves the Pelkeys. She weeps all the way back to the orphanage and keeps asking Parker to turn around and take her back.

She tells Parker that she really loves the Pelkeys. She tells her that the Pelkeys were going to adopt her. Parker does not agree. She tells Sally that even the townspeople had told her what a very bad girl Sally is. Parker says Sally had better start behaving, too, or it will be reform school for her. Sally doesn't know what she is talking about.

The one aim of this house is to do our utmost for the children's spiritual and temporal benefit. We sometimes deplore their lack of piety but we must remember that piety cannot be imposed, it must be humbly begged for. The first means is a good example and the greatest of all lessons. Then try to install in their minds and hearts love for Our Blessed Lord and His Immaculate Mother by all means we can find. This seed may take time to germ but it will grow some day to our eternal credit. Kindness too is a great weapon; no heart resists it.

—Reports of Provincial Superior of Official Visits
to St. Joseph's Orphanage, November 4, 1942

BACK AT ST. JOSEPH'S, THE NUNS TELL SALLY THAT SHE IS MEAN AND CRUEL and evil, and that no one wants her. They tell the other girls at the orphanage that Sally is bad, and that is why she is back.

The beautiful doll with rosebud lips is taken away, and Sally is kept apart from all the other girls. She isn't allowed to talk to them or share a table with any of them at mealtimes. The nuns put hospital curtains around Sally's bed, as if she has an infection and they don't want it to spread. Sally sits with

Eva in the kitchen at mealtimes. When the girls sing "Goodnight, Irene" to Irene each night, Sally tries to join in from behind her curtain.

Harriet Parker explains to Sally that she had been separated from the other girls because the nuns don't want her teaching them about the outside world. But Sally has no idea what she learned about the world that the nuns think is dangerous.

For a while the Pelkeys visit Sally at the orphanage on Sundays. Mr. Pelkey brings dolls and chocolate in pretty boxes that he says Sally can store jewelry in once the chocolates are eaten. But the nuns say it isn't fair for Sally to have something the other children cannot have. The dolls are taken away and Sister Cecile tells Sally that all the girls can share the chocolate, but once the nun takes the box, Sally never sees any of it again.

The Pelkeys take Sally home with them for the weekend a few times, but Sally can't bear the tension of going to their house, which is familiar and comfortable, and then having to return to the orphanage, which she dreads.

She decides to make the Pelkeys stop loving her so she doesn't have to go back to their house. She wants them to forget her so she can just go ahead and rot or die, just like all the other kids who had disappeared and never been seen again. She takes things from Mrs. Pelkey's pocketbook, like a little ring, a small picture, and a keychain. On one visit she calls Mr. Pelkey an SOB, which is the worst thing she can think of.

The plan works. The Pelkeys stop visiting.

Later that year a social worker from the orphanage takes Sally to the Burlington Mental Hygiene Clinic. Sally tells the doctor that she wishes she knew how to play the games that the other girls at the orphanage play. She doesn't know how to play their ball game or "Cowboys and Indians." She wants the other girls to like her better.

The doctor reports that Sally is cooperative, spontaneous, and outgoing, but testing shows that she appears to be "seriously retarded." Her vocabulary is very limited, the doctor reports, and when she is presented with absurd sentences as part of an IQ test, she can't tell the difference between statements that describe things that are normal and real and those that are unreal or impossible.

*We must be aware my dear Sisters that education is by far the most ex-
cellent art of reaching the students. We must first show them dignity
and Christian upbringing. It is the Holy Spirit that elevates these young
people's soul.*

*—Reports of Provincial Superior of Official
Visits to St. Joseph's Orphanage, April 23, 1948*

IT TURNED OUT THAT THE NUNS WERE RIGHT ABOUT SALLY BRINGING BACK
things from the outside world into the closed world of the orphanage. She
has changed. They still beat her and lock her into frightening spaces, but
after her time with the Pelkeys, Sally decides she isn't going to scream anymore. She is going to stick up for other children, too, and when she is in
trouble, she is not going to cry. Sometimes after she had been in the attic or
the nuns beat her for doing something wrong, she makes a point of folding
her arms and smiling at them once they are done.

Her refusal to cry makes all the nuns angry, but Sister James Mary seems
to take it the most personally. Sally no longer fits into the pad box, so Sister
James Mary tells her to climb inside a big empty metal water tank in the
attic. Sally was so stubborn, Sister James Mary said, she wouldn't cry or do
anything. This may be the most confusing part of life with the nuns. They
want Sally to cry when they want her to cry. It shows they can make her do
what they want. But if she cries when they don't want her to cry, then they
really give her something to cry about. When they do that, they won't stop
until Sally stops crying.

Sister James Mary makes Sally climb up a little ladder on the outside of
the tank. Then she pulls the lid shut.

At first, alone in the dark, Sally screams to be let out. But the echoes in
the tank make it sound like other people are in there with her. It just about
scares her to death. So she makes herself very quiet instead.

Sally tries not to move and doesn't push against the lid. It is hard to tell
how much time has passed. It is so still and so black, she is pretty sure that
two days have passed by the time Irene finds her.

"This can't happen again." Irene said. "To forget a child . . . to be so long with nothing to eat." But it did happen again.

#328. Since a child learns largely through observation it is essential that the teacher be a living example of the principles of conduct she desires to help her pupils develop, namely integrity, justice, charity, courtesy, reverence, obedience to authority, self-discipline, and respect for human dignity.

—*Customary of the Daughters of Charity, Servants of the Poor, Providence Mother House, Montreal, 1959*

EVERY YEAR IN MAY, ONE SPECIAL GIRL, A MEMBER OF THE SODALITY OF the Blessed Virgin Mary, crowned a statue of the Virgin as part of a ceremony in the grotto at the back of the orphanage. The grotto was like a small stone mountain, made of chunky rocks that projected up out of a neat green lawn, shaded by two enormous oak trees. Halfway up to the grotto's tallest point, a little recess held a white statue of Mary, her hands clasped in prayer, her eyes lifted to the sky. At the bottom of the wall, to the left, was another statue of a woman praying to her.

In the May procession, the nuns and the girls followed the chosen one in a line to the grotto. A page boy dressed in a little suit carried a bunch of ribbons, with the ends held by a cluster of small girls wearing white fluffy dresses with gauzy veils. They looked like tiny angels. The chosen girl wore a perfect white satin dress, so long that it covered her toes, and a veil that draped past her waist. A tall ladder was set up next to the Virgin Mary, and the chosen girl climbed it to lay her crown. Other children made speeches and gave readings, and everyone prayed. Even the chaplain said a few words.

By this time, Sally was allowed to mix with the girls again, but there were always events like this from which she was excluded. Her sister Sherry was petite, quiet, and mild. Sally hardly ever saw her, though the nuns often asked why she couldn't be like her. After Sally's return from the Pelkeys, Sherry crowned the Virgin.

Otherwise, life went on. The older girls worked in the laundry, sorted apples and potatoes in the cellar, looked after smaller children, and cleaned the priest's quarters, in addition to going to school. They mopped the floors of the hall by pushing each other around on the mop. It took ages to do, but if it wasn't clean before a visitor came, the nuns chased them down the corridor and hit them with the wooden handle of the mop.

No one ever spoke about menstruation at St. Joseph's, but when Sally got her period for the first time, she was given a little blue book titled *The Mother's Friend*, whose contents she was forbidden to discuss with anyone. She also received a plastic belt, safety pins, and a bag of long white rags that she washed in secret in a sink in the attic with a bar of lye soap.

Living in the older girls' dormitory had some advantages. There was a little more room to move in the parlor that had a radio, comfortable furniture, and a table in the center for homework. There were dance recitals, and sometimes a woman came from outside the orphanage to teach the girls how to tap dance, but Sally didn't dance anymore. There was also singing, but Sally hadn't sung for a very long time. One freezing day in later years, when a group of the girls had been sent outside to loiter in the yard for hours on end, one of them looked up and spied a group of at a least a dozen nuns in a room dancing. They were wearing their usual dresses but not their habits, twirling one another around. The nuns' skirts lifted and swirled as they spun, until eventually one of them noticed the rapt child staring up at them and quickly pulled down the shades.

In the summer, there were sporting events like relay races and egg and spoon competitions, and softball, which Sally loved because she was a solid pitcher. Winter was especially fun for Sally, who was a good skier and knew how to handle a toboggan. When the local firemen came to create an ice rink for the orphans, as they did every year, Sally and the other girls rifled through the jumble of old and donated skates in the attic. If Sally was lucky, she would find a pair that fit. If she wasn't lucky, Sister Claire would be waiting outside to push her over on the ice.

The girls knew that the nuns secretly borrowed the skates. They found telltale water in the cubbyhole where the skates were hung. At night they sneaked out of bed to cluster at the window and watch the nuns trying to glide over the ice. The women would often squeal and fall on their behinds, and the girls would collapse, laughing and hopeful. Maybe one day one would slip and break her neck?

Christmas was special. On Christmas Eve, the nuns walked through the dormitories, each carrying a candle and singing hymns in French. Even after they had gone, Sally could hear the beautiful singing from far away. Later in the night, all the children got out of bed for midnight mass. On Christmas morning, there was a box of cold cereal and a grapefruit for breakfast. Later in the day, the sound of sleigh bells heralded the arrival of Santa with six helpers. He called each child's name, one by one, and he gave them coloring books, pick up sticks, toy trains and trucks.

For her freshman year of high school, Sally attended Pomeroy, a school outside of the orphanage, but the nuns made her leave that school when she was fourteen. Sally was the only girl from the orphanage who was attending, and they said they could not afford to keep sending her. Anyway, they added, her marks were not good enough for high school. Sally scored a sixty-nine average that year; her teacher, a Sister of Mercy at Pomeroy, told her that if she had received a seventy, it would have been high enough for her to continue. The nun said she could bump it up by one, but she refused to do so because Sally was too stubborn. For example, when she asked Sally about outer space, Sally replied, "What do I care about the moon and the stars? I'm not going up there."

From that point on, Sally worked full time at the orphanage and ate all her meals with Eva in the kitchen. She was paid five dollars a month to wake up at three-thirty in the morning to prepare breakfast with one of the other women who worked in the kitchen. She unpacked the cans and big bags of flour from the trucks. She stirred huge containers of hot cereal and loaded a cart with bread for the children's breakfast. She went to the big refrigerator to skim the cream off the milk and place it in a special pitcher. The cream, along with bowls of fruit, eggs, toast, and coffee, went onto the dumbwaiter for the nuns and the priest. The milk went to the children, who also got a boiled egg once a week on Sunday nights, along with a meat sandwich and a dessert. Sally washed all the pots and the pans to get them ready for lunch, and cleaned both the children's and the nuns' dining rooms.

In the kitchen, Sister Dominick was Sally's nemesis. She insisted that Sally clean the big mixer while the paddles were still turning. It was painful, and Sister Dominick added insult to injury when she laughed out loud at how stupid Sally was to do it. When the nun left the room, the woman who came in to help at the orphanage showed Sally how to turn off the mixer. Sally was so grateful. But when Sister Dominick returned and saw that the mixer was still, she insisted that Sally turn it back on again to clean it.

While younger girls went to school, sewed together, or mooned around in the yard singing "Oh! My Papa," Sally ironed, pressing the nuns' bandeaux, which needed a lot of starch. But at least the ironing was peaceful and could go on for hours with no one else around. At night she got down on her knees and prayed to God that if she ever grew up and got married, if He didn't think she could take care of children properly, to please not let her have any.

```
             CHRONICLES
        ST JOSEPH'S ORPHANAGE
           BURLINGTON, VT
      July 1st 1952 to July 1st 1953


JULY
BAPTISM
6—A little foundling, two weeks old, was baptised in our
chapel today by Father Devoy, and given the name of Ma-
ria Goretti, whose feast it is. May her heavenly patroness
care for her always.
```

THE THIRD CHILD THAT DISAPPEARED FROM SALLY'S VIEW WAS A GIRL. Sally was helping with the little children in the nursery, and one of her favorites was a sweet little girl named Mary Clark.

Mary Clark did not cry tears but instead made strange, sad little sobbing sounds. The nuns in the nursery hated the sound of any child crying, but Mary Clark's sobbing-not-crying sounds made them especially angry.

The nuns did everything they could to make the little girl weep. They slapped and punched her and kicked her feet out from under her, and once they had her on the ground, they laid into her with their boots, kicking her over and over. They made the other girls make fun of her and laugh at her, and locked her in a closet and called her names. Twice, Sally watched them rub onions in Mary's eyes.

Finally Sister Jane of the Rosary—she of the "green pill" and the wooden clappers—grabbed the little girl by the scruff of her neck and announced to Sally and the other girls that she was taking Mary to Mother Superior. Anybody who couldn't cry, she said, was "completely nuts."

That was the last time Sally saw Mary Clark. A few weeks later, one of the older girls announced that "Mary had it made!" She was with her parents, the other girl said. Mary Clark had gone home for good.

```
            CHRONICLES
        ST JOSEPH'S ORPHANAGE
           BURLINGTON, VT
     July 1st 1952 to July 1st 1953


JULY
DEPARTURE OF SISTER JANE OF THE ROSARY
7th—Sister Jane of the Rosary leaves for Mount Providence
after spending almost twenty-seven years in the girls de-
partment. The merit of such an amount of devotedness, and
the unfailing reward that will follow in time and place,
cannot be computed in human terms. He, for whom she de-
voted herself so nobly, and who saw all and who knows all
will settle accounts to the last iota. Our deepest grati-
tude so well deserved is our warmest token.
```

THE FOURTH GIRL WAS SIMPLY PUSHED DOWN THE STAIRS BY A NUN. THERE was nothing unusual about that. Sally had been pushed down the stairs many times. This time, though, the girl didn't get up again. Sally ran to help with Irene following right behind her.

Irene told Sally to keep the girl awake and to get her to talk. Sally tried but the little girl just moaned. She had a huge bump coming up on her forehead and her eyes were turning black and blue.

They took her to the hospital in a taxi. When they got there, someone pointedly asked, "Another accident?"

A doctor took the girl from Sally. Then she and Irene sat and waited for a very long time. Eventually the doctor returned and said the girl would stay in the hospital. Irene and Sally should go.

Later Sally asked a nun if the girl was okay, and the nun said she was. Then the nun explained further, saying what Sally knew was coming, and what she finally suspected was not actually true. The girl was not coming back, the nun said, because she had gone home for good.

```
                    CHRONICLES
                ST JOSEPH'S ORPHANAGE
                  BURLINGTON, VT
             July 1st 1953 to July 1st 1954


FEBRUARY
CHAPEL REDECORATED
6—Today we re-enter our little chapel all refreshed with
paint of the most lovely tints: blue, peach, and ivory. Our
Lord must be happy to return to this beautiful home af-
ter blessing our community with His Presence since Janu-
ary 18th.
                SORROWFUL TRAGEDY

8—Our house which is completing its century is confronted
this day with one of the most tragic events of these hun-
dred years.
    Francis H. Blair, born at Barre, Vermont, November 21st,
1921, admitted to St Joseph's Orphanage, July 21st, 1926,
returned to his father, July 1, 1932, dies in the electric
chair at Windsor, Vermont.
    Francis grew up a smart boy, apt in school, fond of play
but always ready to help. He made his first communion and
was confirmed while here. In general he was a promising,
```

good young man. After leaving the Orphanage he unfortunately met with companions who were his undoing, and led
him to great misfortune, and from one mishap to another
he was finally condemned to the electric chair. This was
God's mercy for him, as while in prison Francis met Father
William Ready, who gently brought him back to God and
the reality of his state.

SALLY THOUGHT THERE WAS A CHANCE THAT THE FIFTH CHILD—A YOUNG
girl—would die. But she didn't, because Sally, the stoic, tearless, word-poor
redhead, saved her life.

A skinny girl named Patricia Carbonneau had joined Sally's group. They
worked together in the second nursery, looking after the children, serving
them lunch, washing the dishes, and cleaning the kitchen, including the
windows. The nursery was on the second floor, and the windows had to be
washed inside and out.

It took both girls to clean the windows. First, Carbonneau cleaned the
inside of a window, and Sally climbed up onto the sill and went out through
the window to stand facing into the room. Carbonneau held Sally's ankles, as Sally, standing on the outside facing in, cleaned the glass. The girls
cleaned one window like this, then swapped places for the next window, and
continued with the routine.

One day Sister Priscille came into the kitchen and told the girls it was
time to clean the windows. Sister Priscille was not much older than Sally, yet
seemed to dislike her regardless. If Sally misbehaved, Sister Priscille was always
ready to punish her, even if she wouldn't have punished other girls for the
same infraction. That day, Sister Priscille seemed even angrier than usual.

The nun got the girls started on the job and then walked out of the room.
Sally knew that streaks made Sister Priscille very angry, so she tried as hard
as she could to wipe the windows clean.

By the time Sister Priscille walked back into the room, Carbonneau was
standing outside the last window. The building turned at a right angle where
the last window was, so that where she stood—outside the window facing
in—there was another brick wall to her left. To her right was nothing. Her

back faced the rear annex that contained the chapel about a hundred feet away. Sally held Carbonneau by the ankles, like she usually did.

Sister Priscille came over and gave Sally a good, hard punch on the arm. She told Sally to leave, and she said that she was going to hold Carbonneau's ankles instead.

Sally figured that they mustn't have cleaned the window properly. In that moment, she felt a surge of distrust for Sister Priscille. She could not have explained why, but instead of leaving the room, she stayed and stood behind the nun.

She didn't have to wait long; it happened very fast. Instead of holding Carbonneau's ankles until she finished washing the window, Sister Priscille gave the skinny girl a shove. She started to shake and teeter and fell backward from the sill.

When this happened, Sally was in her mid-teens. By this point, she had seen a little boy thrown from a high window. She watched another plunge beneath the surface of the lake, and did not see him reappear. She had been bewildered by the disappearance of sobbing Mary Clark and the girl who was pushed down the stairs. She herself had been pushed, beaten, and threatened. She had been loved by a family and then cast out again. Whether it was because these things had happened to her, or in spite of them, something inside her awoke. Harriet Parker had told her that she was an uncontrollable, hateful child, and while Sally believed this to be true, some part of her was no longer entirely beholden to the nuns' version of reality. She believed instead the evidence of her own eyes and acted accordingly.

When Sister Priscille pushed Patricia Carbonneau, Sally jumped forward and grabbed the girl by one ankle and one arm. Carbonneau smashed up against the brick wall to her left, and Sally could see how much it hurt when she hit the wall. She felt terrible, as if it were her and not the nun who had hurt Carbonneau. But Sally did not let go. She was terrified that the girl would hit the ground like the falling boy had.

Somehow between the two of them, Carbonneau made it back in through the window. For a while, the two girls hung on to each other, crying. Sally was in shock. Patricia Carbonneau was such a skinny little thing and always seemed to be a good girl. Why would something like this happen to her?

By the time Sally looked up, Sister Priscille had left the room.

CHRONICLES
ST JOSEPH'S ORPHANAGE
BURLINGTON, VT
July 1st 1953 to July 1st 1954

JUNE
CENTENNIAL NOTES
Before closing the chronicles of the Centennial year, these notes are worthy of mention. During the past hundred years 7066 children were admitted. Four boys became priests: two are dead. Father Murphy, S.J., who died in Rome, and Father Bernard Cunningham, who died in Louisville, Kentucky, in 1927. Those still living are Monsignor Carrière, now pastor of Newport, Vermont, and Father Paul Hebert, S.S.E. of St. Michael's College. One boy became a brother of St. Edmund; Brother Andrew. Twenty-six girls became religious in seven different Communities. Sisters of the Hotel Dieu-1; Sisters of Mercy-2; Sisters of St. Joseph-3; Sisters of the Atonement, Graymoor-2; Sisters of the Sacred Heart-1; Franciscan Sisters-1; Sisters of Providence-16; of whom four are dead.

THE LAST CHILD WAS THE BOY IN THE COFFIN. SALLY SAW HIM WHEN SISTER Noelle took her and a group of bad children to the local hospital to learn a lesson about a runaway who had been hurt.

A rumor had been circulating among the children that the runaway fled the orphanage with his cousin to go see his grandmother. As the pair took a wild cross-country jaunt, they crawled under an electric fence. The runaway was wearing some kind of helmet, the story went, and he was electrocuted when he went under the fence.

At the hospital, Sally was not allowed into the boy's room, and instead looked through a special window in the hallway. She did not see a boy; she saw an object on a bed. It was a "black thing" and had no sheets on it.

Three days later, someone told Sally that the boy had died.

Sister Noelle took the same group of naughty children with her again to the boy's wake.

Here again the boy lay, but this time in a small coffin with no lid. A very sad old woman sat next to him. Sally did not want to go anywhere near the boy, but Sister Noelle made her go to the coffin, and told her to kiss the boy.

Sally was trapped. She leaned over the coffin, and all she could see were the holes in the boy's face from being burned.

As she bent down toward him, Sister Noelle whispered that if Sally ran away, what happened to the boy would happen to her.

CHRONICLES
ST JOSEPH'S ORPHANAGE
BURLINGTON, VT
July 1st 1955 to July 1st 1956

MARCH
HOLY WEEK CEREMONIES
29—In keeping with the Roman decision concerning the Holy Week ceremonies hence forward, we had Mass at 5.30 PM. The washing of the Feet took place after the Gospel and it was a very inspiring ceremony. Twelve little boys dressed in Hebrew style took their places on the steps of the altar and our Chaplain, Reverend Father Foster washed each one's feet while the choir sang appropriate Psalms for the occasion. After Mass, a procession along the corridor preceded the placing of the Blessed Sacrament in the Repository that was prepared for our King. Faithful adorers kept watch during the hours of the day and the night.

SALLY IS SEVENTEEN YEARS OLD. SHE'S STILL A LITTLE ON THE SHORT SIDE, A little plump. Her hair is cut above her shoulders, parted on the side. It curls up at the ends. She wears glasses with darkened rims, neat little collared shirts with cardigans, and on special occasions, a dress with a boatneck and full skirt. On days of celebration, she and the other girls wear a tiny, red-collared cape, loosely clasped at the neck with a shiny button. One beautiful day in May, she is finally allowed to don the silky white, scoop-necked bridal dress with its grand veil and climb the ladder in the grotto to crown the Virgin Mary.

Outside the orphanage, Ray Kroc has opened the first McDonald's, *The Catcher in the Rye* has been published, the structure of DNA has been discovered, and the career of the infamous senator Joseph McCarthy is in decline.

Sally, who knows none of these things, has experienced much disappointment and sadness in her short life, but she will not give up on herself. She tells Sister James Mary that the nun can break Sally's body or her bones, but she can never break her mind. Her mind, says Sally defiantly, is *hers*. It's a brave stand, but unfortunately it isn't much help now.

Sister James Mary takes Sally into the attic. Sally has been locked inside different containers up here. But this time Sister James Mary takes Sally up a second set of stairs to the loft in the attic. There are spinning wheels, statues, other bits of storage, and a chair made of wood and iron with leather belts attached to the arms and the legs, and more belts near the top to strap around a person's head.

"Sally, do you know what this is?" Sister James Mary asks. "This is the electric chair, and if you don't stop being a bad girl and defying us, this is what's going to happen to you."

She tells Sally that the chair will fry her, and then tells her to sit in it.

Sally doesn't want to, but Sister James Mary insists. When Sally sits down, the nun straps down her arms and her ankles.

"You will sit there till I say," the nun says. She leaves.

Sally sits in the chair for hours. She thinks about the time she was burned in the orphanage firepit, when her skin turned black and the pain lasted for weeks. But mostly she is thinking about the boy in the coffin who had holes burned in his face, wondering what it would feel like to be strapped in, unable to escape, completely awake and burned alive with electricity.

CHRONICLES
ST JOSEPH'S ORPHANAGE
BURLINGTON, VT
July 1st 1956 to July 1st 1957

MAY

CROWNING OF OUR LADY

30.–Today is the beautiful feast of the Ascension and Memorial Day. Seldom do a holyday and a holiday combine; but we have both today and we take advantage of it to have the crowning. It took place at the Grotto at one o'clock. The procession leading from the chapel to the grotto where an appropriate hymn was sung. Our Blessed Mother was crowned with a wreath of roses by Sally Fredette, one of our senior girls. The Act of Consecration was recited by our seven year old Nancy Lee. Father Foster gave a short talk on our Lady and told them that the act of consecration which they had just recited was not only for today but for a life-time. Another hymn was sung, then all processed back to the chapel where Benediction of the Blessed Sacrament followed. May this outward demonstration to Mary be always remembered by our children and may it help them to be loyal to their Mother of Heaven.

DESPITE WHAT SISTER NOELLE HAD PROPHESIED, SALLY RAN AWAY AGAIN, although she did it by herself and did not run very far. Sister James Mary had given her a very bad beating, and she fled through the hole in the fence of the graveyard next door.

It was like a park. Peaceful, green, and leafy in the summer, with winding paths and gravestones that fanned out beside the paths, tiny white domes, gray crosses, and looming slabs with the names of babies, soldiers, and whole families who were all tucked up, deep down, together forever. It was laid out on an enormous hill that ended in a sharp drop with a view that opened out to the lake.

Sally ran to the bottom of the hill and sat quietly on a nice firm stone. She was alone and at peace, just Sally and the dead, who didn't scream or blather at her like Sister James Mary did, even after the sun went down.

Sally was aware that somewhere out in the world she had a mother and a father, but that was really the extent of her knowledge. She was like a story-book princess stolen as a baby—no real idea who she was, where she came from, or who her people were. She also did not know that other people knew such things about themselves, and was unaware of the enormous hole in her life where stories of family, life, and home might have been. She knew she was a pretty terrible person and not like other people, who were good without trying. She knew that no one loved her. Not even God. She hated her parents because they had put her in the orphanage, but she still defended them when the nuns or other girls made fun of them. She was probably going to be at the orphanage forever, just like Irene and Eva. At least, she thought, she had done something good once when she saved Patricia Carbonneau.

Sally always sat on the same stone in the graveyard, so Irene knew where she was. Sure enough, when dark had fallen, Irene came to take her back.

CHRONICLES
ST JOSEPH'S ORPHANAGE
BURLINGTON, VT
July 1st 1958 to July 1st 1959

NOVEMBER
CATHERINE ARRIVES
24—A baby girl is left on the front door-steps of our Orphanage in this bitter cold weather at 7.55 pm. The tele-
phone rings and when answered, a woman's voice says there
is a box on the front steps. The box is found and Miss
Riley is notified. The five to six hour waif, wrapped in
swaddling clothes, has been deposited in a cardboard box.
The next morning the unfortunate one was brought to De-
Goesbriand hospital for hospital care. Because the feast
day of St Catherine was the first full day of the child's

life, the Sisters named her Catherine. She will be placed
in a foster home later if the police authorities are unable to locate her parents.

SALLY DALE STAYED AT ST. JOSEPH'S FOR MORE THAN TWENTY YEARS. IN
that time, she grew up in an ever-changing population of twenty to thirty
women and up to 350 children and babies, and of all the thousands of children who passed into the care of the Sisters of Providence during that time,
Sally was there the longest.

A few months after she turned twenty-three—though she didn't know
either her age or her date of birth at the time—her sister phoned her.

Sherry, who had left the orphanage and lived in Connecticut, told Sally
that she was pregnant again and thinking about getting a divorce and putting her children in the orphanage.

Sally was flabbergasted and angry.

"Sherry, didn't you have enough of the orphanage?" she asked her. She
told Sherry to send her husband to St. Joseph's to come get Sally. She would
go home with him to help them. A week later her brother-in-law came to
pick her up.

For twenty-one years, the redheaded, freckled pet-turned-devil had been
a prisoner in the orphanage's bleak mansion otherworld. For years she told
the nuns she wanted to leave but they told her that she wasn't old enough, or
worse, that *this* was her home. In the end Sally assumed, just like the nuns
said, that she would be at the orphanage forever. She wasn't even sure that
she wanted to leave after all. But none of that mattered anymore. It was finally over. Sally walked out the door of St. Joseph's for the last time.

Her brother-in-law drove her from Vermont to Connecticut, and all
throughout the drive, she looked out the window, muttering, "What's so
dirty? What's so dirty?" Finally her brother-in-law asked her what she was
talking about. Before Sally left the orphanage, Sister Blanchard had told her
that she was going into a dirty world. But now that she was out in it, Sally
explained, she couldn't see why. She couldn't see garbage or anything like that.

Sally's brother-in-law said, "Oh God."

And that was that. That's all he said. It was the end of it.

CHAPTER 7

The oldest story I came across about a child's death at St. Joseph's Orphanage was from the 1920s. It involved the orphanage cupola, which could only be accessed by a narrow spiral staircase, barely wider than a child, enclosed by narrow-paneled walls. The staircase sat behind a small wooden door in the center of the attic and extended up through the loft, opening out into the tight square space of the cupola, thin glass windows on all sides, with a complete view of the landscape: the lake below the bluff, the mountains behind the lake, and across the road from the orphanage, a line of houses and large empty parklands. In winter, the whole world was covered in snow and the lake appeared to be frozen solid.

The second time I walked through the orphanage attic, bright lights had been strung up between beams, a railing was attached to the loft, and workers were clearing the place out for a renovation of the building. One of them showed me a photo of a pink taffeta dress that he had found stuffed in a corner. Another pointed out scorch marks from fire damage. I picked up an old leather strap from an ancient roller skate that had split in two.

Almost a hundred years before my visit, two boys had been sent to the attic. One was locked behind the cupola door overnight as punishment. The other boy sat on the other side of the door and listened to his friend cry and beg for help through the night until he eventually made no more noise.

Vermont is one of the coldest states in America, with winter temperatures in the single digits and below. The boy locked in the cupola staircase froze to death, so the story went.

It was the most ghostlike tale I heard. The person who told me about it had heard it from another person, who had likewise heard it from someone else. I was never able to find the original source. Most death and disappearance stories were remarkable for being reported by eyewitnesses or for being only once removed from their origin.

Sally Dale had so many stories herself, having been there for over two decades. It was the work of many years to understand what she said about children who died or vanished, working out which of her stories overlapped with other people's and which were unique to her. Who did she see die? Who actually died? For example, did Mary Clark, the girl who did not cry, really go home to her mother? I looked for traces of Mary Clark and got nowhere. I still don't know if she left the orphanage.

Although Sally Dale reported the most deaths, there were many more stories about the death of children who lived at the orphanage told by residents who had lived there in the 1940s, 1950s, and 1960s. As I worked my way through the depositions, trying to build a catalog of incidents, it occurred to me that there was no reason to believe that similar stories wouldn't have also been told about the 1930s and earlier. It was just that there were more people alive from the institutions in later decades to report what they had seen.

The sheer number of stories about drowned children was confounding. It took a long time, a lot of cross-referencing, and many loose threads to get a sense of how many deaths were in just that category. I identified at least four distinct drowning stories. Other stories involved the stairs, though it wasn't so clear if what was being described was injury causing death or only grievous bodily harm. One woman told me about a very strong memory she had of a day in the early 1960s when she and all the girls in her level were getting ready for bed in their dorm. Another girl suddenly ran into the room, crying hysterically, saying, "They killed him, they killed him." The dormitory nun rushed the screaming girl out of the room and shut the door behind her. The woman I spoke to heard later that the nuns had been holding a little boy over the staircase by his feet because he wouldn't stop crying but they accidentally let him go. She didn't know if the little boy died, but she said that the sound of the girl screaming, *They killed him,* would never leave her.

Piecing together all the stories—the drowned, the fallen, the beaten, the frozen, the sick—was like assembling a jigsaw puzzle with thousands of pieces, all in shades of gray. I got confused, missed details, and then found them again. I tried to make stories match up but then realized they did not fit together at all. I struggled with the length of my ever-growing list. I kept returning to five stories in particular. They were so vivid. It felt, if only briefly, that they were in reach.

FOR A WHILE, I WAS TRIPPED UP BY THE FACT THAT SOME OF THE DEATH stories were reported by a woman named Sally who once lived at the orphanage, but she was not Sally Dale.

Sally Miller spent time at the orphanage in the 1950s and early 1960s. She told lawyers about a summer day when a large group of children stood on the shore of Lake Champlain and joined hands to form a human chain. They had been told to slowly walk into the water to search for a boy who was missing. The children usually had to walk in a long way before the water reached their waists. Beyond that point, there was a sharp drop-off. That day, before they got to the drop-off, word came down the line that the boy had been found.

Someone carried the boy to the beach. He was laid out on the sand in his blue and gray striped bathing shorts, legs splayed. Emergency services had been called, and firefighters crouched around him. The sheriff, who had arrived in his patrol boat, stood nearby. It was too late. The boy was dead.

"Someone said he'd hit his head," Sally Miller told the lawyers.

I wondered if this was the same boy that Sally Dale had seen go under and not come up. I compared the dates both women were at the orphanage and the timing of their drowning stories, and I realized he could not have been. The stories did not overlap. I wasn't able to pin down the year that Dale saw a boy go under, but it seemed most likely that she had been younger than ten years old, before 1948. Miller didn't arrive at the orphanage until 1954.

On the second day of Sally's Miller's deposition, she spoke about a different dead child. When she was around eight years old, about a year after she first arrived at the orphanage, Miller noticed that a mass was being held at an unusual time. She came across a nun who looked very sad. The nun explained that the mass was for a little boy who had died. But as she spoke, her mood changed abruptly, and she became angry. For the eight-year-old Miller, the shift was distressing and confusing. Reading her story decades later, it seemed likely that the nun had frightened herself, worried that she had said too much. The nun told Miller she must never talk about it, never say anything about the boy.

Was the child for whom the mass was held the same child who drowned at the lake? In another interview Miller said she thought the conversation with the nun about the mass occurred when she was thirteen years old, and the boy who was pulled from the lake died when she was eight. The memories were quite distinct in Miller's mind. It was hard to tell, though, because the records were not detailed enough to differentiate the two.

I STARTED TO LOOK FOR THE STORYTELLERS. I MADE CALLS. I KNOCKED on doors. My four-wheel drive bounced from side to side on a snow-covered, unpaved road through a forest in the northeast, where the trees were so thick, the road was invisible to satellite. It opened out to a storybook house at the top of a hill where three cars were parked, but no one answered the door. I drove down a lonely highway on a dark autumn night in rural New York, muttering, "steady, steady, steady," when another car appeared from nowhere and sat close behind for miles. It peeled away when the road got busier. I followed a car in Florida through a storm that swept in from nowhere, turning the bright day so black that it was impossible to pull off the road because I couldn't see the edge of it. If the car ahead had driven into the sea, I would have splashed in a moment later. I sat at a table with a woman who told me about the cruelty she suffered at the orphanage as I watched her son, over her shoulder, pinch crystalline rocks out of a plastic bag and place them in a tall glass cylinder. Mostly I drove and drove. More often than not, the person I hoped to find at the end of the trip was no longer there.

On one trip to Burlington, I went looking for a man named Joseph Eskra, who spent time at the orphanage in the 1950s and early 1960s. During the litigation he told the lawyers about searching for a boy who had drowned in the lake.

Eskra said he was twelve years old at the time, and that he had been swimming with his friend Marvin Willette and a group of other boys, between an old raft and a floating log on the lake. As the other boys were climbing on the log, Willette tried to join them. The older boys were bullies and didn't want to let Willette onto the log. Eskra said he argued with them, explaining that Willette couldn't swim properly and should be allowed to hang on. When Eskra later swam back to the shore, the bullies took the log away from Willette. Eskra hollered at them from the shore, but they did not respond. Five or ten minutes later someone shouted that a child was underwater.

The boys who pushed Willette off the log told the adults on the beach that Willette had been swimming near them and had rolled over onto his back with his mouth open at one point and gone under. That was the last they saw of him. Fifteen minutes later they told a brother that Willette hadn't come up.

Years later, other children said they had been at the lake one day and heard that a boy had hit his head on a log and drowned. Others believed, like Eskra, that a boy who drowned had tried again and again to get onto the log but was pushed off. Someone remembered hearing that a vein was hanging out of the nose of a drowned boy as he was pulled back in. The more of such stories I found, the clearer it became that the children were talking about the same day and the same boy. At the time that it happened, though, none of the children had been able to work out the details or even absorb the event because they weren't allowed to talk about it, even among themselves. It seemed likely that this boy was the same one that Sally Miller had helped to look for in the lake. Both she and Eskra were there in the 1960s. Their stories matched.

But Willette wasn't Eskra's only death story.

Eskra described another boy who failed to turn up to dinner one night. A group of about twenty boys then set out with flashlights to look for him.

"We looked all over where we thought he might be," Eskra told the lawyers. "We thought he ran away. We thought maybe he was hiding."

They found him near the swing set. He was tied with his back to a tree, his arms and legs wrapped around it and tied, too. He had frozen to death.

"How do you know that? What do you recall seeing?" the lawyer asked Eskra.

"Well, he was stiff as a board when we shine the light on him," Eskra said, "and of course, we didn't know what to do."

The details on either side of that crystal moment were hard to pin down. Eskra thought that maybe a rescue team had been called to come to get the boy. He thought there was an investigation. He might have spoken to police that night. He thought the dead boy was between eight and twelve years old. He wasn't really sure.

Eskra said he was told later that the dead boy had been playing "Cowboys and Indians," and his friends had forgotten to untie him.

I looked for Eskra for many months. He had spent time in a homeless shelter and had multiple addresses. I hit many dead ends but finally found what seemed to be his current address. He was never at home when I rang the bell. Eventually I tracked down his daughter in another state. When at last I reached her, she said that Eskra had died nine days earlier.

LOOKING FOR SURVIVORS WAS ONLY POSSIBLE AFTER WORKING THROUGH the material of more than two decades earlier and teasing apart who was who. Many of the women had changed their names in marriage, and it wasn't often clear that *this* girl had become *that* woman. Women told stories about other girls who had been at the orphanage, but they used the name they knew, not the married name. Siblings sometimes had different names, and in some cases, they hadn't known until much later in life that they were siblings. One woman I met had changed her given name in honor of a small girl she had once looked after at the orphanage.

Sometimes I came across survivors by accident. After noticing a curious obituary published in 1953, I started looking for a man named Philip Grenon. He had lived at the orphanage but had not, as far as I could tell, been a part of the litigation. He was one of the many men I looked for but could not find, or rather, who I found, like Joseph Eskra, but missed.

The obituary was for a six-year-old girl. It didn't say that she was a resident of St. Joseph's Orphanage but did note that children from the orphanage had attended her funeral. Clearly there was some connection. As was the practice at the time, the obituary named the girl's pallbearers. I recognized some of their names and realized that they had all been boys from the orphanage. By the time I worked out where they lived as adults, all had died. There was one man, though, brother to one of the pallbearers, who had not: Philip Grenon.

Grenon, it turned out, lived right in the middle of Burlington. I tried to speak to him a few times but was never able to connect. Eventually I ended up in conversation with one of his neighbors. Grenon was troubled, she explained. Sometimes he frightened the people in his apartment building. One night, as we emailed back and forth, she told me that the police had been called to his apartment as he was having some kind of terrifying meltdown.

"Now poor Phil is holed up in his room with five police cars parked in the street," she wrote. "He says he has a gun, but I would be surprised."

We continued to email in the hours that followed. Eventually she told me she heard five shots and thought Grenon had perhaps been shot by the police. She was right. Grenon died that night.

FORMER RESIDENTS TOLD ME ABOUT THEIR EXPERIENCES WITH DEATH, OR at least what looked like death, after my *BuzzFeed News* article was published. Anthony Giallella, at Southern State Correctional Facility, had told me about a blond girl wrapped in plastic in the late 1940s or 50s. A man called Joseph Gelineau told me about another girl in the 1960s.

Gelineau belonged to a family who had been closely connected to the orphanage for a long time. An aunt—who he knew only by the nickname Peanut—worked there as a nun. An uncle who was a priest worked for Vermont Catholic Charities and oversaw aspects of the orphanage operation. Another priest relative had regularly visited the orphanage as a seminarian, later becoming bishop of the Diocese of Providence. Yet another relative was a priest with ties to St. Joseph's. In the 1990s, Gelineau told newspapers that he had reported abuse to his uncle and to the man who later became a bishop, but both said it wasn't true.

I visited Gelineau in his home on a hot Vermont day. He was boyish and sweet and vulnerable, and his wife and his ex-wife, both thoughtful, caring women, sat beside him for support. Gelineau remembered fights in his family home about the orphanage: Two of the priests yelling behind closed doors about secrets, and the fact that the one of them was going to go to hell. One day, he heard his Aunt Peanut tell another adult that she had left the orphanage because of the abuse of the children. At this point, Gelineau asked her, if it was that bad, why did you leave us there? She didn't respond, and simply walked away.

Gelineau's memories of his first week at the orphanage in the early 1960s is a collection of distinct images and black holes that have never quite resolved into a coherent narrative. They begin with him and his brother, Raymond, standing side by side. The boys had been looking for their sisters, and emerged in what Gelineau believes was the attic. Gelineau believes he was around eight. His brother was nine months younger.

Standing about twenty feet in front of the boys, with their backs to them, were two nuns. They were animatedly talking to each other, and there was something odd about the way they spoke. Gelineau realized only many years later that the nuns were likely speaking French, a language he wasn't familiar with. His experience only became more surreal after that point.

The boys walked to either side of the two nuns, who were looking down into what he recalls as a large, rounded container in front of them. The boys looked down, too. There was a little girl inside. She was by herself, just lying there. She was wearing a dress with hearts on it. Gelineau can't remember if he saw her arms or her hands, but there was a lot of blood around her, and she wasn't moving, and something was wrong with her face. Gelineau thinks now that the girl was dead, and that was the quality of wrongness he saw.

Gelineau has a sense memory of putting his hands on the lip of the container. After that, a series of things happened. The nuns realized that the boys were there and erupted, screaming and beating the boys. It was a melee. Gelineau's brother screamed back, "We don't understand you. We don't understand you." Next, Gelineau woke up in a cupboard with his brother. It was very humid and hot. He doesn't know how long he was in there. He couldn't recall what they said to him when he was taken out again, but the message was clear: if he spoke about what he had seen, the same thing would happen to him.

Gelineau woke up later, but this time he was somewhere else. He still isn't sure where it was, but it may have been the orphanage infirmary. He was lying in what he described as a hospital bed and his arms and feet were restrained.

That day set Gelineau up for the rest of his time at the orphanage. He said he experienced "total fear" and was "terrified 24/7." Every day "you were just waiting for something to happen to you."

SHERRY HUESTIS WAS ONE OF THE FEW SURVIVING FORMER RESIDENTS I was able to speak to who reported a death in the litigation. I drove for hours from Montreal to visit her in a small town in northern Maine. At first, we spoke out front, with Huestis standing at the edge of the front porch and me in the yard. Twenty minutes ticked by as she weighed whether she wanted to tell her story again. It was so hard, even after all that time.

In the 1990s Huestis told the lawyers that in the middle of the night, the seamstress, Eva, would sometimes pull her out of bed for company as she walked the hallways checking the doors. One night in the 1960s, Huestis testified, awful screams broke the silence. Huestis followed Eva to a room where two nuns were hovering over another nun in the bed. The one in bed had her legs up and wide open. A little baby was coming out.

The next day, Huestis went to her work in the nursery, and sure enough, the little baby was there, sweet and tiny. She had no idea who the baby's father might be. Its skin was much darker than its mother's. Huestis was off to one side when the nursery nun in white robes and habit came in. She picked up a little satin pillow and put it over the baby's face.

The baby flailed its arms and legs at first. But when the nun lifted it up, its limbs dangled by its sides.

Huestis told the orphanage social worker what she had seen. It seemed that the social worker then told the nursery nun. Later that day the nun walked up to Huestis and slapped her good and hard across the face.

Years later, but long before the litigation, Sherry told her sister Sheila, who had also lived at St. Joseph's Orphanage, that she had seen a nun smother a baby in the nursery. Sheila had trained as a registered nurse in 1981 and developed a specialty in pediatric intensive care. When she gave a deposition in the litigation, she acted out the way Sherry said the baby's arms had dropped to its side.

Sheila said, "When she described it to me, I was shocked, because you have to see a baby die before you know exactly how, what happens to the body when they stop breathing. And when she described it to me, I knew that she had seen it."

Sherry invited me in, and we sat in her kitchen of warm wood tones as she told me about the cruelty of the nuns, the misery of the institution, and how she had longed for escape. She wore her long gray hair in neat plaits, and her air of innocence reminded me a little of Sally Dale, even as she narrated a series of unrelentingly gruesome events. She told me the same story about the baby that she had told the lawyers over twenty years before, the same story she had told her sister years before that. When she described the silky texture of the pillow used to suffocate the baby, she rubbed her thumb against her forefinger, emphasizing the feel of it.

I PONDERED THE IMMENSE POWER OF DISBELIEF FOR A LONG TIME. IT BEGAN with survivors themselves. If they reached a point where they were able to believe the evidence of their own eyes, then sometimes they told someone else the story. Survivors had told me about the guileless, shocked, or outraged individuals to whom the death stories were first told. Often their first response was unhelpful, if not blatantly repressive. But as the list of death stories grew, it struck me that as disappointing as their responses were, those individuals did not have the power to keep the stories out of the daylight. It was institutions that disappeared children in the first place, and it was institutions that kept them invisible.

It wasn't just the church. No modern justice system was built to deal with the kind of mass catastrophe, the rolling disaster, that survivors reported.

There were many examples of how the justice system was not set up to deal with orphanage stories, like the FBI agent who had the power to escalate a death claim but did not, the police who returned runaways to institutions without investigating their claims, or the lawyers who refused to take on cases because they were unlikely to win. One of the most significant obstacles to justice was the statute of limitations on claims of childhood abuse.

A statute of limitations determines when or if a case will be heard in court. If a crime or claim is judged to be too old, whatever that means, it's as good as forgotten. Historically, the window of opportunity for survivors of orphanages, or any kind of childhood abuse, to have a criminal or civil case heard has been very narrow, if not entirely shut.

Marci Hamilton, CEO of CHILD USA, a professor, and a lawyer specializing in religious groups who break the law, told me that most of the first sexual abuse cases against the Catholic Church went away because of the statute of limitations. It's only in recent years that people have begun to see how unjust its application has been. We now know that it's common for survivors to come to an understanding of the damage caused by sexual abuse much later in life. It is often the case that the realization does not hit them in a single moment, it evolves over years. Finding the money and resilience to pursue a case legally can take even more time. When courts expect survivors of sexual abuse to follow a calendar that is indifferent to the impact of the crime, they make justice unattainable.

Worse, the more we learn about the long-term consequences of such crimes, the more obvious it is that limitations on childhood sex abuse cases, as Hamilton points out, provide a distinct advantage to perpetrators. Accordingly, some jurisdictions have made changes, and their institutions have begun to reflect the understanding that limitations are unfair to victims. By 2021, at least forty-nine US states and territories had eliminated the criminal statute of limitations on sexual abuse and seventeen states and territories had eliminated the civil statute of limitations on sexual abuse.

The shift in the statute of limitations on sexual crimes against children has been revolutionary. But for the survivors of institutionalized childcare and other kinds of child abuse, it is only partial. In most jurisdictions, the statute of limitations on physical abuse remains extremely narrow. Unlike the reform of sexual abuse limitations, it has gone unchanged and virtually unchallenged. By 2016 only four US states had extended the window for claims of physical abuse. When I first began to learn about orphanages, I asked legal experts about it, and most expected that it would never change.

Considered in light of stories from the orphanage netherworld, this was hard to understand. Children were thrown, pushed, pulled, hit, and physically assaulted in every way imaginable. As a result they experienced lifelong physical and mental harm. Many victims told me that the impact of the sexual and physical abuse was equally terrible for them. For some, the whole thing was backward; in their experience, sexual abuse was a kind of physical abuse, an instance of a larger, diverse category to which they had been so devastatingly exposed. The point was not that sexual abuse wasn't profoundly harmful, but that physical abuse was, too.

The ACE study on the impact of childhood adversity validates survivors' claims. It does not find that one type of abuse is inherently worse than the other or that the different types of abuse are necessarily distinct from each other in practice, but rather that many types of abuse co-occur.

The problem is that the different ways sexual, physical, and other kinds of abuse are judged by the law has shaped the experience of many survivors. This is reflected in government inquiries into institutional abuse. Some have focused largely on sexual abuse as the greater violation, with less acknowledgment of the impact of physical abuse, and as I saw time and time again, an impotent response to stories about child death. In some cases, victims of sexual abuse received financial compensation, but the victims of physical abuse did not. By giving sexual abuse crimes a different status, governments and legal bodies sent a powerful message that physical abuse wasn't as harmful.

Traumatic by itself for victims, this tendency to downplay physical abuse also had a consequential knock-on effect: It made the death stories seem even more surreal. In the orphanage underworld there was a clear progression of violence, beginning with a single hit or push, and in some cases, ending with accidental or intentional death. Critically, the statute of limitations obscured the connection between unrestrained violence against small bodies and one of its inevitable consequences, death, because it shut the door on claims about violence. The stories of physical abuse were not sufficiently explored, so the death stories seemed to come from nowhere, and the storytellers themselves seemed like bizarre isolates.

I wondered what it would have been like otherwise, if a significant number of physical abuse cases had historically been won or lost, litigation pursued, charges laid (or not), and an accompanying mountain of records, references, precedents, and journalism with features, reports, and opinion pieces arguing for or against. In such a world, not only would the victims of physical abuse have received some justice, but the stories about deaths would not have seemed so unreal. All the intellectual and emotional groundwork necessary to believe that children *might* have been killed would have been laid by the courts, law enforcement, insurance companies, and the correctional system, and not left to isolated individuals.

Instead, the history has been shaped by a reinforcing loop between the inaction of the dysfunctional justice system and the attitudes of people who weren't personally affected by it. Most people assume that the laws put in place to protect children make sense. When I tried to explain the death stories, the fact that nothing had been done about them was often construed as a reason for nothing further to be done. That the veracity of the stories had once been up for debate was—illogically—an additional strike against them. Because if it was true, of course, if something that monstrous really had happened, someone would surely have done something about it.

THE ABSENCE OF THE RIGHT KIND OF ENGAGEMENT FROM THE LAW AND the criminal justice system shut down countless cases and, for the victims, warped the reality of the world. But for all that damage, the nefarious work of institutions where the abuse first occurred did even more damage, ranging from obvious stonewalling and lack of cooperation in death and abuse cases, to whispers of conspiracy. It's not simply that those institutions failed to work toward the goal of justice or the moral obligation to do the right thing, or even that their execution was inadequate. In many cases, they were working directly—and effectively—against justice.

CHAPTER 8

Philip White was sitting in his large, third-floor law office one afternoon in 1993 when the mysterious caller arrived. He said his name was Joseph Barquin, and he appeared to be in a state of terror.

White invited him to have a seat and tell his story. Barquin asked White to send his secretary out so the two men could speak privately.

Barquin said he had recently married, and that his new wife had been shocked by the sight of terrible scars on his genitals.

Barquin told White what he had told her: In the early 1950s, when he was a young boy, he spent a few years in an orphanage called St. Joseph's in Burlington, Vermont. It had been a dark and terrifying place run by an order of nuns called the Sisters of Providence. Barquin recalled a girl whose head was smacked so hard into a heater that she "went out like a light." He saw a little boy shaken into uncomprehending shock. He saw other children beaten over and over.

A nun at St. Joseph's had dragged Barquin into an anteroom under the stairs and forcefully fondled him, and then cut him with something very sharp. He didn't know what it was; he just remembered that there was blood everywhere.

Barquin's wife had encouraged him to get help. So on a spring morning, Barquin went to the Diocese of Burlington. He spoke to two priests, one of whom was Father Walter Miller. Barquin said that he wanted help with the cost of therapy, and he wanted an apology. Miller said he would pass the message on, but Barquin had received no response. Now he wanted to sue.

BARQUIN HAD COME TO THE RIGHT LAWYER. AS A PROSECUTOR IN Newport, Vermont, and then as a private attorney, White had devoted his career to challenging and changing the prevailing wisdom about young victims of sexual abuse.

He stumbled into being a state's attorney in 1980. White dropped out of college in 1967, drove around the country, worked as a carpenter and then as a carriage driver in Central Park, smoked some dope, took some acid, had some good trips, had a bad trip, stopped taking drugs, and went back to school. Then he went to law school, where he studied full time while he also worked full time. After completing his degree, he applied for a job at Vermont Legal Aid. It seemed to him like the right fit. He showed up to the interview in a Brooks Brothers suit and found that his interviewers were all wearing plaid shirts and mountain climbing boots. He didn't get the job, but he found work as a prosecutor and eventually ended up in the state's attorney job in Newport, on the Canadian border.

Newport, in the 1970s, was like the Wild West. The town had regular Saturday night drive-by shootings. The state's attorney before White, a deputy sheriff, deputized a prostitute from Montreal so she wouldn't get speeding tickets when she visited him. White began a new regime, pursuing the full range of border town criminality—drunk drivers, cult leaders, drug smugglers, and murderers. Early on, to his puzzlement, he found that when cases of child sexual abuse came to his attention, most people expected them to go away after being quietly dealt with, perhaps with the removal of the child from the home, usually with no prosecution involved.

White encountered the widely held belief that putting a child victim of sexual abuse through the legal process would cause additional trauma and wasn't worth it. Worse, people thought that if the courts began to deal with child sexual abuse, it would stop other victims from coming forward. White suspected that the real problem lay with the fears of first responders—mandatory reporters like teachers and attorneys. When they were nervous about the consequences of reporting, it made people less likely to report. White decided he would make his time as an accidental prosecutor count for something.

White got the social workers working together with the police, who, in his experience, typically saw the social workers as a bunch of dope smokers. He empowered the folks at county mental health services to report abuse. He involved probation officers as well. At the same time, he and some of his colleagues created a set of protocols for reports of abuse, including mandatory counseling for sex offenders, which allowed responders to monitor behavior and intervene sooner, and treatment for kids. It was the early 1980s, and although the system was fragile, White's jurisdiction was only one of four in the country to have written interagency protocols and dealt with the problem head-on.

White's new approach proved incredibly effective. With sensible procedures in place and competent adults on the other side of a child sex abuse complaint, the reporting increased tenfold. The state of Vermont adopted White's approach, making them one of the first American states where law enforcement started to take child sex abuse seriously. His team went into schools to explain to teachers what would happen if they reported abuse. He traveled through Vermont and eventually all over the country to train first responders. He spoke to prosecutors, who told him that they didn't prosecute child sexual abuse because if they lost the case, they couldn't live with themselves. White would reply, "If you don't bring the case, how can you sleep?"

White's team developed a way for children to testify on closed-circuit television so they wouldn't have to tell their story in front of their abuser. Whenever a young client testified, White threw a party, with cake and balloons and streamers. In one case where a number of children had been abused at a daycare, some of the witness's little friends were also there to encourage and congratulate. He told the children that regardless of how the case was decided, they had spoken their truth, and that was the victory.

Bearing witness to the most awful experiences of Vermont's children was hard. White found that it wasn't unusual for a family who spoke out to be attacked by neighbors or other members of the community. It was tough to witness the way children managed the aftermath. With amazement, White watched one abused boy protect his mother from feelings that *she* couldn't bear by doling out information about his abuse in small, tolerable packets.

When it was too much, White would find the steepest ski slope that he could and fly down it, screaming his head off all the way down.

When Barquin found White, he'd built up ten years of scar tissue as state's attorney and left the job to set up a small private practice with another attorney in Montpelier, Vermont. He took a range of cases and planned to continue defending children against monsters and silence.

For all the cases White had worked on, he had never heard a story quite like Barquin's. More than anything, it was Barquin's still palpable fear that impressed him.

Barquin told White that he contacted the Diocese of Burlington, but they did not engage with him. White believed it. He had dealt with the diocese before and knew what it was like to be stonewalled by them. In recent years, White had observed the church besieged by claims about priest sex abuse. In all cases, they had put up a damaging and bitter fight. He believed the Catholic Church to be a brilliant adversary. It hadn't survived so long without protecting itself.

Barquin's assault had taken place decades ago, which would make it hard for White to find corroboration—and easy for the church to question Barquin's memory. As hard as it would be to convince jurors that a priest could be a sexual predator, making that argument about a nun was going to be much harder. In White's experience, most people had a hard time believing that a woman could be predatory.

Still, White decided to take Barquin's case. He filed a complaint in the US District Court at Burlington, Vermont, on June 7, 1993, seeking damages for Barquin's injuries from physical, psychological, and sexual abuse at St. Joseph's Orphanage forty years before. The defendants he named were the Diocese of Burlington, Vermont Catholic Charities, St. Joseph's Orphanage, and, because Barquin didn't know the name of the nun who abused him, Mother Jane Doe.

UNTIL THE MOMENT THAT WHITE FILED BARQUIN'S CASE, THE STORY OF ST. Joseph's Orphanage in the wider Burlington community had been a fading but fondly remembered tale of civic spirit. For decades, local Catholics had rallied for the cause. A bus from the Burlington Rapid Transit Company ferried children and nuns to see the Christmas lights. Older men of the Knights of Columbus, a Catholic fundraising body, dressed as Santa to distribute presents at Christmas. Local Catholic women dressed as elves, raised money, donated secondhand clothes, or wrapped gifts. In the late 1960s, after Vatican II gave nuns more personal freedom to move about the world, one local woman taught a few of the nuns how to drive.

The diocese's response to the lawsuit, which came about a month later, was unyielding. They requested the judge dismiss Barquin's complaint on the basis of the statute of limitations, which in Vermont meant that adults who were abused as children had six years from the moment they realized they were damaged by abuse to bring suit. Bill O'Brien, an attorney who worked for the diocese, as had his father, Bill O'Brien Sr., before him, signed the motion for judgement on the pleadings.

In order to argue for a dismissal based on time limits, the law allowed O'Brien to make his case from a place most non-lawyers would see as one of strange cognitive dissonance. "For the purpose of this motion only," he wrote, "without conceding or admitting any fact," the parties and the judge assumed that what Barquin was saying was true. Briefly then, the court accepted that Barquin had been terribly abused at the orphanage.

The position allowed them to express outrage at Barquin's inaction in the face of what they called the "severe, lifelong nature" of his injuries. Outside the legal world, this position seems to cancel itself: If a person's injuries are extreme and ongoing, how can that person be expected to respond in any kind of normal or legally prescribed timeframe? Thanks to the statute of limitations, this was not a question the diocese had to answer.

Barquin had forty years to work out what had caused his injuries, O'Brien said, during which time relevant evidence or witnesses may have been lost. Bringing a claim from that long ago, he wrote, was a violation of the diocese's rights. O'Brien also lectured White on the First Amendment and other points of law, quoting an opinion from a medical malpractice suit stating that "the law is not designed to aid the slothful in evading the results of their own negligence."

White told Barquin that he might not be alone. He arranged a press conference for Barquin to tell his story. "Either nobody's going to call," he told Barquin, "or the phone's going to ring off the hook." Privately, White thought, if more former residents of St. Joseph's didn't come forward, it would be hard to move ahead with the case.

In his years since leaving the orphanage, Barquin had led an adventurous life. He had worked as a diver, unearthing old shipwrecks and ancient fossils. He had spent time at the famous Naropa Institute in Colorado, hanging out with Ram Dass and Allen Ginsberg. He'd dropped acid with people who knew Timothy Leary. He'd led dolphin encounters. Shirley MacLaine had been in touch. But the day of his press conference, he was afraid. Barquin felt like he was lighting a match inside a dark and ominous cave. He was hopeful that he might inspire others to do the same.

The press conference worked. Barquin did a good job, White thought. He had been direct, straightforward, and simple. White hoped he might hear from a few more former St. Joseph's residents. He heard from forty. Soon a support group called the Survivors of St. Joseph's Orphanage and Friends formed. Participants said it grew to eighty members.

White found that some of the former residents had been at the orphanage at the same time, while others didn't know anyone else who had been there. Some had been there with siblings, but others had been completely alone. Their stories were excruciating and particular, and some of the named abusers—nuns, priests, and laity—seemed to be the same. This was not the kind of case that White was used to. It wasn't the kind of case that anyone was used to. "It was not one priest at one time," White said years later, waving his hands in the air and whirling them around. "It was Dante's inferno."

The survivors' meetings were unpredictable. Some former residents said that the orphanage was the best thing that ever happened to them. Others recounted constant cruelty and physical abuse. Survivors remembered physical toil, emotional cruelty, heinous food. Some threatened violence against clergy members. One woman said she was writing a book. Another, who had been at the orphanage in the 1920s, called to tell her story, weeping in fear that God would punish her for saying it aloud. One man turned up outrageously drunk. Another spoke about how, at home, he would regularly lock himself in a box. Someone wrote to White to warn him that the diocese had sent a spy. *So what?* he thought. *Good!*

Around that time, one former resident died by suicide. Another shot his girlfriend and then himself while his girlfriend's children were at school.

Survivors fought among themselves about what strategy to pursue. At one meeting, a woman was shouted down when she suggested that they all contact the bishop together. Some wanted therapists present at the meetings, but others were appalled by the suggestion.

Eventually White decided to convene a big gathering at the Hampton Inn in Colchester, Vermont, on the weekend of September 18, 1994. It would be the first reunion of the survivors of St. Joseph's Orphanage, Vermont.

As Barquin's case moved forward slowly, White continued to phone, write letters, and request meetings with the bishop on behalf of the other survivors. Months went by and nothing concrete happened, yet his clients were very fragile and on edge. "Once they had reported, that's a place of great risk," White later said. The diocese was so slow to respond to White that as the year went on, he asked the bishop for financial help for survivors—at least enough money to pay for counseling for some survivors who were especially distressed by the process of making a claim. But there was no definitive response to that either.

One of the survivors, Joseph Gelineau, said that members of his family were clergy who had been closely involved with the orphanage and that he had reported the abuse to them many years before. His uncle, Father Edward Gelineau, who had been the director of Vermont Catholic Charities, told a reporter that the statement was "a lie." He suggested that Joseph had been misled by psychologists trying to get him to explore his childhood memories. Bishop Louis Gelineau of Rhode Island, a cousin in the same family, told the reporter that Joseph's statement was "absolutely false."

Meanwhile the diocese's director of communications published an op-ed in the local Catholic press in what she called a "teachable moment." "No, we aren't perfect," she wrote, admitting that the church's responses to child sexual abuse across the country had been tainted by denial. "But we are trying." She argued that the problem rested not so much with the church as with all of society. "Now we can only pray that our country will take a look at the plank in its own eye and join us in the journey to wholeness."

In November 1994, White scored an unprecedented victory, not just for Barquin but for all abuse survivors in Vermont. A judge in the US District

Court of Vermont made a decision about the church's appeal to dismiss Barquin's case. The claim of assault and battery could not be heard by the courts, determined the judge, because the Vermont statute of limitations ruled out cases brought more than three years after the assault occurred. But it was different for the sexual assault claim.

Vermont's law allowed victims six years to pursue their abuser. Critically, that six years was counted not from when the abuse occurred, but from the moment that victims understood they had been injured. It was a way of acknowledging the fact that people didn't always understand how their lives were damaged by what had happened to them as children. Indeed, it wasn't unusual for people to take a very long time to connect the abuse with what happened in the rest of their lives.

The modified statute had been on the books only for a few years in Vermont, but before Joseph Barquin's claim, no judge had ruled on it. This time, the federal judge allowed it. The decision wasn't completely binding, and it didn't mean that a judge would not ultimately rule against Barquin based on the statute of limitations, but at least the church couldn't have him disqualified before his story was told. Barquin would be heard by a judge and get a chance to go to court. It was a great start—Barquin's case could proceed.

AS THE ST. JOSEPH'S SURVIVORS GROUP GAINED MOMENTUM IN BURLINGTON, Joseph Barquin emerged as an extraordinary force for change. Since the judge had allowed his sexual assault case to go forward, he was proving himself to be a tenacious litigant, rallying others to the cause and even doing his own investigative work. He visited a number of Sisters of Providence nuns at the local motherhouse, interviewing them on tape: "Who was the sister that was a real disciplinarian?" But his outsize role and expectations complicated matters. Having been the first to come forward, he believed that his ideas should carry extra weight. His relationship with White deteriorated over what Barquin perceived to be a lack of respect. His relationship with the group frayed as well. Eventually a delegate said several members felt threatened by Barquin.

White came to the painful conclusion that he could not continue to represent Barquin, and encouraged him to find new counsel. White planned to focus on the claims of the other former residents. But as all that was going on, White's doctor told him that he had adult-onset diabetes. He had two children, one of them a newborn, and it became clear that his firm was too small to provide all the resources needed to handle all the cases coming his way. White realized that if he was going to represent the orphans with integrity and competence, he would have to sacrifice everything else. "I'd basically have to leave my family, find a miracle drug for my diabetes, and find a new law firm," he said later.

Around the same time, the bishop made a formal offer: each person would get $5,000 in exchange for waiving their right to further legal action.

White hated to see the cases end like that, but he knew that the statute of limitations would have prevented some of the plaintiffs from ever getting their day in court. And for many of them, $5,000 was serious money. He told his clients that he could not advise them what path to choose, but if anyone wanted to settle, he would help.

The *Burlington Free Press* reported that according to church officials, a hundred people accepted the payment for abuse they said they suffered. Plaintiffs said as many as 160 individuals, who had been at the orphanage from the 1930s to the 1970s, pursued the bishop's offer.

For every one of those he represented, White sent a letter to Bill O'Brien, the diocese attorney.

"Dear Bill," one of the letters said, "K remembers that Sister Madeline and Sister Claire . . . slapped her head and face, pulled her hair, struck her face with the backs of their hands, so that their rings split her lips, and tripped her and knocked her down."

"Dear Bill, . . . If L was caught not paying attention, the nuns would take a needle and regularly prick his fingertips."

"Dear Bill, . . . To this day, C will not enter a closet if it has a hanging light."

"Dear Bill, . . . The nuns would also force G and other children to hold their arms up at their sides, with their palms up in the air, balancing a book on the palms. If G dropped his arms before the requisite time was up, he would be beaten and forced to repeat the punishment all over again."

The bishop published a letter around the same time. In a larger sense they were all victims, he said, both the children who had been abused and the good priests and brothers and nuns. "If anybody has been hurt by any church official in any way," he wrote, "I am heartily sorry."

The woman who had suggested contacting the bishop at one of White's survivor meetings went ahead and visited him herself. She said he told her that if modern-day laws had been in place when he was a child, his own father would have been charged with child abuse, yet he was able to get over what had happened to him. He didn't understand why other people couldn't do the same.

"They were just kids," the woman later testified that she told him.

"Well, these nuns were just frustrated ladies," he replied, according to her testimony. "They didn't know how to handle children. They hadn't any children of their own."

CHAPTER 9

JOSEPH BARQUIN CONTACTED THE LAWYER ROBERT WIDMAN AFTER HE was referred by a friend of a friend. Widman lived near Barquin in Sarasota, Florida, and Barquin told him about his diving and his dolphin encounters. Despite his stories of freewheeling adventure, he struck Widman as a particularly neat and rather anxious person.

Barquin described his experience at St. Joseph's and explained his work with Philip White. Now that White was unable to continue to represent him, Barquin needed someone else to take on the Diocese of Burlington.

Widman was intrigued. He didn't disbelieve Barquin. He had gone to a boarding school run by Jesuit brothers and knew how cruel clergy could be. He had seen plenty of injustice and depravity in his legal practice. But Widman didn't quite believe Barquin, either. Not yet. He needed to know more.

After working for years as a corporate lawyer, Widman had recently cofounded a two-person law firm. He took the case to Geoff Morris, his new partner. Morris was skeptical, too, but both men agreed that what Barquin was saying had a ring to it. There was enough there to make it worth exploring.

Widman decided to visit Burlington, Vermont. With Barquin's help, he planned to talk to as many of the orphans of St. Joseph's as possible. He gave himself a few weeks to try to get to the bottom of what had happened. If there was more, maybe he would take the case.

WIDMAN AND MORRIS TOURED VERMONT IN EARLY 1996. WITH BARQUIN'S help they met with the survivors of St. Joseph's in houses and homeless shelters and rustic inns. They had searing encounters in the most bucolic settings.

By then, some residents had chosen the diocese's settlement money and receded from view. Others were offended by the offer and wanted nothing to do with legal action. They felt that the church was trying to buy their childhood. The survivors group was still meeting regularly. One of the group's earliest members had started turning up outside the old orphanage building, which no longer hosted any children but was by then the headquarters of the diocese itself. She stood there for hours holding a placard twice her width, on which was written, "WE ARE SURVIVORS of this Orphanage."

It became rapidly clear that gathering all the facts and bringing them all together was going to be a formidable challenge. Widman began to think of the story as an octopus with hundreds of legs. There were so many different experiences. Yet even at the very start of the investigation, Widman saw patterns emerge. People who had been at St. Joseph's in different years, even different decades, described how they had been confined in the same water tank or how they had watched other children be put into the same nursery closet. They remembered a ruler, a paddle, a strap, a small ax, a light bulb, clappers, and a set of large rosary beads. They spoke about lit matches being held against skin. They described a cavernous attic. When they were good, they had gone up there two by two to retrieve Sunday clothes, play clothes, and winter gear. When they were bad, they were pushed, dragged, and blasted up the stairs to sit alone and scream into the void.

The aftershocks of the orphanage had reverberated through lifetimes. Many of the people Widman met had spent time in jail or struggled with addiction, facts that a defense lawyer could use to discredit them in front of a jury. He wanted to help them but wasn't sure if he should take on the daunting job.

WIDMAN HADN'T ALWAYS WANTED TO BE A LAWYER. AFTER EMERGING FROM a few wild post–high school years of hard drinking and fighting, knives carried, guns drawn but not shot, he started to think about social work and helping troubled children. He met with a social worker, who told him that the job was terrible. If Widman really wanted to make a difference, the man said, he should become a lawyer.

Widman's boozy lost years had been a jagged turn in the trajectory he was supposed to take. He grew up in a small farming town about sixty miles outside of Cleveland, Ohio. His mother's uncle had played organ for the bishop. His aunt was the Mother Superior of the Sisters of Notre Dame. A couple of priests were part of the family, too.

When he was fourteen, Widman's parents sent him to Campion Jesuit High School, a boarding school in Prairie du Chien, Wisconsin. His younger brother went to Campion. His sister went to a local school. *Give us a boy*, the Campion Jesuits told the parents of prospective students, *and get back a man*. Widman didn't want to be a Campion man. He played football and basketball in his hometown and he didn't want to leave any of his friends.

There was no art or music or science at Campion. The boys learned Latin, Greek, English and math, and the deep and abiding notion that they would all surely succeed. Campion produced politicians, actors, and authors, a state governor, an NFL player, and an Air Force general. One of Widman's dorm mates, George Wendt, played the character of Norm on the television show *Cheers*. A few years after Widman attended, Vicente Fox, the former president of Mexico, studied at Campion.

Campion boys did a lot of ROTC and played a lot of football. They had their hair cut every month and followed strict clothing regulations. They wrote regular letters home, and for their part, the Jesuit brothers censored what the boys wrote.

The first night Widman went to bed in a Campion dorm, he lay after dark trying to sleep. Campion was situated close to a train track, and late every night a train roared by and blew a loud and shrill whistle. That night, Widman's roommate responded, "Shut up, train!"

A brother who was walking by came into the room. He issued "one JUG apiece," a Campion demerit, to Widman and the talker. Widman protested.

It wasn't him. He hadn't said anything. But the brother was uninterested. He had heard a conversation, and that was that.

Every night before bed, the Campion boys lined up in the hall, and the brother in charge of the dormitory read out the names of boys who had earned a demerit that day, one by one. When Widman's name was called, he was summoned into the brother's room and, upon instruction, pulled down his pants. As the brother wound up with a wooden paddle, Widman bent over and grabbed his ankles. The paddle was about a foot and a half long, maybe a foot wide, and built for the task. For every JUG Widman earned, the brother hit him once with the paddle.

The experience formed one of Widman's abiding lessons. *Life is not fair.*

Illuminating the snow outside Widman's window, a single light glowed in the darkness. He often got up in the middle of the night to sit on the ledge, look out, and think about his parents and the day he left for Campion. Widman's father had taken him to the train station. On the platform, Widman became momentarily distracted, readying himself to board. He turned around to say goodbye to his father, only to find that his father had gone. It was devastating. Widman never got over it.

Night after night, he sat in the cold and thought about that day, and how miserable he was, and the fact that his parents had sent him away. He stayed angry at them until the day they died.

Widman regularly broke all the rules and walked off campus, secretly hoping he would be caught and thrown out. But he probably averaged only one or two JUG sessions a month. It was a constant disappointment.

After Campion, Widman went to John Carroll University in Ohio as an accounting major. But he never went to class. He drank copious amounts of beer and was reliably drunk by two o'clock every afternoon. At the end of his first semester, he received four Fs and a D. It was all rage, he reflected later. Rage that he had felt imprisoned at Campion, rage that his parents had abandoned him. He didn't know what to do with his rage, so he drank.

He got into car wrecks. He hung out in a tenement house with a crew of young men. Drugs, alcohol, pornography—everyone did whatever they wanted. One especially crazy night ended with a police raid. Widman ran but the police chased him. An officer told him to raise his hands. Widman obliged, or at least tried to, but he was extremely drunk. He threw up his hands and accidentally hit the officer in the face.

He spent a few days in jail and then found himself in front of a judge. The judge offered Widman a chance at redemption. If Widman left town and did not come back, the judge said, he would write up his offence as a speeding ticket. John Carroll University kicked Widman out, and there was nothing else to keep him in Ohio. So he made his way to the University of Florida.

Soon after Widman arrived in Florida, he met a smart, confident girl with bright blond hair named Cynthia on a fire escape outside his English literature class. He knew instantly that he wanted only to be with her. They never drank together, but when Cynthia left town for an internship, Widman turned twenty-one and had a drink, and then another. She phoned on his birthday, but Widman's roommate said he was unconscious. She kept calling for two or three days, but Widman was out to the world. Cynthia was shocked and concerned.

By the time he came to, Widman saw clearly that there were two paths ahead of him. Beer was on one path and Cynthia was on the other. He never got drunk again. They were soon married.

By the time Widman began law school, he and Cynthia had a daughter and had moved into the University of Florida's crummy married student accommodations. They got by on food stamps and the fifty dollars a month Widman earned for ROTC, with an extra fifteen dollars every eight weeks when Widman sold his blood. Widman avoided hanging out with the other law students before an exam because their nervous energy threw him, but he loved the law. His professors saw qualities in him that made him perfect for the vocation. He was tenacious, insightful, and able to assimilate vast amounts of information accurately and with ease. Widman also understood how important it was to be on good terms with the other side's lawyers. It wasn't purely strategic. Widman was just a genuinely nice person. There was a lot of smiling and joking when he was around.

Widman started work for the law school's sponsored legal aid clinic. Wearing a thirty-five-dollar suit that he and Cynthia could not afford, he was asked to defend a man who broke the leg of his girlfriend's ten-year-old daughter. At the beginning of the case, Widman went back to his professor and said he could not represent the man. He was repulsed by what his client had done. But his professor told him it was his job, so Widman went ahead. When the victim failed to appear in court, Widman won the case. Later he discovered that his former client had married his girlfriend and was now the girl's stepfather. It was the last criminal case Widman took. He never forgot the sight of the little girl lying in her hospital bed.

Widman also volunteered for a campaign to get one of his law professors elected for local office. The professor, Joe Little, was strict. *You missed three classes, and you failed, the reason was irrelevant.* He was also a creative and tireless defender of civil rights, and Widman found him deeply inspiring.

After graduation, Widman went to work for a commercial law firm. But not long after, his old professor, Joe Little, found himself being sued by the state. He asked Widman for help.

Widman won Little's case, with a large amount of money awarded in damages. Widman also became the top earning lawyer at Nelson Hesse in Sarasota, bringing in millions of dollars for the firm every year. His reward was being able to take time out to do pro bono civil rights work with Little.

Together, Widman and Little defended the Black principal of an elementary school in a southern town who was falsely accused of the molestation of a state senator's daughter, showed that a Florida man who served five years of a fifteen-year sentence had been wrongly imprisoned under the state's three strikes law, and helped a young Chinese woman who had been at Tiananmen Square when Chinese troops shot protestors. Little was the big ideas guy. Widman was the attack dog, though he was less of a brawler and more of a gallant and clever adversary, calmly and resolutely pointing out the flaws in the other side's case.

Widman and Little won some big cases, but over time they lost more. Widman began to believe that the delivery of justice depended less on the law than it did on individual judges, who were, in most of his cases, extremely conservative. After twenty years, Widman decided that the cases were unwinnable, so he stopped taking them.

Around the same time, an attorney friend, Geoff Morris, started a private personal injury practice in Venice, Florida, and asked Widman to join him.

Morris thought Widman was smart and an excellent trial lawyer, and critically, he was very honest. Widman was intrigued. He and his prospective partner seemed to have the same taste in work. The two men spoke about going for cases that were really big, almost impossible. They didn't want lots of little jobs, they wanted to focus on one.

Widman left his law firm and joined Morris in Venice. He wore jeans and sandals every day and took his dog to work. For most of his life, Widman had been a combination of easygoing and fearless. Now he had a lot more time on his hands, so he went looking for a fight.

It wasn't until he made the four-hour drive from Burlington to a modest house in Middletown, Connecticut, to meet Sally Dale, born Sally Fredette, that Widman made up his mind about the St. Joseph's case.

Sally took him in through a mudroom with lots of tiny boots flung about, to a kitchen filled with the inviting smell of home cooking. They sat down at the table and ended up talking for hours.

Then, and in subsequent conversations, she told him about the little boy who was thrown out of a fourth-story window by a nun, a boy who went under the surface of Lake Champlain and did not come up again, and the very sad and frightening story of the little boy who was electrocuted. She told him about beatings and punishments and terrible accidents, like the day the nuns sent her into the fire pit to retrieve a ball and her snow pants caught on fire, and how weeks later, as the nuns pulled blackened skin off her arms and her legs with tweezers and she cried out in pain, they told her it was happening because she was a bad girl.

When Widman walked out of her house that day, he stood in her driveway with tears in his eyes. He couldn't say what it was about Sally—her strange fearless innocence, her stubbornness—but he trusted every word she said. She was the most believable person he'd met in his life.

After they met, Widman asked Sally to write to him about everything she remembered of St. Joseph's. He told her that he didn't care about spelling or anything like that, he just hoped it might help her sort things out. She liked the idea, and over many months, she sent him a series of powerful and detailed letters.

July 12, 1996

I had a dream last night about the orphanage. But the funny part is my eyes were wide open. I saw a sister come into the girls small dorm and she came over to my bed and told me to come with her. She took me by the hand and brought me to her room. She put me on her bed and started to touch me all over, I was so afraid but would not make a sound so she would get mad and swipe me. Then she took my hands and told me to rub her all over while she put her fingers where it really hurt and I did not like it. Then she told me to put her fingers where she had touch me on her and I said no.

She got so mad that she gave me a strapping real hard and sent me back to my bed in the dorm and told me to never say anything about it, so I did what she sayed because I really was afraid she would hurt me again.

1996

I remember when I was real little and would get mad I would throw a temper tantrum. They would get so mad at me they would grab me wherever they could and bring me into the bathroom and put me on my back over the tub and pour cold water into my face until I would stop scream and kicking. The water would come down so hard on me.

1996

As I really got older they used to make me babysit the real little ones in the nursery. There were times when I would see things the nuns were doing to them but did not know where to go to tell someone. Sometimes I would ask them why they did those things and they would say because they were very bad boys or girls.

In the winter we would have these funny looking things that heat and steam would come out off. They would put the little kids on them sometimes just to sit but others they would stand them on it and then push them and of course sometimes there little legs would get caught between the wall and radiator and the little kids would really scream and cry. They would pull them out and some kids would have real nasty burns and blisters from it. If they did not stop crying they would then lock them in the same closet they used to put me in. You could here them but you could do nothing for them because they would keep the keys on them till they were ready to let them out. But what could I do I was still just a kid myself.

CHAPTER 10

WHEN SHE LEFT THE ORPHANAGE, SALLY TOOK THE MEMORY OF HER broken leg, the incident with Patricia Carbonneau, the burned boy, the drowned boy, the boy who was thrown from the window, all the disappeared children, and she locked them in a box in an attic and forgot that the attic had ever existed. Apart from a few conversations about events at the orphanage, she hardly mentioned or thought about it at all.

But in the days and weeks after the St. Joseph's survivors reunion, everything buried inside her began to clamber back into her life, tugging and grabbing at her, punching through the day itself. Sally had headaches, her back was killing her, and she started having flashbacks two or three times a day. She found herself doing things she hadn't done for years, like getting up long before dawn to wash, dry, and put away all the clothes, scrubbing the floors on her hands and knees, buffing it to a shine, and making sure everything in the house was perfectly set.

For most of her adult life, Sally was not interested in digging up memories. Talking about things just brought back the hurt. As it was, every now and then, she felt like crawling into the middle of the road and screaming her head off. It was hard, too, when something bad happened and should have made her cry, but she just stood there with a stupid grin on her face instead, and everyone got mad at her and asked why was she smiling.

Sally's husband said she should love herself but that made no sense. She was nobody. She could look at a photograph and pick herself out, but when she looked in a mirror, she didn't see herself, she just saw nobody. By the time the attorney Robert Widman came to visit, Sally's family told her it was time for her to do something.

It had taken Sally a long time to get to a place where she felt like she could do something. After leaving the orphanage and moving in with her sister Sherry, Sally found a job working for a local doctor. But Sherry didn't like the way Sally started to behave. She worried that Sally had fallen in love with her boss, and she became convinced that Sally wasn't fit for the world outside the orphanage. Sally told the lawyers that Sherry asked a judge to send Sally back to St. Joseph's. According to Sally, the judge asked her a series of puzzling questions like, How are babies born? Sally thought that babies came out of people's backsides. She was surprised and embarrassed to hear that they did not. Still, whatever was wrong with her, it wasn't bad enough that the judge felt she should go back. She was free.

Sally's sister lived downstairs from a family called the McCarthys. They were a warm, loud, happy bunch. Sally was drawn to them, and they welcomed her. She spent more and more time upstairs with them, and a few months after the incident with the judge, she fled Sherry's home permanently to live with the McCarthys. They told her she was part of their family now, and even though she was in her early twenties, she called Mrs. McCarthy "Mom."

Life with the McCarthys was happy in a way that Sally had never experienced. She had a job at the cafeteria at First National. She had her own money. Because she was now the eldest of the seven McCarthy children, she finally got to be a big sister.

She was protective of the little ones. She loved to buy them pizza with her own money. She gave little Melissa her first Barbie doll. She took one of the boys to see Bill Cosby at the local theater. She took two of the teens to see Herman's Hermits. Somehow they were seated in the front row, and when the five handsome men with their suits and ties and funny English accents sang, "Something tells me I'm into something good," everyone started swinging. Sally clapped right along.

One day early on, Sally threw up. She worriedly asked her new siblings if Mom would make her eat her vomit. They were confused by the question but confident that the answer would be no. When Sally told Mom that milk curdled in her stomach, Mom told her to see an allergy doctor. The doctor told Sally that she was allergic to milk. Sally stopped eating dairy, and she stopped throwing up. Around the same time, she had to have her appendix removed. After the operation, the surgeon told Sally that her appendix had been leaking for years. He seemed to think that it explained the pain she frequently felt on her right side at the orphanage.

Sally kept breaking bones though, especially in the winter. It seemed like she was always wearing a cast for some reason or other. She did her best to smile and get on with things and never complain. Once when the family was tobogganing, Sally fell against a tree and broke her arm. She didn't make a fuss because she didn't want to ruin everyone's dinner. It was only when the McCarthys saw that one of her bones was sticking out that they took her to the hospital. It wouldn't be Christmas, the family used to say, without Sally breaking a bone.

Odd things got in the way every now and then. One time Sally went up to the attic, which she usually avoided, and strange things began to flutter in the back of her mind. It was confusing because she actually started to see the attic at St. Joseph's instead of the attic that she was standing in. She couldn't breathe when she was by herself in a small space, like an elevator or a tiny room. The only exception was if there was a thunderstorm. Then Sally hid inside her bedroom closet. The McCarthy kids would stand at the closet door, begging her to come out and teasing her for being such a baby.

Sally's worst day was when she accompanied the family to the funeral of the children's grandmother. She walked into the funeral home and smelled its funny smell, and she began to feel dreadful. *Would Mom make Sally kiss the dead woman?* She asked the children what they thought. The answer again was no, but Sally had turned so pale at the prospect that Mrs. Mc-Carthy sent her straight home.

Sometimes when these things happened, a bit of what Sally had locked away would come out. When she was hurt and did her best to hide it, she told Mom McCarthy about being hit or eating her own vomit. When Grandmother McCarthy died, she told Mom McCarthy she had kissed a burned boy in a coffin. But these were small scraps, and as soon as they burst out, Sally stuffed them back down again.

After nine years with the McCarthys, Sally met a man named Alfred John Potter. By then she was thirty-two years old, and Potter was the only man who had really paid attention to her. Sally figured he was her one chance to have a family of her own. Within six months, they married. They moved into a house near the McCarthys, and soon had two children.

Potter was a heavy drinker, and after they married, he beat Sally and tied her up, and made her do terrible things. For years, Sally felt so tired and miserable that she didn't really care what happened. God could do to her what he did to the boy in the coffin for all she believed she was worth.

When things were really bad, she hid in the house next door with one of the McCarthy boys, but mostly she just tried to make sure she didn't show what she was feeling because she didn't want anyone to worry. The troubles in Sally's marriage became so bad that one day it seemed the state might take her children away. That was when her marriage finally ended. Sally found that she had a bottom line after all. The McCarthys stepped in to help, and Potter left.

Over the following year, Potter broke into the house every now and then to torment Sally, but in time she married Robert Dale. After that, Potter left her alone. Bob Dale, who had been introduced by a friend, seemed very kind, and after their first night of marriage, Sally told Mom McCarthy that she was confused. Sally and her new husband had sex, but Sally didn't have any bruises on her body the next morning. Was there something wrong?

Life with Bob was stable. Sally looked after her children, and when she cleaned the house, she anxiously asked Bob if it was clean enough. It always was. Her back troubled her and she had at least half a dozen surgeries. She took Zantac for chronic stomach ulcers and Fiorinal for headaches. She walked with a cane and had been on disability since 1983. Yet she still avoided getting medical help. When she did go, the doctors were always confused by her broken bones and fixed smile.

She remained close with the McCarthys. Her children called them Auntie and Uncle. Her son, Rob, married a lovely girl, and Sally, who still

watched Shirley Temple films, taught her how to tap, *shuffle-ball-change,*
shuffle-ball-change.

SALLY NEVER STOPPED FEELING THE DEEP HURT OF THE PELKEYS' REJEC-
tion. But she missed them, too, even though the nuns had told her that Mrs.
Pelkey said she was out of control and bad. One day she decided to go see
them in Vermont.

Mrs. Pelkey and Sally's one-time little sister Nancy were thrilled to see
her. At first, all the three women did was catch up and revel in the sweetness of their reunion. Sally shared a few of the not-so-good memories: the
way Sister James Mary beat her hands, the experience of being locked in
the attic. Eventually the story of Sally's departure from the Pelkey house
came out, too. The Pelkeys told her that they had not sent her back to St.
Joseph's at all. They wanted to adopt Sally but Ramona Fredette, Sally's biological mother, refused to authorize the adoption. So Sally was returned to
the orphanage.

Here at last was evidence for Sally that she was actually not a bad person.
If the Pelkeys had wanted her, could she really have been that bad? It started
a chain of thoughts and feelings that ended with her own mother. She needed
to know once and for all if she was the evil person that everyone had said she
was, or if it was her mother who was bad.

Once again, Bob drove Sally to Vermont, this time with the children.
They went to the house where Sally's mother lived. Sally knocked on the
door and a young woman invited them all into the house. When Sally's
mother entered, she said in a cold voice, "My God, Sally."

That voice, those words, that woman—they sent shivers down Sally's
spine. She had her answer, right there. She was not the bad person that
Ramona said she was. This woman did not care for her at all. No mother
should speak that way to her own daughter.

Sally didn't say anything to Ramona. She just walked out.

Later, Sally's stepsister told her that Ramona had said frequently that if
she never saw Sally again, it would be the best time of her life.

Finally, Sally visited Eva DuPaul, the seamstress, cleaner, and all-round
helper who had herself been at the orphanage since the early 1900s, and

who was by then living in an eldercare home, also called St. Joseph's. Eva reminisced about what a naughty girl Sally had been. What about the time the bishop visited, and a nun slammed Sally into the wall of the nursery? It had made such a big dent! Even after Sally was long gone from St. Joseph's, Eva said, they used to point at the hole and tell the little children that's what happened when you were naughty.

Irene McGowan had died, but Eva, God love her, told Sally that she had been a favorite of Irene's until the end. When Irene lay dying, she called out to her little *Fryface*, imploring her to be careful when she was washing the windows lest she fall and get hurt or die.

Eva gave Sally some photographs of herself and some of her friends. It was very strange, Sally thought, because the girls in the pictures were smiling and looking so happy.

AFTER SHE MET BOB WIDMAN, SALLY BEGAN TO WRITE A SERIES OF LETTERS to him and his partner, Geoff. For the first time in her life, she found that when she put pen to paper, she was able to describe things that she hadn't been able to say out loud to anyone else.

> *I was such a little girl when it happened that now I really hope if they died they will be in hell. I know it's a bad thing to say but I can't help it anymore feeling this way. Please forgive me.*

As she lined up the events of her life, she started to see how one thing in her life had led to another, how her stoicism was forced on her.

> *You smile all the time, you be on your best behavior . . . if you fell and got hurt, you got up, you don't tell anybody, you just live with it.*

The nighttime nuns and the brothers had prepared her for her first husband.

> *There are things he did that made me remember what the brothers and the nuns did. Like the tea party and touching me, sometimes it*

would really hurt. But I guess I always believed it was right and okay because that was what they did at the orphanage.

. . . I am sure afraid because they are holding my head under water and just won't let me up. Maybe it was because I told one nun about the games that the brothers wanted to play I did not like it at all.

The more she turned to the past, the more it turned toward her.

Last night one more time I had to dream again with my eyes wide open I really hate this because I thought I had buried all of this a long time ago. It really hurt and makes me sad to think how no one ever cared what happened to all of us kids.

The more she wrote, the more questions she had:

Oh boy another day of this am I going crazy or what. I sure do hate these flashbacks I sometimes wish I was dead or I could get it all so I would never have to dream or have flashbacks again. It would really be nice for a change to believe that all of this never happened and I could really enjoy what I have and begin to like myself no matter what they did to us. God love all the kids that had to pass by in the orphanage in all these years. I really love them all no matter even if I don't remember all of them.

I really hope the ones that went before me are with God and waiting for me with arms open for me to get there to.

But will I ever get there because they always told me I was very bad and evil child.

Bob and Jeff what do you think?

Sally wrote about the children who had gone missing or almost missing. One death reminded her of another.

. . . So I went behind her when she gave Patty a shove and then left not seeing me at all. I saw Patty's arm go out and then for some reason I grabbed her ankle before she fell all the way down. I was so scared she

would hit the ground like the boy did on the boys side when I was real little. I saw the nun push him out the window and I guess I never forgot that.

She wrote about the little girl that she and Irene had taken to the hospital in a taxi after a nun pushed her down the stairs. The nuns had told Sally that the girl had gone "home for good." But when Sally repeated the familiar refrain for Widman, she was clearer about its meaning.

At times when I would look back at what happened, she said about the little girl, I wished they would have done the same to me. At least it would have been a way out.
    I really hope [Irene] is in God's arm every sense she passed away. And also that little boy who was burned and the one that I saw pushed out the window.

She could see how the past affected her and her husband Bob. *I really never understand because he would never force me to do these things*, she wrote. Sally loved Bob. But she didn't like it when he touched her and she always pulled away. They hadn't had sex in years because Sally had reached a point where she declared that she didn't enjoy it, so why did she have to do it? She had never told him about the sexual assaults at the orphanage, she admitted, and she really didn't see how she could.

By the time Sally wrote her last letter, it seemed that the crazy knot of pain and relief inside her could not be untangled.

It seems like today I hate myself and the whole world too. Will it ever stop. I don't want to hate anymore. I just want to let it all go. Sometimes I wish I had as much guts as Bambi and the others who killed themselves. Well I guess I am just a coward about trying to do that. I'm sure they felt the same way I do right now but they did something to make the hurt and ashamed of all about it to go away forever. God Bless them all and keep them in his arms. Bambi was my best friend at the orphanage. And now I can understand why she did what she did.

I guess to let all the hurt go away forever. But us who are cowards just keep letting the hurt go on and on.

Sorry about the spelling Bob or Jeff. Thank you very much for coming to our aid. I thought nobody would ever listen to our story about what happened there. I sure do love both of you for being so kind to all of us. Thanks again.

Love

Sally A Dale.

CHAPTER 11

OR THREE DAYS, WIDMAN AND HIS PARTNER GEOFF MORRIS SHARED A room with two beds in a chintzy bed and breakfast in Vermont's verdant countryside. By day, they spoke to people who lived with monumental trauma and had the stories to explain it. At night, they lay on their beds exhausted and watched *Seinfeld* on a small-screen TV.

Before he became a lawyer, Morris had been a helicopter medevac in Vietnam. He picked up men who had been shot to pieces and tried to hold them together until they reached a field hospital. He was a tall, smart man who Widman found to be honest and loyal. Usually Morris was impatient, quick to make decisions; Widman dealt with the details, but they always came to be in agreement in the end. They started their business on a handshake, a highly unusual practice for lawyers.

Early on, Morris and Widman arranged to meet with a man named Ed Duprey, a gruff, depressed-looking fellow, in their bed and breakfast. Duprey told the lawyers that in 1939 when he was three, his mother died from uterine cancer, and he was sent to the Sisters of Providence. Some of it had been okay, he said, but mostly it was hell. When he wet the bed, the nuns made the other kids laugh at him, and if he said "damn" or "darn," he had to chew a chunk of lye soap until he was sick. Many decades later, he was still scared to put his head underwater, and he couldn't bear being in any room with the door closed. Once, a doctor who was treating him for deafness asked if he'd been hit on the ear a lot as a child. Duprey had indeed been hit on the ear a lot by the nuns, but he was too ashamed to answer the doctor's question.

Duprey told Morris and Widman that when he was fourteen years old and working at a local farm, he was so full of rage and distress—feelings he relived with an alarming intensity as he spoke—that one day he grabbed a sledgehammer from the wall of the barn and hit a cow in the head with it. The animal died instantly.

Duprey vibrated with intense emotion as he told the story but didn't seem to realize it. He looked right through Morris and Widman. For Morris, it seemed obvious that Duprey was reliving the actual moments in which he killed a large animal, right there in front of them. It was a visceral and unforgettable experience.

Later Duprey said that since his time at the orphanage, he was like Mr. Spock on *Star Trek*. He did not trust "human people," and he didn't need love; it wasn't logical. There was a lot that didn't mean anything to him.

Morris believed that taking on the St. Joseph's litigation was the right thing to do. Widman would take the lead while Morris focused on personal injury, including medical malpractice, work in Florida. It was a good balance. It was righteous. Morris also thought that he and Widman would make money.

WIDMAN BEGAN TO TRAVEL TO VERMONT FROM FLORIDA FOR A WEEK OR two at a time. Plane to JFK, then tiny commuter plane to Burlington, and because Widman was a hamburger kind of guy, a Motel 6–style hotel that was a five-minute drive from the pedestrian mall in the center of town. At all hours of the day and night, orphans arrived at his door to tell him their terrible stories. He tracked down the details, looked for verification, widened the net. One person would lead him to five more, and those five would each lead to another five.

He hired Langrock Sperry & Wool, a local law firm in Burlington. Widman was the believer, but he needed the firm's local expertise. They gave him access to a brilliant paralegal, Corinne Brown, who took the sprawling mess of stories, names, and dates that started coming their way and wrestled it into some kind of order. Brown created a big binder that recorded who Widman spoke to, who they named, and what had happened to them. It was an immense, mind-boggling task.

Widman sat with former residents in their homes, or at the offices of Langrock Sperry & Wool, and told them that he would represent them—but that it would be a risky, difficult business. Church lawyers would ask the most painful questions possible. If plaintiffs had ever visited a psychologist or psychiatrist, the lawyers could demand to see their files. If they were divorced, the church would want to talk to their ex-spouses and their children. And after all that, there was no guarantee that they would win.

It was hectic and expensive. Yet even when former residents didn't directly corroborate the stories of Joseph Barquin or Sally Dale, they told stories that were overwhelmingly of a kind—the cruelty to the bedwetters, the terror-filled swimming lessons, the medical negligence. Some experiences had occurred across the long timespan of different witnesses from the 1940s through to the 1970s. Others were particular to an era. A number of women who lived at the orphanage in the 1970s described being assaulted by a priest in a room that was full of furniture upholstered in red fabrics and red draperies, which they had all independently come to think of as "the red room." Other cases cropped up around the edges, too. A few orphans made claims or launched their own suits with different attorneys.

It wasn't all fear and violence. Out of the giant cluster of incomprehensible facts about orphanages, one of the hardest to understand was how atrocities and happiness coexisted there. Even residents who spoke about extreme abuse laughed about sliding down bannisters, being encouraged to sing, and taking pleasure in something they accomplished.

Former residents brought Widman photographs and different tokens of childhood. A woman named Marilyn Noble, who lived at St. Joseph's at the same time as Sally, gave Widman a manuscript called *Orphan Girl No. 58*. She had written it in the 1980s, hoping it would help her children understand her. It was as if Little Orphan Annie had written a memoir about her time on Rikers Island. As a young girl, she had been forced to slap herself fifty times in the face, and when she didn't do it hard enough, the nuns did it for her. When a cut on her hand developed into a throbbing, toxic infection, she had been too afraid to tell the nuns until it was almost too late.

Yet she cherished a memory of when the von Trapps, the Austrian family whose flight from the Nazis inspired *The Sound of Music*, visited St. Joseph's. For the singing of the benediction, Noble was placed next to Maria herself. The kindest and most beloved stepmother in the world leaned down and told Noble that she sang beautifully.

Noble was proud of the fact that in her time at the orphanage, she had been the youngest child to learn the whole mass in Latin. When she was twelve, she had the starring role in the orphanage play. In the opening scene, her character had an eighteenth birthday party. In the next scene, her parents told her they wanted big things for her. She was so pretty. She could be a star! Her character said no. She wanted to be a nun.

Orphan girl number fifty-eight remembered her lines exactly fifty years later. "It is not the beauty of face or figure that man should strive for," she declaimed.

Before a captive audience of children and women whose hair and face were cocooned in starched bindings, the twelve-year-old girl went on: "It is the inner beauty, the beauty of the soul."

In the next scene, she entered a convent to take her vows.

On one trip Widman found himself at the home of Geoff Morris's parents in Providence, Rhode Island. Morris, who thought of his parents as professional Catholics, had gone to bed early and left Widman stranded, trying to make polite conversation with Morris's mother. She didn't believe the stories of the orphans at all and went on for hours about the goodness of the Catholic Church. It was excruciating.

"You son of a bitch," Widman later said to Morris.

Mostly it was Widman in Vermont, wrestling the octopus with hundreds of legs, while Morris built the medical injury practice in Florida to keep the firm afloat. Widman called Morris regularly. *You're not going to believe who I met! Guess who I just talked to?* He updated Morris on the latest stories and the two men talked strategy.

At least a hundred people, and possibly as many as 160, had pursued the diocese's offer either by themselves or through an attorney, many through Joseph Barquin's first attorney, Philip White. The letters White wrote recorded what had been done, when it happened, and in many cases, who had done it. With them, the former residents had essentially created a data-bank of dozens of accused violators and a long and varied list of violations. It was obvious to Widman and Morris that the settlement letters would be critical for their success.

The victims' letters to the diocese included not just evidence about spe-cific events and people, but potentially about the modus operandi of the shadowy figures who haunted the dorms after the sun had gone down, peo-ple whose identity might not be known but whose acts followed a distinct pattern. Any two people who had been hurt by the same person—even if it occurred in the dead of night and they never knew it had also happened to someone else—would have at least put the same act in their letter.

The letters provided critical evidence for Barquin's story, and they would make it hard for the church to say it had never heard about a particular nun's or priest's abuse of one of his plaintiffs. More than any other single testimony or document, the letters told the true hidden history of St. Jo-seph's Orphanage. But now the church was in sole possession of that trove of information.

Widman had to go to a judge to force the defense to hand the letters over. In the meantime, he tried to track down everyone who had sent a letter. They had signed away their legal right to pursue the diocese or the nuns or anyone else responsible. A number had also signed what they be-lieved to be confidentiality agreements, so Widman could not pursue the church on their behalf. Still a former resident who had settled could act as a witness for Barquin or anyone else who wanted to sue the Catholic Church. Widman hoped they would show him their letter. But first he had to find them.

WIDMAN THREW HIMSELF INTO THE DISCOVERY PROCESS. HE LEARNED fast, but the more he heard, the more questions he had. It was hard to find even basic information about how orphanages operated. He could locate no books or studies on the subject. What little press coverage the institutions had received over the course of the century was usually about jolly excur-sions or the happy recovery of a runaway scamp.

The more Widman spoke to people who had lived at St. Joseph's, which was founded in 1854, the clearer it became that the hole in the public record was not an accident. Thousands of people all over the United States had at some time worked in an orphanage, yet none had come forward to reminisce about their time, at least not that Widman could find. The diocesan hierarchy had oversight of the orphanage, and the nuns had lived and worked there, but none of them were forthcoming with their recollections.

It was the same with the children. Siblings who had once been in the same orphanage together had often not discussed it with each other, much less with friends or even spouses. Even after Barquin had come forward and articles about St. Joseph's appeared in the *Burlington Free Press*, many families who were affected—children who had lived there and the elderly parents who sent them—didn't mention it to each other.

SEVERAL FORMER RESIDENTS EXPLAINED TO WIDMAN THAT IN THE EARLIest days of the orphanage, it had housed the aged as well as the young. Louis deGoesbriand, the first bishop of Burlington and founder of the orphanage, had also retired there "to be with the children he so dearly loved," according to the local newspaper. One woman who lived there in the late 1930s recalled lying in bed at night as a child, listening to old souls trudge up and down the long hallways making "screaming and moaning and scraping sounds." She realized only later that the terrifying sounds came from these older residents pushing a chair in front of them, like a walker. Eventually, the older residents left.

The children remained. Hundreds of them. As Widman came to see, however, many of them were not actually orphans. They had been born into local families, Catholic French Canadians, English and Irish Americans and, in a few cases, Black Americans and children of the Abenaki tribe.

Most were extremely poor. One girl drank milk for the first time at St. Joseph's and thought it was the most delicious thing she had ever tasted. Before entering, another girl had seen an egg at the dining table only a few times a year. Lack of money though was usually just one of the problems.

The children's parents were often ill or addicted, imprisoned, divorced, or violent. Some parents delivered their own children to the nuns, believing they were leaving them in a safe place. Many were brought by the state after their homes were deemed unacceptable. Sometimes they ended up in an orphanage simply because their mother was unmarried. They arrived in every imaginable condition, dirty and lice-ridden, covered in bruises, recently raped, or perfectly healthy. No matter where they had come from, many of the children didn't know where they were going until the moment they turned around and discovered that the person who had brought them was gone.

Once the doors of St. Joseph's shut behind them, the children played a part in a strange, private theater, with many actors but no audience. They even took on different identities, as the nuns replaced their names with numbers. The women of the Sisters of Providence were renamed, too, as they took the vows of their order. Léonille Racicot became Sister James Mary. Jeanne Campbell became Sister Jane of the Rosary. Marie-Rose Dalpe became Sister Mary Vianney. Various men moved in and out of the drama: priests, seminarians, counselors, and others, recurring characters who kept their given names and who would appear for a time, then step back offstage and into the rest of the world.

In 1994, members of the survivors group had asked for permission to return to the old brick building, which had stopped admitting children back in the 1970s and now housed a few church offices. Initially they were turned away at the door. Months later, some were allowed to walk through, but usually just one at a time. The diocese reached out to a former resident they believed would testify for them and flew her in from Utah for a tour. They told her that they didn't want plaintiffs in the building because "it would cause false beliefs" and "they could make up things by going through it." To the contrary, the woman found that walking down the long hallways and standing in the empty dorms brought back many vivid memories.

Widman wanted to get in too, but he knew the diocese would be even less likely to arrange a tour for him than for the building's former residents. So one day he just walked in the front door, said he was visiting from out of town, and politely asked if he could look around. The person at reception told him to go ahead.

The grand marble circular staircase that the children had trudged up and had fallen or been thrown down was removed in the 1950s to accommodate an elevator, an innovation that was exciting enough to warrant a series of photographs, including one of a bespectacled nun, mid-laugh and looking as merry as can be, awkwardly pressing buttons with the back of her hand as four grinning, well-dressed children looked on. One of the photos appeared in a local newspaper. "Going up," read the caption. "Sister James Mary and students at St. Joseph's Orphanage, Burlington, try a new elevator as their centenary gift initiated by Bishop Ryan." The replacement staircase, now old and chipped, was narrow and utilitarian. Widman followed it straight up to the top floor.

Stepping through an oddly small door to the massive attic was like stepping into a different universe.

Several orphans had told him it was a terrifying place. Sally had described an electric chair—or something that looked just like one—that Sister James Mary used to strap her into for hours, taunting her that she would fry.

Even for an adult, the shadowy chamber was immense and disorienting. Widman gazed at the rafters and the loft and the door that concealed the spiral staircase to the cupola. Names had been scratched in the wood of the doorframe.

Widman found a huge metal water tank with pipes coming out of it. It had a big lid, and as he stood there and looked at it, he remembered that Sally Dale had told him that nuns made her climb up the little ladder and drop herself in. Then they pulled the lid back over and left.

```
                         CHRONICLES
                    ST JOSEPH'S ORPHANAGE
                       BURLINGTON, VT
                 July 1st 1969 to July 1st 1970


        JUNE
        DIFFICULTIES
        For several weeks past, some of the older boys have at-
        tempted to run away, and it was necessary to have the po-
        lice trace them, after search for them had been done by
        the Sisters in the car. Children will resort to anything
```

to get attention and sympathy, and so these boys did not hesitate to lie as to the cause of their desired freedom. The officers of the police force were very understanding and cooperative, and on only one occasion was the child believed until proof was obtained the lad was lying. These falsehoods could have caused harm to the Center, and it is with gratitude that we sang a silent Te Deum. At the present writing of the Chronicles, things have returned to normal and all the children are happy enjoying a summer of fun and outing which have been planned for them.

WIDMAN DISCOVERED THAT THE SISTERS OF PROVIDENCE AT ST. JOSEPH'S had long published an annual newsletter called the *Chronicles*. It took months to get his hands on a copy. Starting in 1934, the *Chronicles* were written in French in a beautiful looping handwritten script, and published annually until the 1970s, by then typewritten and in English.

Holy days and other important dates were noted, like the start and end of school terms; baptisms; and days of celebration, like the birthday of the Mother Superior; as were welcomes and goodbyes to the many priests who came and went over the years. The *Chronicles* listed special masses with their cast of clergy: the celebrant, the assistant at the throne, the First Assistant Deacon, the Assistant Deacon. There were many one-off items, like a note of gratitude from a local, an invitation from a priest to one of the boys to come and study with him, the death of a nun's family member, or a nun's Golden Jubilee as a professed member of the order. For a decade or two, the *Chronicles* noted when nuns departed for and returned from their annual retreat. The 1954 centennial celebration merited many entries: a lunch for benefactors, an open house for former pupils ("some who travelled a good distance to their dear old home"), a banquet for the priests, and a separate banquet for the sisters. The final entry for each year listed the number of nuns, employees, children, and in the earlier years, older people who lived at the orphanage. It also listed how many sick visits the nuns had made in the community and how much money had been bequeathed or donated to them.

Here and there, the *Chronicles* reported a visit from other Sisters of Providence who came from a connected Canadian orphanage-turned-hospital. "We were very happy to have as our guests thirteen Sisters from Mount Providence Hospital, Montreal," a chronicler wrote in 1968. "As the bus left our yard our hearts sang silently, 'Behold how good it is when Sisters dwell in unity.'" The connection struck Widman as worthy of investigation.

In the 1953 edition, the sisters gave thanks for all the invitations the children had received that year, like the King Brothers Circus, a play called *The Miracle of Fatima*, and a film, *The Robe* (the bishop had granted the nuns permission to go, they noted with gratitude). In earlier decades the children had been taken for rides on the famous Ticonderoga steamboat on Lake Champlain. Here and elsewhere, visits with different stars of the era were recorded. The Great Lester, illusionist and prestidigitator, pulled coins from the children's noses in 1942. Silo the human robot made them all laugh in 1947. Gene Autry, the singing cowboy, brought Champion the Wonder Horse in 1954. In 1958, a little person disguised as a bear entertained the children for an hour.

By the late 1960s, the *Chronicles* still celebrated many of the same good works—camping with volunteers, trips to the circus, outings on the ferry to New York, a bus trip to wave hello to Santa at the airport—all arranged with the help of kind friends of the orphanage. New nuns were welcomed and departing nuns were hailed for their zeal and devotion. But some serious grumbling and significant concerns had started to creep in.

A fire in the boys' dorm was reported in the *Chronicles* in April 1961. Before it could take hold, the sprinkler system and the fire brigade put an end to it. "Providence of God," the chronicler wrote, "We thank Thee for all." In the next decade there was a disturbing increase in fire reports. In April 1968 the *Chronicles* reported a fire had broken out in a dump on the orphanage premises. Firefighters were concerned because the fire was underground and kept flaring up. They had to keep watch on it for three days. In October 1969, the *Chronicles* reported that a fire was set by a boy in the gymnasium, though it was soon discovered and extinguished. In July 1971 the *Chronicles* reported that a barn used as a garage by staff at the Catholic Charities office mysteriously burned down. A *Chronicles* entry for March 1972 announced with much sadness that the local Burlington Cathedral of Immaculate Conception had burned down. The fire was set by a former cathedral altar boy who was described by the sisters as "disturbed." Then an entry in September 1972 noted that the child center had been evacuated after a call was received from local firefighters who said they received a bomb threat for a device timed to go off in fifteen minutes. In fact, Widman spoke to a number of former residents who had, as young boys, set fires at the orphanage or who knew others who had. They had hoped to burn the place down.

The 1969 *Chronicles* mentioned an increase in disciplinary problems, a spirit of destruction and insubordination, and the taxing of nerves. That year's chronicler was much less concerned with the appearance of piety than scribes from previous years. In one entry, she obliquely mentioned that some "runaways" had been telling tales to the police, but she noted that luckily the nuns had been able to reassure the police that the children were lying. Another entry described the children as "selfish, exacting, and ungrateful." The same year, another batch of runaways returned to the orphanage were called "defiant, rude, and insolent until they realized who was BOSS."

Father John McSweeney, who had been Financial Officer and Vicar General of the Diocese of Burlington, told Widman about the annual Bishop's Fund, which had been raising money since the 1940s. It was a professionally managed drive that placed inspiring articles in the local newspaper about all the good that Vermont Catholic Charities had achieved. Indeed, almost every year the fund received more money from the community than the year before. At the bishop's discretion, the money was divided between the diocese itself and its charitable activities, which included the orphanage, an eldercare home, and other programs, like one that sent unwed mothers out of the state to have their babies and leave them for adoption.

McSweeney did not really know how the orphanage was funded, he said. Although, he added, the diocese had used it as a vehicle for fundraising. "The care of children, the orphans, was very appealing to people, and I

think people like to give to that." McSweeney surmised that because the diocese had used the orphanage for a lot of their publicity, some of that money
"eventually probably went to the orphanage."

The sisters, at least as far as their records were concerned, were far more
exacting, making careful note of all assets and expenditures over the years.
In 1935, they estimated the value of their building to be $103,000, and the
land to be $21,909. They collected $10,313 in alms and received $13,169.21
in legacies. They spent $1,942.15 on heat and $15,296.32 on food. In 1953,
they noted various legacies, attached to conditions, such as the Estate of
J. N. Caissy, which required that a high mass be celebrated annually. Every
year it seemed a number of people in the community left a house, a sum
of money, or their whole estate to the good sisters doing God's work at the
orphanage. In 1957, the chancery office wrote to the sisters, acknowledging
that it would pay them interest on the sum of $20,000, and in addition, on a
sum of approximately $10,000 left from the sale of a house on Booth Street
and loaned by the orphanage to the diocese.

Despite all the money and real estate that the orphanage generated simply by existing, the nuns received no personal funds. For a long time, only
their basic needs were covered, and only then by permission of the bishop.
Finally, in 1963 each nun was accorded a yearly salary of $500, plus room
and board, and a Blue Cross hospital plan. The bishop was a bit embarrassed
apparently. He said he never knew the sisters received so little.

The Charter of the Sisters of Providence was as specific and exhaustive as
any secular setup, with strict rules governing the elections of directors and
the nomination of officers, guidelines for what happened with legacies, and
constraints on the behavior of members. No individual could act on behalf
of the corporation. But there were interesting exceptions. For an organization
that supported an extremely conservative cultural worldview, they stipulated
that married women who were members of their community could act *without* the permission of their husbands. The community ran hospitals as well as
orphanages, and the 1885 charter included a curious passage that allowed the
sisters to manufacture and profit from remedies and medications.

In between the lines of the various budgets and minutes of board meetings, a power tussle was detectable. Certainly, the bishop held most of

the cards, but by virtue of their authority over the institution and all its inhabitants, the nuns accrued some power themselves. In 1939, the bishop sternly explained to the Mother Superior that no child was to be released to anyone outside the orphanage without the explicit permission of Vermont Catholic Charities, the social work organization he oversaw. It was unclear from the record exactly what event had triggered the admonition; nevertheless, the bishop made it clear he wanted an assurance that *that* wouldn't happen again.

The initial division of power between the diocese and the Sisters of Providence stipulated that the diocese supplied the money for the orphanage and the sisters supplied the staff. With the advent of Vermont Catholic Charities as a third player, the division was renegotiated numerous times over the years, usually with the bishop reminding the nuns of various things they could *not* do without the approval of Vermont Catholic Charities. Technically, within the orphanage the girls were assigned to the charge of the nuns, but even though the nuns equally looked after the boys, they were ultimately overseen by a priest, who was a representative of Vermont Catholic Charities.

Really, it was remarkable that the nuns retained any authority at all, beginning as they did from a place of explicit obeisance.

The Priest, says one author, is the smile of God on earth. It is his eternal joy that he communicates, for through the priest the joy of God descends into souls. Also to love God is to love the priest. And great, very great is the joy of uniting with God to create priests. It is to enter into the deepest love of the August Trinity.

—*Religious Courtesies, 1956*

IN 1962, THE ORPHANAGE CHANGED ITS NAME TO THE ST. JOSEPH'S CHILD Center. It was probably the one change the orphanage board made in concession to the utterly changed world in which they now operated.

CHRONICLES
ST JOSEPH'S ORPHANAGE
BURLINGTON, VT
July 1st 1970 to July 1st 1971

MAY
STATUE AT GROTTO
11.—The statue of the Blessed Virgin at our outside grotto
had been destroyed by vandals during the year and had
not been replaced.

EVEN BEFORE HE READ THE *CHRONICLES*, WIDMAN KNEW THAT THE SISTERS
of Providence must have been feeling the strain by the early 1970s. The nuns
themselves were older, and recruitment for all religious orders had suffered
enormously in the previous decade.

When the strict rules for life in religious orders were relaxed by Vatican II, some sisters and brothers across the world began to use their birth
names and wear casual clothes, and where sisters had not been allowed to
walk through the world unaccompanied, some were now given permission
to walk down a street by themselves, and even make up their own minds
about where to be, at least to some extent.

Yet if one of the goals of Vatican II was to make life in a religious order
more appealing to the children of the 1960s, it had the opposite effect, being
rather more like opening a valve on a pressure chamber. Everywhere religious orders deflated as women walked away from their vocation, and others
did not join in the first place. According to some estimates, the Catholic
Church lost 80 percent of its members of religious orders.

It was an extraordinary reversal of fortune. For over one hundred years,
the nuns had absolute control of the children, a power that was effectively
given to them by all the good Catholics in their dominion and was ultimately sanctioned by the state. As early as the 1940s, state social workers
visited the orphanage to check on the well-being of children, as had Catholic social workers from Vermont Catholic Charities. But by the mid-1960s,

with the advent of child psychiatry, social work, dental care, medical care, and nutrition studies, there were many more specialists from the outside dealing with the children—albeit often still from within the Catholic world. Even the *Chronicles* noted that state representatives were coming in to check on the amenities and the food.

A few other documents gave Widman some insight into what it felt like to be a Sister of Providence at that historic moment when the power of the order was waning. Some of the early 1970s social worker reports, which Catholic Charities were court ordered to turn over, spoke obliquely about conflict and tensions, and were especially revealing in their odd mix of deference and criticism.

One social worker reassuringly declared that she wasn't suggesting the children "take over," and she carefully noted the good things that the children experienced (siblings together in one place, arts and crafts, sports, cooking programs), but she proposed that the administration consider the children's complaints, like not being able to wash their own hair and having their mail censored, and their fear that they would be punished if they said negative things about life with the Sisters of Providence.

Another social worker, who had only been employed for four months, said that the orphanage staff and the Catholic Charities staff appeared to want to meet the physical, spiritual, and emotional needs of the children, but they seemed to have different ideas about how to do that, particularly in the case of emotional needs. She mentioned the orphanage's unwritten policies, too. Curiously, that page of her report was missing, so it wasn't clear what she thought those unwritten policies were.

A third social worker, who had been at St. Joseph's for almost twenty years, wrote about the orphanage's shrinking population of children. In his time, they had gone from 250 to 52 children, a decline he attributed to changing morals—being a single mother was much less stigmatized than it had been in the 1950s—and to the fact that most of their referrals used to come from parish priests.

The social worker did not mention the likely role of the oral contraceptive pill, the first brand of which was sold in 1960. Nor did he acknowledge that two young women doctors had recently founded the Vermont

Women's Health Center, which was now providing counseling, education, and medical services, including pregnancy termination, to women. Local Catholics were well aware of the service, which advertised itself as "run by and for women." They had aggressively denounced it; one likened it to a slaughterhouse. At one community meeting, a nun from a local Catholic hospital brought a twelve-week-old fetus in a bottle to illustrate her anti-abortion stance.

Still, the clinic received support from the community at large. For a while it was the only clinic in New England that offered pregnancy termination, and it wasn't long before it was struggling to keep up with demand, including a minibus of women from Montreal arriving every two weeks. In 1977, the clinic moved to 336 North Avenue, Burlington, directly across the road from the orphanage property, which was then the headquarters of the Diocese of Burlington. The clinic was still defending itself against attacks (the following year someone lobbed a Molotov cocktail at the front door) but was providing services to around two thousand people a year.

Instead, the social worker wrote about the new idea that people, including a new generation of antiestablishment social workers, seemed to think that institutions were bad and were just warehousing children. The orphanage needed a strong Mother Superior to lead it, the social worker said, but the job was so unpopular that nuns had to be "trapped" into the role. This was a revelation. No one had offered Widman that perspective. But the man did not elaborate on the idea, except to say that it led to a breakdown in communication and cooperation, and it sometimes meant that Catholic Charities spent as much time trying to work out issues with the Sisters of Providence as look after the children.

With a note of emotion, the social worker concluded, "At the very moment in time when the services are at their best, the institution is dying."

CHRONICLES
ST JOSEPH'S ORPHANAGE
BURLINGTON, VT
July 1st 1970 to July 1st 1971

MAY

CONFIRMATION

26.–His Excellency, Robert F. Joyce, Bishop of Burlington, confirmed seventeen of our pupils tonight at seven-
thirty evening Mass. Our aging Bishop was accompanied
by Monsignor Louis Gelineau, Vicar General, Father John
McSweeney, Assistant Chancellor, Monsignor Charles J. Marcoux, Pastor at St. Francis Xavier, Winooski, Vermont, and
Reverend Joseph N. Pray, Pastor in Milton, Vermont. Parents and social workers were present at this imposing ceremony, during which our Bishop spoke with his customary
fatherly approach. The parents, several among them divorced, or remarried, some separated and even unwed mothers with uneasiness and false happiness stamped on their
faces, make it a real puzzle, which only He Who knows all
things and Who alone can judge, may solve. Our sympathy
went out to the innocent parties and the little ones who
have to cope with such a situation. Holy Spirit come down
on Your children, but also on these people who do not understand what the word "parenthood" means.

WIDMAN WANTED TO KNOW WHY THE INDIVIDUAL WOMEN OF THE SISTERS
of Providence were at St. Joseph's in the first place. Many were French Canadian farm girls. In previous decades, Catholic families from Montreal often
had ten or more children, and it was common for families to want one or
two of their children to enter religious life. Usually by the time the youngest
grew up, there was little left for them anyway and joining a religious order
was a sensible option.

Widman learned that Sister James Mary, nemesis of Sally Dale and a
devotee of the theater of pain, with her threats about frying in electric chairs
and locking little girls inside water tanks, had been born in St. Johnsbury,
Vermont. Her father was a farmer, born in Canada. She spent most of her
life in Vermont, moving occasionally from the orphanage to local Catholic

schools, teaching singing and arranging choirs. She was born in 1911 and took the veil when she was eighteen years old. In her personnel file, available to Widman through the discovery process, she was described as *cette musicienne douée d'une voix remarquable* ("a gifted musician with a remarkable voice"). Other sisters commented, *Quand elle parle de ses petits garçons du Vermont, c'est avec beaucoup de tendresse* ("When she talks about her little boys in Vermont, it is with a lot of tenderness"). In 1967, along with many of her sisters, she reverted to her family name. She trained in Gregorian chants and worked as a librarian after her time at the orphanage.

Sister Jane of the Rosary, Sally's sweetheart and one of her abusers, was born in 1896 in Bedford, Quebec. She was middle-aged by the time Sally arrived at the orphanage. Her father was a laborer. She took her vows at twenty-eight years old. After her work with children at St. Joseph's in Burlington, she worked mostly as a receptionist for the order. Her gaiety and humor apparently never left her, even when she was older.

Sister Claire of the Providence, who featured in many survivors' stories, was born Geneva Bellezemere Leonard in Whitingham, Vermont, to French-Canadian parents. Her father was also a laborer. The 1954 *Chronicles* described Sister Claire of the Providence as a former pupil at the orphanage.

Sister Noelle, who Sally said had burned her hand in the iron press, joined the order at age twenty-five. She had been born in Quebec and completed school in sixth grade. Like most of the nuns, she received no training in childcare. Later she worked as a hairdresser for the order.

Mostly the personnel files were sparse. Widman supposed that the girls who had grown up in farm and laborer families were tough and had no problem dealing out discipline. In their minds, they probably didn't think they were doing anything wrong. If they did, it was possible that, just like the children, they were also afraid to complain.

WITHIN THE SISTERS OF PROVIDENCE, A STRICT HIERARCHY WAS OBSERVED. The defense attorneys noted that the nuns took vows of "poverty, chastity and obedience," stressing the nuns' lifelong devotion to charity, though it seemed just as relevant to Widman that the women who joined the Sisters of Providence were sworn to obedience. It wasn't just the children who were effectively incarcerated at the orphanage; strict rules governed when the nuns could leave the grounds and under what conditions. The bishop had to give formal permission for the nuns to engage in any public activities. In 1954, at the orphanage centennial, the bishop arranged for benefactors to give the sisters a six-passenger Ford. The sisters wrote to the Mother General and asked for permission for one of the sisters to learn how to drive. It would be better, the Mother General responded, if the driver were a man. If a nun already had her license before taking vows, she might drive for short trips, but only with another nun who wasn't nervous.

One year, the nuns forbade the children from singing a popular song by Catholic icon Bing Crosby, "Don't Fence Me In."

> *Oh give me land, lots of land, under starry skies above.*
> *Don't fence me in.*
> *Let me ride through the wide open country that I love.*
> *Don't fence me in!*

Coming from the children, it probably sounded like sedition. But maybe it hit close to home for some nuns, too.

AFTER THE SISTERS LEFT ST. JOSEPH'S, SOME OF THE CHILDREN STAYED IN touch, visiting them at their motherhouse with new babies to show off or husbands to introduce. There had been other brief moments of contact over the years. In the 1970s, Sister Philomena Miles wrote a letter to one of her favorite charges from the 1960s. She apologized obliquely for the sad times at the orphanage. In the 1980s, an orphan wrote to the nuns from prison and told them how terrible his life with them had been. Years later, he told me, they wrote a letter in reply, saying that they had believed at the time that they were doing the right thing.

CHAPTER 12

SALLY DALE'S CASE WAS FILED IN THE US DISTRICT COURT OF VERMONT on June 13, 1996. Widman always went with the best case first. Along with his partner, Geoff Morris, and the local firm, Langrock Sperry & Wool, he took twenty-five cases before two different courts. The first twelve cases, including all the out-of-state plaintiffs, went to federal court. The other thirteen went to state court. Widman filed multiple cases because he didn't want all his eggs in one basket. Other St. Joseph's cases cropped up, too, as a few former residents launched suits with different attorneys.

Widman's lawsuits named three defendants: the Roman Catholic Diocese of Burlington, Vermont, represented by Bill O'Brien; Vermont Catholic Charities, represented by John Gravel; and the Sisters of Providence, who hired Jack Sartore, a litigator with a reputation for being uncompromising and often described by local lawyers, though not to his face, as Darth Vader.

Traveling back and forth from Florida for a week or two at a time, Widman continued to drive through Vermont in search of St. Joseph's alumni who might join the plaintiffs or serve as witnesses. The more stories he gathered about black deeds in pastoral surroundings, the more they began to knit themselves together, as happened in the case of the girl who stole a piece of candy.

A<small>T LEAST SIX WOMEN SEPARATELY TOLD</small> W<small>IDMAN THEY REMEMBERED A DAY</small> when they were gathered together to witness a punishment. One thought it happened near the girls dining room. Another thought it was in the room where the children took off their coats and hats. Everyone agreed it happened downstairs.

Three women recalled that a girl was placed facedown over a desk and beaten. Two remembered that the nun used a paddle. One recalled that the nun had started out hitting the girl with a piece of wood two or three feet long, but it broke, and that's when she reached for the paddle. Eventually the handle of the paddle snapped, so she got another paddle and used that one until she was finished. "You could always tell when they were done," one woman explained, "because the last one was the hardest."

All the women remembered that the nun pulled out some matches. One woman thought the nun had a whole box. Another remembered only a single stick. One thought the nun said they were going to "teach her a lesson." Another remembered it as, "This is what happens to people who steal." A third thought the nun said, "This is what happens when you do things like this." But they all remembered that the match was lit and the girl was held.

One recalled that the girl had struggled and cried; another remembered that all the girls cried; one believed that she herself had spoken out, but that no other girl said a word. Still, they all remembered what happened next.

"She lit the match and she held her hand right over the match, and her hand was touching the flames, and I sat there and I cried and I told them to stop," one said. The nun "took matches out of her dress and she burned the tips of each one of her fingers," recalled another. The woman said the girl, weeping, confessed to taking the candy and said she wouldn't do it again.

If the children mentioned the incident, one witness remembered a nun saying, they would never see their parents again.

Piecing together some background details, Widman figured that the girl's name was Elaine Benoit. He was desperate to find her, but none of his searches yielded anything until one day he got a call. He told me what he remembered of it years later.

"I'm Bob Widman," he had said. "What can I do for you?"

His caller asked him if he was looking for Elaine Benoit.

"Yeah, I'm looking real hard."

"Well, I'm Elaine," the woman said.

Widman was stunned. "I've heard this story . . ." he began.

"About the burning?" she said. "That was me." Then she told Widman her story. It was as everyone had said.

The women's stories about the candy thief provided Widman a lesson in how traumatic memory can work. The witnesses all remembered that the girl had stolen some candy and that a nun caught her. Three of them remembered the name of the girl correctly, and although there was no consensus on the nun's identity, most of them remembered that one nun administered the punishment. Specific details diverged, but the story's center held.

Often, the traumatic memories seemed to work just like normal memory, meaning that an episode might blur over time. For some people, the more intense an experience was, the more likely they were to retain it as a vivid narrative. But there was a threshold, at least for some. If an experience was too disturbing, it sometimes vanished. Whether it was actively repressed or just forgotten, it seemed to disappear from consciousness for decades, returning only in response to a specific trigger, such as driving by an orphanage or seeing a nun at the supermarket.

After each interview, Widman took notes on who he met, what had happened to them, and who they named. Corinne Brown, the paralegal, assembled them, and after months and months of gathering data, inside her bursting binder was not just a list of events or a big picture, it was a whole world that had spun quietly for decades on the edge of a small and oblivious community. It was a tiny totalitarian state, a dark castle, a factory of pain. Thousands of children passed through its doors, and when they left years later there was a spell upon them all, and they could not speak about what they had seen.

Every story Widman gathered was a proof of concept for every other. Perhaps it was hard to believe that a child at St. Joseph's was punched in the face—until you heard that another child was held upside down out a window and yet another was tied to a bed with no mattress and beaten. It was impossible to imagine that a nun would hold a child's head underwater until you also heard about the nuns who covered babies' mouths until they turned blue.

Elaine Benoit's burned hand was an unforgettable image. Widman always thought about every story, every account, and every witness in terms of how it would impact a jury. If they were going to hold an organization as powerful as the Catholic Church to account, the jury was going to have to feel the horror of the children's experience. Details mattered. Widman knew this story would work.

FINDING ELAINE BENOIT WAS A NEEDED WIN FOR A PROJECT THAT OFTEN felt out of control. But the toll of hearing one tale after another of mutilation, assault, or bottomless loneliness began to add up. Widman ran regularly in the nearby hills, but in the winter the roads were too icy. He returned to the same cheap motel because he liked the exercise room. At least he could run on the treadmill there and leave the stories behind. If he was in Burlington on a weekend, he hiked for a couple of hours to Camel's Hump in the Green Mountains.

In the evening, Widman distracted himself by wandering Burlington's Church Street Marketplace. The open-air mall was paved with terracotta bricks and teemed with stores and restaurants. When the temperature wasn't freezing, the restaurants fenced off outdoor sections and filled them with happy diners. Widman set for himself the goal of buying one chocolate chip cookie from a different restaurant every night to cheer himself up.

I MET WITH WIDMAN AT HIS HOUSE IN SARASOTA, FLORIDA, ON A BALMY day in spring 2018. He had slightly wild gray hair and a deep tan, and his face crinkled up when he smiled, which he did often. He had retired from legal practice, and that morning, like every other, he had gone for a three-hour bicycle ride. Now he was dressed casually in jeans and sandals. He was seventy, but he stood and moved like someone much younger.

We sat in a bright, airy room that opened out to a garden. Widman explained finer points of law, pausing to illustrate them with stories from his long career. Sometimes his wife, Cynthia, joined us.

I showed Widman some videos of his plaintiffs' depositions. We watched a middle-aged woman with a sweet, soft face and a young girl's voice talk about the day that she was standing in line at St. Joseph's and the girl in front of her vomited. Enraged, the nun who was in charge that day told her to clean it up. When she couldn't find anything to clean it up with, she said that the nun replied, "You know what I mean. You get down there and you lap it up."

It's not fair the woman had thought in response. Widman leaned in and waved his hand at the screen. Earlier he had told me about the time at Campion that he was punished for his roommate's grumbling at the train whistle—the night that he realized life was not fair. He looked at me and nodded, "Shut up, train!"

The woman in the video knew that if she spoke back to the nun, then the other girls in the line would suffer the consequences. So, she testified, "I did what I needed to do to survive and get out of there." As she spoke, she started to cry. "I got down," she said, "and I lapped up that vomit."

Decades later, Widman still remembered many of the details of the fight. He still felt deeply the injustice the former residents had been subjected to.

We watched a video of Sally Dale talking about the boy she saw pushed out a window. "Ooh, she's clear, isn't she?" he said. He sounded proud of her. In the video, Sally recalled looking up to the fourth floor the day she said a boy was thrown out of a window ("I saw the little body coming out"). Widman let out a big sigh. "It's depressing."

Of all the plaintiffs, Sally occupied a special place in his memory. When I asked about her, Widman's eyes watered. Holding his fist to his heart, he said, "I just loved Sally Dale. I just loved her. She was really a special person."

I showed Widman videos of the depositions he had taken from the Sisters of Providence in the 1990s. Twenty years later, he remembered few of the women individually. They had been, unsurprisingly, quite like each other. They no longer wore habits, but everyone's hair was short and mostly gray. Most had glasses, nothing fancy, and none wore any discernible makeup. They wore high collars, crew necks, or otherwise modest shirts.

They looked as if they had lived similar lives of shared purpose from the time they were twenty-two, or sixteen, or even fourteen, and just out of convent school, as indeed they had. The sisters had been told what to do, what to wear, how to cut their hair, what to think, and what not to think for much of their lives. They had taken a sacred vow to obey and had been trained to not question authority or challenge church doctrine. Their habits had conferred a kind of social blessing upon them. They were widely respected and could feel confident that everything they did was deserving of respect—because it was in service of the one true church. By virtue of their vocation, they had spent their entire adult lives preparing to be witnesses for the church. Unsurprisingly, they were very effective in that role.

We watched Sister Fernande de Grace, who seemed a little younger than her sisters. Most of the nuns looked alike with short gray hair, pale faces, eyeglasses, but Sister Fernande de Grace had close-cropped brown hair, wondering eyes, and dark expressive brows. She came across as sensitive, intelligent, and kind, a friendly local librarian or an older graduate student. She said that she had never seen a nun discipline a child. Sitting next to me on the couch, Widman laughed, "They don't look like monsters, do they?"

We watched Sister Gloria Keylor, who had been the head of the order. Widman never forgot her. Sister Keylor had sharp cheekbones and a high forehead, and when she wasn't speaking, her mouth rested in a small, confident smile. She wore a collared shirt and a blazer and came across as polished and highly competent. For Widman, Sister Keylor had been like the bishop, an instantly recognizable type. She was a "CEO of an international company," he said. "It clearly wasn't her first rodeo."

A FEW HOURS NORTH OF SARASOTA IN LAKE CITY, FLORIDA, ON A PRETTY piece of land with many tall trees, I met Walter Coltey, who lived there with his third wife and five big-eyed, high-strung rescue dogs, all part chihuahua.

Coltey entered St. Joseph's in 1953 when he was seven years old. With him at the time was Ray Benoit, who still lived nearby and joined us that day. The men called each other "brother."

After their time in the orphanage the boys spent a year at Don Bosco, which functioned as an annex for older boys, but in 1959 they left together and lived one summer under an abandoned rowboat they called *32 Beach Avenue*. They ate by boosting food from open-air stalls as they ran past. They stuffed spaghetti down their shirts in supermarkets and cooked it on the beach.

Now, Coltey had four children. Benoit had seven, but he was not in touch with any of them. When we met, Benoit was married to his sixth wife. Coltey kicked off the conversation, "I figure at this point, what could anybody do to me? I'm seventy-three."

I had arranged to meet the men because Ray Benoit was the brother of Elaine Benoit, the girl whose hand was burned. He told me she died two years earlier. When she was younger, he said, she was a go-go dancer, but she ended up a recluse. "She locked herself away with her cats," added Coltey. "Elaine lost her mind."

Coltey's sister, Charlotte, had also lived at St. Joseph's. Charlotte told him that a priest used to take her into the chapel, into the room where they got dressed for mass. "He would make her go underneath his robe while he was getting dressed. She never got over it. She had nightmares until the day she died."

I wanted to ask if either man knew about what happened to Elaine the day a nun said she stole some candy. Had she told her brother about the day her hand was burned? Did she show him her scars? I found it hard to pose the questions. Coltey and Benoit were funny and friendly, and the dogs had settled in around us. I struggled to find a way to raise the awful story. What if Benoit had never heard it? Would it hurt him all over again?

The boys' side had some good nuns, the men explained, but those women moved without much power or presence in the tiny totalitarian dystopia. Of the other nuns, Coltey said, "People don't realize that they had unlimited power." He added, "They could do whatever they wanted. And you had absolutely no recourse. There was nothing you could do. Nothing."

Sister Leontine, Coltey explained, "was the type of person that if somebody did something, she'd line all the boys up and she would walk around, and it was like she had a revelation from God, and she would point to one person and she would say, 'You did it!'"

"And you may as well admit to it," said Benoit, "because if you didn't do it and you denied it, she would beat you until you admitted it, and then she would beat you again because she said you were lying to her."

Coltey said his asthma had been so bad at St. Joseph's, he was given last rites three times. "They waited the longest time before they put me in the hospital," he said. He had epilepsy, too. "I fell out of the desk onto the floor.

The nun came and grabbed me by the ear and said, 'What are you faking for? There is nothing wrong with you.' Took me . . . to see Sister Louis Hector, which got me another beating."

Sister Louis Hector was a short, stocky "drill sergeant" who used to send the boys outside to cut a switch from the thorned rose bush in the grotto. If they brought back the wrong kind, the whipping would go for twice as long. "I remember getting hit so hard that you couldn't stand up. . . . You literally were on your knees, crawling. There was two hitting you as you are crawling," Coltey said.

There was one good priest, according to Coltey. His name was Father John Glancy, though Coltey called him "Jolly Joe." He had been the head of Vermont Catholic Charities and was then assigned to a parish in Vermont. Glancy had always been helpful to Coltey and his sister, Charlotte. When Coltey was thirteen years old, he left Don Bosco and became homeless. Then he went to Vermont Catholic Charities to find Glancy. They directed him to Brandon, Vermont, where Glancy let him stay in his parish rectory and gave him a job mowing the lawn in the cemetery. Glancy was the only good one, Coltey told me. He did not want to know, he said emphatically, if I had heard bad stories about him.

Coltey was still a little haunted by Glancy's reaction when he left the rectory. "One day I just said to him, 'I'm leaving,' and he kind of got upset about that because he had gone out of his way." Coltey explained, "To me, he was part of that orphanage, even though he was a good one, he was still part of that orphanage. . . . He had to know about it, that's what I think. I don't think he did but . . . I don't know."

Benoit listed the foods he still couldn't eat today. He particularly remembered the soup for supper—literally chunks of stale bread mixed in water—and the dismal sausage.

"You ever try to eat half cooked blood sausage?" he asked. "Try it sometime."

Benoit told me he took part in a private settlement process with the Diocese of Burlington in the 1990s. He said he spoke to a local reporter at the time. But he didn't remember much else about it. Coltey didn't hear about either a settlement process or the 1990s litigation until long after it was over. He was philosophical. "Looking back on it, you think about it, you got yourself beat, you got smashed in the mouth . . . and at the same time, it is where I lived," he said. "To people it is a horrifying thing. Not to us. It just was."

That said, "If one of them was alive today, I would want to shoot them," Coltey added. "That's just the way I feel. I dream about that. I dream about burning the place to the ground."

I finally asked about the day Elaine was held down and burned in front of all the other girls. Had either man heard about it? Benoit and Coltey shrugged.

"They liked to play with matches," Coltey said.

Did it happen to the boys, too?

Coltey pointed at his groin. "Right here." Sister Louis Hector, he explained, held a lit match under his genitals.

"Why?"

"You'll have to ask her," Coltey said. "I don't know. I must have done something bad."

"I think she was related to the Marquis de Sade," said Benoit.

As WIDMAN TRAVELED BACK AND FORTH TO VERMONT, HIS LIST OF VICTIMS kept growing. So did his list of abusers. A number of former residents remembered Sister Jane of the Rosary, as well as Sister Claire, Sister Pauline, Sister Dominick, Sister James Mary, Sister Albert, Sister Leontine, and Sister Louis Hector. Of the men at the orphanage, Father Robert Devoy and Father Edward Foster, among others, were named.

Multiple laypeople were also accused of molestation and other abuse. Fred Adams, who worked at the orphanage in the 1940s and sometimes wore a Boy Scout uniform, still haunted the lives of many men. Adams told one boy he would one day go to battle for America and needed to be able to tolerate torture if captured. Adams trussed the boy up and hung him from the ceiling. Then he tied a string to his penis. As he pulled on the string, the boy swung back and forth and smacked repeatedly into a hot bulb that was hanging behind him. Adams said, "You can't say anything to jeopardize your fellow man. . . . This is definitely going to happen to you. It's just a learning."

With each new case, more stories aligned. The swimming lessons were a case in point.

Many plaintiffs had claimed it was common to teach the children to swim by taking them out into Lake Champlain in a rowboat and tossing them in. But the nuns had a different story. One said she never went swimming at all, one said she went down to the lake but only to supervise the boys, one said she swam with the girls, and one said that she and many other nuns swam at the lake but only when the children were not there. One said the nuns did not have a rowboat. Even some of the orphans said they had never seen a rowboat at the orphanage, let alone been thrown in the water.

Initially, it was like one of those great tilting historic debates, like the assassination of John F. Kennedy, where one person saw a gunman on the grassy knoll, but with equal certainty another said the knoll was empty. Yet Widman doggedly tracked the thread through every single deposition and document, and eventually the accounts piled up: people who didn't know each other, people who hadn't met since—all shared their story of being rowed out and thrown in.

Leroy Baker said he was thrown in by a nun and a male counselor in the 1960s. They told him to swim or drown. Richard M., who was at the orphanage in the 1940s, said he was thrown in, too. What he remembered most was looking up at the sky from under the water and seeing "that patch of light as you're going down."

WIDMAN DEPOSED A DOCTOR, ROBERT J. MCKAY, WHO HELPED LOOK AFTER the orphanage children in the 1960s. McKay explained that he had volunteered because, "Well just generally, I get my jollies out of helping people and I thought I was helping people, so—." McKay also explained that he made the children available as test subjects to the medical director of a pharmaceutical company, who he "happened to know personally." McKay was paid $1,500, or rather his university department received $1,500 in grants, for experiments where children at the orphanage were given two drugs, liquid Tylenol and liquid hydrochlorothiazide, a diuretic—a drug that makes you pee.

Over a six-month period, the nuns administered the drugs for McKay to determine their taste acceptability. They received no financial compensation, said McKay. The parents of children were not informed. It was, McKay said, "not customary at that time."

It was mind-boggling to contemplate that the same children who were subject to humiliating punishments for wetting the bed were at the same time given a drug that made them more likely to urinate.

The specter of experimentation and the misuse of medication arose in several witness accounts. Monsignor Paul Bresnehan, the St. Joseph's chaplain from 1966 to 1977, a handsome and articulate man who was a leading light of liberal Catholic values in Vermont, told attorneys about medical studies carried out at the orphanage. He said he had a "vague, vague remembrance" that the children had been the subject of a nutrition study. He spoke about programs at the University of Vermont, saying, "We tried to benefit from whatever would be available to us that would help the children, help the sisters."

Bresnehan thought that Dr. Jerold Lucey, who had worked with the orphanage for years, "or one of his people," had also run a rubella study. Lucey was deposed three weeks after Bresnehan and asked if he had been involved in "any nutritional or medication studies involving the children at St. Joseph's." Lucey said no, adding that he'd heard of something like that since then, but that he couldn't remember anything about it.

Multiple residents from the 1940s told Widman they had been subjects in a nutrition study connected to a Dr. John Browe. Widman found medical records for Sally Dale signed by Browe, and a paper by Browe that discussed findings from a series of vitamin studies he conducted on school-age children in the 1940s. In the studies, an experimental group and a control group of children with different degrees of malnourishment were checked at intervals after a vitamin was administered to the test group. In all cases, the children given the vitamin improved but those in the control group did not, and some of the control children even became less healthy over the period of the study. There was no record of whether the malnourished children were given vitamins after the experiment was over.

Other residents believed they had been experimented on in different ways. One person described when the children had to wake up in the early morning and roll over and pull their pants down. Someone came along and inserted something inside them. The children had to stay in bed for a while after that. At different times, the children collected their feces in white cartons that looked like "little ice cream containers." The child's name and the date were written on the container, and the children did their best to get their poop inside it. "Most of the time you did it in your hand," the former resident said.

Another former resident from the 1960s described an odd activity that the nuns called "Feeding the Angel." At mealtimes, the children had to put exactly the same amount of food they had just eaten for supper in a plastic bag and hand it over to the nuns. The same resident also participated in a study on the effects of sending institutionalized children out to regular schools.

One woman who was at the orphanage in the 1970s said that she had been given an injection by a care worker before she was sexually assaulted by a priest. She remembered watching objects in the room change in strange ways after the injection. Later she came to believe that she had been hallucinating as a consequence of whatever substance she had been given.

The experimentation and the use of medication to obtain compliance or affect emotional state shared a cold hard core of dehumanization with the other acts of abuse Widman had learned about. Legally, though, there wasn't a lot he could do with the stories unless he was able to establish more details with documentation from the defense.

SOME RESIDENTS REMEMBERED ADULTS WHO BROUGHT SOME RELIEF AMID the pain and fear. One resident remembered the time she was confined to bed with a long illness and a nun let her listen to the radio, which played a new song called "American Pie" over and over again. It had been a great kindness.

Young counselors came from the outside to help the nuns in the late 1960s and the 1970s. Some were sexually abusive and physically cruel, but a few formed a thin but helpful layer between the nuns and the children, leading activities the aging nuns could not. One counselor sneaked up to the attic with a few boys and hauled out a few decades, worth of decrepit, donated bikes. They spent half the summer fixing them and then took them out for a glorious ride down Vermont's verdant country roads.

Another took a couple of boys to a blues festival at a local auditorium for a sublimely happy night, where they heard the blues, and some tasted wine and smoked a joint, all for the first time.

Sally Miller told the lawyers about being rescued by a nun when she was a girl. The story was complicated because it was the nun who put Miller in danger in the first place. When she lived at the orphanage, Miller also helped at St. Joseph's Home for the Aged, a connected Catholic Burlington institution. One night she was told by a nun to deliver ice cubes to the quarters of a priest who lived there, Father Harold Preedom. The nun, who seemed agitated, told her to put the cubes outside the priest's door and leave as quickly as possible. But when Miller placed the ice down, Preedom opened his door, pulled her inside, and began to assault her.

She got away, but the nun soon asked her to do it again. For Miller, Preedom was a beast-like figure, lurking in his rooms, waiting to grab her. But she did what the nun told her, and the same thing happened, except that when she fled the priest's room, disheveled and crying, she found the nun waiting for her in the hallway. The nun, Sister St. Catherine, raced into the room and began to grapple with the priest. Telling the story years later, Miller said that she froze. "I had never seen a nun touched in my life. And he was pulling at the front of her, she had a long white neck, she was slender but she was a sturdy nun, she worked really hard in the kitchen."

Later the nun said to her, "Don't ever tell, he's a priest, and he's still a priest and don't ever tell." Miller promised she wouldn't. She kept her promise until church defense lawyers asked her about her experience forty years later.

WIDMAN LEARNED THAT ALONG WITH THEIR FINANCES, THEIR DEMO-graphic, and their way of life, the Sisters of Providence's commitment to eighteenth-century-style mortification appeared to have finally run out of steam by the 1970s. The testimony of former residents from that era included fewer stories like being made to kneel on tiny objects, being held upside down, being locked inside containers, or bleeding from being cut.

There was still an atmosphere of coldness, dread, and unbearable lone-liness that permeated all corners of the building. The bedwetters were still tormented (one girl was made to sleep in the shower room for three days). Others recalled being woken up by a nun hitting them, others were subject to full-body assaults, and the "dark menagerie" closet for little bad children was still in use.

Yet what had been an impregnable fortress for more than one hundred years had become vulnerable to intrusion. It was hard to put a finger on exactly when it happened, but odd incursions began to pile up. There were the incidents of vandalism and graffiti, the fires set intentionally by children, and police officers who dared to ask questions when they returned runaways. One mother, who had been an erratic presence in her children's lives, turned up one day. She had heard that the nuns were being cruel to her daughter, so she barreled in, drunk and shouting for justice. She beat up one nun, and it took two other nuns to hold her back. Eventually she left with police. It was an ecstatic moment for her children.

One of her sons, Dale Greene, who had arrived in 1966, became more and more determined to take charge of his own life. There were so few boys in the dorm in those days that he pulled a bunch of lockers into an L-shape to make himself his own bedroom. Every now and then, he would return to find the lockers had been pulled apart, but he would just put them back together again.

He even went toe-to-toe with his least favorite nun, Sister Gertrude, who he called "the psycho." One day Greene and a friend were playing music in the locker room when Sister Gertrude chased a young boy into the room and started to beat him. There was another nun there. Her name was Sister Brenda. She was petite and inexperienced, Greene thought, not even a full nun. But she stood up to Sister Gertrude and the women grappled physically. Sister Brenda yelled at Sister Gertrude, "cussing her out." Greene thought it was awesome. But it was the last he saw of Sister Brenda. He assumed she was fired straight away, but what she did changed him. He had never seen someone stand up to the psycho before.

After that, when Sister Gertrude tried to hit Greene one too many times, he turned on her and yelled, "Hit me and I'll knock your fucking head off."

Sister Gertrude never hit Greene again. In fact, she lost all control. Soon enough, Greene said, "they shipped her out."

Not long after Sister Gertrude left, she was followed by all of her sisters. In 1974, more than a century since they had arrived, the Sisters of Providence left North Avenue for good.

"That last year," Greene said, "we pretty much ran the place."

CHAPTER 13

THE WEEK BEFORE BOB WIDMAN FILED SALLY DALE'S CASE, THE *Burlington Free Press* ran a series of articles about St. Joseph's Orphanage. Sam Hemingway, an investigative reporter and one of Vermont's best-known journalists, delved into the lives of forty orphans, noting that since their time at the orphanage, they had been plagued by addiction, terrible self-esteem, and fear. The series featured a vomit story, accounts of terrible brutality, and creepy sexual encounters. One man even said he had seen the body of an orphanage boy who drowned in the lake in 1961. Hemingway's coverage was fearless. It meant that for the first time, the orphanage stories could not be ignored.

Two days after the case was filed, Hemingway wrote about Sally Dale and her claims that she was locked in a box in the attic and had seen a nun throw a boy from a window on the fourth floor. Geoff Morris was quoted saying that other residents independently recalled the same incident. The story hit the small town like a bomb.

It was shocking enough for Burlington locals when Joseph Barquin came forward three years earlier. Sally Dale's case dragged it all back into the present and made it much worse. Hemingway's article was crystal clear, and yet its meaning was almost impossible to grasp.

The *Burlington Free Press* was inundated by callers, plenty of them hostile to Sally. A former orphanage chaplain, Monsignor Bresnehan, told the paper it was "just simply unbelievable." Which, for most people, it was.

Widman believed Sally's story about the boy being thrown through the window. But whenever Sally or another orphan told Widman about witnessing a death, his silent reaction was that there were no bodies, no witnesses, and no proof of any kind. He thought, *What the heck am I going to do with this?*

These were the hardest stories to piece together: How many deaths were claimed? Who saw them? When in the forty-odd-year period covered by the litigation had they occurred? The orphanage was in operation for over 120 years. Thousands of people passed through its doors. It stood to reason that there would have been fatalities, if only from natural causes. But the defense never offered an accounting of who had died and how, except in a few narrow instances when forced.

ONE WOMAN, WHO CALLED THE *BURLINGTON FREE PRESS* AFTER THE ARTICLE about Sally Dale was published, spoke so fast she was almost impossible to understand. She said that she was the child that Sally described—a nun named Sister Priscille had tried to push her from a window at St. Joseph's.

The caller found her way to Bob Widman and told him that at the orphanage she was known as Patricia Carbonneau, but she was Patty Zeno now. When she read about Sally seeing a child thrown from a window, it was like someone had slapped her in the face.

In the years since she had left St. Joseph's, Carbonneau had thought as little about the orphanage as possible. For a long time, she wouldn't even drive past it, taking a long circuitous route instead. Confusingly, at one time, she placed her daughter in childcare there. Her attitude was a kind of helpless, *What else was she going to do?* She dropped her daughter off with the nuns and then didn't think about it.

Carbonneau's ability to wall off the first part of her life from the present shattered when she read Sam Hemingway's article. She didn't even read the whole thing. She didn't register that Sally had been talking about a boy. All she knew was that life changed forever in that moment. Carbonneau believed that the Hemingway story had to do with her, and she urgently needed to do something about it.

Carbonneau told Widman that the tension between her and Sister Priscille had been building for a long time, ever since she was eight years old, and she and a group of girls were sitting around a small wooden radio in the recreation room when Sister Priscille was in charge. The nun was not that much older than the girls, but it was impossible for them to see themselves in her. Sister Priscille was small and had a large nose. She was often unkind and always seemed to be frustrated.

Carbonneau asked Sister Priscille if the radio could be turned up, but the nun said no. She asked again and Sister Priscille smacked her face. In response, she stood up and shoved her chair sideways, but the chair, to her horror, skidded across the floor and hit Sister Priscille in the leg. Carbonneau did not wait around to see what the woman's reaction would be. She just "ran like the dickens."

Carbonneau ended up in the basement kitchen. She begged the nun in the kitchen to hide her. The nun, whose name Carbonneau could not remember, pointed out the kitchen's massive mixing kettle. She warned Carbonneau that if Sister Priscille asked her where the runaway girl had gone, she'd have to tell her. Then she turned her back and pointedly looked the other way. Carbonneau got inside the kettle and pulled the lid over herself. Miraculously, Sister Priscille passed through the kitchen without looking inside the cookware or asking the other nun.

From that day, even greater tension simmered between Carbonneau and Sister Priscille. The next time they clashed was a day when the older girls stood in a line, waiting to bathe, wearing their towels. Carbonneau spoke out of turn and Sister Priscille reacted angrily. She seized the girl and lifted her off the ground by grabbing two fistfuls of skin on her back.

Mayhem erupted. Carbonneau, who was very thin ("They used to call me the human skeleton"), dropped down and wriggled from the nun's grasp. She crawled under a bed. Sister Priscille tried to kick her as she scooted back and forth beneath it. She moved under one bed, then another, crawling toward the door. She ran and found her older sister, who told her to go to Vermont Catholic Charities next door to tell the director, Father Glancy.

A SMALL STONE BUNGALOW WITH A GABLED SECOND STORY WAS SITUATED next to the orphanage. Originally, the director of the Lakeview Sanitarium had lived there. The sanitarium, which stood between the bungalow and the orphanage, had since been bought by the church and was used as an extension of the orphanage called the Don Bosco School. Older boys from the orphanage and elsewhere lived there with a priest and some resident brothers. Vermont Catholic Charities had set up an office in the little stone house.

The office was located at a great enough distance that sounds from the orphanage could not be heard, but it was close enough that it only took a minute or two to walk there.

After talking to her sister, Carbonneau burst into the offices and told Father Glancy her tale. The priest sat and looked at her but didn't respond. She left dejected. Later, she knew he had heard at least some of what she said, because a few days after she spoke to him, Sister Priscille cornered her and said, "You will pay for it."

In the weeks that followed, Sister Priscille started waking Carbonneau at night, leaning over her bed and holding a flashlight under her face. To Carbonneau, the nun looked like Satan herself. All Sister Priscille said was, "You will pay for it."

One day Carbonneau found to her great relief that Sister Priscille had been transferred away from the girls' department. For a while her life was peaceful. But then she was sent to work in the second nursery with a girl named Sally, where Sister Priscille was in charge.

Sally and Carbonneau had to get the children out of bed, do their hair, make their meals, and bathe them. The work didn't bother Carbonneau, but the way Sister Priscille treated the children did. She made them kneel for ages or stand facing a corner. She shut them in the closet where they screamed and screamed. Once, after Carbonneau had undressed and bathed the little children, Sister Priscille told her she was immoral. The young nun then sewed a bunch of tiny calico skirts for the little children to wear in the bath so they never looked at their own private parts.

The last straw came the day Carbonneau and Sally were wiping down the nursery kitchen. Sister Priscille walked in and said it was time to clean the windows. Carbonneau and Sally took turns washing the inside and the outside, and when it was her turn, Carbonneau climbed out and stood on the second-floor sill. When the window was almost done, Sister Priscille walked back in. Carbonneau—hanging on to a little bit of wood outside the building—was struck by terror.

Sister Priscille told Sally to go do something else, and as Sally moved aside, the nun took Carbonneau by the ankles and mouthed the words, "You will pay." Then she pushed her.

A lot happened in the next few sickening seconds. Carbonneau spun away from the window, somehow leaving her left foot on the sill while her right side swung out and slammed into the brick wall on her left. She had no idea where her hands were. Was her left hand hanging on to the side of the window? Was her right hand gripping the brick wall? Out of nowhere, Sally appeared and grabbed at her left ankle and arm, and with Carbonneau's body pressed hard up against the wall, somehow the two girls managed together to get her back inside. The whole time Sister Priscille stood in the room watching. Carbonneau heard her call Sally *la rouge*. Then she saw her leave.

MANY SURVIVORS TOLD WIDMAN ABOUT AN UGLY ASSAULT BUT DID NOT remember their abuser's name, only that it was a nun, priest, janitor, or scout leader. Maybe there had been a child witness, but usually they couldn't remember the child's name, either. Yet here was Patricia Carbonneau. She remembered the incident at the window as clearly as Sally Dale did. It was like the story of Elaine Benoit, whose hand was burned in punishment, only this time the victim could have died. Carbonneau was exactly the kind of witness Widman needed.

Carbonneau told Widman that she had not seen Sally except once after the reunion. At first Sally didn't recognize her. Carbonneau, who was once so skinny, was now overweight. When the women recognized each other, they spoke about the nuns slapping them if they laughed during prayers in the hallway, and Sally being put in the attic a lot. Sally asked Carbonneau if she remembered the way they all used to sleep on their sides facing the same direction with their hands in prayer tucked under their cheeks.

"Yeah," Carbonneau said, "but do you still do that?"

"Yes, I do, Patty," Sally had replied.

Carbonneau asked Sally if she remembered catching her at the window. Sally said yes and added, "You know Patty, to be honest, maybe it was luck on my side."

The conversation between the two women didn't go further than that. Carbonneau still believed that she was the shameful, guilty party in the event, at least in part.

Carbonneau wasn't the only one who remembered the story. Another woman told Widman that at the time of the incident she heard a story about a nun who became so angry that she pushed a girl out a window, and that Sally Dale (then Fredette) had grabbed the girl and helped her in.

Other women described the way they would climb out the window and stand facing in to wash the glass while another girl held them by the ankles.

For Carbonneau, publicly saying that Sr. Priscille had tried to push her off the window ledge was an intense and disorienting experience. It was equally confusing that when people heard the story, they blamed Sister Priscille rather than Carbonneau. Somehow that was almost worse. For a while, it threw Carbonneau completely off balance—she became briefly convinced that Sister Priscille was tapping her phone. Eventually she realized the nun was gone for good.

For Sally, life with Sister Priscille also became worse after that day. Sister Priscille told all the girls that Sally's mother was the devil, which made Sally the devil's child. She grabbed Sally by the arm and twisted it. She pulled down Sally's pants in front of all the girls and whipped her hard. That made the other girls laugh at Sally, which was almost as bad as the whipping.

One day, Sister Priscille pushed Sally up the stairs, and Sally fell and hit her knee hard on the marble step. When Sally started to cry, Sister Priscille told her that if she kept crying, things would get a lot worse for her. But that night, things got worse anyway. Sally's knee was so swollen that she showed it to Irene. Irene told the Mother Superior that she had to take Sally to the hospital.

When Sally returned to the orphanage, her leg was encased in a stiff, white cast. But no one said out loud that it was broken.

The nuns told Sally she was faking it because she wanted attention, which, to be fair, they said all the time to everyone, not just her. They also said she was well known to make believe. Sally often had a terrible pain on her right side, but she was always told to stop pretending and not to complain. When any girl was hurt, the nuns encouraged the others to laugh at her or call her a baby or force her somehow to stand on her sore leg or use her sore arm, and just get on with things.

The night after Sally's leg was broken, she had trouble sleeping. The doctor had told Irene to give Sally aspirin at nighttime, but the nuns said not to give it to her. Late at night Irene came quietly into Sally's room and gave her some anyway.

THE DEATH AND NEAR-DEATH STORIES ACCUMULATED. IT WASN'T JUST PATRICIA Carbonneau or Sally Dale. It was Sally Miller, who, along with a large group of children, had looked for a boy in the lake. It was Joseph Eskra, who also recalled the boy who died at the lake and remembered with the same clarity and conviction the night he saw a frozen boy tied to a tree. It was Sherry Huestis, who watched a newborn baby being smothered by a nun dressed in white. Each gave a deposition. Yet the idea that all these heinous acts could have unfolded in one's own town without anyone knowing was too much for most people to take in. The church's attorneys made the most of that skepticism.

Widman also collected stories from former residents, who separately described being made to kiss an old, dead man in his coffin at the orphanage. It was uncanny how many remembered the event. Yet the response of the defense was often to challenge the plaintiffs' memories and even their very grasp of reality.

David Borsykowsky, one of the attorneys for the Sisters of Providence, said to one woman:

"Now if I tell you that there is no record, no memory, no information that there was ever a funeral or ever a dead person at St. Joseph's Orphanage, and that none of the sisters and none of the people responsible for children at St. Joseph's have any memory or any record or recollection of any such event, does that help you to know that it didn't happen at St. Joseph's?"

That was where the conversation ended. Borsykowsky didn't actually say, and perhaps didn't know, whether any deaths or funerals had transpired at St. Joseph's. He just asked the plaintiff what she would say if he said that.

Joseph Eskra told Borsykowsky about the day that Marvin Willette drowned at the lake, and about the boy who never came to dinner and who Eskra later found tied to a tree, frozen.

"That boy, for example, the boy who was—you say was frozen to death?" Borsykowsky asked Eskra. "That was something I've never heard about."

Eskra took Borsykowsky at face value and tried to be helpful. "If you went back in the records, which I presume back then they kept records in Burlington, you would see if you looked through the deaths that there was something there, unless they hid it from the newspapers or from the records."

"Okay. We've been looking for that and so far we haven't been able to find it," said Borsykowsky. "We view with skepticism much of what you've described."

Borsykowsky then asked Eskra a series of questions. The focus was entirely on Eskra's personal history. Borsykowsky appeared to spend far more time trying to elicit compromising details about Eskra than he did trying to work out if a child had died at St. Joseph's, as witnessed by Eskra.

He asked if Eskra ever served time in jail by order of a judge?

Eskra hadn't.

Had Eskra ever been arrested for harming somebody, or for stealing, anything like that?

No.

Had Eskra ever had a problem with drugs or alcohol, using too much?

No.

Did Eskra have any major health problems?

Not that he knew of.

Had Eskra ever been denied access to his children due to accusations of sexual abuse?

No.

Had Eskra ever had any kind of psychiatric, psychological treatment, or counseling for drugs or alcohol or anything like that?

Eskra said he saw a counselor for six months when he left the orphanage, but not much came of it. He said the doctor was nuttier than he was. He also said he had once been fired over a sexual harassment complaint, and an ex-girlfriend had accused him of rape but retracted her accusation.

It was true. Eskra had led a complicated life. Yet despite Borsykowsky's best efforts, his story remained strong.

In August 1996, about three years after Joseph Barquin's suit was first filed by Philip White, the diocese agreed to resolve it through mediation rather than a trial in open court. Widman wasn't surprised. In the relatively short time that he had known Barquin, he had watched with fascination as his client became an intense irritant clamped tight to the church's side. Widman thought of him as a pit bull. Emerging from a lifetime of silence and fear, Barquin was compelling in front of a microphone. And he had been a powerful leader, at least until relations with the group had deteriorated. He had inspired many reluctant former residents to join him in speaking out.

The mediation was not an easy process, and there were a few false starts. In the end, Barquin said, the church settled for a significant amount of money—and a provision that the agreement and the amount be kept secret. (I was unable to obtain any of the documentation for the settlement.)

In his final meeting with the chancellor of the diocese, Barquin and the chancellor asked their attorneys to leave the room, and with only a mediator present, they hashed out the details of the settlement. Both men wept.

On the record, the church maintained its skeptical stance. Earlier, Barquin told defense attorneys that in the painful years before getting help, he had an out-of-body experience while lying on the floor in his room with his dog nearby. It was a scene that the defense for the Sisters of Providence later invoked when they summed up the case for the judge. Even though the diocese had settled, they compared Barquin's strange traumatic moment with his entire story of abuse, holding out both with disdain: ". . . in addition to his memories of alleged experiences at the orphanage," they wrote, Barquin "recalled having an out-of-body experience involving an extraterrestrial and a miniature poodle named Candy."

Still, Barquin's sense of reconciliation with the giant institution proved to be a powerful one. He reversed course and started contacting Widman's other plaintiffs, trying to persuade them to abandon their legal counsel.

In an interview with the *Burlington Free Press*, Barquin said he wanted to find a non-adversarial way for his fellow orphans to resolve their claims. "Rage and anger is never going to work for the future of these people," he told the reporter. Barquin began to phone Sally Dale to suggest that he could have the bishop and some nuns drop by her house to talk about things. Horrified by the suggestion, she said no.

CHAPTER 14

Two months after Widman filed Sally Dale's case, he filed a case for Donald Shuttle: *I lived in fear every day I was there.* In September, he filed a case for Marilyn Noble: *She kept hitting me and hitting me and hitting, telling me to admit the truth. And I told her I was telling the truth, that I didn't do it. And she kept hitting me until finally I said okay, I did it, to stop the hitting.* W. R.: *They put a poker in a wood stove. . . . I watched the poker get red. Then I watched it get white.* And Robert Cadorette: *He said, Bob, where are you, where are you, and then I came out of the bushes, and that's when he grabbed me and took me down to the lake—and that's when he tried to drown me.*

It had been obvious to Widman from the beginning, and even more as the stories of his witnesses accumulated, that he needed to bring all the plaintiffs together in front of the same jury in a consolidated trial. Each former resident's account helped explain the context of every other account. In isolation, any one account was more easily picked apart and cast into doubt. The plaintiffs would be vulnerable outcasts going up against one of the most powerful institutions in the world. Together they had a chance.

Joining the cases was critical for practical reasons, too. The plaintiffs would need to call on each other as witnesses, but if each case was tried separately, they would have to return to the court and tell each story perhaps a dozen times in front of strangers, an experience many would find unbearable. The expert witnesses would have to be summoned repeatedly, and the court would need to assemble different juries for each case. The cost would be extraordinary.

AS HE PUSHED THE CASES FORWARD, WIDMAN PREPARED FOR THE WITnesses for the defense. They were a diverse group, including people who had lived at the orphanage as children, their husbands or wives, and even acquaintances. They also included some of Sally's relatives.

Widman knew ahead of time, more or less, what the defense witnesses would say, and he followed the same general outline for them all. But he always hoped for an accidental revelation. It was possible that when they were talking about their experiences, the defense witnesses might include details that corroborated the stories of the plaintiffs. They might name priests or nuns who had been at St. Joseph's in a particular year. If he was lucky, it might be the same year that his clients had described encounters with them.

Some defense witnesses had come to the attention of the church's attorneys because they had written letters to the newspaper when stories about the litigation first broke. Widman had seen the letters himself. Others came forward as the news filtered through their families. Widman was startled to discover that at Sunday mass in each Vermont parish, priests were reading a letter from the bishop to parishioners, explaining that terrible allegations had been made against the sisters and asking for anyone who had been to the orphanage and had a good time to come forward.

Most defense witnesses said they had not seen, nor could they recall, any force-feeding, vomiting, or hitting. The food was very good, there was plenty of it, it was fine. They were never addressed as a number, they had a lot of free time and happiness, and at Christmas, they were given an abundance of presents: games, toys, mittens, and gloves. Everyone remembered outings on the Ticonderoga, the paddle wheel steamboat that toured Lake Champlain, and a few reminisced about their parents visiting every Sunday.

One woman pulled a photo of Sister Mary Charity out of her wallet during her deposition. She said she carried the photo with her everywhere. Others remembered the nuns with great admiration. Sister Jane of the

Rosary was "warm," Sister Mary Vianney was "loving," Sister Claire was "stately" with "a sense of humor," Sister Madeline was "the comedian," and Sister Pauline was "a real lady." Father Devoy was "a very nice, gentle man," a "saint." He always had candy for the children.

One man recalled that two nuns had a friendly rivalry going to see who could do the most for their kids. To Morris, it sounded an awful lot like *The Bells of St. Mary's*, with Bing Crosby as Father Chuck O'Malley and Ingrid Bergman as the beautiful Sister Superior Mary Benedict. The tension between the two characters in the 1945 film was all due to their concern for the welfare of the orphans.

Eva DuPaul, the seamstress who had lived at the orphanage from 1910 until 1982, when she moved to the St. Joseph's Home for the Aged, told Widman that in all of her seventy-two years at the orphanage, she had never seen a nun yell at a child or hit them. She said that she had never been asked by Sister James Mary to discipline Sally.

Mostly, the defense witnesses appeared to share a feeling of shock and outrage at the plaintiffs' claims. One man who had never been to the orphanage came forward because his wife, who had spent time at St. Joseph's, was upset about the allegations. Another man who spent a year at the orphanage and grew up to work in law enforcement and the department of social welfare, recalled reading about the case in the newspaper. "How could these people suddenly reappear twenty to thirty years after they had been at the orphanage and make these allegations?" he asked. Where did they come up with them? It made him feel "disgusted."

Widman walked them through a series of questions. He was never confrontational. After all, he wanted them to let their guard down. At first, though, no matter what he asked, the witness would often respond no, or rather, "No, no, no."

Eventually, the truth that Widman sought began to trickle out. Often, at some point in the questioning, a witness would allow that one of the punishments alleged by the plaintiffs did, in fact, occur. Taken together, the testimonies of the defense witnesses actually confirmed much of what the plaintiffs said.

One woman, who was so fond of the Mother Superior that she had stayed in touch with her for years, recalled that she was made to slap herself in the mouth. But, she said, by way of excuse, she didn't have to hit herself hard. She also remembered Sister Jane and the girls making fun of disabled children, in particular a girl with a speech impediment. Widman asked if the disabled girl had been embarrassed, but the woman replied that the girl wasn't the sort of person you could embarrass. Another woman recalled being thrown in the lake from a boat. She said it cured her fear. Another was punished for wetting the bed, but she said that it didn't bother her. Another recalled being made to sleep in the same direction with hands under her head, but she said it was not a big deal.

One woman responded, "I don't recall" to every question, but when asked if "I don't recall" meant that something didn't happen or if she just didn't recall it, she replied, "I don't recall."

The plaintiffs and defendants differed most in who they held responsible for the punishment that was meted out to the children. The woman who hit herself in the face fifty times said that she had to do it because she talked a lot. Another who was rapped with the clappers said that it made her a better person. Another man said plainly that he was hit because he deserved it.

One man who spent a year and a half at St. Joseph's said he didn't believe that anyone had ever been locked up in the attic, although he also said that he hadn't realized before the litigation that the building had an attic. The attorneys asked another man about a boy named Robert Cadorette, who claimed that Brother Gelineau—the bishop of the Diocese of Providence, Rhode Island, at the time of the litigation—tried to unzip his pants. The man replied that if Brother Gelineau had been that way inclined, he could have found someone better than Robert Cadorette to do it to. Even when witnesses were asked about cases where a nun or priest at St. Joseph's had given sworn testimony affirming a report of sexual abuse, like the case of a nun who walked in on a maintenance man assaulting a boy, they said they found it hard to believe.

Not one person said they recalled one of the events that Sally or the other plaintiffs recalled, although they were usually confident that it must have happened a different way. Really, their most significant contribution to the litigation was their disbelief.

In some cases, the defense witnesses painted an altogether implausible picture—one woman said there was no discipline at all at the orphanage, and another said that none of the sisters ever raised their voices. Others recalled discipline but said it was mild. There was a demerit system ("one check if you were sassy"), and maybe they had been whacked with a ruler or a pointer or the clappers.

It was curious, too, that while some defense witnesses had been at St. Joseph's with siblings who all agreed it was a good place, others said their siblings refused to discuss the orphanage with them but would not say why. Witnesses on both sides were confused by the definition of sexual abuse. When one witness for the defense was told that his younger brother testified that his genitals were touched by Frank Rule, one of the lay helpers at the orphanage, the witness said he wasn't sure that qualified as sexual abuse. Perhaps there was a conspiracy, he wondered, to get rid of Frank Rule?

A few declared—believably—that they were treated much better at the orphanage than they would have been at home. One woman spoke about the way the nuns accepted her brother with Down syndrome into the day school at St. Joseph's in an era when there were almost no services for children like him. In those days, she said, you didn't even see anyone out on the street with Down syndrome because their families kept them home out of shame.

Widman usually asked the defense witnesses if they would characterize the alleged acts, like forcing a child to eat their vomit, as abuse. Almost everyone seemed to agree that in theory those things were child abuse. But somehow their view was different when it happened at the orphanage. (One woman, who herself had gone on to become a nun and look after children in a daycare, stated that she didn't think that making children eat their own vomit was necessarily abuse in any context.)

It wasn't just former residents who had a hard time believing the nuns could have done anything wrong. One woman, a social worker at Vermont Catholic Charities, where Sally's social worker Harriet Parker had worked, said that on principle she would have believed the children over the sisters, but the children never said anything to her that resembled any of the claims that were made in the litigation.

The social worker, who was at the orphanage for five years in the early 1950s, said that as far as she could tell, there wasn't even any corporal punishment at the orphanage. When Widman put it to her that he knew of a case where a grandparent had visited St. Joseph's and found black and blue marks all over her grandchild, the social worker replied that the families those children and their grandparents came from were not particularly stable and were probably more susceptible to fabrications.

"So if children who are now adults reported these types of things happening, it would be your belief that they are fabricating?" Widman asked.

Yes, she said, it would. In her experience, the nuns were valiant women who loved and protected the children and dedicated their whole lives to looking after them.

"What if a group of women independently testified that they saw a nun burn a girl's hand with a candle?" Widman asked. Would she have a hard time believing it?

Yes, she said, absolutely. It was like "something out of *Oliver Twist*."

Did she think it might be the case that children would find it difficult to describe abuse they had gone through?

The social worker said she found it amusing when people came forward after forty or fifty years to claim that they had been sexually abused. In her experience, when it happened, someone else always knew about it. Maybe even just a friend at school. But these days it was fashionable to say you had been sexually molested. Perhaps people had heard that someone else was awarded a million dollars when they said their stepfather assaulted them. It was a way to get "a little notoriety," a "place in the sun."

WIDMAN INTERVIEWED SALLY'S OLDER SISTER, SHERRY, IN VERNON, CONnecticut, along with two defense attorneys. Earlier, Jack Sartore had asked Sally for Sherry's contact details, but Sally would not hand them over. Sherry had been in and out of mental health institutions, said Sally, and she was going through a particularly difficult time. Sally was not in regular contact with Sherry or her family, but they said that becoming involved in the litigation could tip Sherry over the edge. Now, it seemed, Sherry did not agree. Here she was, only she was a witness for the defense.

Sherry did not believe any of the plaintiffs' stories.

"Oh, Sister Jane, she was very—everybody liked her. She was a very nice sister," Sherry told Widman.

Yes, Sister Jane had spanked Sherry once, using something that was not a razor strap but looked like one, and it had hurt a lot, and it felt unfair at the time. But now, Sherry said, "I feel she was just trying to discipline the way a mother would."

In a photo album titled "Homer and Sherry, Forty Years of Joy," Sherry showed the attorneys photos of the orphanage and said they gave her happy feelings. She said that she had not been having any trouble in her marriage in the 1960s. It was Sally who called her and suggested leaving the orphanage to come to stay with her.

Sally and Sherry's mother, Ramona Fredette, who had probably seen Sally fewer than half a dozen times in her life, also made a statement for the defense.

Whatever he felt on the inside, Widman was as courteous and calm with Fredette as he was with everyone else. Fredette said that everyone at the orphanage had been very pleasant to her. Her daughter had always seemed happy when she visited. There were no bruises on her body.

It was a strangely flat interview, although Fredette reserved some energy for her daughter. She had looked after Sally until she was two years old, and confidently declared that if Sally needed to, she always knew how to throw a tantrum.

Sally had given Widman a long list of orphanage friends. It included a young woman known as Bambi, who Sally had adored, but who died by suicide after leaving the orphanage. Sally believed that the other girls on the list had seen what she had seen. Some had been part of the bad crowd the nuns focused so much attention on. In the end, though, like Sally's family, many became witnesses for the defense.

Sally said that Joan Blanchard had been present the day a nun pushed a little girl down the stairs, and Sally had to take her to the hospital with Irene. But Blanchard, who had herself become a nun for a while after her time at the orphanage, said she didn't see anyone pushed down the stairs,

and that the orphanage made her a better person, and that she barely remembered Sally. When Widman asked her if the children were punished
physically by the nuns, she said no. But when he asked what the teachers
used clappers for, she said, "Your knuckles."

Adrienne and Marie St. Pierre, twin sisters who were at St. Joseph's for
more than ten years, were also in Sally's clique. Adrienne St. Pierre said she
had been a close friend of Sally's, and that Sally was not abused, nor was
there any abuse at the orphanage. Marie St. Pierre likewise said there was no
truth in any of it. She did not remember Sally being treated badly, only that
she was once sunburned, and it was very painful.

Joyce Delisle, who Sally remembered as being in the same group of bad
girls, didn't recall any abuse. She didn't believe it was possible. Yet Delisle,
who was placed at the orphanage at fourteen months and left in 1953 when
she was in eighth grade, gave an interesting testimony because, where many
defense witnesses painted a luminous picture of their time at the orphanage
(*to have known Sister Rose is equal to have known Mother Teresa*), Delisle, a
registered nurse, offered a more hardboiled account.

Delisle said that her time at the orphanage had given her stamina, endur-
ance, and tolerance, and that she lived her life by a credo she had learned
there: "If something bad happens, it will pass and, you know, things will
come good again."

As for Sally, Delisle hardly remembered her, except for one vivid day
that had stayed with her for years when that red-haired, freckled Sally Dale
(known then as Sally Fredette) was up on stage in the gym surrounded by
people. Delisle didn't know why Sally got to be up on stage. She wanted to
get up there as well, but the nuns wouldn't let her, and it didn't seem fair.
Sally sang "God Bless America" in a big booming voice, said Delisle, and all
the nuns just loved her to pieces. She was a favorite really, a pet, because of
her singing and because she spent a lot of time with Eva and Irene.

Delisle knew that she had been friends with Sally, because her mother
told her so, but she did not believe she spent all that much time with her.
Actually, she thought Sally was missing quite a lot of the time; it was like she
didn't even go to school.

The only violence Delisle said she remembered was when Sister Jane
would hit the girls with a wooden clothes hanger. When the attorneys

asked her if it had been hard, she said, "It didn't leave a red mark, let me put it that way."

Delisle's memory of Sister Jane was more nuanced than other witnesses'. She had been an old, impatient woman, someone you did not want to upset, said Delisle, who stayed away from her as much as she could.

Sister Jane had slapped Delisle in the face, but as Delisle explained, it was different in the 1940s. Back then, children weren't supposed to look adults in the eye at all, and if they did, it was insolent and it earned them a slap. One of the attorneys put it to Delisle that another woman said Sister Jane had pushed her head underwater as punishment, but Delisle didn't think that sounded like Sister Jane. She said that it would have been more her style to get someone else to do it for her.

VIVID THOUGH THE ACCOUNTS OF ABUSE WERE, WIDMAN WAS NERVOUS about how they would fare in the litigation. In sex abuse cases across the United States, defense lawyers had started to challenge memory and the strange ways it sometimes behaved. Privately, Widman was mystified by the various and inconsistent ways that plaintiffs' childhood memories manifested. Widman's belief in Sally was unshakable, but some of the survivors remembered some things and not others, some had forgotten everything, while others hadn't forgotten a single painful moment. He and his wife, Cynthia, discussed it. She explained to him the kind of dissociation and repression she saw in her clients. She understood, in a way that he was only beginning to, the confusing and strange ways people reacted to trauma.

The incident of the candy thief had been a natural experiment in traumatic memory. But not every event was corroborated, and the statute of limitations ruled out all physical abuse and every single incidence of sexual assault, rape, and harm that had been inflicted on the survivors—with one exception. It was a catch-22. The only cases when the statute didn't apply were the ones where his plaintiffs had only recently remembered what happened or realized how much harm it had done.

This was one of the ways the statute of limitations distorted the process of seeking justice. It meant that much of the energy during the litigation went toward proving if someone had a memory, when they had that memory, and what the value of that memory was, rather than to directly ascertaining whether children had been raped or sexually assaulted, and whether the institution had covered up these crimes.

In Bennington, Vermont, Widman deposed two siblings, a brother and sister, former residents of St. Joseph's who were witnesses for the defense.

The sister, a slight woman in her forties, spoke positively about her time in the orphanage. At some point, he mentioned the name of the nun who had sewn with the girls and was said to have sexually assaulted more than one of them.

All of a sudden, the woman became immobile, mute. It was like she was having a seizure.

"Are you okay?" Widman asked her.

She said, "Oh my god."

He asked her again if she was okay, and she said, "I remember."

Everyone froze.

She said, "I remember what that nun did to me."

For one beat, no one moved. Then, Widman recalled, pandemonium broke out. The defense attorneys started yelling and screaming. What had Widman done? Had he given her money? Widman himself was frantic. "What are you talking about?" he asked her.

The woman said that she remembered what the nun had done to everyone, and that she had done it to her, too.

Widman could hardly believe it. Right there, in the middle of her deposition, one of the defense witnesses had recovered a memory of her own abuse at St. Joseph's. The woman continued to serve as a witness—but for the plaintiffs.

WIDMAN ALWAYS DID HIS BEST TO BE GENTLE AND FRIENDLY WITH DEFENSE witnesses, all the better to put them at ease. That mattered less with the male clergy than the former residents. The priests on the witness list were comfortable being questioned—not usually defensive, mostly resolute—and they gave nothing up.

Father Foster, once orphanage chaplain and a monsignor by the time of the litigation, waited until the end of his deposition, then chided Widman for failing to ask him about one important topic. Taking control of the moment, he delivered an impassioned speech praising all the sacrifices the nuns had made. The women had worked so hard, laboring through the day and sitting up till dawn with the children if they were sick. Some of the ladies were quite intelligent, and if they made mistakes, it was understandable; even the poor girls, who were right off the farm in Quebec and didn't have a lot of skills and training, sacrificed their own families to do the work of the orphanage. Sure, bad things may have happened, but wasn't that true in any family? Didn't everyone flounder sometimes? Goodness knows, the children at St. Joseph's weren't easy to deal with. Some of them had even been offenders, and yet the Sisters of Providence had given everything they had and asked for nothing in return.

Most of the priests were comfortable giving as little information as possible. Foster had been chattier. He reminisced about the five-mile hikes he and other seminarians led to Burlington Airport, where a truck would meet them and the orphanage boys with gallon cans of Kool-Aid, and all the field days with baseball and boxing and basketball. "We put on a minstrel show," he said. "And the kids did everything, the singing and they were the end men, and they loved that, and there was a competition to see who got their face blackened."

In an aside with Widman about the little donation cards that school children would slot coins into, Foster explained that the money had gone to China, where people sold their babies. "You bought babies," he said. "You know, the Chinese used to sell their babies. So these missionaries would buy the babies with the money these kids would get and baptize them." He didn't say what happened to the babies after the priests baptized them.

Widman asked Foster about a layman who had been accused of abuse. He had heard a story about a nun walking into a room in the 1950s and finding the man in the act of abusing a boy. She had apparently reported the incident to Foster, who then got rid of the man. It was true, Foster said, though he didn't have much to add. The man had actually been torturing the boy. There were large red marks on his behind. But as was their practice, the priest explained, they simply told the man to leave. The police weren't called and no one else was told.

Though he was considerably more voluble than most of the priests Widman deposed, Foster was equally vague in response to questions that he reasonably should have known the answer to, such as whether Father Devoy,

Foster's immediate predecessor, died at the orphanage or whether any children attended his funeral. The question arose because, in addition to the unique murder stories, many plaintiffs said they remembered the terrible prospect of having to kiss or touch an old man in a red robe laid out in a coffin in the chapel at the orphanage. Some believed that man had been Devoy.

For much of the litigation, the stories about deaths at St. Joseph's had swirled in a cloud but refused to coalesce into anything that Widman could work with. But the Devoy story was strong. Many witnesses had independently raised it. Yet for a long time, no witness for the defense—no nun, priest, doctor, or layperson—could remember that anyone had ever died at St. Joseph's. Most of them said there had never been any funerals at the orphanage at all, or at least none they could remember.

The same hazy cloud settled over many topics, like whether nuns had been down to the beach, or whether the orphanage had owned a boat. Which adults lived at the orphanage? Who visited in the summers? Who was legally responsible for the lay workers? Who did anyone ultimately report to?

Widman asked Foster in particular about Sally Dale's tea party. She had named Foster as an abuser and had separately described one of the brothers as pretty, blond-haired, and blue-eyed. Foster fit the bill. He was the only seminarian who was consistently at the orphanage from 1945 through 1950, when Sally swam at the lake.

Widman asked him about spending time at the lake with the children. Had Brother Foster and another brother put on the tea party?

There were times when they might have been at the lake at the same time as the girls, Foster said. "But they were always separate. The boys went every day. The girls might have gone twice a week."

"So there were times—" Widman began.

"They were completely separated," said Foster.

When Widman asked Foster if he'd ever seen any sign of sexual abuse at the orphanage, the priest said firmly, "Never, ever. Never, I never had the least indication of that, either as a chaplain or as a seminarian." In his view, it would have been an impossibility.

Another of Widman's plaintiffs claimed that Foster had abused her, too. She said that one day when she was slipping through the gym to the boys' side to find her brother, Foster caught her and forced her to give him oral sex behind the curtains in the gym. But the story didn't go anywhere. It was an isolated case; the woman was the only other resident to directly accuse Foster, and his response was unequivocal. "Absolutely not," he said. "Unconditionally no."

WIDMAN PUT BISHOP KENNETH ANGELL OF THE DIOCESE OF BURLINGTON on the stand. The bishop's attorneys told Widman that he didn't need to swear him in. He was a bishop, after all.

If anybody needed to be sworn in, Widman said, it was the bishop. The answer did not endear him to either the bishop or his attorneys, but that was fine with Widman. He wasn't there to make friends.

Angell's presence struck Widman as primarily perfunctory and bureaucratic. He didn't seem to have real concern about the victims. He gave Widman the company line. He arrived in Burlington in 1992 to replace Bishop Marshall, just before the first orphanage case went to court. He could reasonably claim that he had no firsthand knowledge of the institution.

Widman pressed him about documents in the diocese's possession that could validate the orphan's stories, but the bishop was noncommittal on whether such documents might exist. He said he didn't think there was anything that would help.

Widman pushed about what Angell might have learned since he had been in the office. But Angell said he didn't know of any written allegations of abuse by the nuns in the 1940s and the 1950s.

Eventually Widman obtained a number of the priest's personnel files from the diocese through subpoena, and the bishop's view was seemingly confirmed. There was nothing in them; they were useless. It was hard to believe the files of men who had been with the church for decades could be so thin. Some of them contained just one page.

The bishop said that the abuse of children was immoral and abhorrent. As a young seminarian, he had been trained to watch out for it, he said. Not that there was a need for that. "It was unthinkable really in my time," he said, "that such things would happen."

WIDMAN AND MORRIS DEPOSED ABOUT TWENTY NUNS. MANY HAD BEEN born in Canada and were raised speaking French. They joined the Sisters of Providence when they were teenagers or young women, and from the time they entered, lived out vows of poverty, chastity, and obedience, wearing the same uniform and eating the same food. They talked about their pride in their long years of service, being moved around for most of their lives. Some taught at local Catholic day schools or another orphanage in Chicago, or returned to the motherhouse in Montreal. They were moved around inside the orphanage as well. They looked after children for a while, then spent months in the kitchen, then worked in the sisters' dining room.

For the most part, the emotional tenor of the nuns' depositions was muted. The women were tentative, polite, careful. Some were more confident in their English than others. Mostly, they didn't remember any abuse or recall seeing any discipline. Or remember anything a child might have done that would have required discipline. Or recall hearing about a priest at St. Joseph's having sexual relations with a child. Or hearing of a priest anywhere having sexual relations with a child. Or remember any deaths, accidental or otherwise.

Out of all the depositions I read or watched, only two nuns said they could remember a child's death, a boy who drowned in 1961.

Sister Donat, once a Mother Superior, acknowledged that the children did have to sleep with their hands on the pillow. It made supervision easier, she said.

Sister Ladislas said she saw Sister Leontine slap a child in the face. Sister Miles said that she herself once slapped a child in the face. She felt terrible about it. Another used the paddle, but never on the skin, and only when it was badly needed. Others said the rules of the order strictly forbade physical discipline.

Sister Louis Hector—the nun that Walter Coltey said had burned him on the groin—was a notable exception. She was hypertense and grouchy, and she didn't seem to care who thought so.

Sister Fernande de Grace, the brown-haired, kind, librarian type, described herself as a "lively nun" who liked singing and playing guitar with the children. She had no problems, she said, and she had never touched a child in anger. Widman asked her about records he had obtained showing that she had hit a boy so hard he was sent to the hospital. The documents stated that she had been sent away the same day to receive counseling from a psychiatrist in Montreal—a significant response, considering that corporal punishment for children was not uncommon in that era.

Once confronted, Sister Fernande de Grace admitted to the incident. She had only hit the boy on the bottom, the hips, and the right arm, she said, and she had used a paddle, and it had only lasted a few minutes, and he hadn't cried at all. The doctor's notes from the time reported that the boy was beaten with a paddle and a belt, but Sister Fernande de Grace said that was wrong. It was only the paddle. She regretted it.

WHEN I SPOKE TO WIDMAN ABOUT THE NUNS' DEFENSE, I HAD BEEN ESPE-cially curious to learn if he remembered the story of Julienne Sauvageau. She grew up in a family with ten other children in Montreal and left school at sixteen to join the order. She worked for years at the Sisters of Providence orphanage in Chicago and only came to St. Joseph's in Vermont in 1970.

When Sauvageau was deposed in the 1990s, she said that most of the children didn't want to be in the orphanage. It wasn't their home. But she and her sisters had tried their best. They had games and toys, and sometimes when the children came back from time with their family, they were upset and dirty so the nuns would give them a hot meal.

Sauvageau said she had never disciplined or punished a child in any way, and she had never seen or heard about any other sisters hitting any of the children. She did not have a temper, and there was no demerit system, and she had never called a child stupid or lazy. She did recall one girl who wore a back brace and who used to cry a lot, but Sauvageau said that she had explained to the girl that it was for her own good.

It was put to Sauvageau that another orphan claimed to have seen her bouncing a girl in a back brace off the walls of the bathroom because she hadn't cleaned them properly. She said that that was not true.

What about a girl called Cindy Delisle? Had Sauvageau had any problems with a girl called Delisle at the orphanage?

No, Sauvageau said, she hadn't.

At the time, Delisle was the only girl at St. Joseph's who was Black. Had there been difficulties with Delisle being the only person of color there?

Sauvageau didn't think so. When asked if Delisle was well integrated with the rest of the girls, Sauvageau said yes.

Did she have any physical or mental problems? Did she have a weight problem? No, Sauvageau said. Delisle was the same as the other girls.

It wasn't Widman who had interviewed Sister Julienne Sauvageau that day. She had been deposed by a local attorney, so Widman couldn't tell me about the mood in the room, or the look on Sauvageau's face, or how she held herself when she said things like, "I never did punish the children. Not in any way."

I searched in vain for a video of Sauvageau's deposition. In the end, all I could find was an incomplete transcript. On the page, she came across as sincere, even calm, and her English inflected with French-Canadian was charming. ("Was French your first language?" "Yes. French, yes. Canada French.")

The attorney asked Sauvageau if she thought that Delisle had smelled bad? "Well, you know," she said, "the colored people, I guess they have a certain smell, but—." Sauvageau explained that she had noticed the smell but never mentioned it to Delisle.

I sought out Delisle even before I came across Sauvageau's transcript. She was the only child I had heard of whose family took her out of the orphanage *because* she was abused. It was some time before she was willing to sit and talk with me.

Delisle hadn't been part of the litigation, except for writing an affidavit on behalf of another girl, and she hadn't taken any settlement money. They weren't going to buy her childhood, she told me.

She was at St. Joseph's from 1966 to 1973, and when she left at thirteen, she was shocked to find that the kids in her new public school were being taught math she had learned years before. That was the good bit about the nuns. They were strict with academics, she said. The bad bit was everything else, especially being the only Black child at the orphanage. I asked Delisle what it had been like. "It bites!" she said. "It bites."

In front of everyone, the nuns would tell Delisle that she was fat, and that she smelled and needed to take more showers. They withheld dessert, but only from her. Sister Julienne was the worst. She had been "a hitter," who used to carry a big orange plastic bat around. She often woke Delisle up with a beating for some infraction that Delisle had committed but not even noticed.

"You would just get woken up . . . whup . . . bang . . . and you knew . . . up!" The assaults were so frequent and awful that other girls who were in the room told me they couldn't fall asleep until the inevitable beating was over. If it wasn't Sister Julienne hitting Delisle, it was another nun on Sister Julienne's orders.

Sometimes Delisle provoked the nuns without even really knowing why. She would find herself losing control of her body in the classroom or drifting away and paying no attention, and the nuns would tell her she was having a fit or daydreaming again. Much later a doctor told her she had epilepsy.

Delisle was tired a lot of the time, too. Most nights, Eva DuPaul came to pull her out of bed and tell her it was time to clean up, so Delisle would drag herself to the bathroom and start working through every stall, and then every sink, scrubbing for hours, often with a toothbrush. After she fell back into bed, she would have to get up again an hour or two later.

Delisle's aunt, who was also her legal guardian, once gave Delisle a hair styling product. Delisle hated it, so she gave it to another girl. Sister Julienne saw what Delisle had done, and for some reason became enraged. All the girls had just come back from swimming, and Delisle was wearing shorts and still wet when Sister Julienne started to beat her. Sister Julienne hit Delisle so hard that the skin on the back of her legs split, and by the time she was finished, Delisle had bruises wrapped around each leg.

The next day, Delisle went to her aunt's house for the weekend for an outdoor family event, as planned. She argued with her aunt about not wanting to wear shorts. In the end, her aunt insisted, and Delisle headed to the bathroom to change. When she came out with her severely bruised legs exposed, her aunt "went nuts." She called the diocese and told them Delisle was never coming back. She sent someone else to pick up Delisle's belongings.

Delisle barely thought about the orphanage again until years later. She had just moved house and odd things had started happening. The smell of the basement reminded her of the orphanage, and she began to sense weird flashes of movement, like an explosive hand movement at the back of her head. When that happened, time would shift, and suddenly she would find that she was nine years old again. Delisle thought that she was going crazy, so she went to a psychologist, who told her she was not going mad. She was having flashbacks.

Delisle remembered being pushed out the back of the orphanage in the winter with other children, door locked behind them until dinner, none dressed properly for the bitterly cold weather. They huddled in doorways and against any object they could find to get away from the brutal wind roaring up off the lake. She remembered photographs at Christmas of all the children opening presents, and once the photographs were done, all the presents were taken away, never to be seen again. She remembered being ushered into the auditorium year after year for a grand event, a visiting troupe of performers on the stage, wearing blackface, singing and dancing, doing the cakewalk, and Delisle the only Black person in crowd. It felt very strange. "I was just a little kid," she said. Later, looking back, she thought, *Oh my God! What were they doing?*

Many years after Delisle left the orphanage, she was shopping in a local supermarket with her husband, when suddenly in the aisle before her was a smiling old lady who wrapped her arms around Delisle in an affectionate greeting. It was Sister Julienne Sauvageau, acting as if she were one of Delisle's long-lost loving parents.

Delisle introduced her daughter and husband, and the women had what must have looked like a pleasant catch-up. Delisle must have seemed okay, even more or less happy, but on the inside she had turned to stone.

When the conversation was over, Delisle simply left her shopping in the cart in the aisle and walked away. She told her husband she was done, and she left the store. Her husband came after her and asked what the heck was going on. He said that she had turned three shades of pale.

Once the shock wore off, Delisle was furious—what made that woman think she could address her like that? She fumed, but in the end, she told me she was angrier at herself. She felt like, once more, she had given her power away to Sister Julienne.

Other women who had been at the orphanage with Delisle told me they vividly remembered Sauvageau picking on her, especially the humiliating comments about her weight and cleanliness, and Sauvageau's orange bat.

When Sister Julienne Sauvageau was deposed, the plaintiff's attorney asked her if she had once bumped into Delisle at a local supermarket.

"Oh yes," Sauvageau said. "She was very happy. I was happy to see her, too."

CHAPTER 15

I<small>N DOWNTOWN</small> B<small>URLINGTON, IN A REDBRICK BUILDING WITH LARGE</small> arched windows, Sally Dale sat surrounded by men in the conference room of Jack Sartore, the lawyer for the Sisters of Providence.

It was November 6, the first day of her deposition. At least four more would follow. Robert Widman sat on her right. Her husband was nearby.

"He kind of hit, and—" Sally placed both hands palm-down before her. Her right hand slapped down on the left, rebounded a little, then landed again.

For just a moment, the room was still. "Bounced?" one of the many lawyers present asked. "Well, I guess you'd call it—it was a bounce," she replied. "And then he laid still."

Sally, speaking under oath, started again. "The first thing I saw was looking up, hearing the crash of the window, and then him going down, but my eyes were still glued." She pointed up at where the broken window would have been and then she pointed at her own face and drew circles around it. "That habit thing, whatever it is, that they wear, stuck out like a sore thumb."

A nun was standing at the window, Sally said. She straightened her arms out in front of her, palms up. "But her hands were like that."

Sally figured the nun pushed the boy through the window in 1944 or so, because she was moving to the big girls' dormitory that day, and girls usually moved when they were six.

Sally pointed out her scars for the camera. Here was where Sister Blanche pressed the iron into her hand. Here was the broken left pinkie from when a nun, later named as Sister Claire, kicked her legs out from under her on the ice. Here were the scars from when she slapped out the fire on her snow pants. Here was the problem with her ribs that made it so hard to breathe, from where the nuns pounded her with their fists. Here was where this wrist was broken, and then this wrist; here was the elbow and the scar on the knuckles on both hands, and here was the knee that was fractured.

Did she believe the knee was fractured? Sartore asked.

"Well, why would they have put on that white thing?" she asked.

"Is that a yes?" Sartore asked.

Sartore, a big man whose build had been shaped by long years of competitive swimming, knew how to pace himself. He was cool and implacable for almost the entire nineteen hours. As an interviewer, he was masterful, switching directions deftly and often, so that plaintiffs could not be certain of his next move. Pressing Sally for facts one minute, he would pivot and ask her to speculate on strange, impossible questions about the nature of time and the workings of memory, before pulling back and lightening up, pausing a beat, then circling back around to prod and probe.

Sally was neither combative nor timid, occasionally overly literal, often simply polite: "No, sir." "Yes, sir." "No, sir, not really."

She wept at the memory of how her hands got injured when Sister Dominick ordered her to clean the kitchen's big mixing machine while it was still on and the paddles were whipping around, and again when Sartore asked her about her mother, who came to the orphanage only once that Sally could remember.

When the litigation began, Sally filled out a questionnaire for the defense, and in response to a question about whether she had been sexually abused, she responded no. By the time the deposition began, her answer was yes. Sartore zeroed in.

It wasn't that her story had changed, Sally explained, it was that she hadn't known what sexual abuse was. She just knew that she didn't like it.

Did Sally think of it as abuse back when she was at the orphanage, Sartore asked? No, she didn't. Back then she had not even heard that term. She didn't know what it was.

The brothers who abused her down at the lake—how did she know they were actually men rather than boys from the other side of the orphanage? She held up her fingers several inches apart, unmistakably suggesting the length of a penis. Then she broke off in a goofy laugh, looking around at Widman. "What can I say?"

But she cried when Sartore circled back to what happened in the nuns' bedrooms. She spoke about it as a child would. When the nun made Sally put her hands down below, the nun got "sweaty or wet or something."

When Sartore pushed Sally for more and more detail, it became too much, and she thumped the table, declaring, "I got to take a break."

ONE OF THE REWARDS FOR BEING GOOD AT THE ORPHANAGE WAS AN ACTIVity that the sisters had called "serving God." God, at least for those purposes, turned out to be Father Devoy, the resident chaplain.

Devoy had his own rooms and dining table, where he was often joined by seminarians. Sally told Sartore that when she was quite little, she had done her very best to be good for a whole week, and for once it had worked. At the end of the week, Sally got to go into God's rooms. She set his table and took in his food and placed it on the table before him.

She managed to put the plate down without spilling anything, but when she turned to walk away, Father Devoy put his hand under her skirt. He yanked down her underpants, touched her backside, and told her that she had cute buns. The next time he tried it, the headstrong girl spilled the soup in his lap.

Sartore sounded outraged at Sally's inference. "Will you agree with me that a grown man, an elderly man, a priest, could pinch the behind of a little girl without it constituting, quote, sexual abuse?"

Sally declined the invitation to undermine herself. "I can't answer it," she said. "Because I thought if you swore, okay, it is like a form of sexual harassment."

Sartore wouldn't let go. "What was there, if anything, about the way Father Devoy grabbed your behind that constituted sexual abuse?"

"Because he used to say how cute they were," Sally explained. "You have cute little buns," she recalled him saying.

"And so for a sixty- or seventy-year-old man to pinch a little girl's bottom and say you have cute buns, you now consider that sexual abuse?" Sartore asked.

"I don't know as I say sexual abuse," Sally said. "I just don't see it was right, whether it was an old man, young man, to do that to a child."

As Sartore and Sally moved from past to present and back again, small, vivid memories punctuated the larger grim narratives. Sally recalled, still mystified, that sometimes in summer a nun would wake the children in the middle of the night because an ice cream truck had come by with leftovers. The children had to eat as much as they could, right there on the spot, because there was nowhere at St. Joseph's to keep it.

Sally had brought some old photos. Here was Sally herself with Sister Peter, the Mother Superior, and Bishop Brady. Here was Doris Jacob in the kindergarten; it must have been around 1945. Here was Sally in a tiny cap and gown that Irene made for kindergarten graduation.

Sally's face creased with deep pain when she spoke of the boy who was pushed from the window, the boy who disappeared into the lake, and the boy burned beyond recognition.

As she was recalling the boy who fell, Sally was asked, "How do you know it's not your imagination?"

Crying, she replied, "Because I still see the boy."

Later Sartore asked Sally if she thought the boy was dead.

"Yes, I did."

"Do you think he was dead today?"

"Yes, sir."

Sartore asked if the boy came out the window head or feet first.

"Body first," Sally said.

About the incident with Patricia Carbonneau and Sister Priscille, he asked how had Sally forgotten that day.

"I don't know if it was just hidden back there," Sally said, pointing to the back of her head, "and I refused to bring anything out until that final day at the reunion."

Sally had been inconsistent in some of her claims. She said her memories came flooding back at the reunion, but she had given an interview detailing some of the abuses a year before that. When shown a report of that interview in her deposition, she said she had no recollection of giving it. In one interview she described herself as older when she kissed the boy in the coffin. But in another interview, she said she was around four or six when she kissed a boy in a coffin. It wasn't clear if there were one or two coffin incidents. Sally said at first that Sister Jane of the Rosary was the only nun she really liked. Later she described Sister Jane as an oppressive and abusive figure. And in her account of the day that one adult after another was told to beat Sally but could not bring themselves to do it, some details and a name varied.

But Anna Salter, an expert in the psychology of predators and victims, testified that it was common for a child to be attached to someone who abused them, and that what tended to come through with recovered memories was the overall narrative—not necessarily all the specific details. Even if all the details were remembered, the victim might be too embarrassed to describe them.

Nonetheless, Sartore kept returning to the workings of memory. Had Sally consciously pushed her memories away? No, Sally said, she didn't think it was conscious. "It's just I didn't want to hurt anymore."

Could Sally have called up her memory of seeing the boy who fell if someone had asked her about it before the reunion?

Sally wasn't sure. She explained many times that she didn't think her memories had ever been entirely lost, but maybe they were hidden. Or buried.

On the fourth hour of the third day of the deposition, when Sartore came back around to the boy, he sounded a bit bored by the events.

"Did you ever see a nun try to push anyone else out a window besides, uh, the little boy you saw when, uh, in 1944 and this episode with, uh"—Sartore sighed—"Patricia, in 1948 or 1949?"

But he was fully engaged when he asked Sally what allowed her to summon those recollections. How did Sally remember events that she said she forgot fifty years ago? Could she now recall any memories she had between

1961 and 1994 of events that she said occurred in the early 1940s? When did her memories become repressed? When did she forget the thing she forgot?

I SPENT A LONG TIME TRYING UNSUCCESSFULLY TO TALK WITH LAWYERS DAvid Borsykowsky, Bill O'Brien, and Jack Sartore. Borsykowsky gave a quick and unequivocal no and didn't respond to written questions I sent him. I tried to contact O'Brien in many ways, but he remained elusive; months after I called, he was disbarred and jailed for defrauding a client. Sartore initially said no, but after my repeated attempts to connect, he invited me to his office in downtown Burlington, which I visited on an autumn day. The man whose voice I recognized so well from the deposition tapes came sweeping into the reception area, guiding me into his wood-paneled office and offering me a seat at a green table. I had wanted to meet him for a long time, and now here he was—Darth Vader, in business casual.

Sixteen years after the St. Joseph's case, he remained a formidable presence, big and broad-shouldered, polite but unsmiling.

Responding to my inquiries, he paused occasionally, kept his face perfectly expressionless, and fixed me with a very long, uncomfortable stare. As the seconds ticked by, I felt I was being sized up, inspected for weak spots.

Sartore grew up outside of New York City and moved to Vermont in 1971, when there were still French-language traffic signs in Winooski. He had just been made managing partner at his law firm when the St. Joseph's cases came to him "out of the blue." One of his partners had a connection with the Canadian counsel for the Sisters of Providence in Montreal, and put the Sisters in touch with Sartore. He said it became a time of "extreme busyness," as St. Joseph's was the largest set of cases he had handled. When the litigation began, he would sit in his office late at night, just trying to get a handle on who was who: "It was a huge cast of characters."

He found the names particularly difficult. The women who had been at the orphanage had often changed their names once or twice by marriage. Some had changed their first and last names because they wanted to distance themselves from who they had been as a child. "Sometimes they just called themselves different things at different times. Sometimes brothers and sisters would have different names."

When the plaintiffs named the nuns, Sartore said, their names were often incorrectly cited, too. He said that the sisters "were wholly depersonalized from the other side. They were referred to as 'a nun.' A big nun came and hit me and did this or that. An ugly nun did that. Well, who knows how these kids experienced it. The nuns wore habits at that time. They were wholly obscured but their face." Later when I referred to the nuns, he scolded me: "Don't say the nuns, say the sisters."

He was wary when Widman turned up from out of town. "You don't know this guy. You don't know if he is a real asshole, you don't know if he is a good guy. It turned out he was a good guy, but he was a pretty aggressive lawyer and he knew which end was up. He knew how to handle a case."

Sartore traveled to Montreal to interview the sisters. Over the course of five or six years, he said, he interviewed nearly a hundred. "They're old gals," he said. "And they sit there with faces that are just beaming and they have memories that are astonishing. *I was ordained on June 12, 1947, and I had my jubilee on June 12, 1997,* and *I arrived at St. Joseph's Orphanage on July 31, 1953.*

"They told me they were praying for me," he said.

The nuns acted with dignity and grace, Sartore said, and they earned his respect. He asked them if they remembered children, like Sally Dale. "Oh, Sally Dale, she was such a sweet young girl," they would say to him.

Sartore then explained to the nuns what Sally was saying. "They'd say, 'Ooh, oh my goodness.'"

The depositions were a chance to learn the facts. "What happened physically? What happened psychologically? What happened sexually?" Sartore asked. "Whose hands were where, when? And who was there and who knew it?"

They were also, he said, a dry run for the combat of a trial, a chance to see how witnesses would present, whether they would cry, whether they seemed genuine.

He compared it to a medical examination. "The doctor probes physically. Does this hurt? He or she is going to have some response, but your professional response is, okay, that's stopped, that hurts, we'll move on. We've got information there, and we'll move on."

I asked about Sally Dale's nineteen-hour deposition, which I had found excruciating to watch. She had been so stoic, yet I could see his poking and prodding caused her a great deal of pain. I wondered if he had reservations about going after her that hard? "My job isn't to be her therapist," he said.

Sartore told me that in the 1990s he used to joke that the best witness you could have in a trial was two nuns. That aside, a trial was not what he wanted. Trials are arduous and taxing, with no upside and many possible downsides. He said, "A trial is an alternative to war."

Speaking of Widman, he said, "You've got a guy who knows where the money is and can get it. He tries these cases . . . gets a couple or three witnesses going against the rulings that we're seeking . . . all of a sudden this thing spirals out of control, and you're looking at big money. Your job is to protect the money."

In that event, he said, "You haven't done the sisters any good by putting them through this and you've allowed a terrible outcome to occur."

"They'll tell you all the time that it is a search for the truth," he concluded. "It's not a search for the truth, it's a search for an outcome."

As for the stories about dead children, Sartore said, "We accounted for every death of a child in the city of Burlington for years, to our satisfaction." Sartore thought some children at St. Joseph's died in the 1918 influenza epidemic. For any death after that, he said, "You could find a hospital record or you could find a death certificate. Did we ultimately go to the lengths of verifying those documentations? No. But there was rational documentation."

When he read Sally's account of the boy who was pushed out the window, he drove to the orphanage to look around and try to make sense of the details. While he was there, he bumped into Bill O'Brien, the attorney for the diocese, who said he was doing the same thing.

He speculated about the nun who Sally saw. "Could she have thrown somebody out of a window, and the body was spirited off and dismembered and people danced around the fire and who knows? You can spin any kind of speculation out of that." But as far as he was concerned, the stories of dead children were for the most part just stories, the result of "kids talking to each other late at night, or in the hallways, or whatever it may have been. Things that grew up to be the mythology of the organization." Sally's falling boy story struck him, he said, as "hallucinatory."

About four years after the St. Joseph's case ended, the *Boston Globe* Spotlight team exposed how the church covered up the sexual abuse of children in Boston, igniting a worldwide scandal and critically damaging the moral stature of the Catholic Church. I wanted to know how Sartore's convictions had fared since then. Surely it had become more possible to imagine that a nun might say something untrue? Maybe, he said.

And that was as far as he would go. Sartore stayed rigorously professional. If he had any doubts, it was clear he would not share them. "I'm not going to relitigate the case," he said.

MUCH OF SALLY DALE'S CASE RESTED ON THE IDEA OF MEMORY, WHICH HAD become a bone of contention in many court cases, most of which involved the Catholic Church. Bessel van der Kolk, Widman's expert witness on trauma from Harvard, explained that for more than a hundred years, psychologists and psychiatrists working with victims of trauma had documented buried memories that burst into the open, as well as troubling gaps where time had seemingly vanished. Cases of amnesia and recovered memory had been observed in war veterans, survivors of natural disasters, and survivors of the Holocaust. Repressed memory was commonplace in such traumatic circumstances. He spoke about soldiers who told the exact same stories in 1989 that they had in 1946. He cited a study of child victims whose recovered memories were later validated in interviews with the predators who molested them.

It was obvious to Van der Kolk that Sally Dale and the other residents were severely traumatized. The stories from St. Joseph's reminded him of people tortured by the police in Argentina. Even though he saw four or five hundred new cases of trauma every year, including victims of rape, war, disaster, and surgery gone wrong, he had never met a group of people who hated themselves as much as Burlington's orphans, he said. One of the men he interviewed was the most withdrawn, schizoid personality he had ever come across. He was not even depressed, said Van der Kolk. He was an empty shell.

The pain of the St. Joseph's victims didn't only come from the original trauma, Van der Kolk said. It was magnified because they had been silenced. "People who go through a public tragedy like the Oklahoma City bombing get a lot of acknowledgement and sympathy," he said. Likewise, the victims of an incident like Oklahoma City don't get told it was their fault. But Sally and her fellow residents were doubly hurt—by the original abuse and then by the litigation.

The defense, for their part, kept trying to reframe the impact of the orphanage on the former residents' lives. When the impact of trauma could not be denied, they asked if the residents' traumas may have come from their family life before or after the orphanage. Here, Sally Dale could serve as the control to a terrible experiment: it wasn't possible to attribute her trauma to her family of origin or foster home experiences after she left the orphanage because almost everything that shaped her from the age of two had come from the nuns.

What about Sally's abusive first husband? Could her trauma have come from her time with him? Anna Salter, Widman's expert on predators and victims, said it was hard to pull those things apart. Often one thing led to the other, meaning that what happened at a younger age was not only traumatic by itself, but could also make victims more vulnerable to later trauma.

Across all the depositions of the plaintiffs and the psychologists, the defense returned again and again to the idea that the orphans did not have a firm grasp of reality. They asked one man if he had ever abused his children. He said no.

"Not that you remember," the defense attorney replied.

Wasn't it the case that trauma was overdiagnosed in society these days? No, said Van der Kolk, it was underdiagnosed.

Surely tough discipline was typical of the era when the victims lived at the orphanage? This was not a case of tough discipline, the experts explained. What happened at St. Joseph's had more in common with systematic torture than an education system. Prisoners of war testified to the ubiquity of mock executions—like hanging someone upside down outside a window or sitting them in an electric chair and telling them they are going to fry. It was a known torture technique, said Salter.

What if the orphans had somehow, intentionally or unintentionally, created a fiction about their time at the orphanage when they met at the reunion? Salter was baffled by the suggestion that a group of middle-aged people could conspire so expertly to create such convincing backstories, complete with long histories of telltale symptoms, all to support a group fantasy. Where was the research, she asked, to suggest that anything like that was possible?

What about Sally and the deaths? Could she have made them up? "You would have to ask instead," Van der Kolk said, "what made her such a creative genius that she could make up those stories and cry and whimper, and basically be a better actress than Meryl Streep."

Salter believed that Sally Dale saw a boy thrown from a window, and she had no doubt that Sally was made to kiss a burned boy in a coffin.

Likewise, Van der Kolk found no reason to doubt Sally's story about the falling boy. He could not say whether the boy died, as he had not been there. But he had been particularly struck by the way that Sally spoke about the boy plopping down to the ground and bouncing up again. Children tended not to manufacture that kind of visceral detail.

Borsykowsky wanted to know if Sally could have taken two things that terrified her at two different times and woven them together. Could she, for example, have seen a boy pushed by a nun, and separately a falling boy who landed on the ground with a bounce? Could she take a memory of a boy plopping down with another memory of a sister in a window? Could she have seen a coffin in one incident and heard a nun's voice telling her that something was going to happen to her in another? Could she have once seen a corpse and another time have been made to kiss a boy?

It was conceivable, Van der Kolk said, but he did not believe that Sally had done so.

Borsykowsky put it to Van der Kolk that memories can shift over time. Van der Kolk agreed, yes, memories could be subject to later interpretation, he said. Still, he did not believe Sally was suggestive; rather, she was "one stubborn little girl."

THE DEFENSE LAWYERS KEPT ASKING THE ORPHANAGE SURVIVORS, *How many times?*

It was hard enough for some of them to tell Widman about the abuse they suffered. Most of them found it excruciating to sit in front of a bunch of fancy church lawyers and tell the story again and again as it was subjected to hostile scrutiny.

Dale Greene was thirty-nine when he gave his deposition in 1997. Handsome and smart, he had been a gifted athlete and a top altar boy at St. Joseph's in the early 1970s. But now he was recovering from a stroke, which his doctor attributed to stress. He needed a cane to walk.

Greene told the attorneys that a counselor assaulted him in his bed in the boys' dorm at St. Joseph's probably ten or twenty times. He remembered anxiously lying in bed, always worrying, never knowing which boy the counselor would pick in that night's dread-laden lottery. How many times did the counselor crawl into bed with you? Give us a number. Over what period of time did the assaults occur? he was asked. Greene found it hard to say.

"Did this happen once a week to you?" they asked.

"To me," said Greene, "I'd say it was more than once a week."

"Was it twice a week?"

"I'm not sure."

"But you think it was more than once a week?"

"Yeah," said Greene.

"At least once a week he'd come in to you and want this done?"

"Yeah," said Greene. The defense paused, lingered over another detail, and then returned to the counting.

"So you think he came in once a week and tried something with you. Might have happened ten or twenty times to you. Is that accurate? Is that your best recollection today?"

"Yeah, he came in at least once a week, probably more," said Greene.

"So if he did it ten or twenty times, this would have lasted ten or twenty weeks, is that right?"

"It lasted for a year or two," said Greene.

"Then why only ten or twenty times if he came in every week?" defense asked.

"Because—it might have been more."

"Well, I'm just trying to—"

Greene became exasperated.

"I'm not sure how many times it was," he said. "I know that it went on for a few years. As far as a count goes, I'm not sure. I have no idea. I mean, all I remember is he would abuse us, he'd abuse somebody every night, every single night that he worked." Greene added, "And as far as how often, I don't know. But it went on for years."

"Do you think," defense replied, "it was for you personally a weekly event?"

THE DEFENSE ATTORNEYS ASKED PLAINTIFFS TO ESTIMATE THE FREQUENCY of their rape or molestation by day, by week, by year, and then overall. Then they would get the plaintiff to compare the estimates and count—so if it was x times a week, that would be y times in total, right? Inevitably, the figures didn't quite add up.

David Borsykowsky asked one plaintiff, who said she was digitally raped by a nun, how far the nun had penetrated her. "Do you know whether she inserted her finger more than a half inch into your vagina?" he asked. The woman had been five years old at the time. She couldn't tell. "Do you know whether she inserted her finger more than a quarter inch into your vagina?" Borsykowsky asked.

Defense attorneys asked plaintiffs if they had personally done anything to provoke being punched in the face. They also asked if plaintiffs could precisely define sexual abuse. ("Do you have any belief that you were sexually abused at the orphanage?" one man was asked. "And what is that based on?" "It's based on getting hit in the penis with a paddle," he replied.) Sometimes the defense questioned whether a plaintiff had even been at the orphanage, until the plaintiff provided proof.

Given all that, it was remarkable how few times plaintiffs blew up in anger. When Greene said that he had seen all kinds of stuff, the defense asked him: "You say all kinds of stuff, but can you tell me what kind of stuff you saw?"

Greene struggled to explain. "It's years and years and years ago," he said. "You don't understand, it's—this is fucking frustrating."

"Well, I understand that it is," said the defense.

"No, you don't understand how it is," said Greene, "because you're standing there with a fucking tie on, had a fucking easy life all your life, and I'm the one that went through all the bullshit in that fucking place, and now you're sitting here telling me what to do and asking me questions and telling me to be direct and bullshit."

A lawyer asked Greene if it was true that "the first time you ever thought about any of these things, any of the abuse you suffered at the orphanage, was when you found out you could get some money for it?"

Greene had had enough. He launched into the most impassioned soliloquy of the entire litigation. He spoke for himself, and, whether he realized, for everyone else in his position.

I answered it already, the same question. I found out—when I found out that there was a lawsuit, I wanted to be involved in it. Not because I was going to get money. Because I was going to finally straighten out shit that happened to me all my life and should not have never happened. No one should ever have to get put in a child center and get beat on by some women that they don't even know. No one should have to be molested by some frickin' counselor. And there's not a frickin' court in America that would ever say that it's true that you should. And you guys here are representing people that you know nothing about.

I mean, you weren't there. I was there; it wasn't pretty, it wasn't a fun place to be. You got beat on every day for something as simple as talking to your own sister; and for a nine- or ten-year-old little kid, that's not right. Now I'm not trying to be a hard-ass here, and if I'm disrespectful, I'm sorry. But you guys are upsetting me.

I mean, you don't understand what it was like there. And it wasn't a nice place. And if you guys really—if you knew anything about it, if you have kids that were there, or if you had any relatives that were there, you wouldn't be on that side of the table right now.

I mean, you don't understand, it wasn't—it was a nightmare. Now it wasn't a total nightmare; there were some good times there, too. Don't get me wrong. The schooling was pretty good, and we got to do a lot of stuff as far as sports and shit like that. But I mean, overall it sucked—excuse me.

We got beat all the time for stupid stuff. We—you had to do things you didn't want to do, you were unable to do. Or you had to eat things a normal person would not eat; but because they served it, you had to eat it. And if you didn't eat it, you got beat. And if you got sick and threw up, you had to even eat your own puke.

Now that ain't right.

The single irreducible idea at the core of many of the moves made by the defense was how monstrous—how unthinkable—the stories of the plaintiffs were. The citizens of Burlington found them hard to contemplate, as did the priests, the nuns, and the staff assisting with the depositions. The defense produced psychiatrists and psychologists who echoed the view as a professional stance.

One psychiatrist employed as an expert witness for the defense said as much when he wrote an assessment of one plaintiff's claims. The plaintiff said that she was abused multiple times in her life. She had been abused before and after she went to the orphanage, and she had been abused at the orphanage.

The psychiatrist took at face value the woman's story of abuse before and after her time at St. Joseph's, but he was skeptical about the abuse she said she had suffered at the orphanage. In fact, he wrote that when he considered her claims along with the claims of the other plaintiffs, the overwhelming number of abuse stories was concerning. The sheer volume of complaints was, for him, a strike against everyone's credibility.

He wrote that the cumulative reports of former residents "are so extraordinary that one would have to imagine a massive conspiracy by an institution full of sadistic predators."

He meant, of course, that the story was so packed with extraordinary details that it strained credulity. Really, he was stating the logical conclusion of the evidence presented in the litigation: For more than a hundred years, the people of Vermont had, knowingly or unknowingly, sent their children in reverent offering to the huge house on the hill outside of town. The obedient servants of the Catholic God took the children in, and in return, behind the locked doors of St. Joseph's Orphanage, out of their own pain and misery, and with all their immense entitlement, they devoured them.

CHAPTER 16

IT WAS HAPPENING IN CANADA, TOO. IN MONTREAL, LESS THAN A HUN-
dred miles north of Burlington, former residents of Catholic orphanages
were coming forward to say that as long ago as the 1930s and as recently as
1965, they had been subjected to the most extraordinary abuse.

Just as with St. Joseph's, the movement had started with a few voices and
grown quickly. Just as with St. Joseph's, the local press ran articles about the
allegations, with protestations from people defending the nuns. Just as with
St. Joseph's, one of the orders of nuns who ran the orphanages was the Sisters of Providence. Widman went to Montreal to learn more.

He found his way to an office building where the ex-orphans of Catholic
French Canada had rented a room. "There was this whole wall covered in
newspaper articles and pictures and chronologies," he said later. "It was obvious that this was their war room."

The group called themselves the Children of Duplessis. Widman was
greeted by a man who spoke only French. Widman only knew enough to
understand *Parlez-vous français?*, but the man gave Widman a book that had
been written about the group and tried his best to tell his story. Widman got
the basics. "Basically, these nuns shit on these kids to make money and the
government went along with it."

The group called themselves the Children of Duplessis after Maurice Duplessis, Quebec's conservative Catholic premier for much of the 1940s and 1950s. Duplessis observed that orphanages received only half the amount for each resident that hospitals and mental institutions received. So, working with the church and the medical establishment of the province, he engineered a plan to reclassify thousands of abandoned children as mentally deficient.

As many as five thousand children who had previously shown normal intelligence were diagnosed as "mentally handicapped." Their education ceased, and they were pulled out of the orphanages and moved into mental institutions. Often it was the defiant ones who were shipped off first. Some orphanages were simply rebranded as asylums, and untrained nuns were elevated to the status of psychiatric nurses, armed not just with wooden paddles but with all the tools for treating mental illness in the 1950s, including restraints and intravenous sedatives. Here, the nuns, who Widman surmised were mostly French Canadian farm girls, managed wards instead of dormitories.

The lives of former residents of these institutions looked like the lives of the former residents of St. Joseph's in Burlington. Many struggled with addiction and other damage. Some died by suicide. But those who survived were ready for a fight. For Widman, the connections between the groups were stark. The Sisters of Providence, who ran St. Joseph's Orphanage in Burlington, also ran an orphanage in Montreal called Mount Providence. That institution had been rebranded as a hospital in 1955. Sisters were assigned to both Mount Providence and St. Joseph's of Burlington from the same motherhouse. Some women had worked in both institutions. Widman had read entries in the St. Joseph's *Chronicles*, where a party of visiting nuns from Mount Providence had been welcomed to St. Joseph's.

The Children of Duplessis were considerably more organized than Widman's plaintiffs in Vermont, partly because there were many more of them, at least five thousand and possibly as many as six thousand. They weren't all from homes run by the Sisters of Providence. They had spent time in orphanages run by the Sisters of Mercy, the Grey Nuns of Montreal, the Sisters of Charity, the Little Franciscans, and two orders of seminarians. They filed more than a hundred criminal complaints against individual members of religious orders. The attorney for the Children of Duplessis filed a class-action petition asking for more than $1 billion in compensation.

In 1945, when seven-year-old Alice Quinton arrived at Saint-Julien, in Saint-Ferdinand-d'Halifax, a patient approached her and said her name was Alice as well. Saint-Julien, the other Alice explained, would "tame" Quinton. "You will be corrected," she said.

Quinton had been housed in various institutions from birth, starting with the D'Youville Nursery, run by the Sisters of Providence. She was then sent to the Maison Sainte-Domitille, a convent. At seven years old, she and eleven other orphans were taken to Saint-Julien Hospital, an enormous institution with more than a thousand patients, originally founded by nuns as a girls' school and a hospice.

Not long after she arrived at Saint-Julien, Quinton started to cry. She had seen a woman walking around who "was not normal." Quinton asked the nun if she could go back to Laval-des-Rapides, where the Maison Sainte-Domitille was. "If you behave, you'll be treated well," the nun said.

The daily routine at Saint-Julien was as miserable as the one at St. Joseph's in Burlington. Mlle Madeleine Grimard—a woman described as a boarder who seemed to occupy a role similar to that of Eva and Irene at St. Joseph's—would comb each girls' hair in the morning and then, to punctuate the task, slap them in the face.

When Quinton wet the bed, she was beaten with the struts of a chair. Later in class, which took place inside the buildings at Saint-Julien, Sister Ste. Edith chose a child to take to the front of the room, making her bend over, pull up her skirt, and pull down her underpants. Then the nun strapped her bare skin in front of everyone with the leather strap she kept in her pocket.

Once when Quinton was about eight years old, she accidentally hit some iron bars and made them clang as she was leaving a school catechism contest. Sister Ste. Edith ordered her to run a cold bath and change into her white *jaquette*, a garment that was open on the sides, which the girls normally wore in the bath. Once she was in the freezing water, the nun made Quinton bend over, and then scrubbed her back hard with a floor brush. She left the stunned Quinton in the bath in terrible pain, not knowing what to do. A few minutes later the nun returned to tell her to get dressed.

The worst beating Quinton experienced occurred the day she was told she could not attend an event she had been looking forward to. In front of a supervisor, Mlle Marie Dumas, the headstrong Quinton vowed angrily that she would get revenge. In response, Dumas beat her with a broomstick with such unhinged aggression that Quinton felt something break in the base of her spine. For years afterward, she had difficulty sitting and walking. She received no treatment despite being in a hospital. It wasn't until she was twenty-nine that Quinton had a needed operation so she could use her back normally again.

Quinton witnessed as much abuse as she received. She saw girls beaten with chains and little children's heads thrust under cold water. She once saw a young woman who was mentally disabled in a way she did not understand bite another child. The biter was then taken to a doctor, who removed all her teeth.

Quinton especially remembered a little girl of about five years old named Michelle, who was often bruised and marked from beatings. It was said that Michelle had a brain tumor. She arrived at Saint-Julien able to talk, but by the end she could not. "She was between the sky and the earth," Quinton said later. Michelle cried out in pain at night and was beaten all the time, and she died before she turned six years old. Quinton thought it was as likely that the beatings killed the child as the tumor.

QUINTON WAS PUT IN A STRAITJACKET WHEN SHE WAS AROUND THIRTEEN and Sister St. Paul Antoine caught her talking. Quinton had to put on the straitjacket and lie face down on a bed as the nun beat her with a variety of tools at hand: a jump rope, a metal-tipped ventilation cord, a thick board.

That day was nothing compared to the time Sister Marie Dolores made Quinton put on the straitjacket along with a pillowcase over her head. The nun tied Quinton to a bed frame with no mattress and a pot beneath her to catch her excrement. She left her there for three weeks. Each day, one of the asylum's other residents came in to inexpertly feed Quinton. The woman brought her soup, meat, potatoes, tea, and dessert—all mixed into one bizarre brew.

In the 1990s, Quinton sketched the room as viewed from the side and from above: the bed with its metal slats and the pot beneath it, and the front and the back of the straitjacket, showing how the arms were crossed over in the front and detailing the jacket's high collar and corset-like threading on the back.

The caption "Les instruments de torture" was written in beautiful cursive script on the picture of the straitjacket. Quinton also drew a crude needle captioned "Piqûre Largactil" (Largactil shot). The range of sedatives that the sisters of Saint-Julien administered by injection included chlorpromazine, an antipsychotic marketed under the brand names Largactil and Thorazine. It was most familiar to Americans Widman's age for its excessive use as depicted in the film *One Flew Over the Cuckoo's Nest*.

Quinton was given Largactil and other sedative injections by the nuns starting at the age of fifteen. Sister Ste. Thérèse du Crucifix was one of the nuns she remembered injecting it. When she was twenty-one, she was punished for laughing in chapel when one of the other girls passed gas. She was placed in a cell for a week, receiving Largactil and sedative shots from Sister Marie Julie.

When she was older, the nuns sent Quinton to work with some of Saint-Julien's medical staff. She assisted with daily tasks. One of her jobs was holding down the legs of patients who were receiving electroshock therapy.

After Quinton left Saint-Julien, she did not share much about her experiences with anyone until she met historian Pauline Gill. They first met in 1989 after Alice had appeared on a popular Quebec television program with other Duplessis orphans. Gill interviewed other former residents and featured Quinton's story in *Les Enfants de Duplessis*, the book given to Widman by one of the Children of Duplessis in Montreal.

After the book was published, Quinton made a statement to the police. At one point during the investigation, Quinton asked the police whether Sister Marie Dolores was dead. They said yes, and she began to weep. "They asked why I cried," she said later. "It was because I really wanted to take her to court."

Like Sally Dale, Quinton had a solid recall of the girls she was incarcerated with, like Augustine Noël and Marian Kelly. She could pick them out in a photo and tell their stories. She also remembered many of the nuns, especially the ones who made her life most miserable.

On a cold October day in 2017, I drove to Longueuil, Quebec, two or three miles across the St. Lawrence River from Montreal. Alice Quinton lived there in a small, white brick apartment building on a street full of them. A tiny lady with a gruff but animated demeanor, she beckoned me and a translator in to sit at the kitchen table, which she spent the next few hours covering with photos and documents from her own research.

Quinton showed me a group photo of nuns and pointed at Sister Ste. Jeanne Gabrielle, third row, second from the left. "That was the one who killed the five-year-old," she said. She pointed at Sister Marie Dolores, the one who made Quinton put on a straitjacket with a pillowcase over her head. "Look at her face, that old cow!"

She showed me the pictures she sketched of the time she was tied down in the straightjacket. There she was, a stick figure, strapped down to a bed frame, with tangled, black, shocked hair and an incongruous little smile— the kind children automatically place on any face they draw—but with two dashed-line tear tracks coming out of each eye.

Like Sally Dale, Quinton spent most of her young life inside the orphanage system. She lived at Saint-Julien until she was twenty-four years old. She still struggled with many health issues because of the beatings she received. She needed dialysis three or four times a week. Yet she was full of an intense energy, fragile but dogged.

I asked her if anyone she knew at Saint-Julien had died. She told me about the little girl with the brain tumor, Michelle, and about another friend, Evelyne Richard, an orphan-turned-deficient who was especially defiant. Sometimes when a nun walked by, Richard would yell, "Big ass!" to scandalize the nun. Richard died in the hospital wing at Saint-Julien when she was eighteen years old.

Everyone knew, Quinton said, that Sister Ste. Thérèse du Crucifix dosed Richard with Largactil. The day after Richard died, Quinton, who was sixteen at the time and working in the medical wing of the hospital, put her ear against a door and overheard medical staff talking about Richard's autopsy. Quinton said that she heard a doctor and a nurse say that the girl was given too much Largactil and her heart swelled to twice its normal size before giving out.

Quinton remembered watching as a big black hearse, *Morgue Fleury* printed on the side, drove up to the hospital cold room to take her friend's body away. The same car glided up and away often. Quebec's government, generous with the church as always, allowed the nuns to sell the unclaimed bodies of orphans and others to medical schools for ten dollars per body.

PAULINE GILL, THE AUTHOR OF *LES ENFANTS DE DUPLESSIS*, REMAINS THE world expert on the Canadian orphans. She and I spoke on the phone with the help of a translator. Gill spoke little English and I understood only a little French, but even I could understand Gill's response when the translator asked if she'd ever heard of children being placed in electric chairs.

I had first come across stories about the use of electricity as a means of punishment and control when I met Hilly, who lived at the Ballarat Orphanage in 1950s Victoria, Australia. I had touched the patches on his skull where no hair grew, where pads attached by nuns delivered some kind of electric shock. Sally Dale had spoken about being strapped into a chair designed to hold people down, and being told she was going to "fry"—the word Sister James Mary used. Even though I'd already heard Hilly's story, I still found Sally's chair story hard to take in, and I couldn't find any corroboration from other residents of St. Joseph's despite asking many of them about it. Then Kimberly Murray, who led Canada's Missing Children Project, told me about the journey of discovery her team had taken with stories about electric chairs in Canadian institutions. It was one of those tales that, if you didn't know it was true, might seem farfetched, the stuff of horror stories. Still, I asked the translator to ask Gill if she had heard of such things.

Gill responded, "*Ah oui, la chaise électrique!*" She knew all about them.

When I asked Gill about murder at orphanages, she said that in the 1990s after she gave a reading of her book, a woman who identified herself as a former nun spoke to her and confirmed that what she had written was surely true. She also said that she knew where the bodies of children at one of the orphanages had been buried. Gill would not give me the name of the woman. She suspected that she was dead by now.

FOR WIDMAN, THE PARALLELS BETWEEN THE ORPHANS OF MONTREAL AND the orphans of Vermont weren't just in the past. What was happening publicly in Quebec was instantly recognizable to him. Thousands of people in Montreal had stepped forward with specific, detailed stories, most of which aligned tightly, but the nuns of the province, through a spokesperson, had responded by speaking of *their* hurt.

The clergy of Montreal said that the children's stories simply could not have happened, and that they were essentially unbelievable. The only concession they made was to suggest that individual incidents may have occurred.

In Burlington, a spokesperson for the diocese had said, "Now we can only pray that our country will take a look at the plank in its own eye and join us in the journey to wholeness." In Montreal, a professor of Quebec history told a reporter for the *New York Times* that, really, all of "Quebec society was to blame."

Widman also heard that a similar story was unfolding in Ireland. Adults who had grown up in residential schools run by Christian Brothers and different orders of nuns were starting to discuss how they had been assaulted, raped, and brutalized. The police were investigating some of the cases, but the Irish government did not seem to be doing much. The statute of limitations ruled out the pursuit of criminal charges, yet it seemed clear that a storm was building there, too.

FOR WIDMAN, THE STORIES FROM AROUND THE WORLD AFFIRMED THAT everywhere they had gone, the nuns were often "really bad people." It made him angry. As hard as he had been working, he started working harder, and it was becoming a problem. He was spending a lot of money and making none. Geoff Morris found a few good cases to keep them going, but he had begun to worry about the choice they made.

Widman was concerned for Cynthia, too. The couple had two daughters, but both had grown up and left home by then. Now that he was away from home for one and two weeks at a time, he left Cynthia alone and he came home exhausted. On Valentine's Day he brought home a Labrador retriever.

Long before he started going to Burlington, Widman had come to terms with the idea that to be successful in the law, he—an introvert—had to fake extroversion. He was quite good at it, but it was tiring, and now the St. Joseph's experience had become so onerous, there was little relief.

The weather got warmer and life in Burlington was a bit easier, but still, he worked, heading back to Burlington on July fourth. As Widman sat alone on the plane, far above the Independence Day celebrations, he looked out the window and watched the fireworks blossom, streaming colored light in the mountain towns below. He felt a little depressed and a little alone, but it wasn't a problem. There was too much to do.

CHAPTER 17

IT WAS ALSO HAPPENING IN ALBANY, BARELY 150 MILES FROM ST. JOSEPH'S, in the neighboring state of New York, with survivors of St. Colman's Home. Incredibly, the two cases played out in isolation, yet the similarities were extraordinary: The claims of former orphans—and counterclaims of church supporters—tore each community apart. Day after day, the stories made the front page of each local paper, but not a single person I interviewed from either case seemed to know about the other. When Widman first arrived in Burlington, the orphanage system was a bewildering new world. Because the Vermont Sisters of Providence had a connection to Canada, he followed the trail to Montreal and the scope of the story widened considerably. But he didn't once realize that the same dark secrets were erupting in another small American city nearby.

I came across the Albany story when I first began to look for evidence of orphanages in the US. The parallel history of each place was a powerful example of the system's ability to obscure itself. Both orphanages were nodes in the same network. The children who lived there suffered the same kind of abuse. There were disturbing stories about disappearances and deaths. Yet the absence of national media, the lack of scholarly interest, and the power of the church to squash and intimidate, all combined to isolate the survivors from each other and allow the system to persist. Given how networked and hierarchical the Catholic Church is, I found it hard to imagine that people in the hierarchy weren't tracking both cases at the same time.

The Albany case had one crucial difference, though: orphanage survivors had managed to get a police investigation.

The fight began with Bill Bonneau, who had seen his three younger brothers hauled off to St. Colman's back in the 1950s. Only two made it out. The youngest, Gilbert, died at the home when he was eight. Doctors said it was meningitis.

But in 1978, more than two decades later, Bill got a phone call from a stranger who said her name was Marion Maynard. Bill told me that Maynard had an urgent message about Gilbert: Before Gilbert died, he was beaten by a nun. Maynard said the nun, Sister Fidelia, had savagely hit Gilbert in the head and he died the next day. For decades, Maynard had kept the story to herself, but she happened to see the nun in Troy, New York. The sighting triggered a sudden, intense recognition. Filled with a sense of great urgency, she raced home and started to work her way through all the Bonneaus in the phone book.

Bill was so stunned by the call that, though he did his best to scribble down everything Maynard was saying, he didn't think to ask her for a contact number. She ended the conversation promising to call him back. But days and then weeks and years came and went, and the call never came.

ONE OF BILL'S BROTHERS PLACED AN AD IN THE LOCAL NEWSPAPER BEGGING Marion Maynard, or anyone who knew her, to get in touch with him. The ad ran for many years. It wasn't until 1995 that a local reporter named Dan Lynch noticed the ad and wondered if it came with a story.

The article Lynch wrote for the *Times Union* in Albany asked, "Did Gilbert die after a beating by a nun? Was he a victim of a brutal institutional environment? Has the truth surrounding his death been covered up?" Lynch went on a tour of the orphanage led by a nun named Sister Regina. When he asked her about allegations of abuse and murder, she asked him to look her in the eye. The claimants were liars, she said.

Lynch's article ignited the same kind of angry, distressed chaos that was engulfing Burlington at the same time. Dozens of former St. Colman's residents came forward to talk about their time at the orphanage. One spoke of being thrown down concrete stairs, one was forced to kneel for hours in punishment, one was hung upside down in the laundry chute, and one was forced to eat his own vomit. Multiple witnesses said a nun stood on a boy's leg until it broke. One heard it break.

The same nuns were identified by separate people. Some said a nun named Sister Regina pushed children down the stairs and took them into the laundry to assault them in private. Long after the children had grown up, they still remembered that when she hit them, Sister Regina would say, "Look me in the eyes."

A laywoman known as Kitty who had lived at the orphanage and helped with the children was described by a number of survivors. Like Irene and Eva at St. Joseph's, Kitty had entered St. Colman's in the early twentieth century with many siblings when she was very young. One by one, her brothers and sisters left, but Kitty stayed until old age. One man remembered her because she used to hang him upside down in the third-floor laundry chute threatening to drop him.

Devout local Catholics fought about the stories on talk radio and called newspapers and police to say that the people reporting abuse were themselves crazy. Some were confident that even though they themselves had never been to St. Colman's, the nuns would never have behaved like that. A few said that they spent some time at St. Colman's and all the nuns were lovely. One described her time there as a pajama party.

In Burlington, only a few hours away, Robert Widman was hearing the same thing. To him, it seemed that whenever he put forward a witness who said St. Joseph's Orphanage was hell, the opposition put forward a witness who said it was like Disneyland. It didn't take long for the sprawling mess to come down to one person's word against another.

As in Burlington, a support group for survivors formed. They occasionally protested in front of St. Colman's, which still housed the Sisters of the Presentation of the Blessed Virgin Mary and some children in their care. A reaction group called Pro Colman formed and protested against the protestors.

Neither the order that ran the home, nor the bishop, nor any representative of the Diocese of Albany made a formal apology or acknowledged the stories of the St. Colman's survivors group. The attorney for the Sisters of the Presentation said that nothing worse than a smack on the wrist or "the fanny" had ever taken place, a claim that was so obviously implausible, he later qualified it by adding that, of course, there had been discipline appropriate for the time.

Bishop Howard Hubbard ran a permanent letter in the newspapers asking for victims of sexual abuse to get in touch to allow the church to begin a healing process. Members of the St. Colman's survivors group said they left messages on an answering machine at the advertised number, but they were never called back.

The police opened an investigation into Gilbert Bonneau's death, but it quickly expanded to include the deaths of an older man with a disability who, according to an aid worker, was deprived of oxygen by the nuns; Andrew Reyda, an orphan who, according to a witness, was savagely beaten by a nun shortly before he died in 1943; and Mark Longale, who died in 1963.

Longale's mother said a doctor at the hospital initially said her son had injuries consistent with a bad blow or fall. But she was told later that the autopsy showed that her son's appendix had burst. In the 1990s, a witness told the police that she had seen a nun brutally beat the boy days before he died.

In 2018, a lawyer for St. Colman's told me the institution declined to comment.

St. Colman's was situated on Watervliet Street in the suburb of Colonie, in Albany County, New York, which meant that the investigation was handled by the small Colonie Police Department. When I asked journalist Dan Lynch about it, he said that their response had basically been, "What the hell do we do with this?"

Seen through the survivors' eyes, Albany was part of an ancient empire whose agents ran their own gulag on the outskirts of town. Behind the doors of their prison, they tortured the weakest, loneliest, and smallest members of society, while they were respected, even adored, as paragons of charity when they were out and about in the world. There was nothing in the training, culture, or history of small-town American policing that prepared officers to see the institution that way or to identify systematic atrocities. In addition, at the time, Bishop Hubbard had enormous political power.

The police called the Bonneaus and expressed their displeasure that the family had gone to the newspaper before calling them. In truth, it was the newspaper that had gone to the Bonneaus, and up to that point, the police had ignored the Bonneaus altogether. But now the police felt obliged to engage.

The Colonie police assigned one officer, Michael Ruede, to the case of St. Colman's. He found it almost impossible to get a handle on the task. No one he knew had dealt with anything like the case of the orphanage children and the nuns, and he was also expected to continue working on his other cases at the same time. Ruede was not Catholic, but his colleagues began to tease him that now he was going to go to hell.

Ruede collected almost seventy separate witness statements, an enormous undertaking. The district attorney also forwarded complaints to him, like a letter from a man whose three children were abused at St. Colman's. But unlike other investigations he'd run, no one from the DA's office really followed up with him on the witness statements he collected. Communication from the district attorney was not encouraging.

"Perhaps you have heard of this and I would suggest that you call him," wrote the district attorney, forwarding a letter from the father of three victims. "I am sure you will be receiving accurate factual information (!) from him."

Ruede felt for the people he interviewed. They were clearly distressed. He liked the Bonneaus and found their story compelling. But it bothered him that the St. Colman's case had become a social movement. By the time he got to some of the complainants, they had been meeting up at candlelit vigils outside St. Colman's or swapping stories in each other's living rooms. That was not how crime investigation was supposed to work. Witnesses should be kept separate. How else could he be sure that they hadn't gotten together and concocted a story, or at the very least, put ideas and names and even incidents in one another's heads?

More than a few of the St. Colman's survivors were addicts and seemed unstable to him. Legally, Ruede didn't think the investigation made a lot of sense either. The statute of limitations was surely going to rule out most of the complaints. Nonetheless, he took the case seriously.

I VISITED RUEDE IN FLORIDA IN 2016, AND WE SAT IN HIS PRETTY, GREEN backyard next to a small pool with an upright concrete alligator. He was retired from the police force and spent half the year in New York and half in Florida. He told me the St. Colman's case was the craziest thing he had worked on in his life.

If the allegations from St. Colman's came to light now, he said, there would be a whole team on it, with police and investigators from the district attorney's office. But at the time, he told me, "It was a hot potato" that no one wanted to touch. "It was an evil thing."

Back then, Ruede said, he sincerely believed that the Catholic Church would not lie. It wasn't until after the revelations about priest sex abuse in Boston in 2002 and the wave of exposure that swept the country afterward that he knew he had been wrong.

It wasn't that he didn't believe the witnesses at the time, Ruede explained, but it was hard to know what to do with their stories. They were just so far outside anything he had experienced.

He crossed a personal Rubicon when an older man he knew pulled him aside and quietly revealed that he had spent some time at St. Colman's as a child. Ruede had worked for the man before joining the police force and had always admired him. Ruede's former boss told him that when he was at St. Colman's, the nuns beat him every night before bed.

But even without his friend's testimony, it was clear to Ruede that something was very wrong with the childcare institution. When he visited the little old nuns of St. Colman's and sat down with them and their lawyer, he said, the experience reminded him of sitting down with a group of regular criminals. Ruede sat across from Sister Regina, the nun who had taken Dan Lynch on a tour through the building and said all the former residents were liars. When Ruede described the allegations to her, she reared back in her seat with her hands across her heart, gasping as if in shock. "Totally phony!" Ruede told me. It was clear to him that he was going to get nothing from the nuns. They just blew smoke, he said.

The Sisters of the Presentation wouldn't provide any documents, so Ruede got a subpoena and obtained Gilbert's bedside notes, which he found curious. It appeared that the number of days Gilbert had spent in the infirmary had been altered. Ruede obtained Gilbert's death certificate. It said the cause of death was meningitis.

Ruede looked for Marion Maynard and Sister Fidelia, too. He never found Maynard, but Sister Fidelia, it turned out, was once called Beatrice Dwyer. She left the order around the time of Gilbert's death and moved away from Albany. She died in the 1980s.

Ruede asked the sisters for a list of all the residents of the home in the 1950s, but they said they no longer had that information. Instead, the Mother Superior put together a list of residents for Ruede from her memory. She also signed a statutory declaration that no one named Marion Maynard had ever been an orphan or lived at St. Colman's.

Technically, the Mother Superior's statement may have been true. Yet when Ruede interviewed Sister Fidelia's own brother, the man told Ruede that he remembered a girl named Marion Maynard who had once worked in the kitchen with his sister.

Ruede had long ago archived his case notes, but I brought a copy with me to Florida. As he and I worked our way through them, many carried different connotations for him now that, post-Spotlight, he knew the Catholic Church lied.

Among the case notes was information about the death of Andrew Reyda. Under subpoena, the Sisters of the Presentation had produced notes, a contemporaneous log of Reyda's illness and death. But Ruede's old records contained two versions, and they were different.

It appeared that one had been used as a draft for the other—there were handwritten mark-ups on one version that were written directly into the other. But the edited version had been presented as if it were the original unedited log of Reyda's final few days.

Overall, the second set of notes gave a much more defensive account of the death. When Ruede compared the two sets of diary pages, he observed how hard the writer had strained to construct a picture of the nuns' innocence.

THE INVESTIGATION INTO THE DEATH OF GILBERT BONNEAU DRAGGED ON through the tenures of two different district attorneys. Three forensic pathologists considered the case, one of whom examined Bonneau's remains, which the family paid to have exhumed after more than forty years. All three pathologists agreed that there was no evidence that the boy died of meningitis. Finally, a witness who lived all the way in Florida came forward to say that he'd seen Bonneau in the infirmary bloody and screaming—and that he kept screaming until one of the nuns straddled him, put a pillow over his face, and smothered him. The man said he knew nothing about the investigation. He had simply posted a message to an internet forum that Bill Bonneau's brother stumbled across.

Despite all the evidence that the Bonneaus had managed to gather, the district attorney never brought any charges, and no lawyer ever agreed to take the case and file a civil suit. Having failed to find the justice they sought, the family made a formal request, asking if at least the cause of death on Bonneau's death certificate could be changed from meningitis to unknown, in keeping with the three pathologists' reports. The request was denied.

Many glaring anomalies in Bonneau's case were never cleared up. For example, Bill Bonneau was at the hospital the night his brother Gilbert died, and no one could explain to him why, if Gilbert died of an infectious disease, he had a bandage wrapped around his head.

CHAPTER 18

I N BURLINGTON, THE DEFENSE FOUGHT EVERYTHING WIDMAN THREW AT them. This was not surprising. Across the US in the 1990s, an increasing number of dioceses were fighting sex abuse cases, mostly to do with the assaults of parish priests. A few years earlier, the Archdiocese of Philadelphia countersued a boy's parents for failing to discover—and thus do anything about—the fact that their local priest was molesting their son.

Lawyers for the church argued that it was prejudicial against *them* to let orphanage plaintiffs join cases in a consolidated trial and ask a jury to hear stories from such a long span of time. They challenged Widman's witnesses, arguing that if they weren't at St. Joseph's at the exact same time as a given plaintiff, their experience wasn't relevant and would prejudice a jury. Sartore, the lawyer for the Sisters of Providence, later described the legal strategy as "traditional divide and conquer."

They fought Widman's attempts to get the letters that Philip White had written on behalf of the survivors who took the initial $5,000 settlements. For Widman, the letters would have been invaluable, practically a database of abuse and abusers. They could have offered proof that residents who didn't even know each other faced the same tortures—and more importantly, that people in charge should have been aware of the problems. (Widman was also unable to get the letters directly from White, for reasons neither lawyer could later recall.)

The defense refused Widman on the grounds that he hadn't filed a specific list of the documents that he wanted. It was another catch-22: The only way Widman could file a specific list of the letters was if the defense told him who the letters had been written for. But they refused.

When the bishop asked former orphans to share their stories with him, the defense argued, he had done so out of compassion. He had given the survivors settlement money out of concern for their well-being. Sharing the letters with Widman, the argument continued, would undermine the bishop's efforts to help the former residents, compromise the church's freedom of religion, and violate the privacy of the people on whose behalf they were written. Ultimately, the lawyers claimed, releasing the letters would harm the former residents' relationship with the church.

Most of all, the defense's strategy in all communications was to emphasize the length of time that had passed since the alleged abuse took place. Long enough, the implication was, that no plaintiff's memory, no matter how compelling, could ever be reliable. Long enough that no allegation, no matter how concrete, could ever be verified.

At every opportunity, the lawyers called the residents' claims, some of which dated back to the 1940s, "ancient," "antediluvian," and "impossibly stale." "Some claims were already stale before the onset of WWII!" proclaimed one memo from Sartore. "Indeed the hackneyed adjective 'stale' is hardly descriptive for these superannuated claims."

It was a smart strategy. For the plaintiffs, it was also a cruel one. From their perspective, their long silence was not an accident; it had been forced on them, a direct result of the abuse they had suffered.

How many times had the children learned the lesson that no one was interested in their pain? If you cry, you cry alone. If you smile, the whole world smiles with you. How many times had they been punished for speaking up, leaving them to conclude that no one in power was interested in their problems? That their pain had no meaning inside or outside the orphanage walls? Again and again, they learned that their firsthand observations were not valid. The nun told Sally she had a vivid imagination. *We are going to have to do something about you, child.*

It took years—decades—for the survivors of St. Joseph's to undo that indoctrination, to learn to trust their own perceptions, to reclaim their own experiences.

WIDMAN'S VICTORIES—FINDING ELAINE BENOIT, THE GIRL WHOSE HAND was burned, connecting Sally Dale's and Patricia Carbonneau's stories, filing all those cases—had been intense and a long time coming. They were also short-lived. The defense found two witnesses who testified that if someone else saw the letter that Philip White sent to the diocese on their behalf a few years earlier, it would have been an invasion of their privacy. The federal judge then ruled that the diocese did not have to hand over the letters to Widman.

The judge allowed that if individual orphans gave permission for the diocese to release their letters, they could. The onus was then on Bill O'Brien, the attorney for the diocese, to write an individual letter to each orphan and ask them.

But the letter the defense wrote asked people to get in touch if they wanted to go public. It shifted the burden of contact onto the letter writers. When the attorneys didn't hear back from any of them, they claimed the non-response was a no.

Widman's local attorneys hounded O'Brien. They wanted to see evidence that the letter to the former residents had been written and sent at all. They got none of it. No former orphans stepped forward to say they would like to share their letters. All the information, all the corroboration, all the validation, and the naming of abusers—all of it would stay in the hands of the church, and no one else could touch it.

At the same time, Widman and his team had been pushing for a joint trial of all plaintiffs. The diocese argued that a jury would be prejudiced by hearing stories from such a long span of time. They said that producing the information would infringe on the church's freedom of religion, and they accused some plaintiffs of being engaged in a politically motivated smear campaign.

They challenged Widman's witnesses, arguing that if the person wasn't at St. Joseph's at the exact same time as the plaintiff, their experience wasn't relevant and would unfairly prejudice a jury. In some cases, when they weren't challenging the right of former residents to speak, they questioned their actual existence. When residents spoke about how awful it was to watch another child be abused but couldn't identify the name of that child, the defense scoffed that the plaintiffs couldn't even name the "phantom victims." Some recalled specific priests, but the diocese said they never had priests with that name.

In the end, the same judge ruled against Widman on the joint trial, too. He was never going to see the letters and there would be no joint trial. Now all of Widman's shattered plaintiffs would have to go it alone against the Catholic Church.

WIDMAN'S TRIPS TO BURLINGTON HAD BEGUN TO BLUR TOGETHER. HE hadn't been home for the Fourth of July, and he planned to be in Vermont for Thanksgiving, too. This time, Cynthia came to stay with him. Amid the stress of Widman's work, separation wasn't good for either of them.

The couple booked a room at the Trapp Family Lodge for a weekend, but as they drove down a country road, they hit a patch of ice. Widman lost control of the car and they landed in a creek. After they emerged from the vehicle—"I'm alright, are you alright?" "Are you alright? I'm alright"— Widman looked up to see an older woman staring down at them from the road. She shook her finger at him, "You were driving too fast." Widman realized the woman was Rosemarie von Trapp.

Widman was inclined to argue, but then took stock of the situation and thought better of it. Von Trapp was up on the road and dry while he and Cynthia were stranded with their car. They carefully climbed out of the creek, and von Trapp drove them to their lodge.

It was rare that Widman took breaks like this; he was usually more worried about his clients' stress levels than his own. Later in the litigation, one deposition required Jack Sartore and the other defense attorneys to visit Sarasota, Florida, so Widman and Cynthia took them to Siesta Key, a barrier island, to go swimming and have dinner. The island was renowned for its pure white sand and clean, inviting water. For once, Widman recalled,

Sartore, who had sternly avoided even minor friendly chitchat, submitted to being social.

It was a lovely day that turned into a beautiful evening. The group sat outdoors and ate a delicious fish dinner, and had a civil discussion about the case.

By that point, Widman had deployed every legal strategy he could. Likewise, the defense had done what they could to pull the stories apart, pull the survivors apart, and pull the history of St. Joseph's to pieces. They tried to make it look like a series of unfortunate, isolated events rather than a pattern.

It had been an epic battle, and the toll on plaintiffs was significant. They needed counseling, support, and enough money to get on with their lives. Widman told Sartore that his plaintiffs deserved an apology and needed to be able to get counseling for the rest of their lives. He asked Sartore if he would settle.

Sartore was one of the best lawyers Widman had faced. Widman figured that if the bishop of Burlington had any real concern for the victims at all, his offer would be a win-win.

But Sartore was immovable. He wouldn't even consider it—there would be no money for therapy and there would be no apology.

The case crawled onward.

By spring of 1998, after the judge ruled that the church did not have to turn over the letters and the survivors could not have a joint trial, things began to fall apart. Now the survivors would have to bring their own cases as individuals. There would be no chance to stack the stories up, to show the similarities, let the patterns emerge, and overwhelm disbelief.

Some plaintiffs dropped their cases. A judge dismissed another five. He ruled against Marilyn Noble because of the statute of limitations. She had written her unpublished memoir, *Orphan Girl No. 58*, in the early 1980s for her children. But the memoir, she told me, was used as evidence that she had been aware for almost two decades of the damage she had suffered. Thus, the law recognized the abuse that caused Noble's suffering, but punished her for not pursuing her abusers sooner.

Sally Dale's case was dismissed too. The judge ruled that the statute of limitations barred her claims of emotional and physical abuse. Most of the memories hadn't come flooding back until the reunion, but over the years, small bits of the larger story had leaked out. Sally once told someone about having been forced to eat vomit. She told someone else that she had been beaten and banished to a terrifying attic. These incidents were enough, the judge said, to have obliged Sally to take legal action at that time or forever lose her chance.

The judge threw out Sally's sexual abuse claims, too—not because of the statute of limitations, but because she could not prove that anyone in power at the orphanage had known what was happening to her. Yes, he conceded, she told a social worker about the seminarians who molested her at the lake, but there were no records to show that her complaint was passed on to any-one who had the authority to investigate it.

It was a blow, but Widman kept fighting. He and the attorneys at Langrock Sperry & Wool were working on a theory they called the "dirty institution."

All along, the church had been arguing that if any abuse had taken place, it would have been the sole responsibility of the individual abuser—not the Mother Superior, not the order of nuns, not Vermont Catholic Charities, and not the diocese. If the victim could not offer proof that they had reported the abuse to someone in authority, then those in authority were not responsible.

Widman's idea was to argue that the sheer scale of abuse made it impos-sible that those in authority did not know. He believed that after hearing story after story after story, any reasonable person would agree. He just had to bring those stories to trial in front of a jury of their peers, in front of "real people," as he put it. Widman planned to appeal the rulings.

The appeal faced long odds. The process could take a year. Some of the plaintiffs were unwell and might die. Others were already coming apart from the stress. And even if they all made it to the courtroom, there were no guarantees that they would win.

Still, a victory for the plaintiffs could have catastrophic effects for the diocese—and for the church as a whole. Widman saw this, even though he didn't know at the time that US bishops had been swapping pedophile priests among parishes and across state lines for decades. The bishops could do the math, though. If a precedent was set, an untold number of cases could follow.

The path ahead had become far riskier for both sides. In the end, Widman said later, he blinked, and they blinked. In early 1999, the defense agreed to settle.

ONCE HE HAD AN AGREEMENT IN PLACE, WIDMAN WENT TO THE PLAIN-tiffs and said, I'm going to tell you what I would tell my daughter or my wife. He said he didn't think it was worth going ahead. They should take some money now while they still had a chance.

A plaintiff named Barbara Hammons figured at least they'd gotten their story into the newspapers, and some people now believed it. But when she got her settlement check and saw the paltry dollar amount, she laughed out loud. She thought about the church and how much money it had, and every cruel, awful, scarring thing the nuns and the priests had done. *Jeez! Could you spare it?* she thought. Hammons said she wasn't allowed to tell me the exact amount—but it wasn't even enough to buy a secondhand car. At least she paid off some of her bills.

Leroy Baker, who had filed a suit with another attorney, got a call to tell him that the church had offered to settle. Baker testified that he had been molested, abused, and emotionally devastated when he was at St. Joseph's, and he was tired and extremely angry with the whole process. He told me he had received a $10,000 settlement and insisted the attorneys give him the money in cash. When they did, he said, he walked three blocks to his old landlord, paid the rent he owed, and headed to the closest bar. The money was gone in a week and a half.

Sally Dale wanted to keep fighting. Having been abandoned at St. Joseph's when she was just two years old, she had been through so much. She was there through the early years, when the nuns treated her like their pet, putting her onstage to sing for everyone. And she was there when they hauled her out of bed in the dark for special private tortures. She was there when she was nine and a loving Vermont family tried, without success, to adopt her, and through her teens, when the nuns told her that she wasn't old enough to leave St. Joseph's and would live there forever.

She was twenty-three when her older sister's husband picked her up and drove her away at last. Of all the orphans who had passed through St. Joseph's wooden doors, Sally had been there longer than most.

She had suffered so much and worked so hard for the lawsuit. She wanted her day in court, however brutal it might be. But there was nothing else to do. She couldn't fight the battle alone.

She said goodbye to Widman and to the others, put her papers in a thick leather briefcase, and went back to her quiet life with her husband in Middletown, Connecticut, baking cookies for the neighborhood children.

MORE THAN ANYTHING ELSE, WHAT THE ST. JOSEPH'S PLAINTIFFS WANTED was recognition: they wanted the world to acknowledge their agony, and to say it should never have happened. What they got instead was a small check, the amount of which was yet another secret.

After the case was settled, Widman headed back to Florida and started to specialize in legal malpractice cases. Morris, his partner, continued to practice personal injury law, and the firm became very successful. Widman also taught an ethics class at the University of Florida Law School. He didn't take abuse cases again.

When I first met him, Morris said, "We made a mistake. He meant financially. "It was a bitch." But of course, emotionally it was awful, too.

Jack Sartore stayed in Burlington and specialized in business law. He has not worked for the Sisters of Providence again.

All the characters in the drama moved on, happily or unhappily, to the next events in their lives—all except the children whose disappearances still haunted the plaintiffs. The boy who was pushed from the window, the boy who went underwater and never came back up, the girl who was thrown down the stairs, poor Mary Clark who did not cry tears, the drowned Marvin Willette, the frozen boy, and the burned boy in the coffin.

THE DEFENSE HAD LEANED HARD ON THE IDEA THAT THE EVENTS IN QUESTION were simply too far in the past—too old to prove or disprove. They were lost to time. I had my own doubts about whether the stories could be properly investigated, let alone verified, after so many intervening decades. Initially, I had trouble believing they could all be true in the first place. Could the nuns have been that indifferent to human life? I asked Widman what he thought on a visit to his Florida home. How could I believe the story of the burned boy? Had he been electrocuted after crawling under a fence? Was he wearing a metal helmet? Had Sally been made to kiss his blackened corpse?

"That is why I didn't take it to trial," Widman said when I expressed my doubts. A jury would have been as skeptical as I was.

He explained that lawyers are "risk managers." The stories of the deaths were weak, supported by very little evidence, certainly not by a body. "You don't try the weak claims," he said, "because the weak claims ruin the strong claims."

In 2018, the orphanage building, repository of all those secrets, was scheduled to be completely gutted and renovated to make way for a new apartment complex, to be called Liberty House. I feared that the passage of time had destroyed the chance to learn about what happened at St. Joseph's, and especially to the children who had gone missing.

But then, after years of accumulating public records, private journals, legal transcripts, and personal interviews, I gained access to a cache of documents Robert Widman never saw.

ACT III

Secret priests tribunal, located at the Hall of the Tribunal, Diocese of Burlington, formerly St. Joseph's Orphanage, North Avenue, Burlington, Vermont, 1981

McSweeney-Willis

P.N. 206/80

DEFINITIVE SENTENCE

In nomine Domini. Amen.

With Pope John Paul II happily reigning in the third year of his pontificate, John A. Marshall being Bishop of Burlington, the Officialis and the four Prosynodal Judges of the Diocese of Burlington meet to hand down the decision in the first instance in the case of the Reverend Alfred Willis, Defendant, a priest of the Diocese of Burlington, summoned before this Tribunal on the motion of the Reverend John R. McSweeney, J.C.L., Promoter of Justice of the Diocese of Burlington. The Judges are the Reverend Bernard F. Depeaux, Praeses, the Reverend Walter D. Miller, J.C.D., Ponens, the Reverend Monsignor Edwin T. Buckley, S.T.D., the Reverend Monsignor Raymond A. Adams and the Reverend Brendan W. Lawlor. The competence of this tribunal is established by reason of the site of certain alleged crimes and by reason of the domicile of the Defendant. The Reverend Monsignor Paul M. Bresnehan, approved by the Ordinary, represented the Reverend Alfred Willis as Procurator-Advocate. The appointed Notary for this case is the Reverend Michel J. St.-Pierre of the Tribunal staff.

. . .

The Tribunal takes cognizance of the Defendant's cooperation in appearing at his summoned hearing, and this at considerable inconvenience to himself. He was polite in manner. He was read a descriptive list of alleged incidents and given the opportunity to reply to each. For the most part, he avoided replying to the specific allegations. However, he did engage in a certain generic defense—contained in the following dialogue excerpted from the hearing (pp. 596–599).

Fr. D. [Judge] I see. Parenthetically Father, uh–it is–it's extremely important not only for you–and it is a very important for you–but it's also important for all of us, for me, for the Church, that as much as possible–if you can–object to these allegations. Now I–I can't say more than that in my position as a judge, but you're under no obligation to be silent if you can contradict any statements. I've used the word very carefully–'allegation'–all the way through here.

Fr. W. [Accused] Um-hum. Again, I–I guess my understanding is that the initial charge when the'a–when we first came together was–uh–in violation of the Sixth Commandment with'a minors.

Fr. D. [Judge] Boys under sixteen.

Fr. W. [Accused] Boys under sixteen. To that, I have pleaded and continue to plead nolo contendere. Many of these related incidents which are alleged, and certainly many of these circumstantial allegations–there's no truth in that. Many of the—the names which you have used—uhm—there is no truth in that. I don't know that it would serve any useful purpose to say 'Well, in this one, I—I plead that there might be a possibility—this one I just throw out'—because I'm still responding to the initial charge. Uh—eh—am I making myself clear?

Fr D. [Judge] Yes, I think so, Father.

. . .

Fr. W. [Accused] Many of those—uh—testifiers—if that's the proper term—I know would be prejudiced against me. For example—um—oh, one woman who has made sexual advances at me and I have refused her. I notice that her son's name is one of the names used and there's no truth in that. Um—homosexual advances by one of the parents of one of the—the children—um—my refusal of his advances might be—and his allegations may be a result of frustrations in that area—I don't know. And I certainly—I don't want to bring his name forth 'cause I'm not charging him with anything. OK? But I think that, just to bring to the attention of the court, there may be other circumstances than—than what actually appeared before you in testimony. Uhm—but at the same time, I'm not trying to use that as an excuse for something that I've become aware of in my own life. And—and I guess that's the tension that I'm—I'm trying to explain.

Fr. D. [Judge] Well, Father, your statement is commendable—uh—and'a it—it betrays—um—modesty on your part but also betrays, I think, a—a charity to people involved here. I'm not sure that your preference to be silent about specific names is in the best interests of the common good of the Christian community involved in the Diocese of Burlington. I'm not—I don't wish to press you however, not in the least. You're entirely

free. And I don't want to encourage you in this fashion saying "Well, these people have accused you specifically and this gives you every right to accuse
them specifically." So that if you persist in not
wishing to name—particularly the two individuals to
whom you've just referred—uh—I have a certain admiration for you for that. That doesn't matter—whether
I admire you or not—but I'm just saying. It's commendable, I should say. On the other hand, I'm not certain
that it would be in the best interests of the common
good for you NOT to be specific. I just say this to you
again, in my efforts to be as honest and thorough
with you as I possibly can be.

. . .

Having availed himself of the opportunity to read the
Acts in their entirety, the Defendant wished to change
neither his plea nor his stance. He did volunteer the ob-
servation that his own unacceptable moral conduct and
social behavior since ordination has been regrettably
abetted by that which he referred to as religious emo-
tionalism rampant in the communities to which he has
been assigned (p. 602).

. . .

> Given at the Hall of the Tribunal
> Diocese of Burlington
> 351 North Avenue
> Burlington, Vermont 05401
> This 19th day of June, 1981.

CHAPTER 19

WHEN WIDMAN OBTAINED THE PERSONNEL FILES OF VERMONT priests through the discovery process, he was disappointed to find the information in them to be meager and of little value. But in the early 2000s, long after the litigation ended and everyone had gone home, a judge ordered the Diocese of Burlington to hand over the personnel files for dozens of priests who had been accused of sexual misconduct. The files that were surrendered then were much, much thicker, and included some of the same priests Widman had investigated.

The files became available in a 2006 case against the Diocese of Burlington brought by Jerry O'Neill, a Vermont lawyer. O'Neill had pushed hard to get the files on behalf of the victim of an abusive priest named Father Edward Paquette. A judge ordered their release, but even then, it was a fight to get full access. Bill O'Brien, who represented the diocese in that case, too, handed over some files but not others, and he unilaterally redacted parts of files, something he was not allowed to do. Eventually, O'Neill got them all, unredacted. Years later he remembered hearing the repeated refrain, "We never expected these files to be ever seen publicly."

Before O'Neill's case went to trial, just as the opening statements were about to be made, the diocese settled with his plaintiff for over $900,000. It was a monumental shift in the landscape. O'Neill said that at the time,

Burlington was the most litigious diocese in the country, trying more cases on a per capita basis than any other US diocese. O'Neill's previous cases had all been settled for relatively small amounts. With this one, he turned the tide against the church.

Critically, the judge also released O'Neill's side from the confidentiality orders that had been imposed upon them, which would have kept the documentation out of public view. In 2016, ten years later, I visited O'Neill to ask if he had come across any priests who had once worked in the orphanage. His path hadn't crossed much with theirs, he said. But he had a set of documents that threw light on the way the diocese worked. He thought I might like to look at them.

The priests' files from the 2006 case included letters from accusers, records from police investigations, a transcript from a secret church tribunal, rehabilitation reports, and a number of the orphanage settlement letters that Widman had fought so hard to get. It was only when I came into possession of them that I began to understand how much information had not been disclosed to Widman and the St. Joseph's survivors, and how much less than the whole truth the Burlington clergy had told under oath. I began to see how much would have been possible—and might still be possible—to prove as fact.

There in the files was Father Foster, once chaplain of St. Joseph's Orphanage and the priest who delivered that spontaneous lecture on the moral purity of the St. Joseph's nuns. For all his eagerness to educate the lawyers, Foster had neglected to disclose one crucial fact: he had recently been sent to the Saint Luke Institute in Maryland, where many priests accused of sexual abuse were "treated."

In a report issued one year after Joseph Barquin first approached the diocese, the Institute reported that Foster had "severe sexual issues" and decades of behavior "unbecoming to a priest." They had advised that Foster, by then almost seventy years old, should have no unsupervised contact with minors. Bishop Angell, who later testified that it was "unthinkable" in his day that a priest might assault a child, was the one who oversaw Foster's case.

This was the first piece of evidence I found in the church's own documents that corroborated the abuse that so many residents of St. Joseph's testified they had endured. But there was so much more.

Saint Luke Institute
because compassion is a gift
<u>CONFIDENTIAL</u>   July 15 1994
Most Reverend Kenneth Angell DD
Bishop of Burlington
Burlington Vermont 05401
RE: Reverend Edward Foster
SLI NO 12959

Dear Bishop Angell:

Thank you for your referral of Father Edward Foster who
is, as you know, a 69-year-old priest from the Diocese of
Burlington, Vermont. Father Foster was referred for evaluation following an accusation from another priest that
Father Foster had sexually abused him when this person
was a minor.

. . .

SUMMARY AND RECOMMENDATIONS: The facts that Father
Foster has presented suggests that he has engaged in
clearly inappropriate behavior with minors, both in the
rubdowns he gave them and sleeping with them in sexually compromising positions. In addition, Father Foster
seems to have had a period of time in his life when he engaged in sexually problematic behavior with at least one
male prostitute and other men he met at gay bars. It seems
likely from this that Father Foster has an important
sexual problem. It is possible that Father Foster has been
unable to discuss the details of these events. It is also
possible that Father Foster, through a combination of
naïveté and with the psychological tendencies discussed
in the psychological testing section, may have allowed
unconscious impulses to control his behavior. This lat-
ter possibility is, in some ways, more alarming. If Father
Foster's behavior was motivated by unconscious impulses,

this behavior could recur without his awareness. The psychological test data suggests that Father Foster has some serious psychological issues and current sexual preoccupations. All this data suggest to us that Father Foster needs substantial psychological treatment for these issues.

. . .

Although we considered recommending residential treatment for Father Foster, we are aware that he has had no outpatient treatment in the past and we are also aware that there are no complaints about his behavior recently. We therefore recommend the following:

1. We recommend that Father Foster begin immediate outpatient treatment that will focus on his sexual issues as well as the personality and psychological issues discussed in this report. At this writing, Father Foster has agreed to begin individual outpatient psychotherapy at Saint Luke Institute.
2. We recommend that Father Foster have no unsupervised contact with minors.
3. We recommend that Father Foster be completely abstinent from alcohol.
4. We recommend that Father Foster begin spiritual direction and find other ways to supplement his spiritual supports.

We believe that Father Foster has many important strengths that will help his treatment. His intellectual strengths, spiritual discipline and motivation to understand his past behavior will all be important assets in his treatment.

In the event that other information becomes available that suggests that Father Foster's difficulties are more severe than we know, the possibility of residential treatment as the only effective treatment for Father Foster remains. At this time, we believe that outpatient treatment will be a sufficient first step in trying to help Father Foster with these issues.

We hope this report is of help to you and to Father Foster. If you have any questions or we could be of other assistance, please do not hesitate to contact us.

In all, I was stunned to discover that at least twelve and as many as seventeen male clergy members who had lived or worked at St. Joseph's or Don Bosco—the connected home for boys on the same grounds as St. Joseph's—had been accused of, or were treated for, the sexual assault of minors. In addition, five laypeople who worked at the orphanage were also accused or convicted of child sexual abuse. And even that wasn't the full tally. There were still more accused priests and laypeople at the Diocese of Burlington summer camps and other local Catholic institutions that St. Joseph's children attended.

Crucially, from 1935 until the orphanage closed in 1974, at least six of St. Joseph's eight resident chaplains—the priests who oversaw the orphanage—had been accused of sexual abuse. Those six—Fathers Foster, Bresnehan, Devoy, Colleret, Savary, and LaRouche—presided over St. Joseph's during most of its final forty years of existence, meaning that during all that time, there were only two years in which the priest in charge of the orphanage did not turn out to be a publicly accused abuser.

The facts about individual priests were stunning, as were the records of their interactions, like the transcript of a 1981 secret priests' tribunal held at 351 North Avenue, the orphanage building that had by then become the diocesan headquarters.

The tribunal had been assembled to determine the guilt of a local priest, Father Alfred Willis, who had been accused of sexual impropriety with children. Priests from the diocesan hierarchy played the roles of judge, prosecutor, and "procurator-advocate," or defense lawyer. With all the pomp of canon law, the men argued a series of claims about the accused. The argumentation was anemic, to say the least. One of the judges began the proceedings by advising the accused that it was extremely important for him—the accused, and for "all of us"—that he object to the allegations. Indeed, Willis counter-accused the parents of the children he had allegedly assaulted, suggesting that their real problem was that he had not responded positively to *their* sexual advances. He refused to name the parents who had allegedly pursued him, though, explaining that *they* weren't on trial. How modest Willis was, observed one of the judges. His reluctance to blame others was commendable.

I recognized the tribunal's procurator-advocate, Willis's defender, Father Paul Bresnehan, as one of the orphanage chaplains, himself accused of sexual abuse during his time at the orphanage. In a letter to the diocese written by Philip White in 1996, one woman reported that Bresnehan forced sexual activity on her when she was eleven, saying that "God was his boss and it was alright." One of the tribunal judges, Father Walter Miller, I learned from the cache, was an accused child rapist. It was he, along with another priest, I later realized, who had been at the orphanage building that fateful day when Joseph Barquin walked in off the street to report that he had once been abused there. Barquin had left that day with the impression that his message would be passed on and that someone would get back to him.

As for Willis, he was defrocked and laicized in 1985, and I found no records that placed him at the orphanage. But the complaints against him were legion. An abuse case brought against him was settled in 2004, and since then, at least six more had been filed.

THE SHEER NUMBER OF PRIESTS IMPLICATED IN SEXUAL ABUSE—SOME OF whom wielded ultimate power inside the walls of the orphanage—was unknown to the plaintiffs in the 1990s, let alone their lawyers and the judges.

Or rather, it was, of course, *known* to the plaintiffs. They had been there when it happened. They told the truth about what they were subjected to, and knew they weren't the only ones.

Take Father Leo Courcy. His file contained complaints from parents and even clergy from other states. In 1994, a letter signed by Bishop Angell acknowledged that Courcy was about to go on trial in New Mexico. The priest had been accused of the sexual abuse of a boy years before. In 1997, documents were produced during the orphanage litigation that identified Courcy as a visitor to the orphanage in 1960 when he was a seminarian. So by then, the diocese knew Courcy was an accused abuser *and* that he had once lived at the orphanage where a large group of people were now claiming that they had been abused.

In fact, Bishop Marshall, Angell's predecessor in the Diocese of Burlington, had known there were problems with Courcy. In the 1970s, when Courcy requested work from Marshall, the bishop asked his vicars and members of the Personnel Board about the priest. They told him that Courcy's history in the diocese included many disturbing stories.

Indeed, Bishop Joyce, Marshall's predecessor, knew it, too. Courcy's personnel file noted a 1959 complaint from Sister Madrin at St. Joseph's Orphanage, addressed to the bishop. The note advised him "to watch Courcy because of abnormal conduct with the boys." That was merely one of the first examples of a long list of documents and correspondence about the priest's mental health and rehab and legal history, much of it occasioned by his disturbing interactions with young boys, and all of it preceding the St. Joseph's litigation, recorded faithfully but not in any way acknowledged by the Diocese of Burlington.

Consider the case of Father William Gallagher. During the orphanage litigation, a former resident reported that Gallagher had raped him at the orphanage in the 1960s. Nothing was done, yet Gallagher's file showed that a representative of the diocese knew in 1987 of assault accusations against him.

What of Father Rouelle? He was deposed during Sally Dale's case when a former resident made an allegation of sexually inappropriate behavior. The boy had been "obese," "erratic," and had a "wild imagination," Rouelle told Widman in 1997. The priest noted that he'd been following the story of the orphanage in the newspaper and thought it was "a bunch of hogwash." But Rouelle's personnel file, never seen by Widman, included one of the letters that Widman had tried so hard to obtain, about another man who grew up at the orphanage and was taken for drives and molested by a man he believed to be Rouelle. Like Foster, Rouelle had been sent to Saint Luke's Institute in 1995, two years before he spoke to Widman. He was accused of sexually abusing a young male relative.

THE CACHE CONTAINED ECHOES OF OTHER EVENTS DESCRIBED BY SURVI-vors of the orphanage, like Katelin Hoffman, who lived at the orphanage in the 1970s and who played a significant role in the 1990s survivors group. During the litigation, Hoffman described seeing a stack of Polaroids of naked children, some of whom she personally recognized, in a drawer in the priest's quarters at the orphanage. She told me about them again in 2016. I believed Hoffman but I wasn't able to find out much more about her account at the time; it appeared to be an isolated event.

Yet as I read through the cache, I was struck by a detail in the file of Father James McShane, who served in Vermont for more than thirty years. In the mid-1970s, staff members at Camp Holy Cross said they found sexually explicit slides of children in McShane's cabin. They recognized one of them as a boy from the camp. The images were taken to Bishop Marshall, who, they said, berated them for looking inside the priest's cabin and took possession of the images, saying he would deal with them.

McShane was not the only priest in the Diocese of Burlington who was alleged to have used or created child pornography. Walter Miller, secret judge of the secret Willis tribunal, stonewaller of Joseph Barquin, and chancellor of the diocese, was accused by two men who were installing a modem in his house in 2001. The men told authorities they saw child pornography on Miller's computer, and then, becoming nervous that they would be blamed for it, deleted evidence of it from the computer. Miller gave them an unusually large tip when they left, they said. One of the men believed it was because Miller knew they had seen something inappropriate on his computer and he tipped them to keep them quiet. Another man who spent time in a different Vermont boys home reported in 1992 that Father Robert Baffa liked to take nude photographs of him and other boys at the home.

THE FILE OF FATHER JOSEPH DUSSAULT OFFERED EVEN MORE DISTURBING insight into the endemic nature of the problem. Dussault was not named by plaintiffs as an abuser in the litigation, but that may have been because his time at the orphanage was too long ago. I found records of his presence at St. Joseph's Orphanage as far back as the 1930s. He was the nun's confessor at the time, and although he had no formal assignment with the children,

editions of the *Chronicles* celebrated his good acts, like taking children from
the orphanage to the cinema. Dussault's personnel file revealed that Bishop
Joyce asked another priest to investigate claims of "sexual impropriety" with
young boys against Dussault in 1959.

Dussault's case mattered because it showed the long line of credibly accused priests who spent time at the orphanage, and the diocesan reports
about them, went back even before the window of the litigation and the
plaintiff's period of residence, as long as that was. The diocese's defense had
vociferously complained that asking a jury to hear complaints from a period
as long as fifty years was unfair to *them*, but Dussault's history meant there
was no reason to believe that the line of priests exploiting, using, and abusing children at St. Joseph's, and then covering it up, had ever been unbroken.

THE DOCUMENTS RELEASED BY THE DIOCESE IN 2000 WERE INVALUABLE
not only because of what they contained, but also because they proved that
evidence still existed, if only you knew where to look. That validation sent
me back to places I had previously searched, like the archives of newspapers, which had come online during the time I had been reporting the story.
There I found more about the St. Joseph's chaplain, Father Devoy, the one
Sally said had pulled down her underpants. Sartore had treated Sally's objec-
tion to that gesture as so outlandish as to be almost incomprehensible. But
Sally was not the only plaintiff who described being abused by Devoy.

During the litigation, one man said the priest had taken him to the
Hotel Vermont in the 1940s and abused him there on the roof as the sun
set. David Borsykowsky had deposed the man with a heavily disbelieving
tone. Yet I stumbled across a 1943 *Burlington Free Press* article that suggested Devoy had been in the habit of taking young orphanage boys to
that hotel. The article reported "an unheralded visitation" by Father Devoy
at the meeting of the Catholic Order of Foresters at the Hotel Vermont
with another "boy from the orphanage." Devoy explained to the surprised
foresters that he and the boy had come to the hotel because the boy was
very interested in forestry.

CHAPTER 20

FATHER DEVOY, LONGTIME CHAPLAIN OF THE ORPHANAGE, TORMENTER of Sally Dale, and escort of young orphanage boys to local hotels, was also the priest whose body, plaintiffs claimed, lay in an open casket at the orphanage. Quite a few former residents said they were told to kiss him, and it haunted them for years after. Devoy was chaplain for twenty years, and his death would have been a major moment in the life of the orphanage, yet many nuns and priests found it hard to remember. Devoy acted as a kind of mentor to Father Foster in the 1940s, and Foster was Devoy's immediate successor as chaplain. He acknowledged that he attended Devoy's funeral but said he did not remember any children there.

In all the depositions I read, no nun or priest acknowledged that children had attended the funeral or seen Devoy in his coffin. It wasn't until 1998, two years into the litigation, that the Sisters of Providence finally noted in an affidavit that Devoy died at the orphanage in 1955.

Over the years, many people handed me folders, briefcases, boxes, and loose bundles of papers. Deep in one cardboard box, I opened a manila folder and found a photograph of a dead elderly man in a coffin and a glum group of children standing beside it. Some gazed transfixed at the dead man's face, others appeared to be looking at his body, one girl was staring at some object a thousand yards away. The caption read, "Saddened by the loss of their pastor, children of St. Joseph's Orphanage pay their final respects to the Rev. Robert Devoy whose body lay in state yesterday at the orphanage."

IF THE NUNS AND PRIESTS WERE SO RELUCTANT TO TALK ABOUT SUCH AN ordinary event as the passing of an elderly man, what might they have withheld about other deaths?

I looked at every death certificate for Chittenden County and Burlington from the 1920s through the 1980s. I spent nights running through them, backward and forward. It was relatively easy to find the 1961 notice about Marvin Willette, the boy whose body had been hauled out of Lake Champlain and laid on the sandy shore. But he was the one child whose death was not in dispute, having been featured at the time on the front page of the local paper. (I even found it mentioned in St. Joseph's *Chronicles*.)

Despite the hazy cloud that hung over the deaths of orphanage children, I found death certificates for six St. Joseph's residents in the 1940s alone, including an eight-year-old boy who died of leukemia in 1942. The other five were infants who died of meningitis, malnutrition, and dehydration, and in one case, "no cause determined." Another two children died in the 1950s and 60s. Since 1916, at least twenty-six orphanage children and a nun and priest died, some of them right there at St. Joseph's or at a local hospital.

One of the orphanage doctors was asked under oath about orphanage children dying. He said he didn't recall any deaths at all, adding that if anything like that had happened, it would likely be something he would remember. But I found two death certificates for babies from St. Joseph's that he himself had signed.

I found another death certificate for a baby girl who died shortly after a breech birth. Her home address was listed as "311 North Avenue," the address of Vermont Catholic Charities offices next door to the orphanage. No one lived there.

I looked for Sally Dale's falling boy. Sally said that she and a nun came around the back of the orphanage and were looking toward the rear of the big building when he was pushed from a window on the fourth floor. I was not able to find a certificate for him or any other witnesses or documents to confirm the story. In the end, it was the word of Sally Dale against the word of the church.

I called a forensic anthropologist who worked for the FBI's Forensic Anthropology Center in Knoxville, Tennessee, known widely as the "Body Farm." Researchers there investigate the processes by which people die and what happens to their bodies in the aftermath. I wanted to run the details of Sally's story by someone who understood, if not about orphanages, then about the physics of death. When I described the weird detail of the boy's body bouncing, the man said that was exactly what would happen with a young child's body falling from approximately that height.

Sally's falling boy was not the only story of a child who had been pushed from a window. Robert Cadorette, who was at St. Joseph's in the early 1940s, said Sister Claire tried to throw him through a closed window. She broke the glass with his head, but because he put a hand on either side of the window, she could not push him through. He recalled her saying, "You be a bad boy and I'll throw you out again." Many years later, Cadorette said he crossed paths with the same nun at a care facility for the elderly. When he confronted her with what she had done, she looked at him and remarked, "Oh, you're the one."

Sally herself said that Patricia Carbonneau was pushed out a window by Sister Priscille, and Carbonneau independently confirmed it under oath. I spoke to Carbonneau's daughter, who told me that she was unwell and it was not possible to speak with her. So I went looking for Sister Priscille.

OLD NUNS ARE HARD TO TRACK DOWN. THE NAMES THE ST. JOSEPH'S plaintiffs knew them by often applied only to their years of service. Before Vatican II, postulants had to pass a series of tests before they could join an order, and then they had to disavow their former lives and their former selves, giving up their birth names and taking on new ones. After Vatican II, some women changed back to their original birth names. Others left their order and changed their names then.

The point of taking a new name in religious life is to become born anew in the new order. But a new name can also make a person hard to find. To locate a member of a twentieth-century religious order, a reporter needs the assistance of the order, and if the order doesn't want to assist, there's not much the reporter can do. Fortunately, I found a list of the Sisters of Providence in one of Widman's old binders. It included the last known addresses of women who had left. In many cases, they dated to the 1960s or 1970s. I went through it in the hope that some of the women were still around.

Some had died, and others simply could not be found. What used to be a local Sisters of Providence motherhouse near St. Joseph's in Winooski, Vermont, had by then become a facility for assisted living. A few of the Sisters of Providence remained there, along with elderly nuns from other local orders. From the front door, visitors were buzzed into reception, where they had to state their name and business so they could be buzzed through another locked door. I visited three times to ask for Sister Lorraine Boyer, who was once Mother Superior of St. Joseph's. Neither she nor any other nun wished to speak to me. I knocked on doors all over Burlington and the surrounding countryside, and spent what felt like years calling old phone numbers. I called one number, asking by name for a woman who had once been a St. Joseph's nun. The woman who answered had the same name but was not the woman I was looking for. Being of French Canadian descent, though, she knew what I was talking about when I explained I was looking for survivors of a Burlington orphanage. She had grown up in an orphanage, too, she said. It had been an entirely different place, and it was also a nightmare.

Sister Priscille was my last hope. I knocked at the Quebec apartment that was listed for her, and a tiny, birdlike eighty-eight-year-old with a huge smile opened the door. Yes, yes, she nodded. She was Sister Priscille.

Welcoming me into her home, she took a seat in a large armchair, surrounded by half-full boxes. She was about to move apartments, she said. If I'd arrived a few days later, I would have missed her. Priscille's English wasn't perfect, but it was good enough to tell me the broad outlines of her life.

She was one of fifteen children in a Quebec farm family, named for an older sister who had died. "It was the time of apples," she told me. All the children were outside, she said, and her sister, who was only four, had eaten too many green apples. They poisoned her and she died in the night. There was a dreamlike quality to the story, as if Priscille had been told it when she was very little and had never updated it as an adult. I understood, though, that Priscille's mother had been devastated, and when Priscille was born, she named her for the little girl who died. Priscille grew up, like all her siblings, helping her mother inside and out, regularly getting up at three o'clock in the morning to milk the cows.

When Priscille was eighteen, she told me, she and a sister joined the Sisters of Providence. Priscille did not want to be a nun, but she didn't want to be married either. She knew she could look after herself. "I wanted to be free," she told me. But her mother wanted to have nuns in the house, so Priscille consented to please her and to avoid having to marry. One of her first postings was to a hospital in Alberta.

Compared to farm labor—the nuns arose at five in the morning—convent life was not so hard, but Priscille didn't like being under other people's control. In the mid-twentieth century, convents were no longer medieval cloisters, but they weren't completely unlike medieval cloisters. In many orders, family members and other visitors were allowed only into a reception area at certain times, and they never crossed the threshold into the nuns' domain. At St. Joseph's, perhaps because it was essentially a foreign mission, there was a room where the parents of nuns could stay when they visited.

Priscille wasn't allowed to walk down the street. She was allowed to read only religious books. She wasn't supposed to talk out loud or develop close friendships. When she became close with another young nun, the sisters separated them. "You do that! You do that!" the older nuns would say to her. I wasn't a martyr, Priscille said. I wasn't suffering. Rather, she was strict with herself. She tried to just get on with things. She would say to herself, "I do what I have to do."

She managed to sneak in some fun anyway, sliding down the banisters, swimming at the lake in summer, and sledding down the big hill in winter. She used to laugh out loud, she said, and was punished for it. But, she defended her young self, *it's natural to laugh like that.*

The sisters would tell her she wasn't serious enough, but in the end they scolded her so much that she didn't care anymore.

At the orphanage, she said, "I loved to take care of the boys. The girls, less." Priscille herself was barely older than they were. "Some of them, just to see your face, and they hate you," she told me later.

Priscille recalled how the children would come to the sisters. They were from broken families and were found on the streets, in barns, and in boxes at the front door. Or the police would bring them to the orphanage. Sometimes their hair would be full of lice. Priscille never caught any, she said, because her hair was covered by her habit.

Priscille remembered Eva and Irene. Eva was "cute," she said. But Irene was an "authority." When Priscille had to go and get clothes from the attic, Irene would tell her what she could and couldn't take, as if they were her own dresses.

I told Priscille that some former residents of St. Joseph's claimed that brothers and priests had touched the children sexually. "I never saw that," she said. She told me that she put small skirts on the little children in the nursery to cover their privates when they took a bath.

I told Priscille that some of the former residents also said the nuns punished them. She said no, at first, then she said she knew of one such nun. "She was a bad nun all the time," she said. She began to mention other nuns who she had heard were cruel.

Once when she was eighteen, she had herself become so angry that she shook a boy, she admitted. But she felt terrible about it, and she reported it herself.

I told Priscille that a woman named Patricia Zeno, then Patricia Carbonneau, said that a nun at St. Joseph's had pushed her out a window.

Yes, said Priscille, pointing to herself. It was she.

It became difficult to understand Priscille's English at this point. She said that she had actually told Carbonneau to get out of the window, but that the girl had fallen. Another girl had grabbed her. "When she blame me at that, I could not remember if I was pushing her."

I asked Priscille why she thought Carbonneau blamed her. "What did she gain?" she asked. "I always said to myself that girl wants money. That's all she wants."

Priscille said that she had a photo and a statue of the Mother Superior that she would like to show me, but they had all been packed away. She gave me her new address and told me to visit her after she moved. Once she was unpacked, she said, she would show me what she had.

I did as she suggested, but the second time I visited Priscille, she looked disappointed to see me. The atmosphere between us had changed completely since our last conversation. Yet she invited me in, and we sat down.

I reminded her that she said she had a photo to show me. No, she said. She did not have any photo. She did not have any stories, either. I tried to engage her about what it was like to wear a habit, what the other nuns were like, whether she used to write home to her family.

"Why did you ask me all those questions?" At eighty-eight, she said, you don't get everything right.

"That would put me in prison, sometime?" she asked.

No, I explained, no one was going to put her in prison. I knew sometimes nuns hit the children, but that some of them, like Priscille, had been just girls, too.

"We had permission to kick the children," she said.

"To kick the children?"

"Yes. We have permission. But today I know we don't have permission."

Again Priscille's English became difficult to follow. But she managed to make one point clear: "We try and do the best. I knew what I did, the time I was with the other nun, it took place, what I did, I do the best for the children, and I loved them and I didn't want to hurt any one of them."

I visited the Montreal motherhouse for all the Sisters of Providence. No one was willing to speak to me formally. I took a guided tour through the museum, a series of interconnected rooms celebrating the work of Émilie de Gamelin, who founded the order in 1844. Glass cabinets displayed a native headdress from the American West, a pretty, bejeweled teapot from Egypt, and other mementoes from missions. A beautiful wooden abacus and other teaching aids represented the sisters' various efforts in education, including an institution for children who were blind and deaf.

Three mannequins modeled the nuns' traditional garb. The face of one was surrounded by a white collar and the forehead was completely covered so that only the smallest part of the face showed. The other mannequins represented a postulant and a novice, with three starched white tubes propping up the top of the habit.

The display for *Les orphelinats* had a photo of the nursery at St. Joseph's, a photo of children at their desks, and another of children at repose in an activity room. The accompanying glass cabinet included a tiny pair of white shoes, wooden blocks, hard plastic baby dolls, and an ancient teddy bear, which still had a jaunty air, even though its right eye hung down the side of its face from a wrinkled cotton thread.

A beautiful framed poster on one wall laid out the statistics for the work of the sisters in 1940. It listed 3,361 professed sisters, 107 novices, and 2,451 orphans. In that year, St. Joseph's in Burlington housed many children, yet a considerable number must also have lived in other homes run by the Sisters of Providence in Canada and the US.

It was an extraordinary number, yet the museum space dedicated to the orphans was small and the number of mementoes strikingly few. If the women disappeared when they took new names in the order, and the children became invisible when they entered an orphanage and were assigned a number, it appeared that when the orphanages closed for good, everyone vanished again.

Priscille had made up her mind to leave the order in the 1980s. She told her mother that she no longer wanted to be a nun, but her mother didn't want her to say it out loud, let alone do it. She told Priscille that her life was at the convent and that *she* should change. Priscille asked her mother whether it was she herself or her father who decided when she married. Priscille's mother told her that it was she herself who had decided when to marry. So Priscille said, "Let me decide then." Priscille was sixty years old.

Normally a woman had to leave the order within a year of deciding to go, but Priscille stayed for three more years. She asked the Sisters of Providence for a car, which they gave her along with some money. She went to live with her mother and her sister-in-law. One night, she said, her brother and her sister-in-law took her disco dancing. Even after they came home late that night, she told me, they stayed in the living room and just kept on dancing.

I asked Priscille about the rumors that young girls had been pregnant at St. Joseph's, but she said she never saw anything like that. There was a nun who became pregnant at the motherhouse once, she had heard. But she didn't know if it was true. "We were all young, young girls, you know," she said. Some of the other sisters didn't even know how women became pregnant. But Priscille grew up on a farm and saw the animals do it. It was the same thing.

During the litigation, Widman had tried to find Priscille. He asked quite a few nuns, under oath on the stand, if they knew where Priscille lived, and they had all said no. The implication was that no one was in touch with her anymore.

Priscille told me that at that time of the litigation, she went to Montreal along with four other sisters. They spoke to attorneys there and told them what had happened. "I told the lawyer everything," she said.

OF ALL THE STORIES ABOUT DEAD CHILDREN, SALLY'S ACCOUNT OF THE burned boy always seemed to me to be the most far-fetched. It worried me. If it were a fantasy or some kind of post-traumatic delusion, what did it mean for the rest of her testimony? I wanted to look for the burned boy, but I didn't even have a name.

One night, as I scrolled through the death certificates again, I found him. It had been an accident. On April 18, 1955, Joseph Millette, thirteen years old, died from overwhelming electrical burns. It happened at a power station after Millette crawled under a high-tension wire and made contact through a metal helmet.

Sally Dale had been right all along.

According to a newspaper report, Joseph Millette, the son of Mr. and Mrs. Charles Millette of 27 Washington Street, Burlington, Vermont, was electrocuted at the Green Mountain Power transformer station in the Winooski River gorge. He was wearing a German World War II army helmet, a souvenir from the war. A power line had sent 33,000 volts through his body. He died two days later.

The article named Millette's companion that day as Peter Schmaldienst. Schmaldienst was living in Connecticut and in his seventies when I phoned him. I told him that I was looking for information about a boy who had been electrocuted at a power station in Burlington. "I knew him," Schmaldienst said. "I was with him when he was electrocuted."

Schmaldienst and Millette had been hiking to Essex Junction and decided to follow the railroad tracks instead of hitchhike. They came across a chain-link fence with a hole in it. "We each had an army helmet with us because we were young kids, we were playing, you know." Schmaldienst said that Millette's German helmet was harder to take off than his own American model. He was a few yards past the fence when he realized that something terrible had happened. By the time he got back to his friend, the boy's clothes were on fire, and he was unconscious.

Sally had said the boy ran away from St. Joseph's. Schmaldienst told me he didn't think that was right, though the boy might have been at the orphanage at some earlier time. I found a photograph of Millette in a local newspaper from 1948. He was a resident at the orphanage when it was taken. It wasn't possible to say how long he had remained there.

Evidence of that one accidental death didn't prove that other children died at the hands of nuns, as Sally and others believed. But it proved the strength of Sally's memories, even the most improbable.

SALLY'S EXTRAORDINARY ELECTRIC CHAIR STORY WAS FINALLY CORROBO-rated, too. Sally told Widman about her mock execution at the hands of Sister James Mary, but no one else at the time confirmed her story or the existence of the chair in the attic. Years later I asked many former residents about it, and no one said they had seen it or even heard of it until 2016, when I spoke to a woman who had spent a year at St. Joseph's, and by then lived in Texas. She had nothing to do with the litigation or the settlement, and she did not know Sally Dale. She didn't know I was trying to verify Sally's story when she spontaneously told me about an unforgettable day in 1960 when she and her sister crept up to see the attic.

The woman saw a rack of girls' clothes that went on for fifteen feet, trunks with tiny clothes in them, and boxes of photos of the orphanage in the 1800s. Little girls in the old photos wore uniforms. "Some were all in white, some just had the drapery, some just looked different, beautiful. It was just unreal." Then, as she and her sister explored, the woman suddenly spied what she called a "torture chair."

The woman, who had been an antiques dealer for twenty-five years, told me that the chair was mission style with "leather straps where they strapped down your arms, leather straps where they strapped your legs down to the leg, and this area where they could strap your head to where you couldn't move." She and her sister were so frightened they fled the attic, but the specter of the chair stayed with them. Some time later, they considered reporting a cruel nun to the Mother Superior, but it occurred to them that the cruel nun might put them in the torture chair, so they decided not to speak up.

A former resident suggested that when the diocese bought the sanitarium next door to the orphanage to turn it into Don Bosco, home for boys, some of the sanitarium's equipment might have been stored in the orphanage attic. Perhaps that's where the chair had come from?

Alternatively, the *Chronicles* of St. Joseph's recorded the visit of a delegation of nuns from Mount Providence, Canada, in 1968. Maybe the nuns from the Montreal mental-hospital-and-erstwhile-home-for-orphans-turned-deficients had brought *la chaise électrique* with them.

MANY MYSTERIES REMAINED UNRESOLVED. DESPITE JOSEPH ESKRA'S detailed testimony, I couldn't find any mention of a boy at St. Joseph's Orphanage who had been tied to a tree or frozen to death. I couldn't find any other members of that evening's search party either.

But sometimes a death certificate or some other bit of information rescued a story from the status of fable and planted it firmly in the world of the real, or at least moved it closer. I didn't find out what happened with the boy who was said to have frozen to death in the attic in the 1920s. But I did find a death certificate for fourteen-year-old James Whitehead. He had been a resident of St. Joseph's Orphanage for eleven years and nine months, and he died in 1925 of pneumonia. Was the story about him? I don't know.

There were other stories I didn't so much piece together as become an unwitting part of. After my *BuzzFeed News* article was published, a Vermont reader reached out. She told me that her mother was the eldest of eleven children from a very poor family. In the late 1920s, they had been taken away from their parents and sent to St. Joseph's Orphanage. The woman's aunt, her mother's little sister, came down with spinal meningitis at the orphanage, and—so her mother said—the nuns made her carry her mattress on her back to the attic to ride out her illness there. That was where they put children with a fever, she said. The woman's mother could hear her sister crying through the locked door, but there was nothing she could do. Her sister died there, she said, alone in the attic.

The woman asked her mother, "Why didn't you do something? Why didn't you say something?" But her mother, who was quite old by then, covered her face with her hands, clutched her crucifix, and said, "I couldn't. They would have done the same to me."

I recognized the name of my caller's aunt, Charlotte Snay. For the previous few years, her death certificate, along with the death certificates of other children from St. Joseph's, had been taped to the wall of my office. I often stood in front of them, wondering if there was some telltale piece of information on the record I had missed. According to her certificate, Charlotte, resident of St. Joseph's Orphanage, died in 1933 of bronchopneumonia at a local Catholic hospital. She was twelve years old. I had not been able to tell it from the record on my wall, but I was not surprised to hear that her death had involved cruel mistreatment, and that she had been mourned and missed and remembered by her family for many decades after.

I told the woman that I was looking at Charlotte's death certificate as we spoke. She told me there was a needlepoint hanging on her wall that had been made by Charlotte at the orphanage in 1932, which her terrified sister took with her when she left. It said, "God sees me."

OTHER STORIES BECAME CLEARER WHEN THE DELICATE THREADS OF DIFferent stories that I'd been chasing suddenly started to wind around each other. In the 1990s, Sally Miller told a lawyer about the day a boy drowned at the lake. Joseph Eskra reported a similar story about a boy named Marvin Willette. Once I knew the details of Willette's death, it became clear that this must have been what Miller was talking about. Miller was at the orphanage from 1954 to 1957 and then again from 1960 to 1961. Willette died in 1961, and the details of that day—as described by Miller—lined up with the drowning stories from other former residents, like Joseph Eskra, who didn't know Miller but was there at the same time.

I was puzzled for years about the second dead boy that Miller mentioned. She spoke about seeing a distressed nun who told her that a mass was being held for a young boy who died. The nun told Miller she must never talk about it. Miller thought she might have been about eight years old when she had the encounter with the nun. She said she was about thirteen when the boy, who turned out to be Willette, died at the lake.

Death is such an extraordinary claim, and the details in Miller's deposition were so sparse, it was hard to be confident that her second story had much substance, and that another child really had died in the relatively short time Miller was at the orphanage. I wondered whether the big mass had actually been for the drowned boy, Marvin Willette, and if Miller had perhaps confused the timing of the incident.

I should have treated Miller's memories as solid from the start. I now realize that Miller's second dead boy was probably Joseph Millette, the boy who was electrocuted in 1955.

Miller was born in 1947. Her first stay at the orphanage was from 1954 to 1957. She thought the mass for a dead boy occurred after she had been at the orphanage for about a year when she was about eight years old. Joseph Millette died in 1955, about a year after Miller first entered the orphanage, when she was about eight. Like Sally Dale, Sally Miller turned out to be a wholly reliable child witness of a surreal otherworld.

THE DISPERSAL, OBLITERATION, AND CONCEALMENT OF DOCUMENTS, THE destruction and shattering of lives and realities, stretching back so many decades and extending violently into the present, was monumental. Still, all that remained—the publicly available documents, those that were withheld from Widman and later surfaced, the newspaper articles, the death certificates, and the legends handed down over generations in local families— once assembled, fully validated the nightmarish world the plaintiffs had described.

Yet how effectively had time and power erased so many events in which dozens or even hundreds of people had consciously participated, like Sally

Miller's high funeral mass for Joseph Millette, an event that fully engaged the engine of a complicated institution like the orphanage and was embedded within the much larger institution of the diocese. All those people who were physically present at the time, all the records they generated, all those ephemeral but widely shared moments of straightforward reality—the experience of a dead child and the events following his death—had almost completely disappeared. How close the church and the passage of time came to rendering the claims of Sally Dale and all of her fellow survivors a gothic collection of unverifiable myths.

More is out there. I believe that someone somewhere knows about Eskra's frozen boy. Or at least they did before they died. Someone surely was there when Sally Dale saw a boy thrown from a boat, never to surface again. They wrote about it in their diary, or told their therapist, parole officer, or children, who maybe loved them, but didn't quite believe them, and worried that their elderly parent was losing a grip on reality.

The cloistered and cruel world of the orphanage may seem utterly fantastical, but the events that took place there belong very much to reality, and their lingering traces are out there, in records and memories, waiting to be found.

CHAPTER 21

I HAD HOPED ANTHONY GIALLELLA MIGHT LEAD ME TO MORE THAN REC-
ords and memories. His story had led me to the family who owned the
Lewis Mausoleum, and shortly after we spoke, on a sunny, cool day that was
almost but not quite mud season in Vermont, I returned to the mausoleum
and stood before it. Much had changed around the structure.

Next door, what had been St. Joseph's Orphanage was barely recognizable. The massive main building was altered inside and out, and was now
dwarfed by the new modern building attached to it and others built nearby.
Even the stone cottage that had once housed the offices of Vermont Catholic
Charities, the building where Sally Dale met the Pelkey family for the first
time, was now merely part of a larger structure that projected out behind it.
The terraces and slopes at the back of the orphanage had been flattened by
dozers, which had cleared away the remains of the past, making way for yet
more buildings to come.

The mausoleum, despite all the convulsions of world history that had occurred since I was last there, looked exactly the same: the staunch stone
walls and the rusted doors, slightly bowed out but otherwise frozen, were
impassable, except for telltale leaves and a pine cone projecting from a narrow gap at the top. Squirrels had entered in the previous decades, even if no
one else had.

I met two men there. They brought shovels, rakes, and hammers and stood in front of the doors, looking at them from different angles and sizing them up, analyzing why they were stuck and how they might get them open.

I believed Giallella when I met him in 2019. Or at least I believed that he believed what he was saying. I recognized that the other stories he told me, as outlandish and extraordinary as they sounded, were true. He had bounced back and forth between describing the events of that terrible day and describing what he felt about it—he wondered if it was a dream, he hoped that it hadn't happened. It was when I spoke to two men who had heard Giallella's story years before that it became irrevocably stuck inside me.

Giallella's probation officer from 2001 still remembered meeting him for the first time. Giallella told him he had worked as an enforcer for the Syndicate in the Garment District of New York. He told him about the time he saw a fellow inmate murdered, and the time he had received shock treatment in a state hospital. He told him that his ex-wife died in one of the Twin Towers on 9/11. Members of his family were still receiving compensation for the tragedy. He spoke about nightmarish abuse by nuns and priests and laymen in an orphanage. He told him about helping hide the body of a young girl. He had a lot of extraordinary tales. *Is this guy a big storyteller?* The probation officer asked himself. *What's real and what's not?*

As he got to know Giallella, he noted that the stories never changed, and the ones that Giallella returned to most were the stories about the orphanage. Many men on probation told stories to intimidate or to appear tough, but Giallella was clearly tormented by his. It wasn't that Giallella hadn't committed heinous crimes, or that he wasn't still dangerous. He was hypervigilant, and if you came at him the wrong way, he'd knock your legs out, the man said. But Giallella seemed to have genuine remorse, and when he told the story about the young girl, it was clear that he had been petrified.

Giallella's psychologist from around the same time described an experience like the one that I had. He told me about a "medley" of back-and-forth with Giallella saying what had happened, and then saying *Surely it didn't happen.* The psychologist said it was as if "his senses were telling him that this really happened, but he couldn't believe it had happened." The memory was unintegrated, he thought, stored inside Giallella in an unprocessed form. It was also, he thought, too much to be made up. He came away from their meetings feeling that Giallella's account of the girl was real. A lot of traumatic things had happened to him, the psychologist said, but far and away the worst was his time at St. Joseph's.

In North America and elsewhere in the world, even as most investigations and inquiries have been focused on the living, some of the twentieth century's missing children had begun to return anyway.

In 2015, as I was tracking down survivors of St. Joseph's, a commission formed by the Irish government began an investigation into the nation's mother and baby homes. Twentieth-century institutionalized childcare in Ireland comprised residential schools that looked a lot like the orphanages of America, including Artane, run by the Christian Brothers, where a former resident told me he saw a young boy fall from a great height. It also included mother and baby homes, where unmarried women gave birth. The homes were managed by Catholic nuns and had long been rumored to be places of great cruelty.

The Irish government investigation was announced in response to the work of Galway historian Catherine Corless, who a few years earlier had published the results of research into the Mother and Baby Home in Tuam run by the Bon Secours Sisters, near where she had grown up. Corless worked her way through local records of the home and deduced that almost eight hundred children had died there, and that their remains were unaccounted for. She told a reporter that when she first began her research, she spent time talking to the residents of a housing estate built over the site of Bon Secours. The residents told Corless about an unmarked grave near the estate's playground and finding bones there. Corless deduced that the bones that turned up in the unmarked grave belonged to the missing children. She was proved right. In 2017 a preliminary archaeological investigation determined that significant quantities of human remains had been deposited in a septic tank at the site.

Corless's work confirmed that the stories were everywhere. Everywhere there had been orphanages, everywhere children had been institutionalized in the twentieth century, there were stories in living memory of dead and missing children. Until she went looking, the death stories from the mother and baby homes had not been treated with the gravity they deserved. Like the stories told by Sally Dale, Sally Miller, Anthony Giallella, Joseph Eskra, Joseph Gelineau, Sherry Huestis, and many others, they had mostly gone away.

Catherine Corless's discovery forced a reluctant government to commit to a forensic investigation that is still ongoing. Her actions also lit a fuse beyond her own country. In 2016, when the Irish government announced the mother and baby home investigation, Gordon Blackstock, a Glasgow-based Scottish reporter for the *Sunday Post*, received a call from a man who told him, "There's a Tuam in Scotland."

The caller was referring to Smyllum Park, an orphanage run by the Sisters of Charity in Lanark, southeast of Glasgow. Opened in 1864 and closed in 1981, the orphanage occupied a grand building that had since been redeveloped into upscale apartments. But in a pattern repeated elsewhere in the world, survivors came forward in the 1990s to pursue justice in the courts. At the time, the Scottish statute of limitations meant that if victims hadn't reported abuse within three years of it occurring, or by the age of nineteen, they lost their opportunity to do so.

The stories from Smyllum Park were like the stories from St. Joseph's and all the other institutions elsewhere in the world. Children were beaten with all manner of implements. Children who wet the bed had their wet sheets draped around their heads. Children were made to eat their own vomit. One man told a reporter that he had seen his friend kicked in the head by a nun. The child spent time in the orphanage after his injury and was later taken to the hospital, where he died shortly after.

I spoke to Blackstock in 2022 and asked if he'd ever heard stories about children being subject to some form of electrocution. Within an hour, he forwarded information from Scottish survivors of institutional childcare, in this case, from a place called Nazareth House in Aberdeen. A former resident of that orphanage told a reporter that nuns had attached a contraption with alligator clips to a rubber sheet on his bed. If he wet the bed, he received a shock. The Aberdeen nuns belonged to the Sisters of Nazareth, the same order that ran the home in Victoria, Australia, where Peter Hill,

"Hilly," said that nuns attached pads to the back of his head and delivered electrical shocks. It was also the same order that ran the orphanage in Western Australia where Therese Williams said she saw her friend, Eileen Sinnott, kicked across the yard by a nun.

In the early 2000s, a former resident of Smyllum Park found records that indicated there were at least 100 to 150 bodies of children from the institution buried in a mass grave at the local St. Mary's Cemetery. It was the deaths of these children that Blackstock's caller wanted him to investigate. Blackstock interviewed survivors and learned, in addition to all the now familiar stories, about cases where children had been seriously injured, like a young boy who was accidentally hit in the head with a golf club by a man who worked at the orphanage. Instead of being taken to the hospital, Blackstock was told, the boy was kept at the orphanage and died two weeks later.

Blackstock visited St. Mary's Cemetery. He saw a small dilapidated memorial stone for children from the orphanage, and next to that section, a series of graves for nuns from the order that ran Smyllum Park. The nuns' graves had recently been done up with glossy headstones made of enduring black marble. It was shocking to Blackstock that the order had let the children's memorial fall into such disrepair when the nuns' graves had been treated so well.

Working with Ben Robinson from BBC Radio 4, Blackstock approached the Sisters of Charity, who made it clear that they wouldn't share any records to help the investigation. He then got a researcher to go through death certificates from 1864 to 1981 that had been lodged in the area. She located 403 certificates for children who died at Smyllum Park.

By the time Blackstock's story was published, Scotland had removed the statute of limitations for civil litigation of claims of both physical and sexual childhood abuse. The Scottish government also launched its own abuse inquiry around the time of publication. Smyllum Park was the first home to be investigated. That focus, plus the work of Blackstock and Robinson, led to the reestablishment of a police inquiry into a number of the former residents' claims. At the time of writing, six women, five who had worked as nuns for the Sisters of Charity and one lay worker, were awaiting trial on criminal charges of physical abuse.

In Canada, the whereabouts of long-missing children from residential schools are finally being identified. In 2021, Kimberly Murray, who led Canada's Missing Children Project, was hired to set up the Six Nations Survivors Secretariat investigation into missing children and unmarked burials at a Mohawk residential school in Brantford, Ontario. Known as the Mohawk Institute and called "Mush Hole" by survivors, it is thought to be the oldest residential school in the country, and the one on which many other schools were modeled. The school operated from 1828 to 1970 and was run by the New England Company and the Anglican Church. In 2021, the Six Nations Police, as part of a joint task force with other agencies, also launched an investigation into allegations of death at the school. Survivors had told police that the remains of a child were uncovered in the 1980s and then reburied at the site in an unmarked grave. So far, the group has used LIDAR to search ten of the six hundred acres that must be searched. They have purchased three ground-penetrating radar machines and trained members of the community to operate them.

The Six Nations group was launched after an Indigenous community in British Columbia announced in 2021 that it had located the probable burial site of over two hundred children at the Kamloops Indian Residential School in the territory of the Tk'emlúps te Secwépemc community. Former residents of the school, once run by the Catholic Church, said they recalled being awoken in the middle of the night and made to help dig graves. In recent years, locals told a reporter that a tourist found a child's rib bone at the site.

The Kamloops Indian Residential School discovery prompted multiple investigations. In July 2021, the Penelakut Tribe announced that it had located the unmarked graves of more than 160 children at the site of the former Kuper Island Indian Residential School, run by the Catholic Church. The chief of the Stz'uminus First Nation on Vancouver Island, from which many of the Kuper Island Indian Residential School children were taken, told the *Globe and Mail* that she had heard many stories from relatives about mistreatment at the school, including the story of a girl who died when she was pushed out a window. Since May 2021, investigations have begun at many of the country's 139 residential schools. It's thought that more than 1,300 unmarked graves have been identified so far.

As a consequence of the movement in Canada, the US Department of Interior began an investigation into 408 federally funded residential schools for Indigenous children located in thirty-seven states. (An additional eighty-nine boarding schools that did not receive federal funding have also been identified.) In the United States, even though the federal government had significant involvement in and control of the schools, at least half were run by religious organizations or influenced by religious engagement of some kind. A May 2022 report released from the Department of Interior did not include an exhaustive list of burial sites, but it identified at least five hundred deaths. "As the investigation continues," the report states, "the Department expects the number of recorded deaths to increase."

IN VERMONT, THE REPORTS OF MISSING CHILDREN REMAIN UNRESOLVED. Yet the gathering of all the stories in a post-Spotlight era and in light of the findings from many government inquiries around the world made true change finally possible.

On April 8, 2020, at the Vermont State House in Montpelier, on a rainy spring morning, Representative Sarah Austin of Colchester stood before the assembled legislature and read out a concurrent house resolution declaring that the statute of limitations for civil actions based on childhood physical abuse was now repealed in Vermont. She attributed the change to the efforts of a group of the orphanage's former residents. After she read the resolution, the group, who was present, stood up while all the elected representatives of their state clapped and cheered for them.

Austin did not say, but it was also the case, that this was the first time in United States history that limitations on childhood physical abuse in civil actions had been lifted by a governing body.

Because of these changes, perpetrators may now be held responsible for the physical harm they do to children in Vermont, even long after the event. Perpetrators are also less likely to benefit from the way that crimes without a statute of limitations may be obscured by the statute of limitations on re-lated crimes.

In fact, much change had already occurred in Vermont in the previous two years. In September 2018, after the August publication of my *BuzzFeed*

News article about St. Joseph's Orphanage, the Vermont state attorney general, the mayor of Burlington, the Burlington Police Department, the Vermont State Police, the Burlington Community Justice Center, and other state agencies announced that there would be both a criminal task force to investigate the claims of survivors and a restorative justice process for survivors to gather, engage with the state, and finally be heard.

On October 10, 2018, *BuzzFeed News* published an additional article reporting the details of a state investigation into priest sexual abuse in the Diocese of Burlington in the early 2000s, which had been kept secret. One day after the *BuzzFeed News* article was published, the diocese announced that it would form a committee to make public any credible accusations against Vermont priests. The process took one year, and on August 19, 2021, the diocese published a list of forty credibly accused priests. The list included many of the men identified by orphanage survivors, as well as others who had abused and terrorized the children of Vermont in parish churches and summer camps. I was contacted by a man who told me he had asked the bishop to publish such a list for many years; the bishop told him it would never happen.

Included in the diocesan list was a Father Edward Gelineau, who had worked as director for Vermont Catholic Charities. In the 1990s, Joseph Gelineau, his nephew, publicly said that he told his uncle about abuse at the orphanage. At the time, the priest told reporters that Joseph's claim was a "lie" and suggested that his nephew had been manipulated by psychologists.

The *BuzzFeed News* orphanage article, along with activism from former gymnasts that was occurring at the same time, contributed to the May 2019 repeal of the statute of limitations on civil actions for childhood sexual abuse in Vermont. Since then, another wave of cases against the Diocese of Burlington has been launched by survivors of priest sexual abuse. Jerry O'Neill, the lawyer whose 2006 case against the diocese changed the course of sexual abuse litigation against the church in Vermont, has pursued twelve cases since the list was published. Four have been settled and eight are pending as of this writing.

When the *BuzzFeed News* article about priest sexual abuse was first published, a spokesperson for the diocese said that by the time of the early 2000s investigation, most of the accused priests were "barred from presenting themselves as priests, functioning as priests, or wearing a collar." He added, "Many were laicized. Most are now dead." The implication was that publishing a list of names would not make a difference to people's lives. But of the cases that Jerry O'Neill has since pursued, at least three came to him specifically because of the list.

The St. Joseph's Orphanage Task Force, launched by Attorney General T. J. Donovan, produced a report in 2021 that officially validated many of the claims of former residents. Detectives of the Burlington Police Department interviewed dozens of survivors who had been at the orphanage between 1940 and 1974, as well as friends and family. The report recorded the beatings—the slaps, the broken bones, the broken teeth—the emotional abuse and intense cruelty, the threats, the verbal abuse, the shaming, and the sexual abuse by men and women. It included many statements by survivors, who detailed what happened to them in their own words.

The Task Force stated that it unequivocally supported the former residents of the orphanage. "No historical context," the report stated, "excuses the failure to protect these children."

The Sisters of Providence did not cooperate with the Task Force investigation. The order is based in Montreal, across an international border. None of the usual leverage a state government might use to investigate an organization in such circumstances was available.

As part of the restorative justice process, a group of former residents assembled for the first time in May 2019. The first meeting vibrated with almost unbearable intensity. The group called themselves the Voices of St. Joseph's Orphanage, and during their regular meetings over the next few years, they developed a mission to protect children "both now and in the future, and hold accountable those who abuse them."

In addition to their role in the repeal of the statute of limitations on childhood physical abuse, survivors worked on advocating for changes to the language of the law to include psychological and emotional abuse. They also published a book, staged an online performance of their writing, recorded oral histories, worked with the Burlington Parks Department to create a memorial space near the shore of Lake Champlain where the children of the orphanage used to swim, trained childcare providers about the impact of their experiences, advocated for legislative change to ensure that care recipients can access their records, and created a museum exhibition that must surely be the first accurate and true portrayal of orphanage life in the United States, as well as the first to honor the thirteen thousand children who spent all or part of their childhoods under the care of the Sisters of Providence and the Diocese of Burlington at St. Joseph's Orphanage in Burlington, Vermont.

NEXT TO THE GOLDEN-DOMED STATE HOUSE IN MONTPELIER, VERMONT, the Vermont History Museum now houses the exhibition of the Voices of St. Joseph's Orphanage. In April 2022, the day the resolution was read out, survivors held a celebration at the museum. Walter Coltey, who I first met in Florida, was there. So was Sheila Cardwell, sister of Sherry Huestis (the woman who said she saw a baby smothered), and who the diocese wrongly thought would defend them in the 1990s. Katelin Hoffman, who was at the reunion that Sally Dale attended in 1994, was not at the museum, but she had been a critical part of the process driving toward that day. Other survivors who told me their stories in previous years were there. Some I met for the first time.

Standing in front of an exhibit poster that bore a photograph of the old orphanage building, Brenda Hannon, who I had not met before, told me she was at the orphanage from 1959 to 1968. She said that a nun had once attempted to throw her out a window. She was nine and was making beds in the big girls' dorm. Inspired by the film *Peter Pan*, she tied a pillowcase around her neck, climbed onto the windowsill, then leaped onto a bed yelling, "I can fly!" Hannon did it over and over, until she suddenly felt herself grabbed from behind by a nun as she was climbing back onto the windowsill. The nun lifted Hannon and threw her into the window, saying, "So you think you can fly?"

Gesturing at the poster, Hannon pointed at a window on the left side of the building where it happened. I asked her if she remembered the name of the nun who pushed her. She looked off into the middle distance for a moment, then said, "I want to say . . . Sister Claire?"

In the 1990s, Robert Cadorette testified that a nun named Sister Claire tried to push him out a window in the 1940s. (When he confronted her decades later, she had remarked, "Oh, you're the one.") That same Sister Claire, more formally known as Sister Claire de la Providence, may have resided at the orphanage when Hannon was there; at the time, she taught in a local parochial school. There was, however, another Sister Claire, Sister Claire Hélène, who worked in the girls' department in Hannon's time.

It's likely that the Sister Claire featured in Hannon's story was Sister Claire Hélène, with the implication that there were at least two women with the same religious name who tried to push children out of a window at St. Joseph's, not counting, of course, Sister Priscille. Of these three women, only Sister Claire de la Providence was resident at the orphanage in the early 1940s when Sally Dale said she saw a boy thrown out a window. At the time, that Sister Claire was in charge of one of the boys' dormitories.

I had pursued the story of the first Sister Claire, born Geneva Leonard, with great interest for years. Survivors of St. Joseph's reported her repeatedly in the 1990s for abuse. She had also served in the 1950s at Mount Providence, the Canadian orphanage turned-hospital where many Children of Duplessis were abused. As a child, she had herself also been a resident at St. Joseph's Orphanage. I came across this pattern a number of times.

When I interviewed Anthony Giallella about his time at the orphanage, he was incarcerated, serving a sentence for the sexual abuse of a young girl. He told me about the extreme sexual and physical abuse he suffered at the orphanage at the hands of a man named Fred Adams, and Adams was not the only one who had abused him.

Being abused as a child does not mean a survivor will themselves abuse children. It is true, however, that people who are abusers have often been abused as children. Many of the stories of the orphanage reveal how the cogs of this machine, which perpetuated itself over generations, interlocked.

In a similar way, Patricia Carbonneau, the girl who said Sister Priscille pushed her from a window, later sent her daughter to childcare at the orphanage. In a pattern that seems hard to fathom—especially when abuse is hidden and trauma is unacknowledged—other residents also sometimes sent their children back through the system that had hurt them so badly.

CHAPTER 22

THE LONG FALLOUT OF ORPHANAGE LIFE IS STILL UNFOLDING, TOO. Only in the last few years have formal inquiries validated the idea that it can take many, many years for victims to testify to abuse. Walter Coltey, who told me in 2016 about Sister Louis Hector—who made the boys cut switches from the thorned rose bush in the grotto—also told me about a priest connected to the orphanage, Father John Glancy, "the only good one," who had been supportive of him. Glancy was once head of Vermont Catholic Charities, and he had taken Coltey in when he was a homeless teenager.

When I first met Coltey, he told me *not* to tell him bad stories about Glancy. If there were any, he said, he didn't want to know. But as he worked with the survivors group, uncomfortable memories began to bother him. Toward the end of the restorative justice process, he said to himself, *You want other people to tell their story, but you're not telling yours.* So on the day of the museum celebration in Montpelier, Coltey told me about the summer he lived with Glancy.

At thirteen, Coltey was homeless, and he had asked the priest for shelter. Glancy said yes but added, "There will be issues if you stay here." Coltey didn't know what that meant, and he didn't ask. Glancy also told Coltey that he would come into his room every night to pray. From his second night at the rectory, about an hour after Coltey had gone to bed, Glancy came into his room, but the priest didn't kneel down as Coltey expected. Instead, Glancy got into bed with the boy. Every night for the next two months, Glancy molested Coltey and he made the thirteen-year-old perform sexual acts on him.

At the time, Coltey was a child who had no support and nowhere else to live, but he still feels enormous guilt and a sense of responsibility for what happened. "He didn't force me," he said.

Glancy is not on the list of the diocese's accused priests.

I had already learned that the overwhelming majority of priests who acted as chaplain for the orphanage from at least 1935 onward were accused abusers. Since then, with the publication of the names of credibly accused priests, the church has effectively conceded that the chain of succession at the institution was essentially a chain of accused pedophiles. These men oversaw a set of abusive visiting male clergy, resident abusive nuns, and abusive lay workers.

Now, with Coltey's story about John Glancy and the diocese's list of credibly accused priests, including Paul Bresnehan and Edward Gelineau, it appears that the three priests who headed Vermont Catholic Charities, the organization that oversaw the orphanage from at least 1950 to 1983, were also accused abusers. As well as heading Vermont Catholic Charities, Bresnehan, as mentioned, also worked as the chaplain of the orphanage.

For those who were not abusers, the imperative to be silent was reinforced over and over. In a familiar refrain, a 1941 visitor from the motherhouse, essentially an assessor from the head office, reminded the resident nuns, "No inquisitive questions about those who come and go."

Language often forces us to distinguish between predators and the hierarchy that protects them, especially when describing the Catholic Church. But in this story, there are no clear lines between the two.

It's taken a long time, modern search technology, and enormous investment from state and national governments, news outlets, and many individuals to begin to grasp the scale of the story of St. Joseph's Orphanage and the other orphanages mentioned in this book. In some ways, the story was too big to be told before. Increased scrutiny only makes it bigger.

For example, on May 17, 2022, Mitchell Garabedian, the lawyer whose work was critical to the 2002 Spotlight investigation, announced that he had represented a victim who was abused in the 1960s by a priest of the Burlington Diocese named Roger W. Carlin. The victim, who was nine years old at the time, said that he reported his abuse to another priest but was told it was a mortal sin to talk about it to anyone. Carlin's name rang a bell. I went back through my notes and realized that he had worked at Vermont Catholic Charities in the 1950s as a social worker before he was ordained. The tally of abusive male clergy who once had access to the orphanage children rose yet again.

As of this writing, Roger Carlin was not on the list of the diocese's accused priests.

Harold Preedom, the priest who assaulted Sally Miller in the 1960s at the St. Joseph's Home for the Aged, is also not on the list of the diocese's accused priests. But Miller described the assault in sworn testimony in the 1990s and again to me in 2022.

Roger Colleret, an accused priest named in 2019 by the Diocese of Charleston, who worked briefly as chaplain at St. Joseph's Orphanage in Vermont, is also not on the list of the diocese's accused priests.

None of the names of the women accused of sexually and physically abusing children at St. Joseph's Orphanage in the Diocese of Burlington—identified by their victims in sworn testimony more than twenty years ago—have been published either by the diocese or by the Sisters of Providence.

Much work remains to be done. Accounting properly for the history of twentieth-century institutional childcare will take many volumes written by many authors. Fundamentally, it requires accepting the pernicious and widespread presence of abuse and abusers, whether from a legal or scholarly or humanitarian perspective. The terrible reality, so rarely grappled with, is that abusive practices weren't just inherent to the operation of institutions, they were, as argued by historian Shurlee Swain about Australian institutions, essential.

Hand in hand with this reckoning must come a rigorous attempt to measure the multigenerational impact of abuse. In 2015, I spoke to Bessel van der Kolk, who had been one of Widman's expert witnesses in the 1990s on the nature and impact of trauma. He believed that, finally, some of America's institutions were waking up to the fact that "this pandemic of child abuse has fantastically large public health consequences."

A true history also requires a sophisticated analysis of human institutions and the dynamic forces that operate upon them—on the institutions as entities and the individuals within them, as well as on the complicated interactions between the two over time.

We have learned much about the impact of trauma on individuals and how information can be repressed within families and even within selves, but there is yet much to learn about the ways institutions block information by insensitive practices, criminal deceit, and unwillingness to follow through on legal mandates.

According to the church's own records, male predators largely filled the upper tiers of the St. Joseph's organizational structure. These men were treated with reverence in the world, while behind the safe, closed walls of the institution, they violated children. It is tempting to assume that the institution had been mostly benign before some unfortunate point in its history when enough bad actors tipped the balance from good to bad. But it's also possible there was never a time *before* predatory behavior was integral to the institution. Maybe it was always there, going all the way back to the founding.

The sworn testimony of former residents described many of the women at St. Joseph's as sexually and physically abusive. Yet the 2019 diocesan list of forty credibly accused clergy who worked under the aegis of the Diocese of Burlington included only men. To be sure, some of the sworn testimony from orphanage victims did not include women's names, but enough of it did. There is no reasonable argument to omit the names of the women on the list and fail to accord their victims the same acknowledgment as the victims of men. Allowing the names of these perpetrators to disappear into history benefits only the perpetrators and the organizations that housed them. Even now, little is known or widely understood about abusive female clergy. Until enough data on this phenomenon is gathered, all victims of women will find themselves less likely to be believed.

It's possible that women at the orphanage were also being sexually abused themselves. The last decade has seen an acknowledgment for the first time that a significant number of nuns all over the world have been sexually assaulted by priests. These crimes, like the crimes against children, were hidden by trauma and by shame and by institutional design, and they were covered up by the abusers themselves.

Accounting properly for the history of twentieth-century orphanages and institutional childcare also requires understanding the factors that helped obscure their reality for so long. A complete history must include an understanding of the forces that kept that history invisible, even as other large-scale injustices of the nineteenth and twentieth centuries have been investigated and exposed.

It's also critical to better understand the forces that helped reveal and expose the terrible history of twentieth-century institutional childcare. At the heart of all those endeavors has been the courage of survivors, starting with the children who ran away from institutions as long ago as the 1930s to try and tell someone what was happening, up to current groups, such as CLAN in Australia and the Voices of St. Joseph's Orphanage in Vermont. The survivors have been supported by, and in turn helped to fuel, social changes beginning in the 1960s when the church began to lose control of the loyalty of churchgoers, the stigma of being a single mother diminished, and social movements arose to give women reproductive control of their own bodies, close the pay gap between women and men, and fight the forces that kept women out of the workplace.

Those influential survivors include very small children, some as young as five, like the ones Philip White worked with in the 1980s before he represented the survivors of St. Joseph's Orphanage. The bravery of those children, and the revolutionary framework of support that White and his team put around them, led to broad social changes in how America deals with childhood sexual abuse now. What those children started is now decades later evolving into a broader movement concerned with all childhood abuse.

White used to say to the children, "These guys can only do what they do in secret. They survive on your silence. When you speak out in public about what they do, you break the silence."

White has reconnected with the parents of some of the children and with the children themselves, now adults. He told me that "the validation they received, and the therapy they received, allowed these kids to flourish as adults." He sees one family every year at an event at Lake Crystal, Vermont. "We use the day to catch up and celebrate," he said.

Bob Widman's work in the 1990s, and that of everyone who supported him, drove the legal process further down the road that finally led to the repeal of the statute of limitations on childhood physical abuse in 2022, more than twenty years later. Likewise, the bravery and commitment of journalist Sam Hemingway, supported by what was then a thriving local press, revealed publicly for the first time what former residents had endured. It also generated even more records that ensured the stories lived on.

Vermont has been one of a very small group of states to lead the United States in almost every stage of the broad social and legal revolution in the way trauma and abuse are handled. The creation of a restorative justice process for the survivors of St. Joseph's Orphanage, in addition to the criminal investigation, was another step on that path. T. J. Donovan, the state attorney general, told me that previous investigations hadn't brought closure or healing or allowed people to talk openly and honestly about harm. It was clear to him that they needed to do something different this time. "Sometimes no courtroom or legal proceeding will address those harms," he said. "We had to create a new alternative system of justice."

America's twentieth-century orphanages are the immediate ancestor of its modern foster care system. Although both systems were in use in the twentieth century, the balance was toward institutionalized care for the first half of the century, tipping slowly toward foster care and other kinds of care after that point. In many cases, the same institutions were repurposed and staffed by the same people. It's impossible to imagine that we can clearly judge the benefits and danger for children in the modern system when we remain blind to the stark realities of the system that preceded it.

ON SEPTEMBER 9, 2018, BISHOP COYNE, THE CURRENT BISHOP OF BURlington, pledged to cooperate fully with the orphanage investigation. He said, "The only way we can get to the truth of these matters is to be cooperative." Yet members of the survivors group told me the following year that the diocese refused to take part in the restorative justice process until the criminal investigation ended. In November 2019, when I asked a spokesperson for the diocese about this seeming contradiction, he replied:

At this point, we await the report of the Task Force. As of now, no criminal charges or completed findings have been shared with VCC or the Diocese of Burlington. Additionally, the "restorative justice" process has nothing to do with the investigation. It is one possible response among many to the findings of the investigation. Entering into a process of "restorative justice" at this time would be premature since the criminal process is not finished.

For the survivors, of course, a process of restorative justice was long overdue. Nor did they think of restorative justice as simply "one possible response." It was the response that they, the victims, wanted.

Marc Wennberg, a restorative justice consultant who facilitated the St. Joseph's Orphanage Restorative Inquiry group for just under three years, invited the diocese to participate in the process when the group first formed. The former residents wanted the bishop to come and speak to them as a group. The diocese responded that while the criminal investigation was ongoing, it would be premature "to commit to any course of action." However, when the criminal investigation concluded, Wennberg asked them again to participate in the Restorative Inquiry. This time they replied, "Since the task force and the Burlington Police Department have completed a thorough and complete inquiry regarding the allegations made by some former residents of the former St Joseph's Orphanage, we see no need for further inquiry."

"It was a completely missed opportunity to support healing," Wennberg said.

Coyne made himself available to talk one-on-one with survivors, but in 2021, Brenda Hannon, the former resident I met at the museum, told a reporter for the *Catholic News Agency* that the group felt Coyne was only having these meetings so he could "control the meeting and the situation."

Hannon also told the reporter that Vermont Catholic Charities refused to release the orphanage records of survivors. She explained that "members are only allowed to see their records, which contain redacted information, while they are sitting in a room with a staff member of Catholic Charities."

Despite all the evidence of their organization's malfeasance, the Sisters of Providence did not produce documents requested by the Task Force, and when the Task Force report was released, they issued a statement saying that "the report focuses on those who allege hardship," but that it was "mute on the important role of religious institutions in rearing and caring for orphaned children." The sisters also said they prayed for "peace and healing."

The Task Force did not find evidence to support the survivors' allegations of murder. To what extent the outcome was shaped by the nature of the investigation—a search for physical evidence based on accounts that were sixty to eighty years old—is unknown. Supporters of the church will take it as closure. But in the absence of full cooperation from the Sisters of Providence, this position appears to signify more a lack of resolution. I asked T. J. Donovan about the extent to which the Sisters of Providence's lack of involvement in the investigation may have affected the outcome. He reiterated that in the United States, people who are the targets of criminal investigation have Fifth Amendment rights to choose not to cooperate with a criminal investigation. The Task Force made a determination based on the evidence they had, Donovan said. "That's our job." He could not speculate, he said, that the absence of something suggested the existence of something. Nevertheless, the Burlington Police Department stated, they reserved the right to reopen the investigation if new information was brought to their attention.

When I learned about the Sisters of Providence's lack of engagement with the investigation, it reminded me of the words of Richard Sipe, the former Benedictine monk and Catholic priest who became a psychotherapist and who had done so much to expose the hidden predatory lives of Catholic priests. "This is the important thing," he said, "the sense of power, and the sense of necessity, and the justification."

For most of the time that I spent investigating the orphanage, I thought that the nuns, like the rest of church hierarchy, were playing the longest game of all. They were lifelong servants of an institution that has garnered the love, loyalty, obedience, minds, and money of millions of people for more than two thousand years. There is nothing else in human history like it. The institution is one of the—if not *the*—most formidable entities in the world. Empires, nations, and theocracies have risen and fallen in the same time the church has evolved, adapted, protected itself, and lived on.

But I now think that the Catholic nuns and male clergy are not playing the same game as everyone else. All this time, survivors have been pursuing justice, but the goal of the Catholic Church is unrelated to the causes and ideals of individuals. The goal of the church is suprahuman and is measured in centuries: it has been working to control history.

It took a while to get the doors of the Lewis Mausoleum at Lakeview finally open. When the men worked their way through its rusted bolts and hinges, they noted with surprise that even though the door had been stuck, it wasn't locked.

I could see three marble boxes built into it—two across the bottom, which filled the structure from side to side, and one stacked on top of the bottom right box. Each box was designed to contain one person and should have been completely sealed.

Two people had been buried in the mausoleum in the 1920s: Alla Mary Lewis, who died in 1926, and one of her sons, Harry Edwin Lewis, who died in 1927. Harry had been a doctor, and when I spoke to his great-great-niece of Phoenix, Arizona, to ask if I could look inside, she felt that he wouldn't have minded, if he'd known, that I wanted to open the doors of his mausoleum to see if a young girl had been placed in there.

Alla was buried in the bottom box on the left side. Harry's marble box was on the top right. According to the records, the box beneath his was empty. An enormous mass of rust-colored leaves and pine cones filled the space next to Harry's box. At first, the men I was with dragged some of the matter out with a rake. Then I took the rake and began to pull out decades of squirrel debris onto the ground. It was hot work, even on that cool day, and as I pulled out more leaves, I could see that the marble side of Harry's box was missing. One of the men I was with believed that it had fallen flat and was lying on top of Alla's box to its right. All the leaves in the mausoleum had accumulated since the marble side had fallen. It was odd for the structure to be open that way.

As I raked and pulled, a weird shape began to emerge from the leaf pile, an enormous, rough-torn piece of metal projecting from the side of Harry's box. Eventually it became clear that the marble boxes of the mausoleum must each have a metal liner. But the side of the liner that secured Harry's crypt had been torn open and sat at an almost forty-five-degree angle to the box, pushing into the space next to it. The liner was bent in the middle and there was a small hole on its right half. Its top righthand corner was bent back, like a dog-eared page in a book. Or like someone had inserted a crowbar between the marble box and the metal liner and bent it back so as to get a purchase on it. It wasn't possible to say for sure what had caused the rupture, but it was very clear that between the time Harry had been buried in the 1920s and that cool spring day in 2022, someone else had been inside the structure and opened up Harry's crypt.

At that point, I couldn't look further. Harry had been laid to rest behind that liner. I couldn't cross that line. But I reported the story and the state of the mausoleum, and the Burlington Police followed up with an anthropological investigation. They found no trace of Giallella's girl, only of Harry. Generations of squirrels had been in there, too. The outside doors had not been forced, but at some point they had been secretly opened and shut, leaving a gap at the top. It appeared that the breach in the liner of Harry's box had occurred at the same time. Over decades the squirrels had pulled in leaves and pine cones and deposited them both inside Harry's box and in the space next to it. It was not possible to definitively say why the liner had been so ripped out or how much natural forces had contributed to the chaos. Nor was it possible to say when exactly someone else had been inside the mausoleum since Harry had been laid to rest.

A 1958 letter from a member of the Lewis family to the superintendent of Lakeview explained that the family had chosen to bury Harry's brother in a grave next to the mausoleum, not in the marble box inside the mausoleum—the one beneath Harry's—that had been assigned to him. The letter explained that the doors were so thoroughly sealed by the weather, it would be too expensive to open the mausoleum up. It seemed likely, then, that the breach in the doors, and the subsequent weathering and rust, and the first forays of the colonizing squirrels, happened before 1958. The incident Giallella described probably took place in the late 1940s.

People who don't believe Giallella's story will conclude that the girl wasn't in the mausoleum because she never existed. To be sure, it's possible that vandals who had nothing to do with the orphanage entered the structure and damaged it. But I believed that Giallella's story, his memory, was solid. If it was, what then? Did I have the wrong little house? Was the girl placed in the mausoleum but taken out again and moved somewhere more permanent?

Not too far up the hill from the Lewis Mausoleum is the City Vault, a structure built into a hill near the cemetery entrance. For most of Lakeview's history, the vault was where the bodies of individuals who died in the deep winter were placed. There they waited until the ground thawed enough for a grave to be dug. Is it possible that Giallella, the nun, and the men walked up the hill, not across it? Could the girl have been placed there temporarily? Or had the Lewis Mausoleum been used like the City Vault? Had it been a place to hide a body, and then to return and remove it later when another safer location could be found?

When the rusted old doors were once more shut, I was left with the overwhelming sense that I had let the young Giallella down. I had let the girl down. It felt that I had come very close to doing what he asked, what all the survivors of those very stark and unforgettable stories implicitly asked, but I failed. I couldn't find the telltale sign with which to close the story, one way or the other. By then, though, I had heard so many of the same stories, I understood that as far as the vastly larger missing piece of American history was concerned, that wasn't all that mattered.

That the experience of a great wrong unanswered, of justice just beyond reach, was so widely shared was what mattered. The expanding undeniable reverberation of all the different stories recounted by all those voices across the world was what mattered. The fact that the history was not yet entirely lost, that it could yet still be hauled back out of the deep black pit that had almost swallowed it—that was what mattered. That there yet is so much more to be recovered, to be reported, to be found again and told, matters.

SALLY DALE WAS NOT THERE IN 2018 TO SEE THE STATE ANNOUNCE AN INvestigation into the orphanage or to participate in the beginnings of a restorative justice process. Yet none of it would have happened without her. She died in 2000 of lung cancer.

But her spirit was invoked in 2022 when Sam Hemingway, the journalist who broke the story of the orphanage in the 1990s, spoke about her before a group of survivors at the Vermont History Museum. Now white-haired and retired, Hemingway had worked with the survivors group throughout the restorative justice process, helping them assemble information for the exhibit.

When I first met Hemingway in 2016, he told me about Sally Dale. Like the lawyer Bob Widman, Hemingway thought Sally was special. He had never forgotten walking up North Avenue with her and her husband, and seeing her catch sight of the orphanage building and freeze, then turn to her husband, weeping. In person, Sally had been "down to earth, folksy and believable." He had always thought of her story and her courage as remarkable. At the museum, he said, "I think she'd be smiling up there, looking down on us today."

Hemingway spoke about the denial of the 1990s when the stories first came out. Readers told him his stories were blasphemous. People he came to think of as true believers complained to his editors that he had been taken in by "sob stories." Then the court cases went nowhere, he recalled, and the victims were shut down again. "Finally in 2022," Hemingway said, "people are willing to hear these stories and believe them."

Hemingway emphasized that it only happened because of the monumental perseverance of survivors—all the survivors in the room that day, and all the ones who couldn't be there.

A few years earlier, when I first met Sally Dale's son, Rob, he brought Sally's old tan briefcase with him, filled with the documents that she had entrusted to him. It made me think about the day that Sally was interviewed by psychiatrists for the defense. They asked her why she was engaged in the litigation. She said that she was tired of carrying things for the church. She just wanted it to carry its own baggage for a while.

Rob told me that for many years Sally had a bucket list of places to visit: Las Vegas, Disneyland, the Grand Canyon in a helicopter, Ellis Island, and the Statue of Liberty. She talked about them all the time, Rob said, especially the Statue of Liberty. One day, some family friends took Sally and her husband to see it.

First, they planned to see Ellis Island, where Sally was eager to look up the names of friends' immigrant ancestors. She was disappointed to find the museum closed. But she still had the statue. So many people who had passed through Ellis Island before her must have seen it the day they arrived, beautiful and grand, holding out the promise of freedom and possibility.

None of the people in Sally's adult life really knew the extent of the cruelty to which she had been subjected, or how she had to fight from the time she was two to keep part of herself alive. But they loved her, and they saw how much the statue meant to her. Rob's father said he barely saw the statue because he couldn't take his eyes off the huge smile on his wife's face.

Sally climbed all the way to the top. After all the pain and the darkness, after the long fight, she had stood high up and safe in the crown of the Statue of Liberty and looked out over the water and the city and the sky. At last, Sally told her son, "You could see everything."

AUTHOR'S NOTE

THIS BOOK COMES OUT OF MORE THAN TEN YEARS OF RESEARCH INTO THE world of twentieth-century orphanages and the experiences of children in them. To write it, I relied on many different sources, including thousands of pages of transcripts from the St. Joseph's litigation in the 1990s and files from Vermont Catholic Charities, which included contemporaneous logs from social workers at the orphanage, medical records, historic photographs, and letters written by priests and other workers in child welfare at the time, as well as handwritten diaries, police records, autopsy reports, transcripts from secret church tribunals, priest rehabilitation reports, orphanage settlement letters, historic newspaper articles, death and birth certificates, and government files and reports from many jurisdictions. I conducted hundreds of interviews with witnesses, family members, and professionals whose work was connected in some way with orphanage stories. Perhaps unusually for this kind of narrative, I describe these resources more than once in the text itself. This is because at the heart of this book are questions about how we can document reality, how we should do it, and how it has actually been done.

All the events described were reported by at least one person but often by many. In cases of abuse, where usually only a survivor reports it, other individuals abused by the same person or in the same institution often described the same kind of abuse.

The historic landscapes of this book, including those as recent as the pre-2017, pre-development grounds and building of St. Joseph's Orphanage in Burlington, Vermont, were either described or photographed by multiple eyewitnesses, validated by historic photos or descriptions, or videoed and photographed by me. My interviews were recorded by audio and in writing, and occasionally photography and video.

Where I describe past weather, it is either based on a witness report or a weather almanac I used to learn about the conditions on a particular date.

I added notes to identify specific source material and to provide context around some events, locations, and the source of written quoted statements where that context does not appear in the text itself. Where a written quote, usually from a deposition, identified an individual as the victim of sexual or physical abuse but I was not able to locate that individual or find instances of them talking publicly about it, I included location and date information in the note but withheld the name.

Where I quote or use information from an interview I conducted, where I am writing about my personal experience, and where my source is mentioned in the text itself and is publicly available, I did not add notes.

In many cases, the material I used is technically publicly available, but practically, it's not easily accessible. In some cases, I am one of the few people in possession of the record. Part of the work of this project, once this book is published, is finding a permanent archival home for these materials.

QUOTATION MARKS ARE USED TO MARK SPEECH, REPORTED AND REMEMbered, and words from written sources. In some interviews, the person I was speaking to would recall—and utter—something they or someone else had said one week earlier, or in some cases, fifty years earlier. The first example of this is my conversation with Rob Dale in Chapter 1, where he says that when Sally told him stories as a young boy he would say to her, "Mom, that doesn't sound right." I quoted these utterances. Where possible, I cross-checked words in deposition transcripts against documents the speaker had themselves produced at the time or later, or in conversation with others who were also there. Generally, the context of any one quote makes it clear if someone's utterance took place in real time, as written, or if it was recalled.

In my reporting, I found that some people tended to be more exact than others, and more exact on certain subjects. Some had reflected regularly on an event for years and had told their story over and over. By the time I heard it, there was a script-like quality to the telling. That did not mean that the story was any more or less likely to be accurate. But sometimes it meant that getting at other forgotten details required persistence. Other people remembered an occurrence for the first time when I asked them about it. It was extraordinary to witness the event, the feeling, the recognition, move across their face in real time.

All these considerations were true of the deposed testimony I consulted. Individuals who participated in the 1990s litigation were asked to range back in time to when they were children, when they had left the orphanage, and of course, their current life in the 1990s. Twenty-five or so years later, I spoke to some of the same people and I asked them to perform the same feats of memory, though this time from a different vantage point.

Trauma was an important factor in recollection. For some people it locked down an event for decades in excruciating specifics. For many people, remembering came at a great cost. Numerous people reported that after they had spoken to me the nightmares and flashbacks that they had experienced years ago came surging back.

As a journalist, I write a lot about science and cognition, and I'm familiar with the literature that seeks to characterize memory, especially long-term memory. My experience in reporting this book was that people tended to be extremely consistent over long periods of time. Occasionally I made a mistake and quoted a decades-old deposition to a former resident, thinking that it was theirs. In all cases, they instantly told me that I had it wrong.

In historic scenes from the point of view of characters, like Sally, where there was no handy transcript or video, I used materials that were created later. In Sally's case, these included depositions, letters, orphanage records, and recorded conversations from the 1990s. I also relied on the memories of many people who knew Sally. In the case of Bob Widman, I spoke to Bob and his wife, Cynthia, many times, I spoke to people who knew Bob, and I had access to much of his documentation from the litigation, including copies of transcripts and notes between him and other lawyers.

Where it was possible to include a version offered by the nuns in their own words, I did that (see Chapter 14). By their own choice, the nuns' versions of events at St. Joseph's were mostly lacking in specificity, if not entirely opaque.

Where I am representing someone's thoughts, I use italics. Either an individual told me what they were thinking, or some, like Sally, later wrote about their thoughts or told someone about them. Likewise, I use italics for emphasis, repeated phrases, Sally's letters, and when I'm personally recalling the meaning of an utterance, rather than the specific words, as in Chapter 2 when Leonie Sheedy says something like, *Are you kidding me?* In that case, I checked the recollection with Sheedy to make sure it was consistent with her sense of our discussion.

I refer to all characters by their last names, except for Sally Dale, née Fredette, whose last name changes during the events described in the book.

THE STORIES IN THIS BOOK WERE THE MOST EPIC, COMPLICATED, AND EXtraordinary that I have come across. Yet what is reported in these pages amounts to only a few threads of a vast, disturbing saga. There were many details and incredible scenes from individual stories, even Sally's, that I could not include. There were so many people who told me about their life or someone else's with great courage and generosity, but who I do not name in the text of the book. To have done so would have turned certain sections into long lists of names. Yet the book could not have been written without all of them. After the *BuzzFeed News* article was published, the former residents of other orphanages across America wrote to tell me stories they hadn't told anyone else before. There are many stories yet to be told.

Since the *BuzzFeed News* article was published, members of the restorative justice group published their own book, *Anthology 2021: The St. Joseph's Orphanage Restorative Inquiry Writers' Group* from the Green Writers Press.

ACKNOWLEDGMENTS

THERE ARE MANY PEOPLE WITHOUT WHOM THIS BOOK WOULD NOT HAVE
been written. Not all of their names appear in the following. My thanks and
admiration to:

Lily Arthur, Charles Bailey, Heather Bell, Nancy Bishop, Rod Braybon,
Keith Broadbent, Margaret Burke, Ashley Cadd, Caroline Carrol, Jack Car-
vill, Brian Cherrie, Oliver Cosgrove, Kathleen Daly, John Devine, Frank
Golding, David Hartmann, Terry Helmann, Barbara Hildreth, Patricia
Hill, Peter "Hilly" Hill, Bob Hoatson, Tim Kosnoff, Marion La Trombois,
Jeff Maher, Gavan McCarthy, Paul Mones, Andrew Murray, Jimmy Neu-
mann, Cate O'Neill, Donald Pier, Maggie Podunivich, Ray Prosser, Ross
Raymond, Donna Scopa, Angela Sdrinis, Vlad Selakovic, Leonie Sheedy,
Jack Smart, Vera Steer, Alf Stirling, Bev Stirling, Margaret Stride, Glendra
Stubbs Knowmore, Shurlee Swain, Joe Turner, Ray Turner, Lois Ann West,
Therese Williams, Kirsten Wright, Tony Young.

Rob Dale, Heidi Dale, Melissa Bailey, and Denise Douglas.

Leroy Baker, Joseph Barquin, Ray Benoit, Sheila Cardwell, Walter
Coltey, Mary Beth Damon, Cindy Delisle, Carolyn Elliott, Courtney El-
liott, Joseph Gelineau, Kathleen Gelineau, Kathy Gelineau, Debi Gevry-
Ellsworth, Anthony Giallella, Dale Greene, Coralyn Guidry, Barbara
Hammons Crady, Brenda Hannon, Debbie Hazen, Katelin Hoffman,
Sherry Huestis, Diana Jones, Dennis Maurice, Sally Miller, Marilyn No-
ble, Shirley Scardino.

Ken Bear Chief, Lisa Chalidze, John Evers, Peter Langrock, Joe Little,
Geoffrey Morris, Kimberly Murray, Anna Salter, Blaine Tamaki, Bessel van
der Kolk, Clara Vargas, Philip White, Bob Widman, Cynthia Widman.

Sheila Ahern, Kate Bochte, David Clohessy, Tom Doyle, Sam Hemingway, Dan Lynch, Terry McKiernan, Richard Sipe, and Patrick Wall.

The St. Joseph's Orphanage Investigative Task Force, Eric Bianchi, Matthew Burlew, Holli Bushnell, Phil Damone, Gordon Faison, Amy Farr, Molly Gray, Dick Kieslich, Thea Lewis, Jerome O'Neill, Emma Ottolenghi, Sister Janice Ryan, Jack Sartore, Peter Schmaldienst, Jeff Shed, Judy Tyson, Marc Wennberg, Steve, and Woody.

John Bangert, Ann Blanchard, Bill Bonneau, Rosemary Bonneau, Elise Boudreau, Dorothy Cotrona, Madeline Duprey, Paul Koren, Tracey Koren, Gus Papay, Susanne Robertson, Mike Ruede, Bob Von Zur Linde.

For your grace and generosity, thank you Linda Nofer and Edward Nofer III.

The Australian part of this story would not have happened without the support of John van Tiggelen and the wonderful team at *The Monthly*. Thank you.

The American part of this story kicked off with a conversation with the extraordinary Mark Schoofs, who at the time was in the process of founding the *BuzzFeed News* investigative team based in New York. Mark, I'm so glad we worked together. Thank you for everything. The story would not have happened without the longstanding support of Ben Smith and the style and scissors of Ariel Kaminer. Jeremy Singer-Vine, John Templon, Kevin Townsend, Emma Loop, Alicia Hosking, Katie Rayford, Matt Mittenthal, Dru Moorhouse, Lukas Vrbka, Nabiha Syed, and Matthew Schafer contributed critical help. Thank you all and to everyone on the investigations and *BuzzFeed News* teams, including the very cheery support of Simon Crerar and others in the once widespread *BuzzFeed News* empire. Double thanks to Emma Loop for helping me with the book, too.

Many, many thanks to Ben Adams and Clive Priddle. And to the team at Hachette, Jeanine Draut, Jaime Leifer, Melissa Veronesi, Miguel Cervantes, and Pete Garceau. Thank you, Vanessa Radnidge. Thank you to Sara Krolewski for your keen eye and smart takes. Many thanks to Debra Hine.

Thanks for your help over many years Alex Kane, Jessica Spitz, and thanks as always, Jay Mandel.

For your beautiful images, many thanks to Ian MacLellan and Nicole Cleary.

Thanks as always for the friendly and generous company of the Invisibles. Lydia Denworth, Anya Kamenetz, and Reem Kassis: consider this an accountability check-in.

Catherine Desmarais, so many thanks and so much admiration.

Thank you to Lucia Dapos, Tony McHugh, Lena Moon, and Simone Young. Thank you Jeremy and Sam.

Thank you, too, Roslyn Oades, Chris Womersley, Angela Kenneally, Jane Harvey, Jodi Coughlan. Thanks for everything, Desmond and Josephine Kenneally. Cheers, Hugh.

Monica Dux and Amanda Schaffer, I am so grateful for your brilliance, generosity, good sense, and friendship.

Shelagh Lloyd, a million thanks. Katherine Milesi and Steven Milesi, for your insight and your support, thank you.

Much love and thanks for being such inspiring creatures: Allegra Lloyd, Orson Lloyd, Babette Lloyd, Austin Jukes, Rohan Jukes, Zoe Jukes, Madeleine Kenneally, and Jessika Milesi. Justin Milesi, thanks for your help, man.

Nat and Fin, I love you so much.

NOTES

Act I

1 **Reports of Provincial Superior of Official Visits to St. Joseph's Orphanage:** Documentation from the Sisters of Providence that was produced during the litigation included annual *Reports of Provincial Superior of Official Visits to St. Joseph's Orphanage; Conseils Pedagogue (Teaching Advice), Daughters of Charity Servants of the Poor, Second edition,* Providence Mother House, Montreal, 1936; *Chronique De l'Orphelinat Saint Joseph,* Burlington, Vermont; *Customary Of the Daughter of Charity,* Servants of the Poor, Providence Mother House, Montreal, 1959; Episcopal Directives outlining the operations and responsibilities of the Diocesan Director and Vermont Catholic Charities at the orphanage, a 1963 contractual agreement between the Diocese and the Sisters of Providence, the 1866 Act to Incorporate the Providence Orphan Asylum and Hospital of Burlington, minutes of Board meetings, financial statements, a list that was alleged to include the name of every sister who worked in Burlington from 1935–1960, and personnel files for the sisters.

Chapter 1

3 **what had once been St. Joseph's Orphanage:** In 1942, an annex was added to the old building. After the Sisters of Providence left, the new annex was occupied by diocesan offices. The diocese sold the orphanage property and buildings to Burlington College for $10 million in 2011, and the college mostly occupied the new annex before it closed in 2016. Parts of the main orphanage building were used briefly over the years for different purposes; some people told me that refugees were housed there for a short while. For the most part it was left untouched.

5 **"You little devil!":** Sally A. Dale, interview by Elissa Benedek and Charles Clark, for Sally A. Dale and Robert A. Dale, Wife and Husband, v. The Roman Catholic Diocese of Burlington, Vermont, Inc., Vermont Catholic Charities, Inc., St. Joseph's Orphan Asylum, Inc., and/or its successors or assigns in interest and Sisters of Charity of Providence, a/k/a/ Sisters of Providence, United States District Court for the District of Vermont, August 26, 1997, transcript, 109.

5   **"Sal, you look good for everything you went through":** Sally A. Dale interview for Sally A. Dale and Robert A. Dale, Wife and Husband, v. The Roman Catholic Diocese of Burlington, transcript, 110.

5   **"You were our Shirley Temple of the orphanage!":** Sally A. Dale interview for Sally A. Dale and Robert A. Dale, Wife and Husband, v. The Roman Catholic Diocese of Burlington, 110.

6   **"No, no, no, no, no, it's not true":** Sally A. Dale interview for Sally A. Dale and Robert A. Dale, Wife and Husband, v. The Roman Catholic Diocese of Burlington, 20.

11 **He told at least one boy:** Chip Le Grand, "Priest's Aboriginal Victims Sue Pope Francis over Church's Failures," *Sydney Morning Herald*, November 27, 2020.

11 **Glennon said he had lost track of how many people he had raped:** Dan Silkstone, "Priest and Predator," *The Age*, October 11, 2003.

11 **pleaded not guilty in all but one:** "Applause as 'Evil' Priest Gets More Jail," *The Age*, October 23, 2003.

11 **Glennon shook his head in disbelief:** Jewel Topsfield, "Notorious Pedophile Guilty," *Herald Sun*, October 10, 2003.

11 **Glennon had regularly visited a boys' orphanage called St. Augustine's:** Broken Rites Australia, http://brokenrites.org.au/drupal/node/97.

12 **made to stand with their backs to the show:** Terry Helmann, conversation with the author, March 16, 2022.

14 **website that aimed to identify all the orphanages in the country:** Find & Connect, www.findandconnect.gov.au/.

16 **the notion that it happens in "distinct categories":** Rosemary La Puma, "De-Categorizing Child Abuse—Equally Devastating Acts Require Equally Solicitous Statutes of Limitations," *U. C. Davis Journal of Juvenile Law & Policy* 20, no. 2 (Summer 2016): 144.

Chapter 2

20 **When Geoff Meyer lived at Royleston:** I first reported Geoff Meyer's story for *The Monthly*. Parts of this chapter first appeared in Christine Kenneally, "The Forgotten Ones," *The Monthly*, August 2012.

25 **subject to medical experimentation:** Commonwealth of Australia, *Forgotten Australians: A Report on Australians Who Experienced Institutional or Out-of-Home Care as Children*, August 30, 2004, 115–117; Robert Milliken, "Vaccines Tested on Australian Orphans," *The Independent*, June 11, 1997; Gary Hughes, "Polio Vaccine Tested at Orphanages," *The Age*, October 25, 2004.

25 **If a boy's heels were worn away:** Frank Golding, *An Orphan's Escape* (Port Melbourne, Australia: Lothian Books, 2005), 41.

25 **photos cut from magazines:** Frank Golding (author of *An Orphan's Escape*), conversation with the author, March 2022.

30 **The inquiry estimated that at least 500,000 children:** Commonwealth of Australia, "Institutional Care in Australia," *Forgotten Australians: A Report on Australians Who Experienced Institutional or Out-of-Home Care as Children*, August 30, 2004. According to Joanna Penglase's *Orphans of the Living* (Fremantle, Australia: Fremantle Press, 2008), no one had attempted before the inquiry to count the number of institutions in the country, let

alone understand how they operated. Institutions were licensed by state governments, but even they kept few records of the places over time. When researchers and family members started to ask questions about institutional care in the 1990s, many government records had already been destroyed (69).

31 **why a parent chose a particular institution:** Joanna Penglase, *Orphans of the Living* (Fremantle, Australia: Fremantle Press, 2008), 69.

31 **Some were visibly successful, like former senator Andrew Murray:** Murray played a critical role in the 2004 Senate Inquiry into Children in Institutional Care, which led to the *Forgotten Australians* report, and the 2013 Royal Commission into Institutional Responses to Child Sexual Abuse established by the Australian government.

31 **The last three people to be executed:** These three were Eric Edgar Cooke (1964), Glen Sabre Valance (1964), and Ronald Joseph Ryan (1967).

31 **Using testimony from more than six hundred former residents:** Commonwealth of Australia, *Forgotten Australians: A Report on Australians Who Experienced Institutional or Out-of-Home Care as Children*, August 30, 2004, section 1.6.

32 **One man traced five generations of wards:** Frank Golding (author of *An Orphan's Escape*), conversation with the author, March 2022.

33 **non-bedwetters were encouraged to laugh at them:** I spoke to numerous former orphanage residents who told me they had wet the bed well into adulthood after being tormented for doing it as a child in an orphanage

33 **"spin it as hard as they can":** Deposition of Randy K. Stevens, for Randy K. Stevens and Laurie Stevens v. The Roman Catholic Diocese of Burlington, Vermont, Inc., Vermont Catholic Charities, Inc., St. Joseph's Orphan Asylum, Inc., and/or its successors or assigns in interest and Sisters of Charity of Providence, a/k/a/ Sisters of Providence, United States District Court for the District of Vermont, April 21 and 22, 1998, transcript, 117.

34 **"signify the total obliteration":** Judith Lewis Herman, *Trauma and Recovery: The Aftermath of Violence—From Domestic Abuse to Political Terror* (New York: Basic Books, 2015).

34 **took his brother's inhaler away:** Commonwealth of Australia, *Forgotten Australians: A Report on Australians Who Experienced Institutional or Out-of-Home Care as Children*, August 30, 2004, 47.

34 **"which meant lying":** *Forgotten Australians*, 122–123.

Chapter 3

39 **the whistling sound of air:** Margaret Stride, conversation with the author, July 2022.

42 **According to her funeral notice:** Funeral notice for Eileen Sinnott, *Geraldton Guardian*, June 26, 1948.

42 **I even found a reference to Sinnott's death:** Alan Gill, *Orphans of the Empire: The Shocking Story of Child Migration to Australia* (Docklands: Random House Australia, 2012), 283.

42 **"just laughing and joking with her little mate":** Gill, *Orphans of the Empire*, 283.

46 **A book about Braybon's life:** Vikki Petraitis, *Salvation: The True Story of Rod Braybon's Fight for Justice* (Australia: Jewel Publishing, 2009).

46 **If Braybon's impressions were correct:** The Victoria Police did not respond to my query about this incident in enough time to include their account of this exchange before this book went to press.

48 **"the orphans' friend," and also as "Keaney the builder":** Margaret Humphreys, *Oranges and Sunshine: Empty Cradles* (London: Corgi Books, 2011), 288.

48 **"exceptional depravity" of the homes run by the brothers:** Parliament of the United Kingdom, "Australia," House of Commons Select Committee on Health, Third Report: *The Welfare of Former British Child Migrants*, July 23, 1998, 51.

49 **the brothers liked blue eyes:** Parliament of the United Kingdom, "Australia," *The Welfare of Former British Child Migrants*.

49 **died from a broken skull:** Parliament of the United Kingdom, "Australia," *The Welfare of Former British Child Migrants*, Appendix 7.

Chapter 4

54 **allegations against priests were probably true:** The Spotlight investigation was revolutionary. However, any history of the Catholic Church and child abuse in the United States must include the essential work of reporter Jason Berry, whose pioneering investigation *Lead Us Not into Temptation: Catholic Priests and the Sexual Abuse of Children* (New York: Doubleday, 1992) lay the groundwork for all that followed.

55 **Where possible, foster care and other kinds of family settings:** *Proceedings of the Conference on the Care of Dependent Children* (Washington, DC: US Government Printing Office, 1909); Paul Lerman, *Deinstitutionalization and the Welfare State* (New Brunswick, NJ: Rutgers University Press, 1982), 110.

55 **In the early 1990s, some limited scholarship:** For general histories of the orphanage system in the United States, see Timothy Hacsi, *A Second Home: Orphan Asylums and Poor Families in America* (Cambridge, MA: Harvard University Press, 1997); Eve P. Smith, "Bring Back the Orphanages?" in *A History of Child Welfare*, ed. Eve P. Smith and Lisa Merkel-Holguin (Oxfordshire: Routledge, 2018); and Richard B. McKenzie, ed., *Home Away from Home: The Forgotten History of Orphanages* (New York: Encounter Books, 2009). In an essay in *Home Away from Home*, Hacsi states, "There is simply no way to know how often children were abused in orphanages . . . to the extent that we know about abuse that did occur, it does not give definitive answers because there is no way of knowing who was abused but never reported it" (246). Hacsi stands out as having gone further than any other contemporary historian in attempting to analyze and create a record of the United States orphanage system. However, by focusing on the challenge of obtaining definitive metrics, he lets himself and other scholars too easily off the hook. By 2009, ample evidence, including written records, witness testimony, and interview transcripts, demonstrated a widespread pattern of abuse that was endemic to the orphanage system. To understate this pattern and its implications is a distortion of history. *Home Away from Home* editor Richard McKenzie is unusual for having an overtly pro-orphanage position, inspired in part by his personal experience. Not long after Joseph Barquin first came

forward to report the sadistic abuse he experienced at St. Joseph's, McKenzie conducted two surveys of orphanage alumni, described in the "Introduction" to *Home Away from Home*. He states that less than 3 percent of respondents said they had negative experiences, 12 percent said they had mixed experiences, and the rest were positive. In 1994, McKenzie wrote in the *Wall Street Journal* that the notion of orphanages as cold and loveless places was "out of date and out of whack." McKenzie and I communicated briefly after my *BuzzFeed News* article was published, and his position was the same. The discrepancy between his views and the experience of the thousands of survivors represented in this book, including those who testified in the half dozen or more legal and government inquiries around the world, is stark. To be sure, McKenzie's experiences and research must be included in the history of the system. Suffice it to say that any analysis of institutional childcare that fails to grapple with an overwhelming body of legal, historical, and governmental evidence is not simply incomplete, it misrepresents the system entirely.

55 **with a few exceptions, remained indifferent:** In 2015, at the beginning of my US investigation, a lawsuit against the Ursuline Sisters of the Western province was settled. The lawsuit included many allegations of extreme sexual, physical, and emotional abuse by more than eleven nuns against children of the St. Ignatius Mission school on the Flathead Indian Reservation in Montana. The victims included both day students and residents at the school. Although the total settlement amount was significant, there were so many plaintiffs that each was said to receive only about $20,000. In *Unholy Orders* (New York: Viking Press, 1990), author Michael Harris tells the story of a series of investigations into the extreme sexual and physical abuse of boys at Mount Cashel Orphanage in Newfoundland, Canada. Legal proceedings and settlement arrangements are still ongoing in the Mount Cashel case.

56 **credibly accused in the United States and other countries:** In common use, the terms *credibly accused, accused, accused abuser,* and the like are a way to talk about reported crimes against children. The terms do not imply that criminal charges have been laid or that civil litigation has taken place, although in certain cases, that may also be true. Generally, the terms describe the status of an accused person when a victim's report is deemed to be plausible and credible by law enforcement, legal representatives, reporters, church officials, and other officials; when there are multiple victims' reports or other evidence that provides validation of the claim of abuse; or when the accused person acknowledges that the victim's report is true.

56 **"When you were in the classroom"** Deposition of Denise Allain, for Sally A. Dale and Robert A. Dale, Wife and Husband, v. The Roman Catholic Diocese of Burlington, Vermont, Inc., Vermont Catholic Charities, Inc., St. Joseph's Orphan Asylum, Inc., and/or its successors or assigns in interest and Sisters of Charity of Providence, a/k/a/ Sisters of Providence, United States District Court for the District of Vermont, December 3, 1997, transcript, 6.

57 **At their peak in the 1930s, there were as many as 1,600 orphanages:** Eve P. Smith, "Bring Back the Orphanages?" in *A History of Child Welfare*, ed. Eve P. Smith and Lisa Merkel-Holguin (Oxfordshire: Routledge, 2018). In *Second Home: Orphan Asylums and Poor Families in America* (Cambridge, MA:

Harvard University Press, 1998), Hacsi offers a more conservative number: 1,321 orphanages in 1933 compared to 1,631. In "Orphanages vs. Adoptions: The Triumph of Biological Kinship, 1800–1933," E. Wayne Carp uses the same number Hacsi does, which he derived from 1933 Census data (*With Us Always: A History of Private Charity and Public Welfare*, ed. Charles H. Parker and Donald T. Critchlow, Rowman & Littlefield, 1998, 123–144). Carp also used census data to determine that there were 2,280 children's institutions in 1933, separate from orphanages. It's not clear how he defines these other institutions, although it seems the distinction is made by the census, which organized the data according to "orphanages," indicating orphan asylums/homes for orphans and "children's institutions," indicating any other kind of residential institution/organization for children. Carp specifies that the numbers he cites "are only approximate" since "census reports grossly under-reported the number and size of institutions. Moreover, the Census Bureau used different classifications of institutions for each report, thereby obviating any consistency" (138). Smith also uses census data, though her numbers for 1933 are from a 1935 census report, not the 1933 report.

57   **it's likely there were still many hundreds of them:** This is based on esti-mates from the records cited earlier and personal communication with Terry McKiernan, who shared a spreadsheet he created that listed 776 residential institutions drawn from the 1950 Official Catholic Directory, including or-phanages, boarding seminaries, and homes for deaf children. At the time, the Catholic Church ran many of the nation's orphanages, but they were not the only providers.

57   **It is likely that more than five million:** With the assistance of *BuzzFeed News* data journalist Jeremy Singer-Vine, I derived this estimate from annual population and stay duration estimates in the following works: Paul Lerman, *Deinstitutionalization and the Welfare State* (New Brunswick, NJ: Rutgers University Press, 1982); Eve P. Smith, "Bring Back the Orphanages?" in *A History of Child Welfare* , ed. Eve P. Smith and Lisa Merkel-Holguin (Ox-fordshire: Routledge, 2018); *Home Away From Home: The Forgotten History of Orphanages*, Richard B. McKenzie, ed. (New York: Encounter Books, 2009); and Timothy A. Hacsi, *Second Home: Orphan Asylums and Poor Families in America* (Cambridge, MA: Harvard University Press, 1997).

58   **increasing criticism from a professionalized welfare community:** Tim-othy A. Hacsi, "Orphanages as a National Institution" in *Home Away from Home: The Forgotten History of Orphanages*, ed. Richard McKenzie (New York: Encounter Books, 2009), 237.

58   **It is likely that the trend to deinstitutionalization:** Paul Lerman, *Deinsti-tutionalization and the Welfare State* (New Brunswick, NJ: Rutgers Univer-sity Press, 1982).

60   **They never responded:** Ken Bear Chief, letter to FBI Field Office, Seattle, WA, August 10, 2010.

Chapter 5

73   **"select cases of mild derangement" and "nervous troubles":** Advertise-ment from *The Vermonter* 1 no. 5, December 1895, CXIV, described in

caption for image of Lakeview Sanitarium, Burlington, Vermont, Cottage Annex, at Llewellyn Collection of Vermont History, Champlain College Special Collections.

74   **"that bad place":** Sally A. Dale deposition for Sally A. Dale and Robert A. Dale, Wife and Husband, v. The Roman Catholic Diocese of Burlington, Vermont, Inc., Vermont Catholic Charities, Inc., St. Joseph's Orphan Asylum, Inc., and/or its successors or assigns in interest and Sisters of Charity of Providence, a/k/a/ Sisters of Providence, United States District Court for the District of Vermont, November 7 and 8, 1996, video 5, at 1:44.

77   **"Jesus Christ! Fredette all over!":** Vermont Catholic Charities, social worker notes from home visit to Ramona Fredette Donalson, July 7, 1945.

78   *Maudit Crisse*: Sheila Cardwell, conversation with the author, April 2022.

79   **"I hate you":** Sally Dale interview with Howard Fitzpatrick, Sally A. Dale and Robert A. Dale, Wife and Husband, v. The Roman Catholic Diocese of Burlington, Exhibit 1023.

79   **"He is here, he is here!":** Marilyn Noble, *Orphan Girl No. 58*, unpublished memoir, 3.

80   **He told the nun, "This child is very honest":** Deposition of Sally A. Dale for Sally A. Dale and Robert A. Dale, Wife and Husband, v. The Roman Catholic Diocese of Burlington, November 7, 1996, video 4, at 1:53.

84   **"Sister?"** Deposition of Sally A. Dale, for Sally A. Dale and Robert A. Dale, Wife and Husband, v. The Roman Catholic Diocese of Burlington, November 6, 1996, video 2, at 1:40.

87   **"You're going to eat it, Sally?":** Deposition of Sally A. Dale, for Sally A. Dale and Robert A. Dale, Wife and Husband, v. The Roman Catholic Diocese of Burlington, November 6, 1996, transcript, 98–99.

89   **"a little puppy with brown eyes":** Deposition of Sally A. Dale, for Sally A. Dale and Robert A. Dale, Wife and Husband, v. The Roman Catholic Diocese of Burlington, November 8, 1996, video 8, at 1:20.

90   **she told Irene that she loved her:** Sally Dale's experience of Irene was critical for her survival, but Sally Miller, who was at the orphanage in the 1950s and the 1960s, experienced Irene as very cruel. Irene called Miller "cream puff" and directed other derogatory language at her. Sally Miller also said that Eva DuPaul was very kind to her. Another witness, Barbara Hammons, described Eva as "cruel, mean, nasty." Another witness said that Eva hung her out the window of the bathroom. The accounts of negative treatment are not canceled out by the accounts of positive treatment some girls received. The point is that the adults treated different children in different ways.

Chapter 6

95   **"Oh, don't worry":** Sally A. Dale deposition, for Sally A. Dale and Robert A. Dale, Wife and Husband, v. The Roman Catholic Diocese of Burlington, Vermont, Inc., Vermont Catholic Charities, Inc., St. Joseph's Orphan Asylum, Inc., and/or its successors or assigns in interest and Sisters of Charity of Providence, a/k/a/ Sisters of Providence, United States District Court for the District of Vermont, November 6, 1996, video 3, at 1:23.

98 **"seriously retarded"**: Elizabeth Kundert, M.D., Report from Vermont Mental Hygiene Clinics, Vermont Catholic Charities, July 5, 1949.

102 **"What do I care about the moon and the stars?"**: Deposition of Sally A. Dale, for Sally A. Dale and Robert A. Dale, Wife and Husband, v. The Roman Catholic Diocese of Burlington, November 6, 1996, transcript, 55.

104 **"completely nuts"**: Deposition of Sally A. Dale, for Sally A. Dale and Robert A. Dale, Wife and Husband, v. The Roman Catholic Diocese of Burlington, November 6, 1996, transcript, 249.

105 **"Another accident?"**: Deposition of Sally A. Dale, for Sally A. Dale and Robert A. Dale, Wife and Husband, v. The Roman Catholic Diocese of Burlington, November 6, 1996, video 3, at 35:00.

108 **"black thing"**: Sally A. Dale interview with Howard Fitzpatrick, for Sally A. Dale and Robert A. Dale, Wife and Husband, v. The Roman Catholic Diocese of Burlington, November 7, 1996, Exhibit 1023, 30.

110 **"Sally, do you know what this is?"**: Deposition of Sally A. Dale, for Sally A. Dale and Robert A. Dale, Wife and Husband, v. The Roman Catholic Diocese of Burlington, November 6, 1996, transcript, 137.

113 **"Sherry, didn't you have enough"**: Deposition of Sally A. Dale, for Sally A. Dale and Robert A. Dale, Wife and Husband, v. The Roman Catholic Diocese of Burlington, November 7 and 8, 1996, video 5, at 1:46 (transcript, 183).

113 **Sister Blanchard had told her that she was going into a dirty world**: Sally A. Dale deposition interview with Howard Fitzpatrick, for Sally A. Dale and Robert A. Dale, Wife and Husband, v. The Roman Catholic Diocese of Burlington, October 29, 1993, Exhibit 1023, 19.

Chapter 7

116 **"They killed him, they killed him"**: Deposition of Deborah Hazen, for Sally A. Dale and Robert A. Dale, Wife and Husband, v. The Roman Catholic Diocese of Burlington, Vermont, Inc., Vermont Catholic Charities, Inc., St. Joseph's Orphan Asylum, Inc., and/or its successors or assigns in interest and Sisters of Charity of Providence, a/k/a/ Sisters of Providence, United States District Court for the District of Vermont, March 7, 1997, transcript, 15–17.

117 **"Someone said he'd hit his head"**: Deposition of Sally Miller, for Joseph R. Barquin, Jr. v. The Roman Catholic Diocese of Burlington, Vermont, Inc., Vermont Catholic Charities, Inc., St. Joseph's Orphan Asylum, Inc., and/or its successors or assigns in interest and Sister Jane Doe, United States District Court for the District of Vermont, May 30, 1996, transcript, 51.

119 **"We looked all over"**: Deposition of Joseph Eskra, for Sally A. Dale and Robert A. Dale, Wife and Husband, v. The Roman Catholic Diocese of Burlington, October 27, 1997, transcript, 20.

123 **He said he experienced "total fear"**: Joseph Gelineau and I discussed his memories a number of times. When I repeated back to him what I had heard, "total fear" and "terrified 24/7," he said the words didn't even come close to the actual feeling of being at the orphanage, the sense that "you knew you were going to be abused, you just didn't know when." In the 1990s, as the litigation against St. Joseph's began, Joseph Gelineau joined the survivors

group. He accumulated a set of documents, full of the horror stories of members of the group. One day a woman who called herself a reporter came to his house and interviewed him. The woman was small and wore baggy jeans and a baggy shirt. She asked if she could copy Gelineau's records for her story and he agreed. "I didn't ask for any ID," he told me. "I should have." The woman took the records away, saying she would bring them back later that day, but she never returned and Gelineau never saw the records again. Someone suggested to Gelineau that the woman had been a nun, sent by the Church. Years later when he contacted Vermont Catholic Charities, they said they were unable to furnish him with much more. This time he received a set of pages, most of which were blacked out, a report card, and the names of his brothers and sister and the dates they were at the orphanage. Years after that when we spoke, he first checked that I wasn't working for the Catholic Church in any way.

123 **She picked up a little satin pillow:** Deposition of Roger Barber, for Joseph R. Barquin, Jr. v. The Roman Catholic Diocese of Burlington, July 10, 1996, transcript, 102.

124 **"When she described it to me":** Deposition of Sheila Cardwell, for Sally A. Dale and Robert A. Dale, Wife and Husband, v. The Roman Catholic Diocese of Burlington, December 9, 1997, transcript, 46.

Chapter 8

131 **White's new approach:** White's jurisdiction also had a written interagency protocol for dealing with domestic violence, including a "no drop" policy, even if the victim recanted.

133 **taught a few of the nuns how to drive:** Dick Kieslich, conversation with the author. Kieslich's mother taught some of the nuns to drive.

133 **"For the purpose of this motion only":** Roman Catholic Diocese of Burlington, Defendant Motion for Judgement on the Pleadings, for Joseph R. Barquin, Jr. v. The Roman Catholic Diocese of Burlington, Vermont, Inc., Vermont Catholic Charities, Inc., St. Joseph's Orphan Asylum, Inc., and/or its successors or assigns in interest and Sister Jane Doe, United States District Court for the District of Vermont, July 16, 1993.

133 **"the law is not designed to aid the slothful":** Defendant's Motion for Judgement on the Pleadings, for Joseph R. Barquin, Jr. v. The Roman Catholic Diocese of Burlington.

135 **the statement was "a lie":** Sam Hemingway, "Cousin Accuses Bishop of Ignoring Abuse," *Burlington Free Press*, September 19, 1994.

135 **"absolutely false":** "Diocese Disputes Abuse Claims," *Burlington Free Press*, September 21, 1994.

135 **"No, we aren't perfect":** Gloria Gibson, "Diocese Responds to Alleged Sexual Abuse by Clergy," *Vermont Times*, November 11, 1993.

136 **"Who was the sister":** Joseph Barquin, transcript of interview with unidentified nun, 1994.

137 **"K remembers that Sister Madeline":** Letter from Philip White, Law Office of Wilson and White, to Bill O'Brien, O'Brien Law Offices, re: K.A., February 2, 1996.

137 **"If L was caught not paying attention":** Letter from Philip White, Law Office of Wilson and White, to Bill O'Brien, O'Brien Law Offices, re: L.D., June 4, 1996.

137 **"To this day, C will not enter":** Letter from Philip White, Law Office of Wilson and White, to Bill O'Brien, O'Brien Law Offices, re: C.B., January 4, 1996.

137 **"The nuns would also force G":** Letter from Philip White, Law Office of Wilson and White, to Bill O'Brien, O'Brien Law Offices, re: G.P., June 4, 1996.

138 **"If anybody has been hurt":** Bishop Kenneth A. Angell, Bishop of Burlington, pastoral letter printed in *Vermont Catholic Tribune*, February 2, 1996.

Chapter 11

158 **He did not trust "human people":** Deposition of Edward Duprey, for Joseph R. Barquin, Jr. v. The Roman Catholic Diocese of Burlington, Vermont, Inc., Vermont Catholic Charities, Inc., St. Joseph's Orphan Asylum, Inc., and/or its successors or assigns in interest and Sister Jane Doe, United States District Court for the District of Vermont, May 30, 1996, transcript, 8.

162 **"to be with the children he so dearly loved":** "Diocese to Raise Fund to Improve Orphanage Here," *Burlington Free Press*, April 27, 1954.

162 **"screaming and moaning and scraping sounds":** Marilyn Noble, *Orphan Girl No. 58*, unpublished memoir, 2.

163 **"it would cause false beliefs":** Sheila Cardwell, conversation with the author, February 2016.

164 **"Going up":** Photo caption from the *Vermont Edition*, February 27, 1955.

165 **"some who travelled a good distance":** *Chronicles of St. Joseph's Orphanage*, July 1, 1953 to June 30, 1954, May edition.

166 **"We were very happy to have":** *Chronicles of St. Joseph's Orphanage*, July 1, 1968 to June 30, 1969, August edition.

166 **"Providence of God":** *Chronicles of St. Joseph's Orphanage*, July 1, 1960 to June 30, 1961, April edition.

167 **"selfish, exacting, and ungrateful":** *Chronicles of St. Joseph's Orphanage*, July 1, 1969 to June 30, 1970, August edition.

167 **"who was BOSS":** *Chronicles of St. Joseph's Orphanage*, July 1, 1971 to June 30, 1972, September edition.

168 **"eventually probably went to the orphanage":** Deposition of Monsignor John McSweeney, for Sally A. Dale and Robert A. Dale, Wife and Husband, v. The Roman Catholic Diocese of Burlington, Vermont, Inc., Vermont Catholic Charities, Inc., St. Joseph's Orphan Asylum, Inc., and/or its successors or assigns in interest and Sisters of Charity of Providence, a/k/a/ Sisters of Providence, United States District Court for the District of Vermont, March 5, 1998, transcript, 20–21.

168 **The bishop was a bit embarrassed:** Bishop of Burlington, letter to Mother Superior, January 20, 1962.

171 **recently founded the Vermont Women's Health Center:** Vermont's Supreme Court struck down its statute prohibiting abortion (in all cases except to save the mother's life) in 1972, a year before *Roe v. Wade*, allowing the health center to be established in 1972, before a similar center was established

in 1974 in Concord, New Hampshire, which appears to have been the second clinic to offer pregnancy termination in New England.

172 **likened it to a slaughterhouse:** "Election Laws, Abortion, Other Issues Discussed," *Vermont Freeman*, October 1, 1972.

172 **arriving every two weeks:** Amy Lilly, "Choice, Before and After: Vermont's First Abortion Providers Give *Roe v. Wade* a Check-up," *Seven Days*, January 16, 2008.

172 **"At the very moment in time":** Raymond Syriac, "Reflections on St. Joseph's Child Center," for Joseph R. Barquin, Jr. v. The Roman Catholic Diocese of Burlington, January 21, 1974, Deposition Exhibit 4.

174 *cette musicienne douée*: This and other comments about Sister James Mary are from the personnel file for Sister Jacques Marie (Léonille Racicot), Hommage a Soeur Léonille Racicot, Sisters of Providence.

Chapter 12

178 **"You could always tell when they were done":** Deposition of Patricia Zeno, for Sally A. Dale and Robert A. Dale, Wife and Husband, v. The Roman Catholic Diocese of Burlington, Vermont, Inc., Vermont Catholic Charities, Inc., St. Joseph's Orphan Asylum, Inc., and/or its successors or assigns in interest and Sisters of Charity of Providence, a/k/a/ Sisters of Providence, United States District Court for the District of Vermont, January 27, 1997, transcript, 60.

178 **"teach her a lesson":** Deposition of Sally Miller, for Sally A. Dale and Robert A. Dale, Wife and Husband, v. The Roman Catholic Diocese of Burlington, February 18, 1997, transcript.

178 **"This is what happens to people who steal":** Deposition of Patricia Zeno, for Sally A. Dale and Robert A. Dale, Wife and Husband, v. The Roman Catholic Diocese of Burlington, January 27, 1997, transcript, 78.

178 **"This is what happens when you":** Deposition of P. A., for Sally A. Dale and Robert A. Dale, Wife and Husband, v. The Roman Catholic Diocese of Burlington, October 15, 1997, transcript, 12.

178 **"She lit the match and she held her hand":** Deposition of G. P., for Sally A. Dale and Robert A. Dale, Wife and Husband, v. The Roman Catholic Diocese of Burlington, September 30, 1997, transcript, 9.

178 **"took matches out of her dress":** Deposition of P. A., for Sally A. Dale and Robert A. Dale, Wife and Husband, v. The Roman Catholic Diocese of Burlington, October 15, 1997, transcript, 12.

181 **"You know what I mean":** Deposition of Sally Miller, for Joseph R. Barquin, Jr. v. The Roman Catholic Diocese of Burlington, Vermont, Inc., Vermont Catholic Charities, Inc., St. Joseph's Orphan Asylum, Inc., and/or its successors or assigns in interest and Sister Jane Doe, United States District Court for the District of Vermont, May 30, 1996, transcript, 12.

185 **molestation and other abuse:** A number of men told me about frequent sexual activity between the boys in the dorms, some of which evolved into a kind of organized hazing assault of new, smaller boys. It is now well known that children who are being sexually abused will sometimes act out those abusive behaviors with other children.

185 **"You can't say anything to jeopardize":** Deposition of Roger Barber, for Joseph R. Barquin, Jr. v. The Roman Catholic Diocese of Burlington, July 10, 1996, transcript.

186 **"that patch of light":** Deposition of R. M., for Sally A. Dale and Robert A. Dale, Wife and Husband, v. The Roman Catholic Diocese of Burlington, February 19, 1997, transcript, 144.

186 **"Well just generally, I get my jollies":** Deposition of Robert J. McKay, for Sally A. Dale and Robert A. Dale, Wife and Husband, v. The Roman Catholic Diocese of Burlington, June 6, 1997, transcript, 155.

187 **"We tried to benefit from":** Deposition of Monsignor Paul Bresnehan, for Sally A. Dale and Robert A. Dale, Wife and Husband, v. The Roman Catholic Diocese of Burlington, June 4, 1997, transcript, 60.

187 **Lucey said no:** Deposition of Jerold Lucey, for Sally A. Dale and Robert A. Dale, Wife and Husband, v. The Roman Catholic Diocese of Burlington, June 25, 1997, transcript, 40.

187 **school-age children in the 1940s:** John H. Browe and Harold B. Pierce, "A Survey of Nutritional Status Among School Children and Their Response to Nutrient Therapy," *Milbank Memorial Fund Quarterly* xxviii, no. 3 (July 1950): 222–237.

188 **sending institutionalized children out to regular schools:** In the absence of records, it is unclear if some of the remembered incidences were cases of medical treatment that were insufficiently explained to the children or if they were organized studies. Former residents from St. Colman's orphanage in Albany, New York, told me similar stories about being given red pills and injections, and never knowing what they were for, or not being able to find any trace of the drugs in their medical records. If St. Joseph's made its children available to other outside organizations for their use, as they did for Dr. McKay, they would not be the only orphanage to have done so. In one famous twentieth-century case, a doctor intentionally induced stuttering in children at an Iowa orphanage in order to study the phenomenon. Sadly, when the study was over, some of the children were unable to stop stuttering. When the experiment was first publicly questioned, it was framed as a tragic and exceptional story, but it is far from the only example. In Ohio in 1943, children at the Soldiers and Sailors Orphanage were used in dysentery studies. All suffered serious side effects. In the worst cases, the children fell sick within thirty minutes of being administered an experimental vaccine. They had high fever, extreme headache, backache, nausea, vomiting, and diarrhea. In Canada, in homes run by Catholic nuns, including the same order that ran St. Joseph's in Vermont, children were used for vaccine trials in the 1960s. In Australia during the same time period, babies in Catholic-run homes were used in vaccine trials as described in Chapter 2. In Ireland, documents subpoenaed from GlaxoSmithKline showed that children in mother and baby homes and other institutions were also used for vaccine trials, including the home in Tuam, which was investigated by Catherine Corless.

189 **"I had never seen a nun touched":** This and other related quotes in this scene are from the deposition of Sally Miller, for Sally A. Dale and Robert

A. Dale, Wife and Husband, v. The Roman Catholic Diocese of Burlington, March 4, 1997, transcript, 7.

Chapter 13

193 **Geoff Morris was quoted:** Sam Hemingway, "Lawsuits Detail Abuse at Orphanage, Nun Threw Child from Fourth Floor, Residents Say," *Burlington Free Press*, June 15, 1996.

194 **"just simply unbelievable":** Sam Hemingway, "Echoes of Abuse Grip Orphans," *Burlington Free Press*, October 27, 1996.

195 **"ran like the dickens":** Deposition of Patricia Zeno, for Sally A. Dale and Robert A. Dale, Wife and Husband, v. The Roman Catholic Diocese of Burlington, Vermont, Inc., Vermont Catholic Charities, Inc., St. Joseph's Orphan Asylum, Inc., and/or its successors or assigns in interest and Sisters of Charity of Providence, a/k/a/ Sisters of Providence, United States District Court for the District of Vermont, January 24, 1997, transcript, 144.

195 **"They used to call me the human skeleton":** Deposition of Patricia Zeno, for Sally A. Dale and Robert A. Dale, Wife and Husband, v. The Roman Catholic Diocese of Burlington, January 24, 1997, transcript, 66.

197 **"Yeah," Carbonneau said, "but do you still do that?":** Deposition of Patricia Zeno, for Sally A. Dale and Robert A. Dale, Wife and Husband, v. The Roman Catholic Diocese of Burlington, November 8, 1996, video 7, at 1:25.

199 **"Now if I tell you":** Deposition of J. H., for Sally A. Dale and Robert A. Dale, Wife and Husband, v. The Roman Catholic Diocese of Burlington, February 12, 1998.

200 **"That boy, for example":** Deposition of Joseph Eskra, for Sally A. Dale and Robert A. Dale, Wife and Husband, v. The Roman Catholic Diocese of Burlington, October 27, 1997, transcript, 39.

201 **"in addition to his memories of alleged experiences":** Sisters of Providence, Defendant Memorandum in Opposition to Plaintiffs' Motion to Stay Discovery Deadlines, for Patricia Zeno and Alfred Zeno v. The Roman Catholic Diocese of Burlington, Vermont, Inc., Vermont Catholic Charities, Inc., St. Joseph's Orphan Asylum, Inc., and/or its successors or assigns in interest and Sisters of Charity of Providence, a/k/a/ Sisters of Charity, State of Vermont, Chittenden County, SS, December 19, 1997.

202 **"Rage and anger is never going to work":** Sam Hemingway, "Orphans Struggle to Escape Past," *Burlington Free Press*, October 28, 1996.

Chapter 14

205 **Sister Mary Vianney was "loving":** Deposition of Phyllis M. McKenzie, for Sally A. Dale and Robert A. Dale, Wife and Husband, v. The Roman Catholic Diocese of Burlington, Vermont, Inc., Vermont Catholic Charities, Inc., St. Joseph's Orphan Asylum, Inc., and/or its successors or assigns in interest and Sisters of Charity of Providence, a/k/a/ Sisters of Providence, United States District Court for the District of Vermont, June 2, 1997, transcript, 89.

205 **"stately":** Deposition of Elizabeth L. Gadue, for Sally A. Dale and Robert A. Dale, Wife and Husband, v. The Roman Catholic Diocese of Burlington, February 13, 1998, transcript, 12.

205 "a sense of humor": Deposition of John Leonard, for Sally A. Dale and Robert A. Dale, Wife and Husband, v. The Roman Catholic Diocese of Burlington, February 23, 1998, transcript, 89.

205 "the comedian": Deposition of John Leonard, transcript, 8.

205 "a real lady": Deposition of John Leonard, transcript, 9.

205 "a very nice, gentle man": Deposition of Marie Thibault, for Sally A. Dale and Robert A. Dale, Wife and Husband, v. The Roman Catholic Diocese of Burlington, December 16, 1997, transcript, 24.

205 a "saint": Deposition of Marilyn Doaner, for Sally A. Dale and Robert A. Dale, Wife and Husband, v. The Roman Catholic Diocese of Burlington, April 23, 1998, transcript, 35.

205 "How could these people": Deposition of Robert McNulty, for Sally A. Dale and Robert A. Dale, Wife and Husband, v. The Roman Catholic Diocese of Burlington, December 10, 1997, transcript, 6.

206 "I don't recall": "Memo from Geoff Morris to Bob Widman on December 18, 1997, re: Deposition of Marie Thibault," for Sally A. Dale and Robert A. Dale, Wife and Husband, v. The Roman Catholic Diocese of Burlington.

207 "one check if you were sassy": Deposition of Patricia Dague, for Sally A. Dale and Robert A. Dale, Wife and Husband, v. The Roman Catholic Diocese of Burlington, October 29, 1997, transcript, 11.

208 "So if children who": Deposition of Phyllis M. McKenzie, 50.

208 "something out of *Oliver Twist*": Deposition of Phyllis M. McKenzie, 53.

208 "a little notoriety," a "place in the sun": Deposition of Phyllis M. McKenzie, 95.

209 "Oh, Sister Jane": Deposition of Sherry Lee Bousquet, for Sally A. Dale and Robert A. Dale, Wife and Husband, v. The Roman Catholic Diocese of Burlington, November 6, 1997, transcript, 10.

209 "I feel she was just trying": Deposition of Sherry Lee Bousquet, 14.

210 "Your knuckles": Deposition of Joan Krawczyk, for Sally A. Dale and Robert A. Dale, Wife and Husband, v. The Roman Catholic Diocese of Burlington, January 21, 1998, transcript, 13.

210 "If something bad happens": Deposition of Joyce Delisle, for Sally A. Dale and Robert A. Dale, Wife and Husband, v. The Roman Catholic Diocese of Burlington, February 2, 1998, transcript, 67.

211 "It didn't leave a red mark": Deposition of Joyce Delisle, 79.

212 but for the plaintiffs: Robert Widman, conversation with the author. I had access to many transcripts and recordings from the litigation, but there were many I never found. I did not find a transcript for the events described here. I asked one of the defense lawyers about this day, but he said he couldn't recall an event like the one Widman described.

213 "We put on a minstrel show": Deposition of Monsignor Edward Foster, for Sally A. Dale and Robert A. Dale, Wife and Husband, v. The Roman Catholic Diocese of Burlington, November 13, 1997, transcript.

213 "You bought babies": Deposition of Monsignor Edward Foster, 138.

214 "But they were always separate": Deposition of Monsignor Edward Foster, 58.

214 "Never, ever. Never": Deposition of Monsignor Edward Foster, 59.

215 **It was an isolated case:** The woman who accused Foster told the lawyers she worked as a prostitute after leaving the orphanage. Another former resident who was sexually abused by nuns, and who saw her sister raped by nuns at St. Joseph's, told a reporter that she became a prostitute at the age of eleven (Susan Youngwood, *Vermont Times*, September 30, 1993).

215 **"Absolutely not":** Deposition of Monsignor Edward Foster, 124.

215 **contained just one page:** Widman obtained files for his plaintiffs from Vermont Catholic Charities. Some appeared to have been altered. The photocopy he received of Sally Dale's file, supposed to be an unaltered verbatim copy, contained two pages where the top part of the page was exactly the same, but the bottom half was different. It looked like someone had cut and pasted pages together but accidentally used the same segment twice.

215 **"It was unthinkable really":** Deposition of Bishop Kenneth Angell of the Diocese of Burlington, for Joseph R. Barquin, Jr. v. The Roman Catholic Diocese of Burlington, Vermont, Inc., Vermont Catholic Charities, Inc., St. Joseph's Orphan Asylum, Inc., and/or its successors or assigns in interest and Sister Jane Doe, United States District Court for the District of Vermont, May 31, 1996, transcript, 48.

216 **"lively nun":** Deposition of Sister Fernande de Grace, for Sally A. Dale and Robert A. Dale, Wife and Husband, v. The Roman Catholic Diocese of Burlington, May 7, 1997, transcript, 12.

217 **Had Sauvageau had any problems** This and other related quotes from this scene are from the deposition of Sister Julienne Sauvageau, for Katelin Hoffman v. The Roman Catholic Diocese of Burlington, August 18, 1998, transcript, 154.

217 **At the time, Delisle was the only girl:** One woman who was at St. Joseph's Orphanage for some years in the 1950s and 60s remembered seeing nuns scrubbing the skin of a "'dark skinned girl' . . . until she bled." She said, "The nun kept telling her she was dirty and she was always going to be dirty." The woman who reported the incident said that she had wanted to play with the girl, but she wasn't allowed to because of her skin color.

Chapter 15

221 **"He kind of hit, and":** Deposition of Sally A. Dale, for Sally A. Dale and Robert A. Dale, Wife and Husband, v. The Roman Catholic Diocese of Burlington, Vermont, Inc., Vermont Catholic Charities, Inc., St. Joseph's Orphan Asylum, Inc., and/or its successors or assigns in interest and Sisters of Charity of Providence, a/k/a/ Sisters of Providence, United States District Court for the District of Vermont, November 8, 1996, video 2, at 1:40.

222 **"Well, why would they have":** Deposition of Sally A. Dale, video 8, at 38:00.

223 **"What can I say?":** Deposition of Sally A. Dale, video 3, at 1:15.

223 **"sweaty or wet or something":** Deposition of Sally A. Dale, video 6, at 40:00.

223 **"I got to take a break":** Deposition of Sally A. Dale, at video 6, at 40:00.

223 **"Will you agree with me":** This and other quotes from this scene are from the deposition of Sally A. Dale, video 8, at 1:48.

224 **"How do you know it's not your imagination?":** This and other quotes from this scene are from the deposition of Sally A. Dale, video 4, at 1:28.

224 **"Body first":** Deposition of Sally A. Dale, video 2, at 1:45.

224 **"I don't know if it was just hidden back there":** Deposition of Sally A. Dale, video 7, at 1:41.

225 **"It's just I didn't want to hurt":** Deposition of Sally A. Dale, video 2, at 0:26.

225 **"Did you ever see a nun":** Deposition of Sally A. Dale, video 7, at 1:42.

229 **"People who go through a public tragedy":** Deposition of Bessel van der Kolk, for Sally A. Dale and Robert A. Dale, Wife and Husband, v. The Roman Catholic Diocese of Burlington, date and transcript page unknown.

230 **"Not that you remember":** Deposition of Roger Barber, for Sally A. Dale and Robert A. Dale, Wife and Husband, v. The Roman Catholic Diocese of Burlington, December 8, 1997, transcript, 52.

231 **Where was the research:** Deposition of Anna Salter, for Sally A. Dale and Robert A. Dale, Wife and Husband, v. The Roman Catholic Diocese of Burlington, date and transcript page unknown.

231 **"You would have to ask instead":** Deposition of Bessel van der Kolk.

232 **"Did this happen once a week to you?":** Deposition of Dale Greene, for Sally A. Dale and Robert A. Dale, Wife and Husband, v. The Roman Catholic Diocese of Burlington, May 20, 1997, transcript, 196.

233 **"Do you know whether she inserted her finger":** Deposition of M. W., for M. W. v. The Roman Catholic Diocese of Burlington, Vermont, Inc., Vermont Catholic Charities, Inc., St. Joseph's Orphan Asylum, Inc., and/or its successors or assigns in interest and Sisters of Charity of Providence, a/k/a/ Sisters of Providence, State of Vermont, Chittenden County, April 9 and 10, 1998, transcript, 99.

233 **"Do you have any belief":** Deposition of C. R., for Sally A. Dale and Robert A. Dale, Wife and Husband, v. The Roman Catholic Diocese of Burlington, April 10, 1997, transcript, 46.

233 **"You say all kinds of stuff":** Deposition of Dale Greene, 152.

234 **"the first time you ever thought":** Deposition of Dale Greene, 214.

234 **"Now that ain't right":** Dale Greene told me that after talking to the lawyers, all the terrible memories of the orphanage came flooding back, and he endured a year of nightmares.

235 **the cumulative reports of former residents:** Albert M. Drukteinis, M.D. J.D., psychiatric evaluation of [name withheld], New England Psychodiagnostics, January 12, 1999.

Chapter 16

242 **she beckoned me and a translator:** Translator, Emma Loop, journalist.

243 **the unclaimed bodies of orphans:** The children were buried without tombstones or markers. No one knows today how many of their bodies were sold by nuns. In the early 2000s, the Children of Duplessis survivors group said that many children were buried in the cemetery next to the Saint-Jean-de-Dieu hospital and asked for them to be exhumed. They believed that exhumation would prove children had been subject to different kinds of surgical experimentation, including experimental lobotomies. The cemetery was closed in

1958 and is now covered by a warehouse for the provincial liquor store. The bodies were never exhumed.

243 **medical schools for ten dollars per body:** "Duplessis Orphans Seek Proof of Medical Experiments," *CBC News*, June 19, 2004.

243 **spoke on the phone with the help:** The translator was journalist Emma Loop.

244 **"Now we can only pray":** Gloria J. Gibson, "Diocese Responds to Alleged Sexual Abuse by Clergy," *Vermont Times*, November 11, 1993.

244 **"Quebec society was to blame":** Clyde H. Farnsworth, "Orphans of the 1950's, Telling of Abuse, Sue Quebec," *New York Times*, May 21, 1993.

Chapter 17

248 **"Did Gilbert die after a beating by a nun?":** Dan Lynch, "Answers to a 42-Year-Old Mystery May Have Eroded Away," *Times Union*, December 21, 1995.

251 **"accurate factual information (!)":** Sol Greenberg, letter to Mike Ruede, February 23, 1996.

Chapter 18

255 **for failing to discover . . . that their local priest was molesting their son:** "The Catholic Church Struggles with Suits over Sexual Abuse: While It Pledges Compassion, Its Lawyers Play Rough Defending Lapsed Priests Suing Parents for Negligence," *Wall Street Journal*, November 24, 1993.

256 **At every opportunity:** Quotes from this paragraph are from the Sisters of Providence, Defendant Memorandum in Opposition to Plaintiffs' Motion to Stay Discovery Deadlines, for Patricia Zeno and Alfred Zeno v. The Roman Catholic Diocese of Burlington, Vermont, Inc., Vermont Catholic Charities, Inc., St. Joseph's Orphan Asylum, Inc., and/or its successors or assigns in interest and Sisters of Charity of Providence, a/k/a/ Sisters of Charity, State of Vermont, Chittenden County, SS, December 19, 1997.

258 **"phantom victims":** Sisters of Providence, Defendant Memorandum in Opposition to Plaintiffs' Motion to Stay Discovery Deadlines.

Chapter 19

270 **"severe sexual issues":** Saint Luke Institute, letter to Kenneth Angell, Bishop of Burlington, regarding Reverend Edward Foster, SLI NO 12959, July 15, 1994.

274 **"God was his boss":** Philip White of the Law Office of Wilson and White, letter to Bill O'Brien of the O'Brien Law Offices, regarding K.T., February 16, 1996.

275 **complaint from Sister Madrin at St. Joseph's Orphanage:** The note addressed to the bishop was written by Sister Madrin, a whistleblower of sorts, who worked at St. Joseph's Orphanage from at least 1959 to 1960. The Sisters of Providence provided significant documentation during the 1990s litigation, including what was supposed to be an exhaustive list of every nun who worked in Burlington from 1935 to 1960, but no trace of Sister Madrin appears in the documents.

275   **The boy had been "obese," "erratic,":** Deposition of Father Forrest Rouelle, for Sally A. Dale and Robert A. Dale, Wife and Husband, v. The Roman Catholic Diocese of Burlington, Vermont, Inc., Vermont Catholic Charities, Inc., St. Joseph's Orphan Asylum, Inc., and/or its successors or assigns in interest and Sisters of Charity of Providence, a/k/a/ Sisters of Providence, United States District Court for the District of Vermont, June 5, 1997, transcript, 27.

275   **"a bunch of hogwash":** Deposition of Father Forrest Rouelle, 31.

275   **molested by a man he believed to be Rouelle:** When Rouelle's file was handed over in 2006, it should have included every document relevant to his tenure as a priest at the orphanage. As such, it included a letter from Philip White about a man who was a former resident of the orphanage and who believed he had been molested by Rouelle. But I came across another letter that reported sexual behavior from Rouelle at the orphanage that had not been included in the 2006 cache, even though it was supposed to be an exhaustive file.

276   **a stack of Polaroids of naked children:** Katelin Hoffman, conversation with the author, 2016.

276   **something inappropriate on his computer:** An investigation into Miller was conducted by Cindy Maguire, Chief of the Criminal Division from the Office of the State Attorney General. On December 9, 2004, she wrote a letter addressed to then bishop Kenneth Angell; it began by saying that on May 14, 2002, the diocese had provided her office with a list of priests who had been accused of child sexual abuse. She then observed that Walter Miller, the current chancellor of the diocese, was not on that list, even though the diocese was aware that there had been allegations of child pornography on Miller's computer at the time that the list was prepared. Maguire went on to explain that those claims, as well as additional claims about the rape and assault of children, were investigated by her office. She noted that allegations of rape and assault fell outside the statute of limitations. However, the child pornography claims, if proven, would fall within the statute of limitations. Maguire then added, "Under the specific facts of this case, we do not believe that sufficient evidence exists to proceed with the criminal prosecution, particularly with the deletion of the computer files." Maguire also described a March 27, 2002, letter from Miller's attorney, provided by the diocese, that asserted their computer expert had evaluated Miller's computer and concluded it did not contain pornography.

277   **"an unheralded visitation":** *Burlington Free Press*, February 1, 1943.

Chapter 20

280   **death certificates:** An entry in the 1943 *Chronicles* dated September 3 described the baptism of three babies, Mary-Ann, aged four months, who was transferred to Fanny Allen Hospital, and twin brothers Alfred and Antoine, aged four months, also transferred to Fanny Allen Hospital. The entry states that the children were made angels by the sacrament of baptism. No other entry in decades of the *Chronicles* connected a baptism announcement with babies or children being made angels, or connected their baptism with a

transfer to the hospital. There are no death certificates for these children. It's unclear what happened to them.

287 **crawled under a high-tension wire:** "Joseph Millette Hit by 33,000-Volt Blast," *Burlington Free Press*, April 18, 1955.

289 **A former resident suggested:** Katelin Hoffman, conversation with the author, 2016.

Chapter 21

295 **most investigations and inquiries:** In 2022, the government of Northern Ireland issued an apology to former residents of orphanages and children's homes after a formal inquiry into institutional abuse.

295 **missing children had begun to return anyway:** In 2013, anthropologists uncovered the remains of dozens of boys in a cemetery at the site of the former Arthur G. Dozier reform school in Marianna, Florida. Records indicated the existence of thirty-one graves in the cemetery, but investigators found the remains of more than fifty individuals. Former residents of the school and their families had been agitating for an investigation for years. Some families had been told their boys had run away from the school, but they had never seen them again. Survivors told stories of extreme physical abuse and there were eyewitness accounts of the deaths of boys, but for a long time no one in power had listened. The results of the cemetery investigation were greeted, finally, with outrage; however, there was a sense in the way the school was discussed that because it was a reformatory, its violent history was specifically shaped, or at least heavily influenced, by that function. In fact, twentieth-century reformatories, training schools, and other institutions of juvenile justice have much in common with the orphanages. Older boys with criminal records were sent to the Dozier school, but there were also boys there as young as five. Survivors of the school reported that many children were sent there only because they had run away from home or simply because they had no family support. The poverty of all connected communities and the way they were treated by society in general, and by the law in particular, are critical to the history of both kinds of institutions. It's only in recent decades that the systems that deal with child protection and with criminal matters have become distinct. In fact, in the first half of the twentieth century, children in some countries were effectively criminalized when they were sent into institutional care. As recently as 2018, the Australian state of Victoria apologized for the fact that in the twentieth century, criminal records were created for children when they were made wards of the state.

295 **the nation's mother and baby homes:** St. Joseph's Orphanage performed some of the same functions as the mother and baby homes. It ran a nursery for babies. Newborns were sometimes left on the front doorstep. In Burlington, the Elizabeth Lund Home, or as it was known in the 1920s, the Home for Friendless Women, also performed many of the same functions, housing young women and girls who were pregnant and finding homes for their babies. Death certificates for the Lund Home indicate there were more than seventy baby deaths in the twenty-five years between 1924 and 1949. Katelin

Hoffman spent time at St. Joseph's Orphanage and also spent two years at the Lund Home, even though she wasn't pregnant.

295　**research into the Mother and Baby Home in Tuam run by the Bon Secours Sisters:** Catherine Corless, "The Home," *Journal of the Old Tuam Society* 9 (2012): 75–82, reprinted by The Children's Home Graveyard Committee, Tuam, County Galway, Ireland.

296　**if victims hadn't reported abuse:** As in Scotland, some states in Australia have repealed the statute of limitations on both sexual and physical abuse in civil litigation. In the Australian state of Victoria, at the time of writing, cases that tried both sexual and physical abuse together had been run, but no single case that tried only physical abuse had taken place. However, one lawyer told me that lifting the statute of limitations in civil litigation created a wedge, so that for the first time, survivors were settling physical abuse cases for significant sums. The law and the history remain tricky; part of the problem is that corporal punishment was once legal, whereas sexual abuse never was.

297　**Blackstock's caller:** Blackstock's caller was a child abuse campaigner who had spent time as a child at another residential home.

297　**first home to be investigated:** The Scottish government inquiry established a redress scheme that offered compensation as an alternative to plaintiffs pursuing abusers through the legal system. Recently, the Sisters of Charity said they were willing to contribute £10 million to the fund. The amount was considerably more than that offered by other involved institutions, some of which contributed nothing. At the same time, however, the sisters did not support a move to place a memorial with all the names of the children at the site. The newly refurbished marble tombstones of the nuns at the same cemetery will, however, last hundreds of years.

298　**New England Company:** The New England Company for the Education and Propagation of the Gospel collected money from investors to conduct missionary work in Canada.

298　**The Six Nations group was launched:** Part of the work of the Six Nations investigation is to bring together the many relevant historical records, some of which are still in the possession of other institutions, such as the archives of the Anglican Church and the New England Company in England.

298　**the country's 139 residential schools:** There were 139 residential schools that operated with government support. Other residential schools did not receive government support and are not included in this count as a result.

299　**this was the first time in United States history:** Vermont is the first US state to totally repeal the statute of limitations on civil actions for child physical abuse. It is also the first state to make the repeal retroactive, such that actions barred by the previous version of the statute of limitations can now be revived. The bill formally passed through both the Vermont state house and senate on April 30, 2021, and the law was formally enacted on July 1, 2021. Louisiana made significant progress in June 2021 when it passed a provision "for physical abuse of a minor resulting in permanent impairment or permanent physical injury or scarring" that eliminates the statute of limitations in those cases. Actions barred by the previous version of the statute of limitations in Louisiana can be "revived" and brought until June 2024, but no later. Since the early 2010s, Florida, Idaho, and Oregon have been the states with the most generous civil statute of limitations policies on physical child abuse. While they have not fully or partially eliminated the statute of limitations, they now permit cases to be brought within several years of "discovery," which could occur later in life. At the other end of the spectrum, Kansas and Kentucky have a one-year statute of limitations that is not influenced by the age of majority, so the action must be brought within one year of the alleged act of abuse, even if the plaintiff is a minor. Wyoming has the same one-year statute of limitations for abuse, and a four-year statute of limitations for negligence, also not affected by the age of majority.

299 **in the previous two years:** A number of legal cases against the Catholic Church were launched in 2019 in Albany, New York, when the state paused the statute of limitations, opening a window for people who had been abused as children to bring cases. In the wake of the publication of the *BuzzFeed News* orphanage article, some of those cases concerned abuse at St. Colman's Home. In 2022, Howard Hubbard, who was bishop of Albany from 1977 to 2014, presiding when the 1990s investigation into St. Colman's Home took place, admitted that he had covered up reports of abusive priests in Albany parishes over many years. Hubbard himself is the subject of at least seven lawsuits, accusing him of sexual abuse. He has denied it.

300 **the details of a state investigation:** Chris McDaniel, "The Secret Results of Vermont's Investigation into Sex Abuse by Priests," *BuzzFeed News*, October 10, 2018.

300 **a list of forty credibly accused priests:** The diocese explained that they modeled their criteria for determining a priest to be "credibly accused" on the criteria used by the Diocese of Syracuse, New York. They explained that a credible allegation was one that met one or more of the following criteria: it was natural, plausible, and probable; it corroborated with other evidence or another source; or it was acknowledged/admitted to by the accused.

300 **Included in the diocesan list:** Louis Gelineau, onetime seminarian who spent time at St. Joseph's Orphanage and later became bishop of Rhode Island, was accused of being abusive by Bob Cadorette in the 1990s litigation. Gelineau's career as bishop was marked by similar accusations, both of abuse and the cover-up of abuse. He is not included on the 2019 list of priests in the Diocese of Burlington.

Chapter 22

307 **inherent to the operation of institutions:** Shurlee Swain, "Institutional Abuse: A Long History," *Journal of Australia Studies* (June 17, 2018):153–163.

308 **a sophisticated analysis of human institutions:** In legal terms, the "dirty institution theory" of Widman and Langrock would be a good place to start.

309 **Those influential survivors include very small children:** There are many stories about the valor and rebelliousness of young children even in impossible situations. In the 1990s, one man recounted how boys in the 1940s at St. Joseph's Orphanage found a dead muskrat down by the lake. They quietly carried it in a box up to the orphanage building, where they placed

it between the sheets of Sister Leontine's bed. Fifty years later, the man remembered clearly hearing the nun scream when she found it. Other boys spoke about finding rulers or other implements used by nuns to beat them, and snapping them in half and throwing them out a window. One girl in the 1960s leaped on a nun who was hurting her sister, unintentionally ripping off the woman's habit. She still remembers the woman melting like the witch in the *Wizard of Oz*. Later in life, an Australian man returned one night to the institution, where a statue of his abuser had been erected. He and a friend had brought tools and, under the cover of darkness, quietly decapitated the statue of their tormentor.

311 **"control the meeting and the situation":** Joe Bukuras, "Diocese, Former Orphanage residents in Vermont Differ in Views of Recovery Process," *Catholic World Report*, June 17, 2022.

312 **"those who allege hardship":** Kevin O'Connor, "Vermont Review of Church Orphanage Finds Misconduct but not Murder," *VTDigger*, December 14, 2020.

312 **"peace and healing":** Don Amato, "Orphanage Report: Investigators Say Authorities Failed to Pursue Abuse Claims," WCAX-TV, December 14, 2020.

INDEX

Abbott, Bud, 65

Abenaki tribe, 164

abortion, 58, 174

abuse

in Australian orphanages, 11–15,
23–25, 30–34, 37–53, 245,
298–299, 309–311

beatings, 33–35, 46, 51, 84, 90,
94, 99, 111, 122, 145, 185–188,
192, 220 221, 236, 242–244,
250–254, 303

burned boy incident, 108–111,
149, 152, 227, 233, 264–265,
289–290

in Canadian orphanages, 13–15,
33, 52–54, 123, 239–249, 291,
300–305

Catholic Church and, 52, 62–63,
125, 132, 163, 182, 231, 254–255,
259–260

crying girl incident, 103–104, 107,
116, 264

drownings, 52–53, 62, 94–95,
117–119, 145, 149, 218, 264,
282, 293

drugs and, 188–190, 240,
243–245

electric chair incidents, 53–54, 94,
105–106, 110–111, 166, 175,
231–232, 245–246, 290–291

electric shocks, 44, 245, 299

electrocution, 108–111, 145,
149–152, 227, 233, 264–265,
289–290, 293, 298

emotional abuse, 16, 24–25, 33–34,
132–134, 166, 190, 262–264,
303–304

forced labor, 24, 31–32, 38–39,
48–50, 100–101, 149, 221

freezing incidents, 52–53, 62,
115–116, 119–120, 201–202,
264, 282, 291–293

illnesses, 44–45, 230, 291–292

investigating, 17–18, 34–35, 37–69,
116–127, 140, 154–157, 195–196,
230–233, 243–256, 264–265,
282–283, 297–303, 309–317

locked up incidents, 20–22, 29, 80,
86–91, 103–104, 110, 115–116,
122, 129, 140, 147, 149–153,
166, 191–192, 195–197, 208,
291–292

molestation, 30, 48–54, 83–84,
146, 187, 210, 231–237,
257–264, 277, 308

physical abuse, 11–12, 16, 24–25,
30–34, 44–57, 60–69, 78–91,
94–113, 115–126, 129–138,
145–147, 154–157, 159–161,
180–192, 196–237, 239–247,
249–264, 272–279, 286–291,
299–305, 307–312

abuse (*continued*)
  psychological abuse, 132–134,
    273–274, 303
  rape, 5, 11, 48–49, 52–56, 203,
    213, 231, 235
  restraints, 66–69, 110, 119–123,
    166, 181, 201–202, 240–245,
    291
  sedatives and, 190, 240, 243–245
  sexual abuse, 5, 11–12, 24–25, 30,
    47–56, 61–69, 83–84, 125–126,
    129–136, 146, 187–191,
    202–217,
    224–237, 252–264, 272–279,
    286, 302–305, 307–312
  staircase incidents, 33–35, 60,
    104–107, 116, 155, 211, 264
  statute of limitations, 124–126,
    133, 136–137, 213–214, 246,
    253, 261–262, 298–304, 312
  straitjackets, 242–244
  suffocations, 123–124, 242–244
  in United Kingdom orphanages,
    33, 39–40, 52, 246, 297–299
  in United States orphanages, 5,
    11–12, 16, 24–25, 30–34,
    44–57, 60–69, 78–91, 94–113,
    115–126, 129–138, 145–147,
    154–157, 159–161, 180–192,
    196–237, 239–247, 249–264,
    272–279, 286–291, 299–305,
    307–312
  whippings, 12, 35, 60, 83, 89–90,
    140–142, 180, 186, 200, 211,
    218–219, 226
  window incidents, 60, 90–91,
    106–107, 112, 116, 149, 155, 183,
    195–200, 223–224, 226–227,
    230, 233, 264, 282–283, 286,
    300, 304–305
  see also death stories; torture
Adams, Fred, 187–188, 305
Adams, Raymond A., 267

adoptions, 26, 30–31, 58, 93, 97, 153,
    169, 263
Adverse Childhood Experiences
    (ACE), 16, 126
Albert, Sister, 187
Albina, Sister, 37–40
"American Pie," 190
Anderson, Hans Christian, 30
Andrew, Brother, 108
Angell, Bishop Kenneth, 217,
    272–273, 276–277
Anglican Church, 300
Archdiocese of Boston, 54
Archdiocese of Philadelphia, 257
Artane school, 52, 297
Assembly of First Nations, 53
Austin, Sarah, 301
Australian orphanages
  abuse in, 11–15, 23–25, 30–34,
    37–53, 245, 298–299, 309–311
  description of, 11–15, 23–25,
    43–45
  investigating, 37–53, 309–311
  survivors of, 63, 245, 298–299
Autry, Gene, 168

Baffa, Father Robert, 278
Baker, Leroy, 188, 263
Ballarat Children's Home, 24–25, 43
Ballarat Orphanage, 25, 245
Bambi (film), 65
Bambi (friend), 156, 211
Barber, Roger, 5–6
Barquin, Joseph
  abuse of, 5, 129–137, 161–164,
    278
  case of, 5, 129–139, 162–163,
    203–204, 276
  story of, 129–137, 139–140,
    161–164, 195, 272, 276
Bayswater children's home, 45–46
BBC Radio 4, 299
Bear Chief, Ken, 59–60

beatings
    investigating, 34–35, 46, 51, 122,
        250–254, 303
    in United Kingdom orphanages, 33
    in United States orphanages,
        33–35, 46, 51, 84, 90,
        94, 99, 111, 122, 145,
        185–192, 220–221, 236,
        242–244, 250–254, 303
    see also whippings
Bells of St. Mary's, The (film), 207
Benoit, Elaine, 180–187, 199, 259
Benoit, Ray, 184–187
Bergman, Ingrid, 207
Bindoon boy's home, 48–50, 63
BishopAccountability.org, 56
Bishop's Fund, 169–170
Blackfeet Nation, 59
Blackstock, Gordon, 298–299
Blair, Francis H., 105–106
Blanchard, Sister, 113, 211–212
Blanche, Sister, 224
"Body Farm," 283
Bon Secours Mother and Baby Home,
    13, 297
Bon Secours Sisters, 297
Bonneau, Bill, 250, 252–256
Bonneau, Gilbert, 250, 252–256
Borsykowsky, David, 201–203, 228,
    233, 235, 279
Boscoe, Sister John, 37
Boston Globe, 54, 61–62, 231
Boyer, Sister Lorraine, 284
Boys' Depot, 20–21, 28–29. See also
    Royleston
Brady, Bishop, 79–80, 226
Braybon, Rod, 45–46, 51
Brenda, Sister, 192
Bresnehan, Father Paul, 189, 196,
    268, 275–276, 308
Broadmeadows children's home, 25
Browe, Dr. John, 189
Brown, Corinne, 160–161, 181

Buckley, Edwin T., 267
Burlington Cathedral of Immaculate
    Conception, 169
Burlington Community Justice
    Center, 302
Burlington Free Press, 56, 137, 164,
    195–196, 204, 279
Burlington Mental Hygiene Clinic, 98
Burlington Police Department,
    302–303, 313–314, 316
burned boy incident, 108–111,
    149, 152, 227, 233, 264–265,
    289–290
BuzzFeed News, 54, 64, 67, 121, 291,
    301–303

Cadorette, Robert, 205, 208, 283,
    304–305
Caissy, J. N., 170
Camp Holy Cross, 278
Campbell, Jeanne, 165. See also Jane
    of the Rosary, Sister
Campion Jesuit High School,
    141–142, 183
Canadian orphanages
    abuse in, 13–15, 33, 52–54, 123,
        239–249, 291, 300–305
    description of, 13–15, 33, 74, 123,
        174, 215, 284–291
    investigating, 300–305
candy thief incident, 179–181, 185,
    213
Carbonneau, Patricia
    abuse of, 106–107, 112, 149,
        196–201, 226–227, 283, 286
    description of, 106–107
    story of, 106–107, 196–201, 259,
        305
    see also Zeno, Patty
Cardwell, Sheila, 123–124, 304
care leavers, 22–28, 31–32
Care Leavers Australasia Network
    (CLAN), 23–24, 26, 28, 31, 311

Care of Dependent Children, 55

Carlin, Father Roger W., 309

Carrière, Monsignor, 108

Castledare boy's home, 48

Catcher in the Rye, The (book), 110

Catherine, Baby, 112–113

Catholic Church
   abuse cases, 52, 62–63, 125,
      132, 163, 182, 231, 254–255,
      259–260
   controlling history, 315
   damage to, 231, 254–255
   defending, 132, 162–163
   goal of, 315
   hierarchy of, 163–164, 249–250,
      275, 308, 314
   lies by, 254–255
   members leaving, 172
   orphanage systems, 15–17, 57,
      300–301, 308–309
   record-keeping, 15
   suing, 163, 254–255, 260

Catholic News Agency, 313

Catholic Order of Foresters, 279

Cecile, Sister, 98

cemeteries
   gravesites, 7, 41–42, 66–68, 73–74,
      111, 295–303, 315–317
   mausoleums, 67–68, 295–296,
      315–317
   unmarked graves, 297–303
   visits to, 66–68, 73–74, 295–303,
      315–317

Cheers (television show), 141

child labor, 24, 31–32, 38–39, 48–50,
      100–101, 149, 221

"child migrants," 31–32, 39, 48–49

CHILD USA, 125

childhood memories, 135, 213–214.
     See also traumatic memories

Children of Duplessis, 239–245, 305

Christian Brothers homes, 11, 34,
      48–52, 246, 297

Chronicles (newsletter), 88, 103–106,
      108–109, 111–113, 166–169,
      172–176, 240, 278–279, 282,
      291

City Vault, 317

Civil War, 57

Claire de la Providence, Sister, 305

Claire Hélène, Sister, 305

Claire, Sister, 101, 137, 176, 187, 207,
      224, 283, 304–305

CLAN, 23–24, 26, 28, 31, 311

Clark, Mary, 103–104, 107, 116, 264

Clontarf boy's home, 48

cold cases, 17–18, 44–46, 63–64. *See
     also* death stories

Colleret, Father Roger, 275, 309

Colonie Police Department, 252–253

Coltey, Charlotte, 185–186

Coltey, Walter, 184–187, 218, 304,
      307–308

Colville Reservation, 59

Corless, Catherine, 297–298

Cosby, Bill, 150

Costello, Lou, 65

Courcy, Father Leo, 276–277

Coyne, Bishop Christopher, 17,
      312–313

Crosby, Bing, 177, 207

crying girl incident, 103–104, 107,
      116, 264

Cunningham, Father Bernard, 108

Dale, Bob, 4–7, 152–153, 156, 158

Dale, Rob, 5–7, 152–153, 318–319

Dale, Sally
   abuse of, 79–90, 97–113, 116,
      223–233
   adult life of, 149–152, 317–319
   background of, 4–8, 12, 17, 37,
      74–78
   case of, 150, 179–183, 195–196,
      198–216, 244–245, 258–265,
      277, 289–295, 317–318

daily life of, 61–63, 77–90, 93–113,
116–117, 145–147
death of, 317
depositions of, 116, 223–233
description of, 4–8, 12, 17, 37,
74–78, 109–113, 317–319
husband of, 4–7, 152–153, 156,
158
later life of, 149–152, 317–319
leaving orphanage, 149–150
letters from, 154–157
marriage of, 152
McCarthy family and, 150–152
medical records of, 189
observations by,
61–63, 77–90, 93–113,
116–117, 145–147, 154–157, 166,
199–200, 277–279, 281–283,
298, 304–305
Pelkey family and, 75, 90 91,
93–100, 111, 153, 295
reunion and, 4–6, 135, 149, 153,
199–200, 226–227, 232–233,
262, 304–305
Robert Widman and, 61, 145 147,
150–157, 179–183, 289–290,
318
Sam Hemingway and, 195–196,
312, 317–318
siblings of, 76–78, 100, 113,
149–150, 210–211
son of, 5–7, 152–153, 318–319
testimony of, 61–63, 150, 161, 183,
195–200, 208–216, 223–233,
289
see also Fredette, Sally
Dalpe, Marie-Rose, 165. *See also* Mary
Vianney, Sister
Dante, 134
Darnell, Simon, 49–50
Dass, Ram, 134
Daughters of Charity, 71, 77, 100
de Gamelin, Émilie, 287

de Sade, Marquis, 187
death certificates, 62–63, 230,
255–256, 282, 289–293, 299
death stories
burned boy in coffin, 108–111,
149, 152, 227, 233, 264–265,
289–290
cemeteries and, 7, 41–42, 66–68,
73–74, 111, 186, 295–303,
315–317
cold cases, 17–18, 44–46, 63–64
crying girl, 103–104, 107, 116,
264
death certificates and, 62–63, 230,
255–256, 282, 289–293, 299
drownings, 52–53, 62, 94–95,
117–119, 145, 149, 218, 264,
282, 293
electrocution, 108–111, 145,
149–152, 227, 233, 264–265,
289–290, 293, 298
freezing incidents, 52 53, 62,
115–116, 119–120, 201–202,
264, 282, 291–295
graves and, 41–42, 111, 297 303
illnesses, 44–45, 230, 291–292
investigating, 17–18, 34–35, 37–69,
116–127, 140, 154–157, 195 196,
230–233, 243–256, 264–265,
282–283, 297–303, 316
mausoleums and, 67–68, 295–296,
315–317
staircase incidents, 33–35, 60,
104–107, 116, 155, 211, 264
suffocations, 123–124, 242–244
suicide, 31, 53, 134, 156, 211,
240
unmarked graves and, 297–303
window incidents, 60, 90–91,
106–107, 112, 116, 149, 155, 183,
195–200, 223–224, 226 227,
230, 233, 264, 282–283, 286,
300, 304–305

deGoesbriand, Louis, 17, 164
Delisle, Cindy, 219–222
Delisle, Joyce, 212–213
Department of Child Welfare, 27
Department of Interior, 300–301
Department of Social Welfare, 207
Depeaux, Bernard F., 267
Devoy, Father Robert, 103, 187, 207,
    215–216, 225–226, 275, 279,
    281–282
Dewar, Ray, 46
Diocese of Albany, 251
Diocese of Burlington, 17, 79, 129,
    132, 139, 169, 174, 179, 186, 217,
    267–279, 302–304, 309–310,
    313
Diocese of Charleston, 309
Diocese of Providence, 121, 208
Dominick, Sister, 102–103, 187,
    224
Don Bosco School, 184, 186, 198,
    275, 291
Donat, Sister, 218
Donovan, T. J., 312, 314
"Don't Fence Me In," 177
drownings, 52–53, 62, 94–95,
    117–119, 145, 149, 218, 264,
    282, 293
drugs, 188–190, 240, 243–245
Dumas, Marie, 242
DuPaul, Eva, 88–90, 98, 102, 112,
    153–154, 207, 212, 221, 241,
    251, 286
Duplessis, Maurice, 240
Duprey, Ed, 159–160
Dussault, Father Joseph, 278–279
Dwyer, Beatrice, 255
D'Youville Nursery, 241

electric chair incidents, 53–54, 94,
    105–106, 110–111, 166, 175,
    231–232, 245–246, 290–291
electric shocks, 44, 245, 299

electrocution, 108–111, 145, 149–152,
    227, 233, 264–265, 289–290,
    293, 298
Ellis Island, 318–319
emotional abuse, 16, 24–25, 33–34,
    132–134, 166, 190, 262–264,
    303–304. See also abuse
England orphanages, 33
Eskra, Joseph, 118–120, 201–203,
    291–294, 298

FBI, 60, 124, 283
"Feeding the Angel," 190
Fernande de Grace, Sister, 184,
    218–219
Fidelia, Sister, 250, 255
Fifth Amendment, 314
First Amendment, 133
First Nations, 53, 300
Fisher, Sister John, 37
flashbacks, 149, 155, 221–222. See also
    traumatic memories
forced labor, 24, 31–32, 38–39,
    48–50, 100–101, 149, 221
Forensic Anthropology Center,
    283
forensic investigations, 46, 255–256,
    283, 298, 316
Foster, Brother, 74, 216–217
    see also Foster, Father Edward
foster care, 21–22, 26–30, 55, 58, 113,
    232, 312
Foster, Father Edward, 90, 109, 111,
    187, 214–217, 272–277, 281
    see also Foster, Brother
Fox, Vicente, 141
Frances, Mother, 37
Franciscan Sisters, 108
Fredette, Henry, 76
Fredette, Joanna, 76
Fredette, Ramona, 76–78, 153, 211
Fredette, Ronald, 76–78
Fredette, Sally

abuse of, 79–90, 97–113, 116,
    223–233
background of, 4–8, 12, 17, 37,
    74–78
daily life of, 61–63, 77–90, 93–113,
    116–117, 145–147
description of, 4–8, 12, 17, 37,
    74–78, 109–113, 317–319
marriage of, 152
McCarthy family and, 150–152
medical records of, 189
observations by,
    61–63, 77–90, 93–113,
    116–117, 145–147, 154–157, 166,
    199–200, 277–279, 281–288,
    298, 304–305
Pelkey family and, 75, 90–91,
    93–100, 111, 153, 295
siblings of, 76–78, 100, 113,
    149–150, 210–211
see also Dale, Sally
Fredette, Sherry, 76–78, 100, 113,
    149–150, 210–211
freezing incidents, 52–53, 62,
    115–116, 119–120, 201–202,
    264, 282, 291–295

Gallagher, Father William, 277
Garabedian, Mitchell, 309
Gelineau, Bishop Louis, 135–138,
    175, 208
Gelineau, Brother, 208
Gelineau, Father Edward, 135–136,
    302, 308
Gelineau, Joseph, 121–123, 135–136,
    298, 302
Gelineau, Raymond, 122
George, 47–50
Geraldton Guardian, 42
Gertrude, Sister, 192–193
Giallella, Anthony, 64–69, 121,
    295–298, 305, 316–317
Gill, Pauline, 243, 245–246

Ginsberg, Allen, 134
Glancy, Father John, 186, 197–198,
    307–308
Glasheen, Kevin, 49–50
Glennon, Father Michael, 9–12
Globe and Mail, 300
"God Bless America," 212
Goretti, Maria, 103
Gravel, John, 179
gravesites
    cemeteries, 7, 41–42, 66–68,
        73–74, 111, 295–303, 315–317
    mausoleums, 67–68, 295–296,
        315–317
    unmarked graves, 297–303
    visits to, 66–68, 73–74, 295–303,
        315–317
Great Depression, 57
Great Lester, 168
Greene, Dale, 192–193, 234–236
Grenon, Phillip, 120–121
Grey Nuns, 53, 240
Grimard, Madeleine, 241
Guidry, Coralyn, 5

"Half-Orphan Asylum," 57–58
hallucinations, 54, 188–190
Hamilton, Marci, 125
Hammons, Barbara, 263
Hampton Inn Colchester, 4, 135
Hannon, Brenda, 304–305, 313
Harvard University, 231
Hazen, Debbie, 5
Hebert, Father Paul, 108
Hemingway, Sam, 56, 195–197, 312,
    317–318
Herman, Judith, 34
Herman's Hermits, 150
Hill, Gordon Lyle, 43
    see also Hill, Peter "Hilly"
Hill, Peter "Hilly," 43–45, 52, 245,
    298–299
    see also Hill, Gordon Lyle

Hoffman, Katelin, 5, 278, 304
Holocaust, 231
Home for the Aged, 191, 207, 309
Home for Wayward and Abandoned
    Boys, 20–21. *See also* Royleston
hospital records, 189, 230
Hotel Dieu, 108
Hotel Vermont, 279
Hubbard, Bishop Howard, 252–253
Huestis, Sherry, 123–124, 201, 298,
    304

illnesses, 34, 42–45, 185–186, 230,
    291–292
Indian Residential School, 300
Indigenous children, 32, 52–53, 57,
    300–301
Indigenous community, 300–301
Indigenous Justice, 53
Institute of the Daughters of Charity,
    71, 77, 100
investigations
    of abuse, 17–18, 34–35, 37–69,
        116–127, 140, 154–157, 195–196,
        230–233, 243–256, 264–265,
        282–283, 297–303, 309–317
    of death stories, 17–18, 34–35,
        37–69, 116–127, 140, 154–157,
        195–196, 230–233, 243–256,
        264–265, 282–283, 297–303,
        316
    by FBI, 60, 124, 283
    forensic investigations, 46,
        255–256, 283, 298, 316
    of missing children, 166–167, 265,
        297–301
    Spotlight investigation, 54, 61–63,
        231, 255, 301, 309
    Task Force investigations,
        300–303, 313–314
Ireland orphanages, 13, 15, 33, 40, 52,
    246, 286, 297
Irwin, Monseigneur, 37

Jacob, Doris, 226
James Mary, Sister, 4, 89, 99,
    110–112, 153, 165–166, 175,
    187, 207, 245, 290
Jane of the Rosary, Sister, 66, 77–83,
    88–89, 94, 104, 165, 176, 187,
    206–208, 211–213, 227
John Carroll University, 142–143
John Paul II, Pope, 267
Joyce, Bishop Robert F., 175, 277,
    279
justice, restorative, 64, 302–305, 307,
    312–313, 317–318
justice system, 124–127

Kamloops Indian Residential School,
    300
Keaney, Brother, 48
Kennedy, John F., 188
Keylor, Sister Gloria, 184
Kieran, Sister, 37
King Brothers Circus, 168
Kitty, 251
Knights of Columbus, 133
Kroc, Ray, 110
Kuper Island Indian Residential
    School, 300

Ladislas, Sister, 218
Lake Champlain, 7–8, 73, 94,
    117, 145, 168, 188, 206, 282,
    303–304
Lakeview Cemetery, 66–67, 73–74,
    315–317
Lakeview Sanitarium, 73, 198
Langrock Sperry & Wool, 160–161,
    179, 262
LaRouche, Father, 275
Lawlor, Brendan W., 267
Leary, Timothy, 134
Leonard, Geneva Bellezemere, 176,
    305
Leontine, Sister, 185, 187, 218

Les Enfants de Duplessis (book), 243, 245

Les orphelinats (museum display), 288

Lewis, Alla Mary, 315

Lewis, Harry Edwin, 315–316

Lewis Mausoleum, 67–68, 295–296, 315–317

LIDAR, 300

Lisa, 8–11

Little Franciscans, 240

Little, Joe, 144

Little, Mrs., 27–28

Little Orphan Annie (film), 30

locked up incidents, 20–22, 29, 80, 86–91, 103–104, 110, 115–116, 122, 129, 140, 147, 149–153, 166, 191–192, 195–197, 208, 291–292

Longale, Mark, 252

Louis Hector, Sister, 106–107, 210, 307

Loyal Order of Moose, 57

Lucey, Dr. Jerold, 189

Lynch, Dan, 250, 252, 254

MacLaine, Shirley, 134

Madeline, Sister, 137, 207

Madrin, Sister, 277

Maison Sainte-Domitille, 241

Marcoux, Charles J., 175

Margaret, Sister, 72

Marie Dolores, Sister, 242, 244

Marshall, Bishop John A., 217, 267, 277–278

Mary Charity, Sister, 206

Mary Vianney, Sister, 80, 165, 207

mausoleums, 67–68, 295–296, 315–317. *See also* cemeteries

Maynard, Marion, 250, 255

McCarthy family, 150–152

McCarthy, Joseph, 110

McGowan, Irene, 88–90, 98–100, 104–105, 112, 154–155, 200–201, 212, 241, 251, 286

McGrath, Mrs., 76–77

McKay, Robert J., 188–189

McKiernan, Terry, 56, 60

McShane, Father James, 278

McSweeney, John, 169–170, 175, 267

medical records, 189, 230

medications, 188–190, 240, 243–245

memorials, 299, 303–304

Meyer, Geoff, 20–22, 26–30, 34–35, 60

Meyer, Leo Joseph, 27

Meyer, Maisie Aileen, 27

Michelle, 242, 244

Miles, Sister Philomena, 177, 218

Miller, Father Walter, 130, 267, 276–278

Miller, Sally, 5, 117, 119, 191, 201, 292–294, 298, 309

Millette, Charles, 289

Millette, Joseph, 289–290, 293–294

Miracle of Fatima, The (play), 168

missing children

investigating, 46, 52–54, 166–167, 245–246, 265, 297–301

runaways, 11–12, 53–54, 108–109, 124, 163, 166–167, 192, 197

searching for, 117, 166–167, 297–301

stories of, 30–34, 46, 52–54, 155–156, 297–301

Missing Children Project, 52–54, 245–246, 300

Mohawk Institute, 300

Mohawk of Kanesatake, 53

molestation, 30, 48–54, 83–84, 146, 187, 210, 231–237, 257–264, 277, 308. *See also* abuse; sexual abuse

Mooseheart orphanage, 57

Morris, Geoff
  background of, 144–145, 154–157,
    159–160
  case against orphanage, 162–163,
    179, 195, 207, 218, 247, 264
  Joseph Barquin and, 139–140
  letters to, 154–157
Mother and Baby Home, 13, 297
Mother's Friend, The (book), 101
Mount Providence Hospital, 168
Mount Providence Orphanage, 13,
    104, 168, 240, 291, 305
Murphy, Father, 108
Murray, Andrew, 31
Murray, Kimberly, 53–54, 245,
    300
museum exhibitions, 287–288, 304,
    307, 313, 317–318

Naropa Institute, 134
Nazareth House, 37–43, 60, 63,
    298–299
Nelson Hesse firm, 144
New England Company, 300
New York orphanages, 57, 249–255
New York Times, 246
nightmares, 45, 185. *See also* traumatic
    memories
Noble, Marilyn, 161–162, 205, 261
Noelle, Sister, 108–111, 176

Oblates of Mary Immaculate,
    53–54
O'Brien, Bill Jr., 133, 137, 179, 228,
    230, 259, 271
O'Brien, Bill Sr., 133
official visits, 1, 3–4, 71–73, 75, 79,
    81, 84–86, 97–99
One Flew Over the Cuckoo's Nest
    (film), 243
O'Neill, Jerry, 271–272, 302–303
Orphan Girl No. 58 (manuscript),
    161

orphanage systems
  in Australia, 11–15, 23–25,
    30–34, 37–53, 63, 245, 298–299,
    309–311
  in Canada, 13–15, 33, 52–54, 74,
    123, 174, 215, 239–246, 249,
    284–291, 300–305
  description of, 3–17
  in England, 33
  in Ireland, 13, 15, 33, 40, 52, 246,
    286, 297
  in New York, 57, 249–255
  number of, 57–58
  in Scotland, 13, 33, 52, 297–299
  types of, 57–58
  in United Kingdom, 3–17, 33,
    39–40, 52, 246, 297–299
  in United States, 13–17, 23–24,
    54–69, 71–91, 97–99, 116–127,
    129–147, 149–157, 163–166,
    172–177, 179–193, 195–237,
    239–247, 249–265, 267–279,
    284–305, 307–319
  in Vermont, 3–17, 23–24,
    54–69, 71–91, 97–99, 116–127,
    129–147, 149–157, 160–166,
    172–177, 179–193, 195–237,
    239–247, 249–265, 267–279,
    284–305, 307–319
  see also specific orphanages
Orphans of the Living (book), 31

Paquette, Father Edward, 271
Parker, Harriet, 74–75, 93, 97–98,
    107
Pauline, Sister, 65, 68, 82, 187, 207
Pelkey family, 75, 90–91, 93–100,
    111, 153, 295
Pelkey, Nancy, 75, 93–96, 111, 153
Penelakut Tribe, 300
Penglase, Joanna, 23–24, 30–31
Pentridge prison, 45–46, 52
Peter Pan (film), 304

Peter, Sister, 226

physical abuse
in Australian orphanages, 11–15,
23–25, 30–34, 37–53, 245,
298–299, 309–311
beatings, 33–35, 46, 51, 84, 90,
99, 111, 122, 145, 185–188,
192, 220–221, 236, 242–244,
250–254, 303
burned boy incident, 108–111,
149, 152, 227, 233, 264–265,
289–290
in Canadian orphanages, 13–15,
33, 52–54, 123, 239–249, 291,
300–305
Catholic Church and, 52,
62–63, 125, 132, 163, 182, 231,
254–255, 259–260
crying girl incident, 103–104, 107,
116, 264
drownings, 52–53, 62, 94–95,
117–119, 145, 149, 218, 264,
282, 293
drugs and, 188–190, 240, 243–245
electric chair incidents, 53–54, 94,
105–106, 110–111, 166, 175,
231–232, 245–246, 290–291
electric shocks, 44, 245, 299
electrocution, 108–111, 145,
149–152, 227, 233, 264–265,
289–290, 293, 298
forced labor, 24, 31–32, 38–39,
48–50, 100–101, 149, 221
freezing incidents, 52–53, 62,
115–116, 119–120, 201–202,
264, 282, 291–295
illnesses, 44–45, 230, 291–292
investigating, 17–18, 34–35, 37–69,
116–127, 140, 154–157, 195–196,
230–233, 243–256, 264–265,
282–283, 297–303, 309–317
locked up incidents, 20–22, 29, 80,
86–91, 103–104, 110, 115–116,
122, 129, 140, 147, 149–153,
166, 191–192, 195–197, 208,
291–292
restraints, 66–69, 110, 119–123,
166, 181, 201–202, 240–245,
291
staircase incidents, 33–35, 60,
104–107, 116, 155, 211, 264
statute of limitations and, 124–126,
133, 136–137, 213–214, 246,
253, 261–262, 298–304, 312
straitjackets, 242–244
suffocations, 123–124, 242–244
in United Kingdom orphanages,
33, 39–40, 52, 246, 297–299
in United States orphanages, 5,
11–12, 16, 24–25, 30–34, 44–57,
60–69, 78–91, 94–113, 115–126,
129–138, 145–147, 154–157,
159–161, 180–192, 196–237,
239–247, 249, 264, 272–279,
286–291, 299–305, 307–312
whippings, 12, 35, 60, 83, 89–90,
140–142, 180, 186, 200, 211,
218–219
window incidents, 60, 90–91,
106–107, 112, 116, 149, 155, 183,
195–200, 223–224, 226–227,
230, 233, 264, 282–283, 286,
300, 304–305
see also abuse; sexual abuse
Poor Sisters of Nazareth, 43
Potter, Alfred John, 152
Pray, Reverend Joseph N., 90, 175
Preedom, Father Harold, 191, 309
Presentation Sisters, 40–42, 251–252,
254–255
priests, accused, 56, 132, 254,
257–260, 267–279, 282,
302–303, 307–310
Priscille, Sister, 106–107, 196–200,
226, 283–289, 305
Pro Colman, 251

Providence Orphan Asylum, 73–74
psychological abuse, 132–134,
    273–274, 303. *See also* abuse

Quinton, Alice, 241–245

Racicot, Léonille, 165. *See also* James
    Mary, Sister
radar searches, 300
rape, 5, 11, 48–49, 52–56, 203, 213,
    231, 235. *See also* sexual abuse
Ready, Father William, 106
Red Cross, 76
Regina, Sister, 250–251, 254
*Reports of Provincial Superior of
    Official Visits to St. Joseph's
    Orphanage* (report), 1, 71–75,
    79–81, 84–86, 97–99
repressed memories, 181, 226–232,
    262, 295–298, 310. *See also*
    traumatic memories
residential schools, 52–53, 246, 297,
    300–301
Restorative Inquiry group, 313
restorative justice process, 64,
    302–305, 307, 312–313,
    317–318
restraints, 66–69, 110, 119–123, 166,
    181, 201–202, 240–245, 291
Reyda, Andrew, 252, 255
Richard, Evelyne, 244–245
Riley, Miss, 112
Robe, The (film), 168
Robinson, Ben, 299
ROTC, 141, 143
Rouelle, Father, 277
Royleston, 19–22, 26–30, 35, 60
Ruede, Michael, 253–255
Rule, Frank, 209
runaways, 11–12, 53–54, 108–109,
    124, 163, 166–167, 192, 197. *See
    also* missing children
Ryan, Bishop, 166

St. Anne's School, 53
St. Augustine's, 11–13, 17, 23, 60
St. Catherine, Sister, 191
St. Catherine's Orphanage, 17, 23,
    25–26
St. Colman's Home, 249–255
Ste. Edith, Sister, 241
St. Francis Xavier, 175
Ste. Jeanne Gabrielle, Sister, 244
St. John of God, 63
St. John's, 51
St. Joseph's Broadmeadows, 25
St. Joseph's Child Care Center, 58,
    171
St. Joseph's Home for the Aged, 191,
    207, 309
St. Joseph's Orphan Asylum, 58
St. Joseph's Orphanage
  abuse in, 5, 11–12, 16,
    24–25, 30–34, 44–56,
    60–69, 78–91, 94–113, 115–126,
    129–138, 145–147, 149, 154–157,
    159–161, 180–192, 196–237,
    239–247, 249–264, 272–279,
    283, 286–291, 299–305, 307–315
  case against, 5, 54–69, 116–127,
    129–147, 160–166, 172–177,
    179–193, 195–237, 239–247,
    249–265, 267–279, 281–305,
    307–314, 317–318
  case settlements,
    137–140, 163, 186–187, 203,
    220, 257–264, 271–272, 276,
    290–291, 302–303
  description of, 3–17, 54–69, 71–91,
    97–99, 115–116, 163–166, 265,
    287, 295
  emotional abuse in, 16, 24–25,
    33–34, 132–134, 166, 190,
    262–264, 303–304
  founding of, 17, 73–74
  investigating, 17–18, 34–35, 37–69,
    116–127, 140, 154–157, 195–196,

230–233, 243–256, 264–265,
282–283, 297–303, 309–317
official visits to, 1, 3–4, 71–75,
79–81, 84–86, 97–99
physical abuse in, 11–12, 16,
24–25, 30–34, 44–56,
60–69, 78–91, 94–113, 115–126,
129–138, 145–147, 154–157,
159–161, 180–192, 196–237,
239–247, 249–264, 272–279,
286–291, 299–305, 307–312
psychological abuse in, 132–134,
273–274, 303
renovations to, 115, 265, 295
reunion and, 4–6, 135, 149, 153,
199–200, 226–227, 232–233,
262, 304–305
sexual abuse in, 5,
11–12, 24–25, 30,
47–56, 61–69, 83–84, 125–126,
129 136, 146, 187 191, 202 217,
224–237, 252–264, 272–279,
286, 302–305, 307–312
survivors of, 3–17, 23–24, 60–64,
120–126, 134–147, 149–157,
179–183, 199–213, 233–237,
239–241, 251–262, 272–278,
284–286, 294–305, 307–319
Voices of, 303–304, 311
Saint-Julien Hospital, 241–244
Saint Luke Institute, 272–274,
277
St. Mary's Cemetery, 299
St. Mary's Mission, 59–60
St. Michael's College, 108, 300
St. Paul Antoine, Sister, 242
St. Pierre, Adrienne, 212
St. Pierre, Marie, 65, 212
Ste. Thérèse du Crucifix, Sister, 243,
245
Salter, Anna, 227, 232–233
Salvation Army, 45–46, 51
Salvation (book), 46

Sartore, Jack, 179, 210, 223–231,
257–261, 264, 279
Sauvageau, Julienne, 219–222
Savary, Father, 275
Schmaldienst, Peter, 289–290
Scotland orphanages, 13, 33, 52,
297–299
sedatives, 190, 240, 243–245. *See also*
drugs
Seinfeld (television show), 159
Servants of the Poor, 71, 77, 100
sexual abuse, 5, 11–12, 24–25, 30,
47–56, 61–69, 83–84, 125–126,
129–136, 146, 187–191, 202–217,
224–237, 252–264, 272–279,
286, 302–305, 307–312. *See also*
abuse
Sheedy, Leonie, 23–26, 28–30,
32–33, 35, 38, 42–43, 51–52
Shuttle, Donald, 205
Sinnott, Eileen, 38–43, 299
Sipe, Richard, 61–63, 314
Sisters from Mount Providence
Hospital, 168
Sisters of Charity, 240, 298–299
Sisters of Mercy, 51, 102, 108, 240
Sisters of Notre Dame, 141
Sisters of Providence
in care facilities, 283–284
commitment of, 111, 191–193, 215,
312–315
depositions of, 182–183, 218–223,
229, 237–241, 260, 281
hierarchy within, 176–177,
249–250, 314
joining, 285–286
lack of cooperation from, 127,
303–305, 313–314
lawyers for, 179, 201–203, 210,
223–235, 257–261, 264, 279
list of, 284
loyalty of, 111, 191–193, 215,
312–315

Sisters of Providence (*continued*)
  in motherhouse, 136, 177, 218, 240,
    283–284, 287–289, 308–309
  names for, 165
  newsletter of, 88, 103–106,
    108–109, 111–113, 166–169,
    172–176, 240, 278–279, 282,
    291
  observations of, 63,
    74–84, 100–113, 116–117,
    129–130, 145–147, 154–159, 166,
    199–200, 277–279, 281–289,
    298, 303–305
  Robert Widman and, 172–177,
    284
  see also specific sisters
Sisters of St. Joseph, 108
Sisters of the Atonement, 108
Sisters of the Hotel Dieu, 108
Sisters of the Presentation of the
  Blessed Virgin Mary, 40–42,
  251–252, 254–255
Sisters of the Sacred Heart, 108
Six Nations, 300
Six Nations Police, 300
Six Nations Survivors Secretariat,
  300
Smyllum Park Orphanage, 13,
  298–299
Snay, Charlotte, 292
Sodality of the Blessed Virgin Mary,
  100
Sound of Music, The (film), 162
Southern State Correctional Facility,
  63–64, 121
Spotlight (film), 61
Spotlight investigation, 54, 61–63,
  231, 255, 301, 309
SS Asturias (ship), 39
staircase incidents, 33–35, 60,
  104–107, 116, 155, 211, 264
Star Trek (television show), 160
Statue of Liberty, 318–319

statute of limitations
  abuse and, 124–126, 133, 136–137,
    213–214, 246, 253, 261–262,
    298–304, 312
  justice and, 124–125, 213–214,
    261–262, 298–304, 312
  murder and, 35
straitjackets, 242–244
Streep, Meryl, 233
Stz'uminus First Nation, 300
suffocations, 123–124, 242–244
suicide, 31, 53, 134, 156, 211, 240
Sunday Post, 298
Survivors of St. Joseph's Orphanage
  and Friends, 134–137, 140,
  149, 305. *See also* St. Joseph's
  Orphanage
Swain, Shurlee, 309

Tardun boy's home, 48–50
Task Force investigations, 300–303,
  313–314
Temple, Shirley, 5, 7, 30, 78, 82, 93,
  153
terrorist attacks, 231–232, 296
Theresa, Mother, 212
Tiananmen Square, 144
Times Union, 250
Tk'emlúps te Secweìpemc community,
  300
torture
  beatings, 33–35, 46, 51, 84, 90,
    94, 99, 111, 122, 145, 185–188,
    192, 220–221, 236, 242–244,
    250–254, 303
  drugs and, 188–190, 240,
    243–245
  electric chair incidents, 53–54, 94,
    105–106, 110–111, 166, 175,
    231–232, 245–246, 290–291
  electric shocks, 44, 245, 299
  forced labor, 24, 31–32, 38–39,
    48–50, 100–101, 149, 221

investigating, 17–18, 34–35, 37–69,
116–127, 140, 154–157, 195–196,
230–233, 243–256, 264–265,
282–283, 297–303, 309–317
locked up incidents, 20–22, 29, 80,
86–91, 103–104, 110, 115–116,
122, 129, 140, 147, 149–153,
166, 191–192, 195–197, 208,
291–292
restraints, 66–69, 110, 119–123,
166, 181, 201–202, 240–245,
291
straitjackets, 242–244
whippings, 35, 60, 83, 89–90,
140–142, 180, 186, 200, 211,
218–219, 226
see also abuse; death stories
Towards Healing program, 41
Trapp family, 162, 260
see also Von Trapp family
Trapp Family Lodge, 260
traumatic memories
childhood memories, 135, 213–214
flashbacks, 149, 155, 221–222
nightmares, 45, 185
repressed memories, 181, 226–232,
262, 295–298, 310
workings of, 179–181, 213–214,
224–231
tribunal, 267–270, 272, 275–278
Truth and Reconciliation
Commission, 53

United Kingdom orphanages
abuse in, 33
description of, 3–17, 33
investigating, 297–299
statute of limitations, 246
United States District Court of
Vermont, 132, 135–136, 179
United States orphanages
case against, 5, 54–69, 116–127,
129–147, 160–166, 172–177,

179–193, 195–237, 239–247,
249–265, 267–279, 281–305,
307–314, 317–318
description of, 13–17,
54–69, 71–91, 97–99, 115–116,
163–166, 265, 287, 295
emotional abuse in, 16, 24–25,
33–34, 132–134, 166, 190,
262–264, 303–304
investigating, 17–18, 34–35, 37–69,
116–127, 140, 154–157, 195–196,
230–233, 243–256, 264–265,
282–283, 297–303, 309–317
physical abuse in, 11–12, 16,
24–25, 30–34, 44–56,
60–69, 78–91, 94–113, 115–126,
129–138, 145–147, 154–157,
159–161, 180–192, 196–237,
239–247, 249–264, 272–279,
286–291, 299–305, 307–312
psychological abuse in, 132–134,
273–274, 303
sexual abuse in, 5,
11–12, 24–25, 30,
47–56, 61–69, 83–84, 125–126,
129–136, 146, 187–191, 202–217,
224–237, 252–264, 272–279,
286, 302–305, 307–312
survivors of, 13–17, 23–24, 60–64,
120–126, 134–147, 149–157,
179–183, 199–213, 233–237,
239–241, 251–262, 272–278,
284–286, 294–305, 307–319
University of Florida, 143, 264
University of Vermont, 189
unmarked graves, 297–303. *See also*
cemeteries; graves
Upper Websterville Elementary
School, 94

Van der Kolk, Bessel, 231–233,
309–310
Vatican II, 133, 172, 283

Vermont Catholic Charities, 74,
121, 132, 135, 168–174, 179,
186, 197–198, 282, 295, 302,
307–309, 313
Vermont History Museum, 304, 307,
313, 317–318
Vermont Legal Aid, 130
Vermont orphanage
case against, 5, 54–69, 116–127,
129–147, 160–166, 172–177,
179–193, 195–237, 239–247,
249–265, 267–279, 281–305,
307–314, 317–318
description of, 3–17, 54–69, 71–91,
97–99, 115–116, 163–166, 265,
287, 295
emotional abuse in, 16, 24–25,
33–34, 132–134, 166, 190,
262–264, 303–304
investigating, 17–18, 34–35, 37–69,
116–127, 140, 154–157, 195–196,
230–233, 243–256, 264–265,
282–283, 297–303, 309–317
official visits to, 1, 3–4, 71–75,
79–81, 84–86, 97–99
physical abuse in, 11–12, 16,
24–25, 30–34, 44–56,
60–69, 78–91, 94–113, 115–126,
129–138, 145–147, 154–157,
159–161, 180–192, 196–237,
239–247, 249–264, 272–279,
286–291, 299–305, 307–312
psychological abuse in, 132–134,
273–274, 303
sexual abuse in, 5,
11–12, 24–25, 30,
47–56, 61–69, 83–84, 125–126,
129–136, 146, 187–191, 202–217,
224–237, 252–264, 272–279,
286, 302–305, 307–312
survivors of, 3–17, 23–24, 60–64,
120–126, 134–147, 149–157,

179–183, 199–213, 233–237,
239–241, 251–262, 272–278,
284–286, 294–305, 307–319
see also St. Joseph's Orphanage
Vermont State Police, 302
Vermont Women's Health Center,
173–174
Voices of St. Joseph's Orphanage,
303–304, 311
Von Trapp family, 162, 260
see also Trapp family
Von Trapp, Rosemarie, 260

Wendt, George, 141
Wennberg, Marc, 313
whippings
in Australian orphanages, 12
investigating, 35, 60, 140
in United States orphanages, 35,
60, 83, 89–90, 140–142, 180,
186, 200, 211, 218–219, 226
see also beatings
White, Philip
background of, 130–131
case against orphanage, 5, 129–139,
162–163, 203–204, 257–259,
276, 311
Joseph Barquin and, 5, 129–139,
162–163, 203–204, 276
Whitehead, James, 291
Widman, Cynthia, 143, 182, 213,
247, 260
Widman, Robert
background of, 141–145
case against orphanage, 165–166,
172–177, 179–193, 195–237,
239–247, 249–265, 271–277,
284, 289–293, 309, 312, 318
interviews by, 56–57
Joseph Barquin and, 139–140
letters to, 154–157
meeting with, 61–62

Sally Dale and, 61, 145–147, 150–157, 179–183, 289–290, 318
Sisters of Providence and, 172–177, 284
visiting orphanage, 165–166
Willette, Marvin, 119–120, 202, 264, 282, 292–293
Williams, Therese, 37–45, 52, 60, 299
Willis, Father Alfred, 267–270, 275–276, 278

window incidents, 60, 90–91, 106–107, 112, 116, 149, 155, 183, 195–200, 223–224, 226–227, 230, 233, 264, 282–283, 286, 300, 304–305
World War I, 57
World War II, 57, 75, 289

Zeno, Patty, 196–201, 286. *See also* Carbonneau, Patricia

Credit: Nicole Cleary

Christine Kenneally is an award-winning journalist and author who has written for the *New Yorker*, the *New York Times*, *Slate*, *Time*, and other publications. Her *BuzzFeed News* story about crimes committed at St. Joseph's Orphanage was viewed more than six million times in six months. It won a Deadline Award and was a finalist for a National Magazine Award, a Michael Kelly Award, and an Online Journalism Award. It was shortlisted for the Fetisov Prize. Her most recent book, *The Invisible History of the Human Race*, was a *New York Times* Notable Book of 2014, among other accolades. Kenneally grew up in Australia and has also lived in New York, Iowa, and England, where she earned a PhD in linguistics from Cambridge University. She lives in Melbourne, Australia, with her family.

PublicAffairs is a publishing house founded in 1997. It is a tribute to the standards, values, and flair of three persons who have served as mentors to countless reporters, writers, editors, and book people of all kinds, including me.

I. F. STONE, proprietor of *I. F. Stone's Weekly*, combined a commitment to the First Amendment with entrepreneurial zeal and reporting skill and became one of the great independent journalists in American history. At the age of eighty, Izzy published *The Trial of Socrates*, which was a national bestseller. He wrote the book after he taught himself ancient Greek.

BENJAMIN C. BRADLEE was for nearly thirty years the charismatic editorial leader of *The Washington Post*. It was Ben who gave the *Post* the range and courage to pursue such historic issues as Watergate. He supported his reporters with a tenacity that made them fearless and it is no accident that so many became authors of influential, best-selling books.

ROBERT L. BERNSTEIN, the chief executive of Random House for more than a quarter century, guided one of the nation's premier publishing houses. Bob was personally responsible for many books of political dissent and argument that challenged tyranny around the globe. He is also the founder and longtime chair of Human Rights Watch, one of the most respected human rights organizations in the world.

· · ·

For fifty years, the banner of Public Affairs Press was carried by its owner Morris B. Schnapper, who published Gandhi, Nasser, Toynbee, Truman, and about 1,500 other authors. In 1983, Schnapper was described by *The Washington Post* as "a redoubtable gadfly." His legacy will endure in the books to come.

Peter Osnos, *Founder*

PELHAM LIBRARY
Pelham, MA

MAR 2 9 2023